ISBN 978-1-329-55137-4

90000

Computer Science
History, Theory and Practice

Contents

1 Introduction To Computer Science   1

    1.1 Computer science 1

       1.1.1 History 1

       1.1.2 Philosophy 3

       1.1.3 Areas of computer science 4

       1.1.4 The great insights of computer science 7

       1.1.5 Academia 7

       1.1.6 Education 8

       1.1.7 See also 8

       1.1.8 Notes 8

       1.1.9 References 8

       1.1.10 Further reading 10

       1.1.11 External links 11

2 Important Topics   12

    2.1 History of computer science 12

       2.1.1 Binary logic 12

       2.1.2 Birth of the computer 12

       2.1.3 Emergence of a discipline 13

       2.1.4 See also 15

       2.1.5 References 15

       2.1.6 Further reading 16

       2.1.7 External links 16

    2.2 Philosophy of computer science 17

       2.2.1 See also 17

       2.2.2 References 17

       2.2.3 Further reading 17

       2.2.4 External links 17

    2.3 Outline of computer science 18

       2.3.1 What *type* of thing is computer science? 18

		2.3.2	Subfields	18
		2.3.3	History	20
		2.3.4	Fields	20
		2.3.5	Basic concepts	20
		2.3.6	Programming paradigms	20
		2.3.7	See also	20
		2.3.8	External links	21
	2.4	Theoretical computer science		21
		2.4.1	History	21
		2.4.2	Topics	22
		2.4.3	Organizations	26
		2.4.4	Journals and newsletters	26
		2.4.5	Conferences	26
		2.4.6	See also	27
		2.4.7	Notes	27
		2.4.8	Further reading	28
		2.4.9	External links	28
	2.5	Theory of computation		29
		2.5.1	History	29
		2.5.2	Branches	29
		2.5.3	Models of computation	30
		2.5.4	References	31
		2.5.5	Further reading	31
		2.5.6	External links	32
	2.6	Information theory		32
		2.6.1	Overview	33
		2.6.2	Historical background	33
		2.6.3	Quantities of information	34
		2.6.4	Coding theory	36
		2.6.5	Applications to other fields	38
		2.6.6	See also	38
		2.6.7	References	40
		2.6.8	External links	41
	2.7	Coding theory		41
		2.7.1	History of coding theory	42
		2.7.2	Source coding	42
		2.7.3	Channel coding	43
		2.7.4	Cryptographical coding	44

	2.7.5	Line coding	45
	2.7.6	Other applications of coding theory	45
	2.7.7	Neural coding	46
	2.7.8	See also	46
	2.7.9	Notes	46
	2.7.10	References	47
2.8	Programming language theory		47
	2.8.1	History	47
	2.8.2	Sub-disciplines and related fields	49
	2.8.3	Journals, publications, and conferences	49
	2.8.4	See also	50
	2.8.5	References	50
	2.8.6	Further reading	50
	2.8.7	External links	50
2.9	Formal methods		50
	2.9.1	Taxonomy	50
	2.9.2	Uses	51
	2.9.3	Applications	52
	2.9.4	Formal methods and notations	52
	2.9.5	See also	53
	2.9.6	References	53
	2.9.7	Further reading	54
	2.9.8	External links	54
2.10	Artificial intelligence		54
	2.10.1	History	55
	2.10.2	Research	56
	2.10.3	Applications	63
	2.10.4	Philosophy and ethics	64
	2.10.5	In fiction	68
	2.10.6	See also	68
	2.10.7	Notes	69
	2.10.8	References	78
	2.10.9	Further reading	82
	2.10.10	External links	82
2.11	Computer architecture		82
	2.11.1	History	83
	2.11.2	Subcategories	83
	2.11.3	The Roles	84

- 2.11.4 Design goals 85
- 2.11.5 See also 86
- 2.11.6 Notes 86
- 2.11.7 References 86
- 2.11.8 External links 87

2.12 Computer engineering 87
- 2.12.1 History 88
- 2.12.2 Work 88
- 2.12.3 Specialty areas 88
- 2.12.4 Education 90
- 2.12.5 Job outlook in the United States 90
- 2.12.6 Similar occupations and field 90
- 2.12.7 References 90

2.13 Computer performance 91
- 2.13.1 Technical and non-technical definitions 91
- 2.13.2 Performance engineering 91
- 2.13.3 Aspects of performance 92
- 2.13.4 Benchmarks 94
- 2.13.5 Software performance testing 94
- 2.13.6 Performance tuning 94
- 2.13.7 Perceived performance 94
- 2.13.8 Performance Equation 95
- 2.13.9 See also 95
- 2.13.10 References 95

2.14 Computer graphics (computer science) 96
- 2.14.1 Overview 96
- 2.14.2 History 96
- 2.14.3 Subfields in computer graphics 96
- 2.14.4 Notable researchers in computer graphics 98
- 2.14.5 See also 98
- 2.14.6 References 99
- 2.14.7 Further reading 99
- 2.14.8 External links 99

2.15 Computer security 100
- 2.15.1 Vulnerabilities and attacks 100
- 2.15.2 Systems at risk 102
- 2.15.3 Impact of security breaches 103
- 2.15.4 Attacker motivation 103

- 2.15.5 Computer protection (countermeasures) 103
- 2.15.6 Notable computer security attacks and breaches 107
- 2.15.7 Legal issues and global regulation 108
- 2.15.8 Government 108
- 2.15.9 Actions and teams in the US 109
- 2.15.10 International actions 109
- 2.15.11 National teams 111
- 2.15.12 Modern warfare 111
- 2.15.13 The cyber security job market 111
- 2.15.14 Terminology 112
- 2.15.15 Scholars 114
- 2.15.16 See also 114
- 2.15.17 Further reading 115
- 2.15.18 References 115
- 2.15.19 External links 118
- 2.16 Cryptography 118
  - 2.16.1 Terminology 119
  - 2.16.2 History of cryptography and cryptanalysis 119
  - 2.16.3 Modern cryptography 122
  - 2.16.4 Legal issues 126
  - 2.16.5 See also 128
  - 2.16.6 References 129
  - 2.16.7 Further reading 130
  - 2.16.8 External links 131
- 2.17 Distributed computing 131
  - 2.17.1 Introduction 132
  - 2.17.2 Parallel and distributed computing 132
  - 2.17.3 History 133
  - 2.17.4 Applications 133
  - 2.17.5 Examples 133
  - 2.17.6 Theoretical foundations 134
  - 2.17.7 Coordinator election 136
  - 2.17.8 Architectures 137
  - 2.17.9 See also 137
  - 2.17.10 Notes 138
  - 2.17.11 References 138
  - 2.17.12 Further reading 139
  - 2.17.13 External links 139

2.18 Database 139
2.18.1 Terminology and overview 140
2.18.2 Applications 140
2.18.3 General-purpose and special-purpose DBMSs 141
2.18.4 History 141
2.18.5 Research 145
2.18.6 Examples 145
2.18.7 Design and modeling 147
2.18.8 Languages 149
2.18.9 Performance, security, and availability 149
2.18.10 See also 152
2.18.11 References 152
2.18.12 Further reading 153
2.18.13 External links 154
2.19 Women in computing 154
2.19.1 Gender gap 154
2.19.2 Benefits of gender diversity 155
2.19.3 Factors contributing to lack of female participation ... 155
2.19.4 Attracting women into computing 157
2.19.5 Relation to gender theory 159
2.19.6 Worldwide timeline 160
2.19.7 Notable organizations 163
2.19.8 See also 164
2.19.9 References 164
2.19.10 Further reading 167
2.19.11 External links 167

3 Text and image sources, contributors, and licenses — 168
3.1 Text 168
3.2 Images 179
3.3 Content license 184

Chapter 1

Introduction To Computer Science

1.1 Computer science

Computer science deals with the theoretical foundations of information and computation, together with practical techniques for the implementation and application of these foundations

Computer science is the scientific and practical approach to computation and its applications. It is the systematic study of the feasibility, structure, expression, and mechanization of the methodical procedures (or algorithms) that underlie the acquisition, representation, processing, storage, communication of, and access to information, whether such information is encoded as bits in a computer memory or transcribed in genes and protein structures in a biological cell.[1] An alternate, more succinct definition of computer science is the study of automating algorithmic processes that scale. A computer scientist specializes in the theory of computation and the design of computational systems.[2]

Its sub fields can be divided into a variety of theoretical and practical disciplines. Some fields, such as computational complexity theory (which explores the fundamental properties of computational and intractable problems), are highly abstract, while fields such as computer graphics emphasize real-world visual applications. Still other fields focus on the challenges in implementing computation. For example, programming language theory considers various approaches to the description of computation, while the study of computer programming itself investigates various aspects of the use of programming language and complex systems. Human–computer interaction considers the challenges in making computers and computations useful, usable, and universally accessible to humans.

1.1.1 History

Main article: History of computer science
 The earliest foundations of what would become computer science predate the invention of the modern digital

Charles Babbage is credited with inventing the first mechanical computer.

computer. Machines for calculating fixed numerical tasks such as the abacus have existed since antiquity, aiding in computations such as multiplication and division. Further, algorithms for performing computations have existed since antiquity, even before the development of sophisticated computing equipment. The ancient Sanskrit treatise Shulba Sutras, or "Rules of the Chord", is a book of algorithms written in 800 BC for constructing geometric objects like altars using a peg and chord, an early precursor of the modern field of computational geometry.

Blaise Pascal designed and constructed the first working mechanical calculator, Pascal's calculator, in 1642.[3] In 1673 Gottfried Leibniz demonstrated a digital mechanical calculator, called the 'Stepped Reckoner'.[4] He may be considered the first computer scientist and information theorist, for, among other reasons, documenting the binary number system. In 1820, Thomas de Colmar launched

Ada Lovelace is credited with writing the first algorithm intended for processing on a computer.

the mechanical calculator industry[note 1] when he released his simplified arithmometer, which was the first calculating machine strong enough and reliable enough to be used daily in an office environment. Charles Babbage started the design of the first *automatic mechanical calculator*, his difference engine, in 1822, which eventually gave him the idea of the first *programmable mechanical calculator*, his Analytical Engine.[5] He started developing this machine in 1834 and "in less than two years he had sketched out many of the salient features of the modern computer. A crucial step was the adoption of a punched card system derived from the Jacquard loom"[6] making it infinitely programmable.[note 2] In 1843, during the translation of a French article on the *analytical engine*, Ada Lovelace wrote, in one of the many notes she included, an algorithm to compute the Bernoulli numbers, which is considered to be the first computer program.[7] Around 1885, Herman Hollerith invented the tabulator, which used punched cards to process statistical information; eventually his company became part of IBM. In 1937, one hundred years after Babbage's impossible dream, Howard Aiken convinced IBM, which was making all kinds of punched card equipment and was also in the calculator business[8] to develop his giant programmable calculator, the ASCC/Harvard Mark I, based on Babbage's *analytical engine*, which itself used cards and a central computing unit. When the machine was finished, some hailed it as "Babbage's dream come true".[9]

During the 1940s, as new and more powerful computing machines were developed, the term *computer* came to refer to the machines rather than their human predecessors.[10] As it became clear that computers could be used for more than just mathematical calculations, the field of computer science broadened to study computation in general. Computer science began to be established as a distinct academic discipline in the 1950s and early 1960s.[11][12] The world's first computer science degree program, the Cambridge Diploma in Computer Science, began at the University of Cambridge Computer Laboratory in 1953. The first computer science degree program in the United States was formed at Purdue University in 1962.[13] Since practical computers became available, many applications of computing have become distinct areas of study in their own rights.

Although many initially believed it was impossible that computers themselves could actually be a scientific field of study, in the late fifties it gradually became accepted among the greater academic population.[14][15] It is the now well-known IBM brand that formed part of the computer science revolution during this time. IBM (short for International Business Machines) released the IBM 704[16] and later the IBM 709[17] computers, which were widely used during the exploration period of such devices. "Still, working with the IBM [computer] was frustrating ... if you had misplaced as much as one letter in one instruction, the program would crash, and you would have to start the whole process over again".[14] During the late 1950s, the computer science discipline was very much in its developmental stages, and such issues were commonplace.[15]

Time has seen significant improvements in the usability and effectiveness of computing technology. Modern society has seen a significant shift in the users of computer technology, from usage only by experts and professionals, to a near-ubiquitous user base. Initially, computers were quite costly, and some degree of human aid was needed for efficient use - in part from professional computer operators. As computer adoption became more widespread and affordable, less human assistance was needed for common usage.

Contributions

Despite its short history as a formal academic discipline, computer science has made a number of fundamental contributions to science and society - in fact, along with electronics, it is a founding science of the current epoch of human history called the Information Age and a driver of the Information Revolution, seen as the third major leap in human technological progress after the Industrial Rev-

The German military used the Enigma machine (shown here) during World War II for communications they wanted kept secret. The large-scale decryption of Enigma traffic at Bletchley Park was an important factor that contributed to Allied victory in WWII.[18]

olution (1750-1850 CE) and the Agricultural Revolution (8000-5000 BC).

These contributions include:

- The start of the "digital revolution", which includes the current Information Age and the Internet.[19]

- A formal definition of computation and computability, and proof that there are computationally unsolvable and intractable problems.[20]

- The concept of a programming language, a tool for the precise expression of methodological information at various levels of abstraction.[21]

- In cryptography, breaking the Enigma code was an important factor contributing to the Allied victory in World War II.[18]

- Scientific computing enabled practical evaluation of processes and situations of great complexity, as well as experimentation entirely by software. It also enabled advanced study of the mind, and mapping of the human genome became possible with the Human Genome Project.[19] Distributed computing projects such as Folding@home explore protein folding.

- Algorithmic trading has increased the efficiency and liquidity of financial markets by using artificial intelligence, machine learning, and other statistical and numerical techniques on a large scale.[22] High frequency algorithmic trading can also exacerbate volatility.[23]

- Computer graphics and computer-generated imagery have become ubiquitous in modern entertainment, particularly in television, cinema, advertising, animation and video games. Even films that feature no explicit CGI are usually "filmed" now on digital cameras, or edited or postprocessed using a digital video editor.

- Simulation of various processes, including computational fluid dynamics, physical, electrical, and electronic systems and circuits, as well as societies and social situations (notably war games) along with their habitats, among many others. Modern computers enable optimization of such designs as complete aircraft. Notable in electrical and electronic circuit design are SPICE, as well as software for physical realization of new (or modified) designs. The latter includes essential design software for integrated circuits.

- Artificial intelligence is becoming increasingly important as it gets more efficient and complex. There are many applications of AI, some of which can be seen at home, such as robotic vacuum cleaners. It is also present in video games and on the modern battlefield in drones, anti-missile systems, and squad support robots.

1.1.2 Philosophy

Main article: Philosophy of computer science

A number of computer scientists have argued for the distinction of three separate paradigms in computer science. Peter Wegner argued that those paradigms are science, technology, and mathematics.[24] Peter Denning's working group argued that they are theory, abstraction (modeling), and design.[25] Amnon H. Eden described them as the "rationalist paradigm" (which treats computer science as a branch of mathematics, which is prevalent in theoretical computer science, and mainly employs deductive reasoning), the "technocratic paradigm" (which might be found in engineering approaches, most prominently in software engineering), and the "scientific paradigm" (which approaches computer-related artifacts from the empirical perspective of natural sciences, identifiable in some branches of artificial intelligence).[26]

Name of the field

Although first proposed in 1956,[15] the term "computer science" appears in a 1959 article in *Communications of the ACM*,[27] in which Louis Fein argues for the creation of a *Graduate School in Computer Sciences* analogous to the creation of Harvard Business School in 1921,[28] justifying the name by arguing that, like management science, the subject is applied and interdisciplinary in nature, while having the characteristics typical of an academic discipline.[27] His efforts, and those of others such as numerical analyst George Forsythe, were rewarded: universities went on to create such programs, starting with Purdue in 1962.[29] Despite its name, a significant amount of computer science does not involve the study of computers themselves. Because of this, several alternative names have been proposed.[30] Certain departments of major universities prefer the term *computing science*, to emphasize precisely that difference. Danish scientist Peter Naur suggested the term *datalogy*,[31] to reflect the fact that the scientific discipline revolves around data and data treatment, while not necessarily involving computers. The first scientific institution to use the term was the Department of Datalogy at the University of Copenhagen, founded in 1969, with Peter Naur being the first professor in datalogy. The term is used mainly in the Scandinavian countries. An alternative term, also proposed by Naur, is data science; this is now used for a distinct field of data analysis, including statistics and databases.

Also, in the early days of computing, a number of terms for the practitioners of the field of computing were suggested in the *Communications of the ACM* – *turingineer*, *turologist*, *flow-charts-man*, *applied meta-mathematician*, and *applied epistemologist*.[32] Three months later in the same journal, *comptologist* was suggested, followed next year by *hypologist*.[33] The term *computics* has also been suggested.[34] In Europe, terms derived from contracted translations of the expression "automatic information" (e.g. "informazione automatica" in Italian) or "information and mathematics" are often used, e.g. *informatique* (French), *Informatik* (German), *informatica* (Italy, The Netherlands), *informática* (Spain, Portugal), *informatika* (Slavic languages and Hungarian) or *pliroforiki* (πληροφορική, which means informatics) in Greek. Similar words have also been adopted in the UK (as in *the School of Informatics of the University of Edinburgh*).[35]

A folkloric quotation, often attributed to—but almost certainly not first formulated by—Edsger Dijkstra, states that "computer science is no more about computers than astronomy is about telescopes."[note 3] The design and deployment of computers and computer systems is generally considered the province of disciplines other than computer science. For example, the study of computer hardware is usually considered part of computer engineering, while the study of commercial computer systems and their deployment is often called information technology or information systems. However, there has been much cross-fertilization of ideas between the various computer-related disciplines. Computer science research also often intersects other disciplines, such as philosophy, cognitive science, linguistics, mathematics, physics, biology, statistics, and logic.

Computer science is considered by some to have a much closer relationship with mathematics than many scientific disciplines, with some observers saying that computing is a mathematical science.[11] Early computer science was strongly influenced by the work of mathematicians such as Kurt Gödel and Alan Turing, and there continues to be a useful interchange of ideas between the two fields in areas such as mathematical logic, category theory, domain theory, and algebra.[15]

The relationship between computer science and software engineering is a contentious issue, which is further muddied by disputes over what the term "software engineering" means, and how computer science is defined.[36] David Parnas, taking a cue from the relationship between other engineering and science disciplines, has claimed that the principal focus of computer science is studying the properties of computation in general, while the principal focus of software engineering is the design of specific computations to achieve practical goals, making the two separate but complementary disciplines.[37]

The academic, political, and funding aspects of computer science tend to depend on whether a department formed with a mathematical emphasis or with an engineering emphasis. Computer science departments with a mathematics emphasis and with a numerical orientation consider alignment with computational science. Both types of departments tend to make efforts to bridge the field educationally if not across all research.

1.1.3 Areas of computer science

Further information: Outline of computer science

As a discipline, computer science spans a range of topics from theoretical studies of algorithms and the limits of computation to the practical issues of implementing computing systems in hardware and software.[38][39] CSAB, formerly called *Computing Sciences Accreditation Board* – which is made up of representatives of the Association for Computing Machinery (ACM), and the IEEE Computer Society (IEEE-CS)[40] – identifies four areas that it considers crucial to the discipline of computer science: *theory of computation, algorithms and data structures, programming methodology and languages*, and *computer elements and architecture*. In addition to these four areas, CSAB also identifies fields such as software engineering, artificial intelligence, computer networking and telecommunications, database systems, parallel computation, distributed computation, computer-human interaction, computer graphics, operating systems, and numerical and symbolic computation as being important areas of computer science.[38]

Theoretical computer science

Main article: Theoretical computer science

The broader field of theoretical computer science encompasses both the classical theory of computation and a wide range of other topics that focus on the more abstract, logical, and mathematical aspects of computing.

Theory of computation Main article: Theory of computation

According to Peter J. Denning, the fundamental question underlying computer science is, *"What can be (efficiently) automated?"*[11] The study of the theory of computation is focused on answering fundamental questions about what can be computed and what amount of resources are required to perform those computations. In an effort to answer the first question, computability theory examines which computational problems are solvable on various theoretical models of computation. The second question is addressed by computational complexity theory, which studies the time and space costs associated with different approaches to solving a multitude of computational problems.

The famous "P=NP?" problem, one of the Millennium Prize Problems,[41] is an open problem in the theory of computation.

Information and coding theory Main articles: Information theory and Coding theory

Information theory is related to the quantification of information. This was developed by Claude E. Shannon to find fundamental limits on signal processing operations such as compressing data and on reliably storing and communicating data.[42] Coding theory is the study of the properties of codes (systems for converting information from one form to another) and their fitness for a specific application. Codes are used for data compression, cryptography, error detection and correction, and more recently also for network coding. Codes are studied for the purpose of designing efficient and reliable data transmission methods.

Algorithms and data structures Algorithms and data structures is the study of commonly used computational methods and their computational efficiency.

Programming language theory Main article: Programming language theory

Programming language theory is a branch of computer science that deals with the design, implementation, analysis, characterization, and classification of programming languages and their individual features. It falls within the discipline of computer science, both depending on and affecting mathematics, software engineering and linguistics. It is an active research area, with numerous dedicated academic journals.

Formal methods Main article: Formal methods

Formal methods are a particular kind of mathematically based technique for the specification, development and verification of software and hardware systems. The use of formal methods for software and hardware design is motivated by the expectation that, as in other engineering disciplines, performing appropriate mathematical analysis can contribute to the reliability and robustness of a design. They form an important theoretical underpinning for software engineering, especially where safety or security is involved. Formal methods are a useful adjunct to software testing since they help avoid errors and can also give a framework for testing. For industrial use, tool support is required. However, the high cost of using formal methods means that they are usually only used in the development of high-integrity and life-critical systems, where safety or security is of utmost importance. Formal methods are best described as the application of a fairly broad variety of theoretical computer science fundamentals, in particular logic calculi, formal languages, automata theory, and program semantics, but also type systems and algebraic data types to problems in software and hardware specification and verification.

Applied computer science

Applied computer science aims at identifying certain computer science concepts that can be used directly in solving real world problems.

Artificial intelligence Main article: Artificial intelligence

This branch of computer science aims to or is required to synthesise goal-orientated processes such as problem-solving, decision-making, environmental adaptation, learning and communication found in humans and animals. From its origins in cybernetics and in the Dartmouth Conference (1956), artificial intelligence (AI) research has been necessarily cross-disciplinary, drawing on areas of expertise such as applied mathematics, symbolic logic, semiotics, electrical engineering, philosophy of mind, neurophysiology, and social intelligence. AI is associated in the popular mind with robotic development, but the main field of practical application has been as an embedded component in areas of software development, which require computational understanding. The starting-point in the late 1940s was Alan Turing's question "Can computers think?", and the question remains effectively unanswered although the "Turing test" is still used to assess computer output on the scale of human intelligence. But the automation of evaluative and predictive tasks has been increasingly successful as a substitute for human monitoring and intervention in domains of computer application involving complex real-world data.

Computer architecture and engineering Main articles: Computer architecture and Computer engineering

Computer architecture, or digital computer organization, is the conceptual design and fundamental operational structure of a computer system. It focuses largely on the way by which the central processing unit performs internally and accesses addresses in memory.[43] The field often involves disciplines of computer engineering and electrical engineering, selecting and interconnecting hardware components to create computers that meet functional, performance, and cost goals.

Computer performance analysis Main article: Computer performance

Computer performance analysis is the study of work flowing through computers with the general goals of improving throughput, controlling response time, using resources efficiently, eliminating bottlenecks, and predicting performance under anticipated peak loads.[44]

Computer graphics and visualization Main article: Computer graphics (computer science)

Computer graphics is the study of digital visual contents, and involves synthese and manipulations of image data. The study is connected to many other fields in computer science, including computer vision, image processing, and computational geometry, and is heavily applied in the fields of special effects and video games.

Computer security and cryptography Main articles: Computer security and Cryptography

Computer security is a branch of computer technology, whose objective includes protection of information from unauthorized access, disruption, or modification while maintaining the accessibility and usability of the system for its intended users. Cryptography is the practice and study of hiding (encryption) and therefore deciphering (decryption) information. Modern cryptography is largely related to computer science, for many encryption and decryption algorithms are based on their computational complexity.

Computational science Computational science (or scientific computing) is the field of study concerned with constructing mathematical models and quantitative analysis techniques and using computers to analyze and solve scientific problems. In practical use, it is typically the application of computer simulation and other forms of computation to problems in various scientific disciplines.

Computer networks Main article: Computer network

This branch of computer science aims to manage networks between computers worldwide.

Concurrent, parallel and distributed systems Main articles: Concurrency (computer science) and Distributed computing

Concurrency is a property of systems in which several computations are executing simultaneously, and potentially interacting with each other. A number of mathematical models have been developed for general concurrent computation including Petri nets, process calculi and the Parallel Random Access Machine model. A distributed system extends the idea of concurrency onto multiple computers connected through a network. Computers within the same distributed system have their own private memory, and information is often exchanged among themselves to achieve a common goal.

Databases Main article: Database

A database is intended to organize, store, and retrieve large amounts of data easily. Digital databases are managed using database management systems to store, create, maintain, and search data, through database models and query languages.

Software engineering Main article: Software engineering
See also: Computer programming

Software engineering is the study of designing, implementing, and modifying software in order to ensure it is of high quality, affordable, maintainable, and fast to build. It is a systematic approach to software design, involving the application of engineering practices to software. Software engineering deals with the organizing and analyzing of software— it doesn't just deal with the creation or manufacture of new software, but its internal maintenance and arrangement. Both computer applications software engineers and computer systems software engineers are projected to be among the fastest growing occupations from 2008 and 2018.

1.1.4 The great insights of computer science

The philosopher of computing Bill Rapaport noted three *Great Insights of Computer Science*[45]

- Leibniz's, Boole's, Alan Turing's, Shannon's, & Morse's insight: There are only **two objects** that a computer has to deal with in order to represent "anything"

    All the information about any computable problem can be represented using only 0 and 1 (or any other bistable pair that can flip-flop between two easily distinguishable states, such as "on"/"off", "magnetized/de-magnetized", "high-voltage/low-voltage", etc.).

See also: Digital physics

- Alan Turing's insight: There are only **five actions** that a computer has to perform in order to do "anything"

    Every algorithm can be expressed in a language for a computer consisting of only five basic instructions:

    * move left one location
    * move right one location
    * read symbol at current location
    * print 0 at current location
    * print 1 at current location

See also: Turing machine

- Böhm and Jacopini's insight: There are only **three ways of combining** these actions (into more complex ones) that are needed in order for a computer to do "anything"

Only three rules are needed to combine any set of basic instructions into more complex ones:

sequence:

  first do this; then do that

selection :

  IF such-and-such is the case,
  THEN do this
  ELSE do that

repetition:

  WHILE such-and-such is the case
  DO this

Note that the three rules of Boehm's and Jacopini's insight can be further simplified with the use of goto (which means it is more elementary than structured programming).

See also: Elementary function arithmetic § Friedman's grand conjecture

1.1.5 Academia

Further information: List of computer science conferences and Category:Computer science journals

Conferences are important events for computer science research. During these conferences, researchers from the public and private sectors present their recent work and meet. Unlike in most other academic fields, in computer science, the prestige of conference papers is greater than that of journal publications.[46][47] One proposed explanation for this is the quick development of this relatively new field requires rapid review and distribution of results, a task better handled by conferences than by journals.[48]

1.1.6 Education

See also: Women in computing

Since computer science is a relatively new field, it is not as widely taught in schools and universities as other academic subjects. For example, in 2014, Code.org estimated that only 10 percent of high schools in the United States offered computer science education.[49] A 2010 report by Association for Computing Machinery (ACM) and Computer Science Teachers Association (CSTA) revealed that only 14 out of 50 states have adopted significant education standards for high school computer science.[50] However, computer science education is growing. Some countries, such as Israel, New Zealand and South Korea, have already included computer science in their respective national secondary education curriculum.[51][52] Several countries are following suit.[53]

In most countries, there is a significant gender gap in computer science education. For example, in the U.S. about 20% of computer science degrees in 2012 were conferred to women.[54] This gender gap also exists in other Western countries.[55] However, in some parts of the world, the gap is small or nonexistent. In 2011, approximately half of all computer science degrees in Malaysia were conferred to women.[56] In 2001, women made up 54.5% of computer science graduates in Guyana.[55]

1.1.7 See also

Main article: Outline of computer science

- Academic genealogy of computer scientists
- Informatics (academic field)
- List of academic computer science departments
- List of computer science conferences
- List of computer scientists
- List of publications in computer science
- List of pioneers in computer science
- Technology transfer in computer science
- Outline of software engineering
- List of unsolved problems in computer science
- Turing Award
- Women in computing

Computer science – Wikipedia book

1.1.8 Notes

[1] In 1851

[2] "The introduction of punched cards into the new engine was important not only as a more convenient form of control than the drums, or because programs could now be of unlimited extent, and could be stored and repeated without the danger of introducing errors in setting the machine by hand; it was important also because it served to crystallize Babbage's feeling that he had invented something really new, something much more than a sophisticated calculating machine." Bruce Collier, 1970

[3] See the entry "Computer science" on Wikiquote for the history of this quotation.

1.1.9 References

[1] "What is Computer Science?" (PDF). Boston University Department of Computer Science. Spring 2003. Retrieved December 12, 2014.

[2] "WordNet Search - 3.1". Wordnetweb.princeton.edu. Retrieved 2012-05-14.

[3] "Blaise Pascal". School of Mathematics and Statistics University of St Andrews, Scotland.

[4] "A Brief History of Computing".

[5] "Science Museum - Introduction to Babbage". Archived from the original on 2006-09-08. Retrieved 2006-09-24.

[6] Anthony Hyman (1982). *Charles Babbage, pioneer of the computer*.

[7] "A Selection and Adaptation From Ada's Notes found in Ada, The Enchantress of Numbers," by Betty Alexandra Toole Ed.D. Strawberry Press, Mill Valley, CA". Archived from the original on 10 February 2006. Retrieved 2006-05-04.

[8] "In this sense Aiken needed IBM, whose technology included the use of punched cards, the accumulation of numerical data, and the transfer of numerical data from one register to another", Bernard Cohen, p.44 (2000)

[9] Brian Randell, p. 187, 1975

[10] The Association for Computing Machinery (ACM) was founded in 1947.

[11] Denning, P.J. (2000). "Computer Science: The Discipline" (PDF). *Encyclopedia of Computer Science*. Archived from the original (PDF) on 2006-05-25.

[12] "Some EDSAC statistics". Cl.cam.ac.uk. Retrieved 2011-11-19.

[13] "Computer science pioneer Samuel D. Conte dies at 85". Purdue Computer Science. July 1, 2002. Retrieved December 12, 2014.

[14] Levy, Steven (1984). *Hackers: Heroes of the Computer Revolution*. Doubleday. ISBN 0-385-19195-2.

[15] Tedre, Matti (2014). *The Science of Computing: Shaping a Discipline*. Taylor and Francis / CRC Press.

[16] "IBM 704 Electronic Data Processing System - CHM Revolution". Computerhistory.org. Retrieved 2013-07-07.

[17] "IBM 709: a powerful new data processing system" (PDF). Computer History Museum. Retrieved December 12, 2014.

[18] David Kahn, The Codebreakers, 1967, ISBN 0-684-83130-9.

[19] http://www.cis.cornell.edu/Dean/Presentations/Slides/bgu.pdf[]

[20] Constable, R. L. (March 2000). "Computer Science: Achievements and Challenges circa 2000" (PDF).

[21] Abelson, H.; G.J. Sussman with J. Sussman (1996). *Structure and Interpretation of Computer Programs* (2nd ed.). MIT Press. ISBN 0-262-01153-0. The computer revolution is a revolution in the way we think and in the way we express what we think. The essence of this change is the emergence of what might best be called *procedural epistemology* — the study of the structure of knowledge from an imperative point of view, as opposed to the more declarative point of view taken by classical mathematical subjects.

[22] "Black box traders are on the march". *The Telegraph*. August 26, 2006. Archived from the original on 8 October 2014.

[23] "The Impact of High Frequency Trading on an Electronic Market". Papers.ssrn.com. doi:10.2139/ssrn.1686004. Retrieved 2012-05-14.

[24] Wegner, P. (October 13–15, 1976). *Research paradigms in computer science - Proceedings of the 2nd international Conference on Software Engineering*. San Francisco, California, United States: IEEE Computer Society Press, Los Alamitos, CA.

[25] Denning, P. J.; Comer, D. E.; Gries, D.; Mulder, M. C.; Tucker, A.; Turner, A. J.; Young, P. R. (Jan 1989). "Computing as a discipline". *Communications of the ACM* **32**: 9–23. doi:10.1145/63238.63239.

[26] Eden, A. H. (2007). "Three Paradigms of Computer Science" (PDF). *Minds and Machines* **17** (2): 135–167. doi:10.1007/s11023-007-9060-8.

[27] Louis Fine (1959). "The Role of the University in Computers, Data Processing, and Related Fields". *Communications of the ACM* **2** (9): 7–14. doi:10.1145/368424.368427.

[28] "Stanford University Oral History". Stanford University. Retrieved May 30, 2013.

[29] Donald Knuth (1972). *"George Forsythe and the Development of Computer Science"*. Comms. ACM. *Archived August 12, 2014 at the Wayback Machine*

[30] Matti Tedre (2006). "The Development of Computer Science: A Sociocultural Perspective" (PDF). p. 260. Retrieved December 12, 2014.

[31] Peter Naur (1966). "The science of datalogy". *Communications of the ACM* **9** (7): 485. doi:10.1145/365719.366510.

[32] "Communications of the ACM". *Communications of the ACM* **1** (4): 6.

[33] Communications of the ACM 2(1):p.4

[34] IEEE Computer 28(12):p.136

[35] P. Mounier-Kuhn, *L'Informatique en France, de la seconde guerre mondiale au Plan Calcul. L'émergence d'une science*, Paris, PUPS, 2010, ch. 3 & 4.

[36] Tedre, M. (2011). "Computing as a Science: A Survey of Competing Viewpoints". *Minds and Machines* **21** (3): 361–387. doi:10.1007/s11023-011-9240-4.

[37] Parnas, D. L. (1998). "Software engineering programmes are not computer science programmes". *Annals of Software Engineering* **6**: 19–37. doi:10.1023/A:1018949113292., p. 19: "Rather than treat software engineering as a subfield of computer science, I treat it as an element of the set, Civil Engineering, Mechanical Engineering, Chemical Engineering, Electrical Engineering, [...]"

[38] Computing Sciences Accreditation Board (May 28, 1997). "Computer Science as a Profession". Archived from the original on 2008-06-17. Retrieved 2010-05-23.

[39] Committee on the Fundamentals of Computer Science: Challenges and Opportunities, National Research Council (2004). *Computer Science: Reflections on the Field, Reflections from the Field*. National Academies Press. ISBN 978-0-309-09301-9.

[40] "CSAB Leading Computer Education". CSAB. 2011-08-03. Retrieved 2011-11-19.

[41] Clay Mathematics Institute P=NP Archived October 14, 2013 at the Wayback Machine

[42] P. Collins, Graham (October 14, 2002). "Claude E. Shannon: Founder of Information Theory". Scientific American. Retrieved December 12, 2014.

[43] A. Thisted, Ronald (April 7, 1997). "Computer Architecture" (PDF). The University of Chicago.

[44] Wescott, Bob (2013). *The Every Computer Performance Book, Chapter 3: Useful laws*. CreateSpace. ISBN 1482657759.

[45] "What Is Computation?". *buffalo.edu*.

[46] Meyer, Bertrand (April 2009). "Viewpoint: Research evaluation for computer science". *Communications of the ACM* **25** (4): 31–34. doi:10.1145/1498765.1498780.

[47] Patterson, David (August 1999). "Evaluating Computer Scientists and Engineers For Promotion and Tenure". Computing Research Association.

[48] Fortnow, Lance (August 2009). "Viewpoint: Time for Computer Science to Grow Up". *Communications of the ACM* **52** (8): 33–35. doi:10.1145/1536616.1536631.

[49] "Computer Science: Not Just an Elective Anymore". *Education Week*. February 25, 2014.

[50] "Running On Empty" (PDF). October 2010.

[51] "A is for algorithm". *The Economist*. April 26, 2014.

[52] "Computing at School International comparisons" (PDF). Retrieved 20 July 2015.

[53] "Adding Coding to the Curriculum". *New York Times*. March 23, 2014.

[54] "IT gender gap: Where are the female programmers?". Retrieved 20 July 2015.

[55] "IT gender gap: Where are the female programmers?".

[56] "what gender is science" (PDF). Retrieved 20 July 2015.

1.1.10 Further reading

Overview

- Tucker, Allen B. (2004). *Computer Science Handbook* (2nd ed.). Chapman and Hall/CRC. ISBN 1-58488-360-X.
  - "Within more than 70 chapters, every one new or significantly revised, one can find any kind of information and references about computer science one can imagine. [...] all in all, there is absolute nothing about Computer Science that can not be found in the 2.5 kilogram-encyclopaedia with its 110 survey articles [...]." (Christoph Meinel, *Zentralblatt MATH*)

- van Leeuwen, Jan (1994). *Handbook of Theoretical Computer Science*. The MIT Press. ISBN 0-262-72020-5.
  - "[...] this set is the most unique and possibly the most useful to the [theoretical computer science] community, in support both of teaching and research [...]. The books can be used by anyone wanting simply to gain an understanding of one of these areas, or by someone desiring to be in research in a topic, or by instructors wishing to find timely information on a subject they are teaching outside their major areas of expertise." (Rocky Ross, *SIGACT News*)

- Ralston, Anthony; Reilly, Edwin D.; Hemmendinger, David (2000). *Encyclopedia of Computer Science* (4th ed.). Grove's Dictionaries. ISBN 1-56159-248-X.
  - "Since 1976, this has been the definitive reference work on computer, computing, and computer science. [...] Alphabetically arranged and classified into broad subject areas, the entries cover hardware, computer systems, information and data, software, the mathematics of computing, theory of computation, methodologies, applications, and computing milieu. The editors have done a commendable job of blending historical perspective and practical reference information. The encyclopedia remains essential for most public and academic library reference collections." (Joe Accardin, Northeastern Illinois Univ., Chicago)

- Edwin D. Reilly (2003). *Milestones in Computer Science and Information Technology*. Greenwood Publishing Group. ISBN 978-1-57356-521-9.

Selected papers

- Knuth, Donald E. (1996). *Selected Papers on Computer Science*. CSLI Publications, Cambridge University Press.

- Collier, Bruce. *The little engine that could've: The calculating machines of Charles Babbage*. Garland Publishing Inc. ISBN 0-8240-0043-9.

- Cohen, Bernard (2000). *Howard Aiken, Portrait of a computer pioneer*. The MIT press. ISBN 978-0-2625317-9-5.

- Tedre, Matti (2014). *The Science of Computing: Shaping a Discipline*. CRC Press, Taylor & Francis.

- Randell, Brian (1973). *The origins of Digital computers, Selected Papers*. Springer-Verlag. ISBN 3-540-06169-X.
  - "Covering a period from 1966 to 1993, its interest lies not only in the content of each of these papers — still timely today — but also in their being put together so that ideas expressed at different times complement each other nicely." (N. Bernard, *Zentralblatt MATH*)

Articles

- Peter J. Denning. *Is computer science science?*, Communications of the ACM, April 2005.

- Peter J. Denning, *Great principles in computing curricula*, Technical Symposium on Computer Science Education, 2004.
- Research evaluation for computer science, Informatics Europe report. Shorter journal version: Bertrand Meyer, Christine Choppy, Jan van Leeuwen and Jorgen Staunstrup, *Research evaluation for computer science*, in Communications of the ACM, vol. 52, no. 4, pp. 31–34, April 2009.

Curriculum and classification

- Association for Computing Machinery. 1998 ACM Computing Classification System. 1998.
- Joint Task Force of Association for Computing Machinery (ACM), Association for Information Systems (AIS) and IEEE Computer Society (IEEE-CS). Computing Curricula 2005: The Overview Report. September 30, 2005.
- Norman Gibbs, Allen Tucker. "A model curriculum for a liberal arts degree in computer science". *Communications of the ACM*, Volume 29 Issue 3, March 1986.

1.1.11 External links

- Computer science at DMOZ
- Scholarly Societies in Computer Science
- Best Papers Awards in Computer Science since 1996
- Photographs of computer scientists by Bertrand Meyer
- EECS.berkeley.edu

Bibliography and academic search engines

- CiteSeer^x (article): search engine, digital library and repository for scientific and academic papers with a focus on computer and information science.
- DBLP Computer Science Bibliography (article): computer science bibliography website hosted at Universität Trier, in Germany.
- The Collection of Computer Science Bibliographies (article)

Professional organizations

- Association for Computing Machinery
- IEEE Computer Society
- Informatics Europe
- AAAI
- AAAS Computer Science

Misc

- Computer Science - Stack Exchange: a community-run question-and-answer site for computer science
- What is computer science
- Is computer science science?

Chapter 2

Important Topics

2.1 History of computer science

The **history of computer science** began long before the modern discipline of computer science that emerged in the 20th century, and was hinted at in the centuries prior. The progression, from mechanical inventions and mathematical theories towards modern computer concepts and machines, led to a major academic field and the basis of a massive worldwide industry.[1]

The earliest known tool for use in computation was the abacus, developed in the period between 2700–2300 BCE in Sumer . The Sumerians' abacus consisted of a table of successive columns which delimited the successive orders of magnitude of their sexagesimal number system.[2]:11 Its original style of usage was by lines drawn in sand with pebbles . Abaci of a more modern design are still used as calculation tools today.[3]

The Antikythera mechanism is believed to be the earliest known mechanical analog computer.[4] It was designed to calculate astronomical positions. It was discovered in 1901 in the Antikythera wreck off the Greek island of Antikythera, between Kythera and Crete, and has been dated to c. 100 BCE. Technological artifacts of similar complexity did not reappear until the 14th century, when mechanical astronomical clocks appeared in Europe.[5]

When John Napier discovered logarithms for computational purposes in the early 17th century, there followed a period of considerable progress by inventors and scientists in making calculating tools. In 1623 Wilhelm Schickard designed a calculating machine, but abandoned the project, when the prototype he had started building was destroyed by a fire in 1624 . Around 1640, Blaise Pascal, a leading French mathematician, constructed a mechanical adding device based on a design described by Greek mathematician Hero of Alexandria.[6] Then in 1672 Gottfried Wilhelm Leibnitz invented the Stepped Reckoner which he completed in 1694.[7]

In 1837 Charles Babbage first described his Analytical Engine which is accepted as the first design for a modern computer. The analytical engine had expandable memory, an arithmetic unit, and logic processing capabilities able to interpret a programming language with loops and conditional branching. Although never built, the design has been studied extensively and is understood to be Turing equivalent. The analytical engine would have had a memory capacity of less than 1 kilobyte of memory and a clock speed of less than 10 Hertz .

Considerable advancement in mathematics and electronics theory was required before the first modern computers could be designed.

2.1.1 Binary logic

In 1702, Gottfried Wilhelm Leibnitz developed logic in a formal, mathematical sense with his writings on the binary numeral system. In his system, the ones and zeros also represent *true* and *false* values or *on* and *off* states. But it took more than a century before George Boole published his Boolean algebra in 1854 with a complete system that allowed computational processes to be mathematically modeled .[8]

By this time, the first mechanical devices driven by a binary pattern had been invented. The industrial revolution had driven forward the mechanization of many tasks, and this included weaving. Punched cards controlled Joseph Marie Jacquard's loom in 1801, where a hole punched in the card indicated a binary *one* and an unpunched spot indicated a binary *zero*. Jacquard's loom was far from being a computer, but it did illustrate that machines could be driven by binary systems .[8]

2.1.2 Birth of the computer

Before the 1920s, *computers* (sometimes *computors*) were human clerks that performed computations. They were usually under the lead of a physicist. Many thousands of computers were employed in commerce, government, and research establishments. Most of these computers were women. Some performed astronomical calculations for calendars, others ballistic tables for the military.

After the 1920s, the expression *computing machine* referred to any machine that performed the work of a human computer, especially those in accordance with effective methods of the Church-Turing thesis. The thesis states that a mathematical method is effective if it could be set out as a list of instructions able to be followed by a human clerk with paper and pencil, for as long as necessary, and without ingenuity or insight .

Machines that computed with continuous values became known as the *analog* kind. They used machinery that represented continuous numeric quantities, like the angle of a shaft rotation or difference in electrical potential .

Digital machinery, in contrast to analog, were able to render a state of a numeric value and store each individual digit. Digital machinery used difference engines or relays before the invention of faster memory devices .

The phrase *computing machine* gradually gave away, after the late 1940s, to just *computer* as the onset of electronic digital machinery became common. These computers were able to perform the calculations that were performed by the previous human clerks .

Since the values stored by digital machines were not bound to physical properties like analog devices, a logical computer, based on digital equipment, was able to do anything that could be described "purely mechanical." The theoretical Turing Machine, created by Alan Turing, is a hypothetical device theorized in order to study the properties of such hardware.

2.1.3 Emergence of a discipline

Charles Babbage and Ada Lovelace

Main articles: Charles Babbage and Ada Lovelace

Charles Babbage is often regarded as one of the first pioneers of computing. Beginning in the 1810s, Babbage had a vision of mechanically computing numbers and tables. Putting this into reality, Babbage designed a calculator to compute numbers up to 8 decimal points long. Continuing with the success of this idea, Babbage worked to develop a machine that could compute numbers with up to 20 decimal places. By the 1830s, Babbage had devised a plan to develop a machine that could use punched cards to perform arithmetical operations. The machine would store numbers in memory units, and there would be a form of sequential control. This means that one operation would be carried out before another in such a way that the machine would produce an answer and not fail. This machine was to be known as the "Analytical Engine", which was the first true representation of what is the modern computer.[9]

Ada Lovelace (Augusta Ada Byron) is credited as the pioneer of computer programming and is regarded as a mathematical genius, a result of the mathematically heavy tutoring regimen her mother assigned to her as a young girl. Lovelace began working with Charles Babbage as an assistant while Babbage was working on his "Analytical Engine", the first mechanical computer. During her work with Babbage, Ada Lovelace became the designer of the first computer algorithm, which had the ability to compute Bernoulli numbers. Moreover, Lovelace's work with Babbage resulted in her prediction of future computers to not only perform mathematical calculations, but also manipulate symbols, mathematical or not. While she was never able to see the results of her work, as the "Analytical Engine" was not created in her lifetime, her efforts in later years, beginning in the 1940s, did not go unnoticed.[10]

Alan Turing and the Turing machine

Main articles: Alan Turing and Turing machine

The mathematical foundations of modern computer science began to be laid by Kurt Gödel with his incompleteness theorem (1931). In this theorem, he showed that there were limits to what could be proved and disproved within a formal system. This led to work by Gödel and others to define and describe these formal systems, including concepts such as mu-recursive functions and lambda-definable functions.

In 1936 Alan Turing and Alonzo Church independently, and also together, introduced the formalization of an algorithm, with limits on what can be computed, and a "purely mechanical" model for computing. This became the Church–Turing thesis, a hypothesis about the nature of mechanical calculation devices, such as electronic computers. The thesis claims that any calculation that is possible can be performed by an algorithm running on a computer, provided that sufficient time and storage space are available.

In 1936, Alan Turing also published his seminal work on the Turing machines, an abstract digital computing machine which is now simply referred to as the Universal Turing machine. This machine invented the principle of the modern computer and was the birth-place the stored program concept that almost all modern day computers use.[11] These hypothetical machines were designed to formally determine, mathematically, what can be computed, taking into account limitations on computing ability. If a Turing machine can complete the task, it is considered Turing computable or more commonly, Turing complete.[12]

The Los Alamos physicist Stanley Frankel, has described John von Neumann's view of the fundamental importance of Turing's 1936 paper, in a letter:[11]

> I know that in or about 1943 or '44 von Neumann was well aware of the fundamental importance of Turing's paper of 1936... Von Neumann introduced me to that paper and at his urging I studied it with care. Many people have acclaimed von Neumann as the "father of the computer" (in a modern sense of the term) but I am sure that he would never have made that mistake himself. He might well be called the midwife, perhaps, but he firmly emphasized to me, and to others I am sure, that the fundamental conception is owing to Turing...

Early computer hardware

In 1941, Konrad Zuse developed the world's first functional program-controlled computer, the Z3. in 1998, it was shown to be Turing-complete in principle.[13][14] Zuse also developed the S2 computing machine, considered the first process-controlled computer. He founded one of the earliest computer businesses in 1941, producing the Z4, which became the world's first commercial computer. In 1946, he designed the first high-level programming language, Plankalkül.[15]

In 1948, the Manchester Baby was completed, it was the world's first general purpose electronic digital computer that also ran stored programs like almost all modern computers.[11] The influence on Max Newman of Turing's seminal 1936 paper on the Turing Machines and of his logico-mathematical contributions to the project, were both crucial to the successful development of the Manchester SSEM.[11]

In 1950, Britain's National Physical Laboratory completed Pilot ACE, a small scale programmable computer, based on Turing's philosophy. With an operating speed of 1 MHz, the Pilot Model ACE was for some time the fastest computer in the world.[11][16] Turing's design for ACE had much in common with today's RISC architectures and it called for a high-speed memory of roughly the same capacity as an early Macintosh computer, which was enormous by the standards of his day.[11] Had Turing's ACE been built as planned and in full, it would have been in a different league from the other early computers.[11]

Shannon and information theory

Up to and during the 1930s, electrical engineers were able to build electronic circuits to solve mathematical and logic problems, but most did so in an *ad hoc* manner, lacking any theoretical rigor. This changed with Claude Elwood Shannon's publication of his 1937 master's thesis, A Symbolic Analysis of Relay and Switching Circuits. While taking an undergraduate philosophy class, Shannon had been exposed to Boole's work, and recognized that it could be used to arrange electromechanical relays (then used in telephone routing switches) to solve logic problems. This concept, of utilizing the properties of electrical switches to do logic, is the basic concept that underlies all electronic digital computers, and his thesis became the foundation of practical digital circuit design when it became widely known among the electrical engineering community during and after World War II.

Shannon went on to found the field of information theory with his 1948 paper titled A Mathematical Theory of Communication, which applied probability theory to the problem of how to best encode the information a sender wants to transmit. This work is one of the theoretical foundations for many areas of study, including data compression and cryptography.

Wiener and cybernetics

From experiments with anti-aircraft systems that interpreted radar images to detect enemy planes, Norbert Wiener coined the term cybernetics from the Greek word for "steersman." He published "Cybernetics" in 1948, which influenced artificial intelligence. Wiener also compared computation, computing machinery, memory devices, and other cognitive similarities with his analysis of brain waves.

The first actual computer bug was a moth. It was stuck in between the relays on the Harvard Mark II.[17] While the invention of the term 'bug' is often but erroneously attributed to Grace Hopper, a future rear admiral in the U.S. Navy, who supposedly logged the "bug" on September 9, 1945, most other accounts conflict at least with these details. According to these accounts, the actual date was September 9, 1947 when operators filed this 'incident' — along with the insect and the notation "First actual case of bug being found" (see software bug for details).[17]

John von Neumann and the von Neumann architecture

Main articles: John von Neumann and Von Neumann architecture

In 1946, a model for computer architecture was introduced and became known as *Von Neumann architecture*. Since 1950, the von Neumann model provided uniformity in subsequent computer designs. The von Neumann architecture was considered innovative as it introduced an idea of allowing machine instructions and data to share memory space. The von Neumann model is composed of three major parts, the arithmetic logic unit (ALU), the memory, and the instruction processing unit (IPU). In von Neumann machine design, the IPU passes addresses to memory, and memory, in turn, is routed either back to the IPU if an instruction is being fetched or to the ALU if data is being fetched.[18]

Von Neumann's machine design uses a RISC (Reduced instruction set computing) architecture, which means the instruction set uses a total of 21 instructions to perform all tasks. (This is in contrast to CISC, complex instruction set computing, instruction sets which have more instructions from which to choose.) With von Neumann architecture, main memory along with the accumulator (the register that holds the result of logical operations)[19] are the two memories that are addressed. Operations can be carried out as simple arithmetic (these are performed by the ALU and include addition, subtraction, multiplication and division), conditional branches (these are more commonly seen now as if statements or while loops. The branches serve as go to statements), and logical moves between the different components of the machine, i.e., a move from the accumulator to memory or vice versa. Von Neumann architecture accepts fractions and instructions as data types. Finally, as the von Neumann architecture is a simple one, its register management is also simple. The architecture uses a set of seven registers to manipulate and interpret fetched data and instructions. These registers include the "IR" (instruction register), "IBR" (instruction buffer register), "MQ" (multiplier quotient register), "MAR" (memory address register), and "MDR" (memory data register)."[18] The architecture also uses a program counter ("PC") to keep track of where in the program the machine is.[18]

2.1.4 See also

- Computer Museum
- History of computing
- History of computing hardware
- History of software
- List of computer term etymologies, the origins of computer science words
- List of prominent pioneers in computer science
- Timeline of algorithms
- History of personal computers

2.1.5 References

[1] History of Computer Science

[2] Ifrah, Georges (2001). *The Universal History of Computing: From the Abacus to the Quantum Computer.* John Wiley & Sons. ISBN 0-471-39671-0.

[3] Bellos, Alex (2012-10-25). "Abacus adds up to number joy in Japan". *The Guardian* (London). Retrieved 2013-06-25.

[4] *The Antikythera Mechanism Research Project*, The Antikythera Mechanism Research Project. Retrieved 2007-07-01

[5] In search of lost time, Jo Marchant, *Nature* **444**, #7119 (November 30, 2006), pp. 534–538, doi:10.1038/444534a PMID 17136067.

[6] History of Computing Science: The First Mechanical Calculator

[7] Kidwell, Peggy Aldritch; Williams, Michael R. (1992). *The Calculating Machines: Their history and development* (PDF). Massachusetts Institute of Technology and Tomash Publishers., p.38-42, translated and edited from Martin, Ernst (1925). *Die Rechenmaschinen und ihre Entwicklungsgeschichte.* Germany: Pappenheim.

[8] Tedre, Matti (2014). *The Science of Computing: Shaping a Discipline.* CRC Press.

[9] "Charles Babbage". *Encyclopedia Britannica Online Academic Edition.* Encyclopedia Britannica In. Retrieved 2013-02-20.

[10] Isaacson, Betsy (2012-12-10). "Ada Lovelace, World's First Computer Programmer, Celebrated With Google Doodle". *The Huffington Post* (http://www.huffingtonpost.com/2012/12/10/google-doodle-ada-lovelace_n_2270668.html). Retrieved 2013-02-20.

[11] http://plato.stanford.edu/entries/computing-history/#ACE

[12] Barker-Plummer, David. [<http://plato.stanford.edu/archives/win2012/entries/turing-machine/>. "Turing Machines"]. *The Stanford Encyclopedia of Philosophy.* Retrieved 2013-02-20.

[13] Rojas, R. (1998). "How to make Zuse's Z3 a universal computer". *IEEE Annals of the History of Computing* **20** (3): 51–54. doi:10.1109/85.707574.

[14] Rojas, Raúl. "How to Make Zuse's Z3 a Universal Computer".

[15] Talk given by Horst Zuse to the Computer Conservation Society at the Science Museum (London) on 18 November 2010

[16] "BBC News - How Alan Turing's Pilot ACE changed computing". *BBC News.* May 15, 2010.

[17] "The First "Computer Bug"" (PDF). *CHIPS* (United States Navy) **30** (1): 18. January–March 2012.

[18] Cragon, Harvey G. (2000). *Computer Architecture and Implementation*. Cambridge: Cambridge University Press. pp. 1–13. ISBN 0521651689.

[19] *"Accumlator" Def. 3*. Oxford Dictionaries.

2.1.6 Further reading

- Ceruzzi, Paul E. (1998). *A History of a Modern Computing*. The MIT Press. ISBN 978-0-262-03255-1.

- Tedre, Matti (2014). *The Science of Computing: Shaping a Discipline*. Taylor and Francis / CRC Press. ISBN 978-1482217698.

2.1.7 External links

- The Modern History of Computing entry by B. Jack Copeland in the *Stanford Encyclopedia of Philosophy*

- Computer History Museum

- Computers: From the Past to the Present

- The First "Computer Bug" at the Online Library of the Naval Historical Center, retrieved February 28, 2006

- Bitsavers, an effort to capture, salvage, and archive historical computer software and manuals from minicomputers and mainframes of the 1950s, 1960s, 1970s, and 1980s

- The Development of Computer Science: A Sociocultural Perspective Matti Tedre's Ph.D. Thesis, University of Joensuu (2006)

Oral history links

- Oral history interview with Albert H. Bowker at Charles Babbage Institute, University of Minnesota. Bowker discusses his role in the formation of the Stanford University computer science department, and his vision, as early as 1956, of computer science as an academic discipline.

- Oral history interview with Joseph F. Traub at Charles Babbage Institute, University of Minnesota. Traub discusses why computer science has developed as a discipline at institutions including Stanford, Berkeley, University of Pennsylvania, MIT, and Carnegie-Mellon.

- Oral history interview with Gene H. Golub at Charles Babbage Institute, University of Minnesota. Golub discusses his career in computer science at Stanford University.

- Oral history interview with John Herriot at Charles Babbage Institute, University of Minnesota. Herriot describes the early years of computing at Stanford University, including formation of the computer science department, centering on the role of George Forsythe.

- Oral history interview with William F. Miller at Charles Babbage Institute, University of Minnesota. Miller contrasts the emergence of computer science at Stanford with developments at Harvard and the University of Pennsylvania.

- Oral history interview with Alexandra Forsythe at Charles Babbage Institute, University of Minnesota. Forsythe discusses the career of her husband, George Forsythe, who established Stanford University's program in computer science.

- Oral history interview with Allen Newell at Charles Babbage Institute, University of Minnesota. Newell discusses his entry into computer science, funding for computer science departments and research, the development of the Computer Science Department at Carnegie Mellon University, including the work of Alan J. Perlis and Raj Reddy, and the growth of the computer science and artificial intelligence research communities. Compares computer science programs at Stanford, MIT, and Carnegie Mellon.

- Oral history interview with Louis Fein at Charles Babbage Institute, University of Minnesota. Fein discusses establishing computer science as an academic discipline at Stanford Research Institute (SRI) as well as contacts with the University of California—Berkeley, the University of North Carolina, Purdue, International Federation for Information Processing and other institutions.

- Oral history interview with W. Richards Adrion at Charles Babbage Institute, University of Minnesota. Adrion gives a brief history of theoretical computer science in the United States and NSF's role in funding that area during the 1970s and 1980s.

- Oral history interview with Bernard A. Galler at Charles Babbage Institute, University of Minnesota. Galler describes the development of computer science at the University of Michigan from the 1950s through the 1980s and discusses his own work in computer science.

- Michael S. Mahoney Papers at Charles Babbage Institute, University of Minnesota—Mahoney was the preeminent historian of computer science as a distinct academic discipline. Papers contain 38 boxes of books, serials, notes, and manuscripts related to the history of computing, mathematics, and related fields.

2.2 Philosophy of computer science

The **philosophy of computer science** is concerned with the philosophical questions that arise with the study of computer science, which is understood to mean not just programming but the whole study of concepts and methodologies that assist in the development and maintenance of computer systems.[1] According to (Tedre 2006), there is still no common understanding of the content, aim, focus, or topic of the philosophy of computer science, despite some attempts to develop a philosophy of computer science like the philosophy of physics or the philosophy of mathematics.

The philosophy of computer science as such deals with the meta-activity that is associated with the development of the concepts and methodologies that implement and analyze the computational systems. [2]

2.2.1 See also

- Computer-assisted proof: Philosophical objections
- Philosophy of artificial intelligence
- Philosophy of information
- Philosophy of mathematics
- Philosophy of science
- Philosophy of technology

2.2.2 References

[1] Turner

[2] http://pcs.essex.ac.uk/

2.2.3 Further reading

- Scott Aaronson. "Why Philosophers Should Care About Computational Complexity". To appear in *Computability: Gödel, Turing, Church, and beyond*.

- Timothy Colburn. *Philosophy and Computer Science*. Explorations in Philosophy. M.E. Sharpe, 1999. ISBN 1-56324-991-X.

- A.K. Dewdney. *New Turning Omnibus: 66 Excursions in Computer Science*

- Luciano Floridi (editor). *The Blackwell Guide to the Philosophy of Computing and Information*, 2004.

- Luciano Floridi (editor). *Philosophy of Computing and Information: 5 Questions*. Automatic Press, 2008.

- Luciano Floridi. *Philosophy and Computing: An Introduction*, Routledge, 1999.

- Christian Jongeneel. *The informatical worldview, an inquiry into the methodology of computer science.*

- Jan van Leeuwen. "Towards a philosophy of the information and computing sciences", *NIAS Newsletter* **42**, 2009.

- Moschovakis, Y. (2001). What is an algorithm? In Enquist, B. and Schmid, W., editors, Mathematics unlimited — 2001 and beyond, pages 919–936. Springer.

- Alexander Ollongren, Jaap van den Herik. *Filosofie van de informatica*. London and New York: Routledge, 1999. ISBN 0-415-19749-X

- Tedre, Matti (2006), *The Development of Computer Science: A Sociocultural Perspective* (PDF) Doctoral thesis for University of Joensuu.

- Ray Turner and Ammon H. Eden. "The Philosophy of Computer Science". *Stanford Encyclopedia of Philosophy*.

- Matti Tedre (2011). *Computing as a Science: A Survey of Competing Viewpoints*. Minds & Machines **21**, 3, 361–387.

- Jordi Vallverdu. "Thinking Machines and the Philosophy of Computer Science: Concepts and Principles"". Idea Books, 2010. http://www.igi-global.com/book/thinking-machines-philosophy-computer-science/40293

2.2.4 External links

- The International Association for Computing and Philosophy

- Philosophy of Computing and Information at PhilPapers

- Philosophy of the Information and Computing Sciences held in February 2010 at the Lorentz Center

- A draft version of *Philosophy of Computer Science* by William J. Rapaport

2.3 Outline of computer science

The following outline is provided as an overview of and topical guide to computer science:

Computer science (also called **computing science**) is the study of the theoretical foundations of information and computation and their implementation and application in computer systems. One well known subject classification system for computer science is the ACM Computing Classification System devised by the Association for Computing Machinery.

2.3.1 What *type* of thing is computer science?

Computer science can be described as all of the following:

- Academic discipline
- Science
  - Applied science

2.3.2 Subfields

Web programming and web designing

- Web programming
- Web designing

Mathematical foundations

- Coding theory – Useful in networking and other areas where computers communicate with each other.
- Game theory – Useful in artificial intelligence and cybernetics.
- Graph theory – Foundations for data structures and searching algorithms.
- Mathematical logic – Boolean logic and other ways of modeling logical queries; the uses and limitations of formal proof methods

- Number theory – Theory of the integers. Used in cryptography as well as a test domain in artificial intelligence.

Algorithms and data structures

- Algorithms – Sequential and parallel computational procedures for solving a wide range of problems.
- Data structures – The organization and manipulation of data.

Artificial intelligence

- Artificial intelligence – The implementation and study of systems that exhibit an autonomous intelligence or behavior of their own.
- Automated reasoning – Solving engines, such as used in Prolog, which produce steps to a result given a query on a fact and rule database, and automated theorem provers that aim to prove mathematical theorems with some assistance from a programmer.
- Computer vision – Algorithms for identifying three-dimensional objects from a two-dimensional picture.
- Machine learning – Automated creation of a set of rules and axioms based on input.
- Natural language processing - Building systems and algorithms that analyze, understand, and generate natural (human) languages.
- Robotics – Algorithms for controlling the behavior of robots.

Communication and security

- Networking – Algorithms and protocols for reliably communicating data across different shared or dedicated media, often including error correction.
- Computer security – Practical aspects of securing computer systems and computer networks.
- Cryptography – Applies results from complexity, probability, algebra and number theory to invent and break codes, and analyze the security of cryptographic protocols.

2.3. OUTLINE OF COMPUTER SCIENCE

Computer architecture

- Computer architecture – The design, organization, optimization and verification of a computer system, mostly about CPUs and Memory subsystem (and the bus connecting them).
- Operating systems – Systems for managing computer programs and providing the basis of a usable system.

Computer graphics

- Computer graphics – Algorithms both for generating visual images synthetically, and for integrating or altering visual and spatial information sampled from the real world.
- Image processing – Determining information from an image through computation.

Concurrent, parallel, and distributed systems

- Concurrency – The theory and practice of simultaneous computation; data safety in any multitasking or multithreaded environment.
- Parallel computing – Computing using multiple concurrent threads of execution, devising algorithms for solving problems on multiple processors to achieve maximal speed-up compared to sequential execution.
- Distributed computing – Computing using multiple computing devices over a network to accomplish a common objective or task and thereby reducing the latency involved in single processor contributions for any task.

Databases

- Relational databases – the set theoretic and algorithmic foundation of databases.
- Structured Storage - non-relational databases such as NoSQL databases.
- Data mining – Study of algorithms for searching and processing information in documents and databases; closely related to information retrieval.

Programming languages and compilers

- Compiler theory – Theory of compiler design, based on Automata theory.
- Programming language pragmatics – Taxonomy of programming languages, their strength and weaknesses. Various programming paradigms, such as object-oriented programming.
- Programming language theory
- Formal semantics – rigorous mathematical study of the meaning of programs.
- Type theory – Formal analysis of the types of data, and the use of these types to understand properties of programs — especially program safety.

Scientific computing

- Computational science – constructing mathematical models and quantitative analysis techniques and using computers to analyze and solve scientific problems.
- Numerical analysis – Approximate numerical solution of mathematical problems such as root-finding, integration, the solution of ordinary differential equations; the approximation of special functions.
- Symbolic computation – Manipulation and solution of expressions in symbolic form, also known as Computer algebra.
- Computational physics – Numerical simulations of large non-analytic systems
- Computational chemistry – Computational modelling of theoretical chemistry in order to determine chemical structures and properties
- Bioinformatics and Computational biology – The use of computer science to maintain, analyse, store biological data and to assist in solving biological problems such as Protein folding, function prediction and Phylogeny.
- Computational neuroscience – Computational modelling of neurophysiology.

Software engineering

- Formal methods – Mathematical approaches for describing and reasoning about software designs.
- Software engineering – The principles and practice of designing, developing, and testing programs, as well as proper engineering practices.
- Algorithm design – Using ideas from algorithm theory to creatively design solutions to real tasks.

- Computer programming – The practice of using a programming language to implement algorithms.

- Human–computer interaction – The study and design of computer interfaces that people use.

- Reverse engineering – The application of the scientific method to the understanding of arbitrary existing software.

Theory of computation

Main article: Theory of computation

- Automata theory – Different logical structures for solving problems.

- Computability theory – What is calculable with the current models of computers. Proofs developed by Alan Turing and others provide insight into the possibilities of what may be computed and what may not.

    - List of unsolved problems in computer science

- Computational complexity theory – Fundamental bounds (especially time and storage space) on classes of computations.

- Quantum computing theory – Explores computational models involving quantum superposition of bits.

2.3.3 History

- History of computer science

2.3.4 Fields

- Programmer
- Software engineer
- Software architect
- Software developer
- Software tester
- Interaction designer

2.3.5 Basic concepts

Data and data structures

- Data structure
- Data type
- Associative array and Hash table
- Array
- List
- Tree
- String
- Matrix (computer science)
- Database

Other

- Abstraction
- Big O notation
- Closure
- Compiler

2.3.6 Programming paradigms

- Imperative programming/Procedural programming
- Functional programming
- Logic programming
- Object oriented programming
    - Class
    - Inheritance
    - Object

2.3.7 See also

- Cognitive science

2.3.8 External links

- Outline of computer science at DMOZ
- ACM report on a recommended computer science curriculum (2008)
- Directory of free university lectures in Computer Science
- Collection of Computer Science Bibliographies
- Photographs of computer scientists (Bertrand Meyer's gallery)

Webcasts

- UCLA Computer Science 1 Freshman Computer Science Seminar Section 1
- Berkeley Introduction to Computers

2.4 Theoretical computer science

This article is about the branch of computer science and mathematics. For the journal, see Theoretical Computer Science (journal).

Theoretical computer science is a division or subset of

An artistic representation of a Turing machine. Turing machines are used to model general computing devices.

general computer science and mathematics that focuses on more abstract or mathematical aspects of computing and includes the theory of computation.

It is not easy to circumscribe the theory areas precisely and the ACM's Special Interest Group on Algorithms and Computation Theory (SIGACT) describes its mission as the promotion of theoretical computer science and notes:[1]

> The field of theoretical computer science is interpreted broadly so as to include algorithms, data structures, computational complexity theory, distributed computation, parallel computation, VLSI, machine learning, computational biology, computational geometry, information theory, cryptography, quantum computation, computational number theory and algebra, program semantics and verification, automata theory, and the study of randomness. Work in this field is often distinguished by its emphasis on mathematical technique and rigor.

To this list, the ACM's journal Transactions on Computation Theory adds coding theory, computational learning theory and theoretical computer science aspects of areas such as databases, information retrieval, economic models and networks.[2] Despite this broad scope, the "theory people" in computer science self-identify as different from the "applied people." Some characterize themselves as doing the "(more fundamental) 'science(s)' underlying the field of computing."[3] Other "theory-applied people" suggest that it is impossible to separate theory and application. This means that the so-called "theory people" regularly use experimental science(s) done in less-theoretical areas such as software system research. It also means that there is more cooperation than mutually exclusive competition between theory and application.

2.4.1 History

Main article: History of computer science

While=of an algorithm in terms of computation. While logical inference and mathematical proof had existed previously, in 1931 Kurt Gödel proved with his incompleteness theorem that there were fundamental limitations on what statements could be proved or disproved.

These developments have led to the modern study of logic and computability, and indeed the field of theoretical computer science as a whole. Information theory was added to the field with a 1948 mathematical theory of communication by Claude Shannon. In the same decade, Donald Hebb introduced a mathematical model of learning in the brain. With mounting biological data supporting this hypothesis with some modification, the fields of neural networks and parallel distributed processing were established. In 1971, Stephen Cook and, working independently, Leonid Levin, proved that there exist practically relevant problems that are NP-complete – a landmark result in computational complexity theory.

With the development of quantum mechanics in the beginning of the 20th century came the concept that mathematical operations could be performed on an entire particle wavefunction. In other words, one could compute functions on multiple states simultaneously. This led to the concept of a quantum computer in the latter half of the 20th century that took off in the 1990s when Peter Shor showed that such methods could be used to factor large numbers in polynomial time, which, if implemented, would render most modern public key cryptography systems uselessly insecure.

Modern theoretical computer science research is based on these basic developments, but includes many other mathematical and interdisciplinary problems that have been posed.

2.4.2 Topics

Algorithms

Main article: Algorithm

An algorithm is a step-by-step procedure for calculations. Algorithms are used for calculation, data processing, and automated reasoning.

An algorithm is an effective method expressed as a finite list[4] of well-defined instructions[5] for calculating a function.[6] Starting from an initial state and initial input (perhaps empty),[7] the instructions describe a computation that, when executed, proceeds through a finite[8] number of well-defined successive states, eventually producing "output"[9] and terminating at a final ending state. The transition from one state to the next is not necessarily deterministic; some algorithms, known as randomized algorithms, incorporate random input.[10]

Data structures

Main article: Data structure

A data structure is a particular way of organizing data in a computer so that it can be used efficiently.[11][12]

Different kinds of data structures are suited to different kinds of applications, and some are highly specialized to specific tasks. For example, databases use B-tree indexes for small percentages of data retrieval and compilers and databases use dynamic hash tables as look up tables.

Data structures provide a means to manage large amounts of data efficiently for uses such as large databases and internet indexing services. Usually, efficient data structures are key to designing efficient algorithms. Some formal design methods and programming languages emphasize data structures, rather than algorithms, as the key organizing factor in software design. Storing and retrieving can be carried out on data stored in both main memory and in secondary memory.

Computational complexity theory

Main article: Computational complexity theory

Computational complexity theory is a branch of the theory of computation that focuses on classifying computational problems according to their inherent difficulty, and relating those classes to each other. A computational problem is understood to be a task that is in principle amenable to being solved by a computer, which is equivalent to stating that the problem may be solved by mechanical application of mathematical steps, such as an algorithm.

A problem is regarded as inherently difficult if its solution requires significant resources, whatever the algorithm used. The theory formalizes this intuition, by introducing mathematical models of computation to study these problems and quantifying the amount of resources needed to solve them, such as time and storage. Other complexity measures are also used, such as the amount of communication (used in communication complexity), the number of gates in a circuit (used in circuit complexity) and the number of processors (used in parallel computing). One of the roles of computational complexity theory is to determine the practical limits on what computers can and cannot do.

Distributed computation

Main article: Distributed computation

Distributed computing studies distributed systems. A distributed system is a software system in which components located on networked computers communicate and coordinate their actions by passing messages.[13] The components interact with each other in order to achieve a common goal. Three significant characteristics of distributed systems are: concurrency of components, lack of a global clock, and independent failure of components.[13] Examples of distributed systems vary from SOA-based systems to massively multiplayer online games to peer-to-peer applications.

A computer program that runs in a distributed system is called a **distributed program**, and distributed programming is the process of writing such programs.[14] There are many alternatives for the message passing mechanism, including RPC-like connectors and message queues. An important goal and challenge of distributed systems is location transparency.

Parallel computation

Main article: Parallel computation

Parallel computing is a form of computation in which many calculations are carried out simultaneously,[15] operating on the principle that large problems can often be divided into smaller ones, which are then solved concurrently ("in parallel"). There are several different forms of parallel computing: bit-level, instruction level, data, and task parallelism. Parallelism has been employed for many years, mainly in high-performance computing, but interest in it has grown lately due to the physical constraints preventing frequency scaling.[16] As power consumption (and consequently heat generation) by computers has become a concern in recent years,[17] parallel computing has become the dominant paradigm in computer architecture, mainly in the form of multi-core processors.[18]

Parallel computer programs are more difficult to write than sequential ones,[19] because concurrency introduces several new classes of potential software bugs, of which race conditions are the most common. Communication and synchronization between the different subtasks are typically some of the greatest obstacles to getting good parallel program performance.

The maximum possible speed-up of a single program as a result of parallelization is known as Amdahl's law.

Very-large-scale integration

Main article: VLSI

Very-large-scale integration (**VLSI**) is the process of creating an integrated circuit (IC) by combining thousands of transistors into a single chip. VLSI began in the 1970s when complex semiconductor and communication technologies were being developed. The microprocessor is a VLSI device. Before the introduction of VLSI technology most ICs had a limited set of functions they could perform. An electronic circuit might consist of a CPU, ROM, RAM and other glue logic. VLSI lets IC makers add all of these into one chip.

Machine learning

Main article: Machine learning

Machine learning is a scientific discipline that deals with the construction and study of algorithms that can learn from data.[20] Such algorithms operate by building a model based on inputs[21]:2 and using that to make predictions or decisions, rather than following only explicitly programmed instructions.

Machine learning can be considered a subfield of computer science and statistics. It has strong ties to artificial intelligence and optimization, which deliver methods, theory and application domains to the field. Machine learning is employed in a range of computing tasks where designing and programming explicit, rule-based algorithms is infeasible. Example applications include spam filtering, optical character recognition (OCR),[22] search engines and computer vision. Machine learning is sometimes conflated with data mining,[23] although that focuses more on exploratory data analysis.[24] Machine learning and pattern recognition "can be viewed as two facets of the same field."[21]:vii

Computational biology

Main article: Computational biology

Computational biology involves the development and application of data-analytical and theoretical methods, mathematical modeling and computational simulation techniques to the study of biological, behavioral, and social systems.[25] The field is broadly defined and includes foundations in computer science, applied mathematics, animation, statistics, biochemistry, chemistry, biophysics, molecular biology, genetics, genomics, ecology, evolution, anatomy, neuroscience, and visualization.[26]

Computational biology is different from biological computation, which is a subfield of computer science and computer engineering using bioengineering and biology to build computers, but is similar to bioinformatics, which is an interdisciplinary science using computers to store and process biological data.

Computational geometry

Main article: Computational geometry

Computational geometry is a branch of computer science devoted to the study of algorithms that can be stated in terms of geometry. Some purely geometrical problems arise out of the study of computational geometric algorithms, and such problems are also considered to be part of computational geometry. While modern computational geometry is a recent development, it is one of the oldest fields of computing with history stretching back to antiquity. An ancient precursor is the Sanskrit treatise Shulba Sutras , or "Rules of the Chord", that is a book of algorithms written in 800 BCE. The book prescribes step-by-step procedures for constructing geometric objects like altars using a peg and chord.

The main impetus for the development of computational geometry as a discipline was progress in computer graphics and computer-aided design and manufacturing (CAD/CAM), but many problems in computational geometry are classical in nature, and may come from mathematical visualization.

Other important applications of computational geometry include robotics (motion planning and visibility problems), geographic information systems (GIS) (geometrical location and search, route planning), integrated circuit design (IC geometry design and verification), computer-aided engineering (CAE) (mesh generation), computer vision (3D reconstruction).

Information theory

Main article: Information theory

Information theory is a branch of applied mathematics, electrical engineering, and computer science involving the quantification of information. Information theory was developed by Claude E. Shannon to find fundamental limits on signal processing operations such as compressing data and on reliably storing and communicating data. Since its inception it has broadened to find applications in many other areas, including statistical inference, natural language processing, cryptography, neurobiology,[27] the evolution[28] and function[29] of molecular codes, model selection in ecology,[30] thermal physics,[31] quantum computing, linguistics, plagiarism detection,[32] pattern recognition, anomaly detection and other forms of data analysis.[33]

Applications of fundamental topics of information theory include lossless data compression (e.g. ZIP files), lossy data compression (e.g. MP3s and JPEGs), and channel coding (e.g. for Digital Subscriber Line (DSL)). The field is at the intersection of mathematics, statistics, computer science, physics, neurobiology, and electrical engineering. Its impact has been crucial to the success of the Voyager missions to deep space, the invention of the compact disc, the feasibility of mobile phones, the development of the Internet, the study of linguistics and of human perception, the understanding of black holes, and numerous other fields. Important sub-fields of information theory are source coding, channel coding, algorithmic complexity theory, algorithmic information theory, information-theoretic security, and measures of information.

Cryptography

Main article: Cryptography

Cryptography is the practice and study of techniques for secure communication in the presence of third parties (called adversaries).[34] More generally, it is about constructing and analyzing protocols that overcome the influence of adversaries[35] and that are related to various aspects in information security such as data confidentiality, data integrity, authentication, and non-repudiation.[36] Modern cryptography intersects the disciplines of mathematics, computer science, and electrical engineering. Applications of cryptography include ATM cards, computer passwords, and electronic commerce.

Modern cryptography is heavily based on mathematical theory and computer science practice; cryptographic algorithms are designed around computational hardness assumptions, making such algorithms hard to break in practice by any adversary. It is theoretically possible to break such a system, but it is infeasible to do so by any known practical means. These schemes are therefore termed computationally secure; theoretical advances, e.g., improvements in integer factorization algorithms, and faster computing technology require these solutions to be continually adapted. There exist information-theoretically secure schemes that provably cannot be broken even with unlimited computing power—an example is the one-time pad—but these schemes are more difficult to implement than the best theoretically breakable but computationally secure mechanisms.

Quantum computation

Main article: Quantum computation

A quantum computer is a computation system that makes direct use of quantum-mechanical phenomena, such as superposition and entanglement, to perform operations on data.[37] Quantum computers are different from digital computers based on transistors. Whereas digital computers require data to be encoded into binary digits (bits), each of which is always in one of two definite states (0 or 1), quantum computation uses qubits (quantum bits), which can be in superpositions of states. A theoretical model is the quantum Turing machine, also known as the universal quantum computer. Quantum computers share theoretical similarities with non-deterministic and probabilistic computers; one example is the ability to be in more than one state simultaneously. The field of quantum computing was first introduced by Yuri Manin in 1980[38] and Richard Feynman in 1982.[39][40] A quantum computer with spins as quantum

2.4. THEORETICAL COMPUTER SCIENCE

bits was also formulated for use as a quantum space–time in 1968.[41]

As of 2014, quantum computing is still in its infancy but experiments have been carried out in which quantum computational operations were executed on a very small number of qubits.[42] Both practical and theoretical research continues, and many national governments and military funding agencies support quantum computing research to develop quantum computers for both civilian and national security purposes, such as cryptanalysis.[43]

Computational number theory

Main article: Computational number theory

Computational number theory, also known as **algorithmic number theory**, is the study of algorithms for performing number theoretic computations. The best known problem in the field is integer factorization.

Symbolic computation

Main article: Symbolic computation

Computer algebra, also called symbolic computation or algebraic computation is a scientific area that refers to the study and development of algorithms and software for manipulating mathematical expressions and other mathematical objects. Although, properly speaking, computer algebra should be a subfield of scientific computing, they are generally considered as distinct fields because scientific computing is usually based on numerical computation with approximate floating point numbers, while symbolic computation emphasizes *exact* computation with expressions containing variables that have not any given value and are thus manipulated as symbols (therefore the name of *symbolic computation*).

Software applications that perform symbolic calculations are called *computer algebra systems*, with the term *system* alluding to the complexity of the main applications that include, at least, a method to represent mathematical data in a computer, a user programming language (usually different from the language used for the implementation), a dedicated memory manager, a user interface for the input/output of mathematical expressions, a large set of routines to perform usual operations, like simplification of expressions, differentiation using chain rule, polynomial factorization, indefinite integration, etc.

Program semantics

Main article: Program semantics

In programming language theory, **semantics** is the field concerned with the rigorous mathematical study of the meaning of programming languages. It does so by evaluating the meaning of syntactically legal strings defined by a specific programming language, showing the computation involved. In such a case that the evaluation would be of syntactically illegal strings, the result would be non-computation. Semantics describes the processes a computer follows when executing a program in that specific language. This can be shown by describing the relationship between the input and output of a program, or an explanation of how the program will execute on a certain platform, hence creating a model of computation.

Formal methods

Main article: Formal methods

Formal methods are a particular kind of mathematics based techniques for the specification, development and verification of software and hardware systems.[44] The use of formal methods for software and hardware design is motivated by the expectation that, as in other engineering disciplines, performing appropriate mathematical analysis can contribute to the reliability and robustness of a design.[45]

Formal methods are best described as the application of a fairly broad variety of theoretical computer science fundamentals, in particular logic calculi, formal languages, automata theory, and program semantics, but also type systems and algebraic data types to problems in software and hardware specification and verification.[46]

Automata theory

Main article: Automata theory

Automata theory is the study of *abstract machines* and *automata*, as well as the computational problems that can be solved using them. It is a theory in theoretical computer science, under Discrete mathematics (a section of Mathematics and also of Computer Science). *Automata* comes from the Greek word αὐτόματα meaning "self-acting".

Automata Theory is the study of self-operating virtual machines to help in logical understanding of input and output process, without or with intermediate stage(s) of computation (or any function / process).

Coding theory

Main article: Coding theory

Coding theory is the study of the properties of codes and their fitness for a specific application. Codes are used for data compression, cryptography, error-correction and more recently also for network coding. Codes are studied by various scientific disciplines—such as information theory, electrical engineering, mathematics, and computer science—for the purpose of designing efficient and reliable data transmission methods. This typically involves the removal of redundancy and the correction (or detection) of errors in the transmitted data.

Computational learning theory

Main article: Computational learning theory

Theoretical results in machine learning mainly deal with a type of inductive learning called supervised learning. In supervised learning, an algorithm is given samples that are labeled in some useful way. For example, the samples might be descriptions of mushrooms, and the labels could be whether or not the mushrooms are edible. The algorithm takes these previously labeled samples and uses them to induce a classifier. This classifier is a function that assigns labels to samples including the samples that have never been previously seen by the algorithm. The goal of the supervised learning algorithm is to optimize some measure of performance such as minimizing the number of mistakes made on new samples.

2.4.3 Organizations

- European Association for Theoretical Computer Science
- SIGACT

2.4.4 Journals and newsletters

- *Information and Computation*
- *Theory of Computing* (open access journal)
- *Formal Aspects of Computing*
- *Journal of the ACM*
- *SIAM Journal on Computing* (SICOMP)
- *SIGACT News*
- *Theoretical Computer Science*
- *Theory of Computing Systems*
- *International Journal of Foundations of Computer Science*
- *Chicago Journal of Theoretical Computer Science* (open access journal)
- *Foundations and Trends in Theoretical Computer Science*
- *Journal of Automata, Languages and Combinatorics*
- *Acta Informatica*
- *Fundamenta Informaticae*
- *ACM Transactions on Computation Theory*
- *Computational Complexity*
- *ACM Transactions on Algorithms*
- *Information Processing Letters*

2.4.5 Conferences

- Annual ACM Symposium on Theory of Computing (STOC)[47]
- Annual IEEE Symposium on Foundations of Computer Science (FOCS)[47]
- ACM–SIAM Symposium on Discrete Algorithms (SODA)[47]
- Annual Symposium on Computational Geometry (SoCG)[48]
- International Colloquium on Automata, Languages and Programming (ICALP)[48]
- Symposium on Theoretical Aspects of Computer Science (STACS)[48]
- International Conference on Theory and Applications of Models of Computation (TAMC)
- European Symposium on Algorithms (ESA)[48]
- IEEE Symposium on Logic in Computer Science (LICS)[47]
- International Symposium on Algorithms and Computation (ISAAC)[48]
- Workshop on Approximation Algorithms for Combinatorial Optimization Problems (APPROX)[48]

- Workshop on Randomization and Computation (RANDOM)[48]
- Computational Complexity Conference (CCC)[48]
- ACM Symposium on Parallelism in Algorithms and Architectures (SPAA)[48]
- ACM Symposium on Principles of Distributed Computing (PODC)[47]
- International Symposium on Fundamentals of Computation Theory (FCT)[49]
- Annual Conference on Learning Theory (COLT)[48]
- International Workshop on Graph-Theoretic Concepts in Computer Science (WG)

2.4.6 See also

- Formal science
- Unsolved problems in computer science
- List of important publications in theoretical computer science

2.4.7 Notes

[1] "SIGACT". Retrieved 2009-03-29.

[2] "ToCT". Retrieved 2010-06-09.

[3] "Challenges for Theoretical Computer Science: Theory as the Scientific Foundation of Computing". Retrieved 2009-03-29.

[4] "Any classical mathematical algorithm, for example, can be described in a finite number of English words" (Rogers 1987:2).

[5] Well defined with respect to the agent that executes the algorithm: "There is a computing agent, usually human, which can react to the instructions and carry out the computations" (Rogers 1987:2).

[6] "an algorithm is a procedure for computing a *function* (with respect to some chosen notation for integers) ... this limitation (to numerical functions) results in no loss of generality", (Rogers 1987:1).

[7] "An algorithm has zero or more inputs, i.e., quantities which are given to it initially before the algorithm begins" (Knuth 1973:5).

[8] "A procedure which has all the characteristics of an algorithm except that it possibly lacks finiteness may be called a 'computational method'" (Knuth 1973:5).

[9] "An algorithm has one or more outputs, i.e. quantities which have a specified relation to the inputs" (Knuth 1973:5).

[10] Whether or not a process with random interior processes (not including the input) is an algorithm is debatable. Rogers opines that: "a computation is carried out in a discrete stepwise fashion, without use of continuous methods or analogue devices ... carried forward deterministically, without resort to random methods or devices, e.g., dice" Rogers 1987:2.

[11] Paul E. Black (ed.), entry for *data structure* in *Dictionary of Algorithms and Data Structures*. U.S. National Institute of Standards and Technology. 15 December 2004. Online version Accessed May 21, 2009.

[12] Entry *data structure* in the Encyclopædia Britannica (2009) Online entry accessed on May 21, 2009.

[13] Coulouris, George; Jean Dollimore; Tim Kindberg; Gordon Blair (2011). *Distributed Systems: Concepts and Design (5th Edition)*. Boston: Addison-Wesley. ISBN 0-132-14301-1.

[14] Andrews (2000). Dolev (2000). Ghosh (2007), p. 10.

[15] Gottlieb, Allan; Almasi, George S. (1989). *Highly parallel computing*. Redwood City, Calif.: Benjamin/Cummings. ISBN 0-8053-0177-1.

[16] S.V. Adve et al. (November 2008). "Parallel Computing Research at Illinois: The UPCRC Agenda" (PDF). Parallel@Illinois, University of Illinois at Urbana-Champaign. "The main techniques for these performance benefits – increased clock frequency and smarter but increasingly complex architectures – are now hitting the so-called power wall. The computer industry has accepted that future performance increases must largely come from increasing the number of processors (or cores) on a die, rather than making a single core go faster."

[17] Asanovic et al. Old [conventional wisdom]: Power is free, but transistors are expensive. New [conventional wisdom] is [that] power is expensive, but transistors are "free".

[18] Asanovic, Krste et al. (December 18, 2006). "The Landscape of Parallel Computing Research: A View from Berkeley" (PDF). University of California, Berkeley. Technical Report No. UCB/EECS-2006-183. "Old [conventional wisdom]: Increasing clock frequency is the primary method of improving processor performance. New [conventional wisdom]: Increasing parallelism is the primary method of improving processor performance ... Even representatives from Intel, a company generally associated with the 'higher clock-speed is better' position, warned that traditional approaches to maximizing performance through maximizing clock speed have been pushed to their limit."

[19] Hennessy, John L.; Patterson, David A.; Larus, James R. (1999). *Computer organization and design : the hardware/software interface* (2. ed., 3rd print. ed.). San Francisco: Kaufmann. ISBN 1-55860-428-6.

[20] Ron Kovahi; Foster Provost (1998). "Glossary of terms". *Machine Learning* **30**: 271–274.

[21] C. M. Bishop (2006). *Pattern Recognition and Machine Learning*. Springer. ISBN 0-387-31073-8.

[22] Wernick, Yang, Brankov, Yourganov and Strother, Machine Learning in Medical Imaging, *IEEE Signal Processing Magazine*, vol. 27, no. 4, July 2010, pp. 25-38

[23] Mannila, Heikki (1996). *Data mining: machine learning, statistics, and databases*. Int'l Conf. Scientific and Statistical Database Management. IEEE Computer Society.

[24] Friedman, Jerome H. (1998). "Data Mining and Statistics: What's the connection?". *Computing Science and Statistics* **29** (1): 3–9.

[25] "NIH working definition of bioinformatics and computational biology" (PDF). Biomedical Information Science and Technology Initiative. 17 July 2000. Retrieved 18 August 2012.

[26] "About the CCMB". Center for Computational Molecular Biology. Retrieved 18 August 2012.

[27] F. Rieke, D. Warland, R Ruyter van Steveninck, W Bialek (1997). *Spikes: Exploring the Neural Code*. The MIT press. ISBN 978-0262681087.

[28] cf. Huelsenbeck, J. P., F. Ronquist, R. Nielsen and J. P. Bollback (2001) Bayesian inference of phylogeny and its impact on evolutionary biology, *Science* **294**:2310-2314

[29] Rando Allikmets, Wyeth W. Wasserman, Amy Hutchinson, Philip Smallwood, Jeremy Nathans, Peter K. Rogan, Thomas D. Schneider, Michael Dean (1998) Organization of the ABCR gene: analysis of promoter and splice junction sequences, *Gene* **215**:1, 111-122

[30] Burnham, K. P. and Anderson D. R. (2002) *Model Selection and Multimodel Inference: A Practical Information-Theoretic Approach, Second Edition* (Springer Science, New York) ISBN 978-0-387-95364-9.

[31] Jaynes, E. T. (1957) Information Theory and Statistical Mechanics, *Phys. Rev.* **106**:620

[32] Charles H. Bennett, Ming Li, and Bin Ma (2003) Chain Letters and Evolutionary Histories, *Scientific American* **288**:6, 76-81

[33] David R. Anderson (November 1, 2003). "Some background on why people in the empirical sciences may want to better understand the information-theoretic methods" (pdf). Retrieved 2010-06-23.

[34] Rivest, Ronald L. (1990). "Cryptology". In J. Van Leeuwen. *Handbook of Theoretical Computer Science* **1**. Elsevier.

[35] Bellare, Mihir; Rogaway, Phillip (21 September 2005). "Introduction". *Introduction to Modern Cryptography*. p. 10.

[36] Menezes, A. J.; van Oorschot, P. C.; Vanstone, S. A. *Handbook of Applied Cryptography*. ISBN 0-8493-8523-7.

[37] "Quantum Computing with Molecules" article in *Scientific American* by Neil Gershenfeld and Isaac L. Chuang

[38] Manin, Yu. I. (1980). *Vychislimoe i nevychislimoe [Computable and Noncomputable]* (in Russian). Sov.Radio. pp. 13–15. Retrieved 4 March 2013.

[39] Feynman, R. P. (1982). "Simulating physics with computers". *International Journal of Theoretical Physics* **21** (6): 467–488. doi:10.1007/BF02650179.

[40] Deutsch, David (1992-01-06). "Quantum computation". *Physics World*.

[41] Finkelstein, David (1968). "Space-Time Structure in High Energy Interactions". In Gudehus, T.; Kaiser, G. *Fundamental Interactions at High Energy*. New York: Gordon & Breach.

[42] "New qubit control bodes well for future of quantum computing". Retrieved 26 October 2014.

[43] Quantum Information Science and Technology Roadmap for a sense of where the research is heading.

[44] R. W. Butler (2001-08-06). "What is Formal Methods?". Retrieved 2006-11-16.

[45] C. Michael Holloway. "Why Engineers Should Consider Formal Methods" (PDF). 16th Digital Avionics Systems Conference (27–30 October 1997). Retrieved 2006-11-16.

[46] Monin, pp.3-4

[47] The 2007 Australian Ranking of ICT Conferences: tier A+.

[48] The 2007 Australian Ranking of ICT Conferences: tier A.

[49] FCT 2011 (retrieved 2013-06-03)

2.4.8 Further reading

- Martin Davis, Ron Sigal, Elaine J. Weyuker, *Computability, complexity, and languages: fundamentals of theoretical computer science*, 2nd ed., Academic Press, 1994, ISBN 0-12-206382-1. Covers theory of computation, but also program semantics and quantification theory. Aimed at graduate students.

2.4.9 External links

- SIGACT directory of additional theory links
- Theory Matters Wiki Theoretical Computer Science (TCS) Advocacy Wiki
- Usenet comp.theory
- List of academic conferences in the area of theoretical computer science at confsearch

2.5. THEORY OF COMPUTATION

- Theoretical Computer Science - StackExchange, a Question and Answer site for researchers in theoretical computer science

- Computer Science Animated

- http://theory.csail.mit.edu/ @ Massachusetts Institute of Technology

2.5 Theory of computation

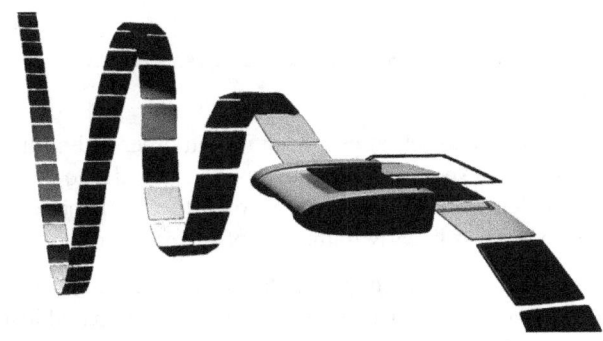

An artistic representation of a Turing machine. Turing machines are frequently used as theoretical models for computing.

In theoretical computer science and mathematics, the **theory of computation** is the branch that deals with how efficiently problems can be solved on a model of computation, using an algorithm. The field is divided into three major branches: automata theory and language, computability theory, and computational complexity theory, which are linked by the question: *"What are the fundamental capabilities and limitations of computers?."*[1]

In order to perform a rigorous study of computation, computer scientists work with a mathematical abstraction of computers called a model of computation. There are several models in use, but the most commonly examined is the Turing machine.[2] Computer scientists study the Turing machine because it is simple to formulate, can be analyzed and used to prove results, and because it represents what many consider the most powerful possible "reasonable" model of computation (see Church–Turing thesis).[3] It might seem that the potentially infinite memory capacity is an unrealizable attribute, but any decidable problem[4] solved by a Turing machine will always require only a finite amount of memory. So in principle, any problem that can be solved (decided) by a Turing machine can be solved by a computer that has a bounded amount of memory.

2.5.1 History

The theory of computation can be considered the creation of models of all kinds in the field of computer science. Therefore, mathematics and logic are used. In the last century it became an independent academic discipline and was separated from mathematics.

Some pioneers of the theory of computation were Alonzo Church, Kurt Gödel, Alan Turing, Stephen Kleene, John von Neumann and Claude Shannon.

2.5.2 Branches

Automata theory

Main article: Automata theory

Automata theory is the study of abstract machines (or more appropriately, abstract 'mathematical' machines or systems) and the computational problems that can be solved using these machines. These abstract machines are called automata. Automata comes from the Greek word (Αυτόματα) which means that something is doing something by itself. Automata theory is also closely related to formal language theory,[5] as the automata are often classified by the class of formal languages they are able to recognize. An automaton can be a finite representation of a formal language that may be an infinite set. Automata are used as theoretical models for computing machines, and are used for proofs about computability.

Formal Language Theory

Main article: Formal language
Language theory is a branch of mathematics concerned

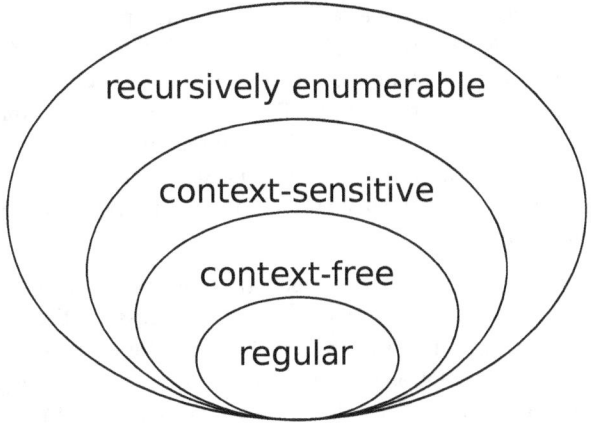

Set inclusions described by the Chomsky hierarchy

with describing languages as a set of operations over an alphabet. It is closely linked with automata theory, as automata are used to generate and recognize formal languages. There are several classes of formal languages, each allowing more complex language specification than the one before it, i.e. Chomsky hierarchy,[6] and each corresponding to a class of automata which recognizes it. Because automata are used as models for computation, formal languages are the preferred mode of specification for any problem that must be computed.

Computability theory

Main article: Computability theory

Computability theory deals primarily with the question of the extent to which a problem is solvable on a computer. The statement that the halting problem cannot be solved by a Turing machine[7] is one of the most important results in computability theory, as it is an example of a concrete problem that is both easy to formulate and impossible to solve using a Turing machine. Much of computability theory builds on the halting problem result.

Another important step in computability theory was Rice's theorem, which states that for all non-trivial properties of partial functions, it is undecidable whether a Turing machine computes a partial function with that property.[8]

Computability theory is closely related to the branch of mathematical logic called recursion theory, which removes the restriction of studying only models of computation which are reducible to the Turing model.[9] Many mathematicians and computational theorists who study recursion theory will refer to it as computability theory.

Computational complexity theory

Main article: Computational complexity theory
 Complexity theory considers not only whether a problem can be solved at all on a computer, but also how efficiently the problem can be solved. Two major aspects are considered: time complexity and space complexity, which are respectively how many steps does it take to perform a computation, and how much memory is required to perform that computation.

In order to analyze how much time and space a given algorithm requires, computer scientists express the time or space required to solve the problem as a function of the size of the input problem. For example, finding a particular number in a long list of numbers becomes harder as the list of numbers grows larger. If we say there are n numbers in the list, then if the list is not sorted or indexed in any way

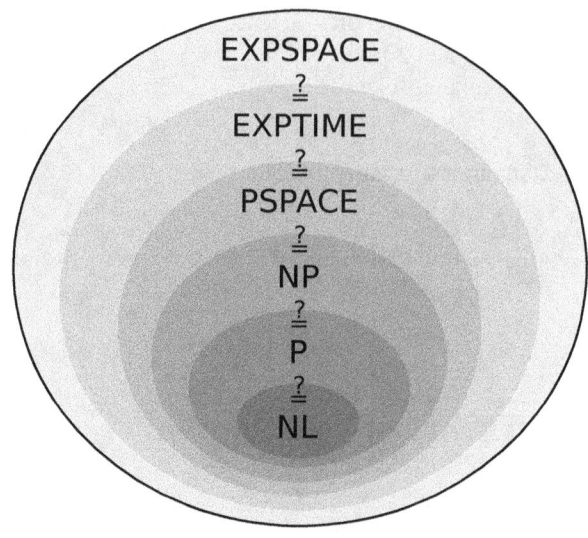

A representation of the relation among complexity classes

we may have to look at every number in order to find the number we're seeking. We thus say that in order to solve this problem, the computer needs to perform a number of steps that grows linearly in the size of the problem.

To simplify this problem, computer scientists have adopted Big O notation, which allows functions to be compared in a way that ensures that particular aspects of a machine's construction do not need to be considered, but rather only the asymptotic behavior as problems become large. So in our previous example we might say that the problem requires $O(n)$ steps to solve.

Perhaps the most important open problem in all of computer science is the question of whether a certain broad class of problems denoted NP can be solved efficiently. This is discussed further at Complexity classes P and NP, and P versus NP problem is one of the seven Millennium Prize Problems stated by the Clay Mathematics Institute in 2000. The Official Problem Description was given by Turing Award winner Stephen Cook.

2.5.3 Models of computation

Main article: Model of computation

Aside from a Turing machine, other equivalent (See: Church–Turing thesis) models of computation are in use.

Lambda calculus A computation consists of an initial lambda expression (or two if you want to separate the function and its input) plus a finite sequence of lambda terms, each deduced from the preceding term by one application of Beta reduction.

2.5. THEORY OF COMPUTATION

Combinatory logic is a concept which has many similarities to λ-calculus, but also important differences exist (e.g. fixed point combinator **Y** has normal form in combinatory logic but not in λ-calculus). Combinatory logic was developed with great ambitions: understanding the nature of paradoxes, making foundations of mathematics more economic (conceptually), eliminating the notion of variables (thus clarifying their role in mathematics).

μ-recursive functions a computation consists of a mu-recursive function, *i.e.* its defining sequence, any input value(s) and a sequence of recursive functions appearing in the defining sequence with inputs and outputs. Thus, if in the defining sequence of a recursive function $f(x)$ the functions $g(x)$ and $h(x,y)$ appear, then terms of the form 'g(5)=7' or 'h(3,2)=10' might appear. Each entry in this sequence needs to be an application of a basic function or follow from the entries above by using composition, primitive recursion or μ recursion. For instance if $f(x) = h(x, g(x))$, then for 'f(5)=3' to appear, terms like 'g(5)=6' and 'h(5,6)=3' must occur above. The computation terminates only if the final term gives the value of the recursive function applied to the inputs.

Markov algorithm a string rewriting system that uses grammar-like rules to operate on strings of symbols.

Register machine is a theoretically interesting idealization of a computer. There are several variants. In most of them, each register can hold a natural number (of unlimited size), and the instructions are simple (and few in number), e.g. only decrementation (combined with conditional jump) and incrementation exist (and halting). The lack of the infinite (or dynamically growing) external store (seen at Turing machines) can be understood by replacing its role with Gödel numbering techniques: the fact that each register holds a natural number allows the possibility of representing a complicated thing (e.g. a sequence, or a matrix etc.) by an appropriate huge natural number — unambiguity of both representation and interpretation can be established by number theoretical foundations of these techniques.

In addition to the general computational models, some simpler computational models are useful for special, restricted applications. Regular expressions, for example, specify string patterns in many contexts, from office productivity software to programming languages. Another formalism mathematically equivalent to regular expressions, Finite automata are used in circuit design and in some kinds of problem-solving. Context-free grammars specify programming language syntax. Non-deterministic pushdown automata are another formalism equivalent to context-free grammars. Primitive recursive functions are a defined subclass of the recursive functions.

Different models of computation have the ability to do different tasks. One way to measure the power of a computational model is to study the class of formal languages that the model can generate; in such a way to the Chomsky hierarchy of languages is obtained.

2.5.4 References

[1] Michael Sipser (2013). *Introduction to the Theory of Computation 3rd*. Cengage Learning. ISBN 978-1-133-18779-0. central areas of the theory of computation: automata, computability, and complexity. (Page 1)

[2] Andrew Hodges (2012). *Alan Turing: The Enigma (THE CENTENARY EDITION)*. Princeton University Press. ISBN 978-0-691-15564-7.

[3] Rabin, Michael O. (June 2012). *Turing, Church, Gödel, Computability, Complexity and Randomization: A Personal View*.

[4] Donald Monk (1976). *Mathematical Logic*. Springer-Verlag. ISBN 9780387901701.

[5] Hopcroft, John E. and Jeffrey D. Ullman (2006). *Introduction to Automata Theory, Languages, and Computation. 3rd ed.* Reading, MA: Addison-Wesley. ISBN 978-0-321-45536-9.

[6] Chomsky hierarchy (1956). "Three models for the description of language". *Information Theory, IRE Transactions on* (IEEE) **2** (3): 113–124. doi:10.1109/TIT.1956.1056813. Retrieved 6 January 2015.

[7] Alan Turing (1937). "On computable numbers, with an application to the Entscheidungsproblem". *Proceedings of the London Mathematical Society* (IEEE) **2** (42): 230–265. doi:10.1112/plms/s2-42.1.230. Retrieved 6 January 2015.

[8] Henry Gordon Rice (1953). "Classes of Recursively Enumerable Sets and Their Decision Problems". *Transactions of the American Mathematical Society* (American Mathematical Society) **74** (2): 358–366. doi:10.2307/1990888. JSTOR 1990888.

[9] Martin Davis (2004). *The undecidable: Basic papers on undecidable propositions, unsolvable problems and computable functions (Dover Ed)*. Dover Publications. ISBN 978-0486432281.

2.5.5 Further reading

Textbooks aimed at computer scientists

(There are many textbooks in this area; this list is by necessity incomplete.)

- Hopcroft, John E., and Jeffrey D. Ullman (2006). *Introduction to Automata Theory, Languages, and Computation.* 3rd ed Reading, MA: Addison-Wesley. ISBN 978-0-321-45536-9 One of the standard references in the field.

- Michael Sipser (2013). *Introduction to the Theory of Computation* (3rd ed.). Cengage Learning. ISBN 978-1-133-18779-0.

- Eitan Gurari (1989). *An Introduction to the Theory of Computation.* Computer Science Press. ISBN 0-7167-8182-4.

- Hein, James L. (1996) *Theory of Computation.* Sudbury, MA: Jones & Bartlett. ISBN 978-0-86720-497-1 A gentle introduction to the field, appropriate for second-year undergraduate computer science students.

- Taylor, R. Gregory (1998). *Models of Computation and Formal Languages.* New York: Oxford University Press. ISBN 978-0-19-510983-2 An unusually readable textbook, appropriate for upper-level undergraduates or beginning graduate students.

- Lewis, F. D. (2007). *Essentials of theoretical computer science* A textbook covering the topics of formal languages, automata and grammars. The emphasis appears to be on presenting an overview of the results and their applications rather than providing proofs of the results.

- Martin Davis, Ron Sigal, Elaine J. Weyuker, *Computability, complexity, and languages: fundamentals of theoretical computer science*, 2nd ed., Academic Press, 1994, ISBN 0-12-206382-1. Covers a wider range of topics than most other introductory books, including program semantics and quantification theory. Aimed at graduate students.

Books on computability theory from the (wider) mathematical perspective

- Hartley Rogers, Jr (1987). *Theory of Recursive Functions and Effective Computability*, MIT Press. ISBN 0-262-68052-1

- S. Barry Cooper (2004). *Computability Theory.* Chapman and Hall/CRC. ISBN 1-58488-237-9..

- Carl H. Smith, *A recursive introduction to the theory of computation*, Springer, 1994, ISBN 0-387-94332-3. A shorter textbook suitable for graduate students in Computer Science.

Historical perspective

- Richard L. Epstein and Walter A. Carnielli (2000). *Computability: Computable Functions, Logic, and the Foundations of Mathematics, with Computability: A Timeline (2nd ed.).* Wadsworth/Thomson Learning. ISBN 0-534-54644-7..

2.5.6 External links

- Theory of Computation at MIT
- Theory of Computation at Harvard
- Computability Logic - A theory of interactive computation. The main web source on this subject.

2.6 Information theory

Not to be confused with information science.

Information theory is a branch of applied mathematics, electrical engineering, and computer science involving the quantification of information. Information theory was developed by Claude E. Shannon to find fundamental limits on signal processing operations such as compressing data and on reliably storing and communicating data. Since its inception it has broadened to find applications in many other areas, including statistical inference, natural language processing, cryptography, neurobiology,[1] the evolution[2] and function[3] of molecular codes, model selection in ecology,[4] thermal physics,[5] quantum computing, linguistics, plagiarism detection,[6] pattern recognition, anomaly detection and other forms of data analysis.[7]

A key measure of information is entropy, which is usually expressed by the average number of bits needed to store or communicate one symbol in a message. Entropy quantifies the uncertainty involved in predicting the value of a random variable. For example, specifying the outcome of a fair coin flip (two equally likely outcomes) provides less information (lower entropy) than specifying the outcome from a roll of a die (six equally likely outcomes).

Applications of fundamental topics of information theory include lossless data compression (e.g. ZIP files), lossy data compression (e.g. MP3s and JPEGs), and channel coding (e.g. for Digital Subscriber Line (DSL)). The field is at the intersection of mathematics, statistics, computer science, physics, neurobiology, and electrical engineering. Its impact has been crucial to the success of the Voyager missions to deep space, the invention of the compact disc, the feasibility of mobile phones, the development of the

Internet, the study of linguistics and of human perception, the understanding of black holes, and numerous other fields. Important sub-fields of information theory are source coding, channel coding, algorithmic complexity theory, algorithmic information theory, information-theoretic security, and measures of information.

2.6.1 Overview

Information theory studies the transmission, processing, utilization, and extraction of information. Abstractly, information can be thought of as the resolution of uncertainty. In the case of communication of information over a noisy channel, this abstract concept was made concrete in 1948 by Claude Shannon in A Mathematical Theory of Communication, in which "information" is thought of as a set of possible messages, where the goal is to send these messages over a noisy channel, and then to have the receiver reconstruct the message with low probability of error, in spite of the channel noise. Shannon's main result, the Noisy-channel coding theorem showed that, in the limit of many channel uses, the rate of information that is asymptotically achievable is equal to the Channel capacity, a quantity dependent merely on the statistics of the channel over which the messages are sent.

Information theory is closely associated with a collection of pure and applied disciplines that have been investigated and reduced to engineering practice under a variety of rubrics throughout the world over the past half century or more: adaptive systems, anticipatory systems, artificial intelligence, complex systems, complexity science, cybernetics, informatics, machine learning, along with systems sciences of many descriptions. Information theory is a broad and deep mathematical theory, with equally broad and deep applications, amongst which is the vital field of coding theory.

Coding theory is concerned with finding explicit methods, called *codes*, for increasing the efficiency and reducing the error rate of data communication over noisy channels to near the Channel capacity. These codes can be roughly subdivided into data compression (source coding) and error-correction (channel coding) techniques. In the latter case, it took many years to find the methods Shannon's work proved were possible. A third class of information theory codes are cryptographic algorithms (both codes and ciphers). Concepts, methods and results from coding theory and information theory are widely used in cryptography and cryptanalysis. *See the article ban (unit) for a historical application.*

Information theory is also used in information retrieval, intelligence gathering, gambling, statistics, and even in musical composition.

2.6.2 Historical background

Main article: History of information theory

The landmark event that established the discipline of information theory, and brought it to immediate worldwide attention, was the publication of Claude E. Shannon's classic paper "A Mathematical Theory of Communication" in the *Bell System Technical Journal* in July and October 1948.

Prior to this paper, limited information-theoretic ideas had been developed at Bell Labs, all implicitly assuming events of equal probability. Harry Nyquist's 1924 paper, *Certain Factors Affecting Telegraph Speed*, contains a theoretical section quantifying "intelligence" and the "line speed" at which it can be transmitted by a communication system, giving the relation $W = K \log m$ (recalling Boltzmann's constant), where W is the speed of transmission of intelligence, m is the number of different voltage levels to choose from at each time step, and K is a constant. Ralph Hartley's 1928 paper, *Transmission of Information*, uses the word *information* as a measurable quantity, reflecting the receiver's ability to distinguish one sequence of symbols from any other, thus quantifying information as $H = \log S^n = n \log S$, where S was the number of possible symbols, and n the number of symbols in a transmission. The unit of information was therefore the decimal digit, much later renamed the hartley in his honour as a unit or scale or measure of information. Alan Turing in 1940 used similar ideas as part of the statistical analysis of the breaking of the German second world war Enigma ciphers.

Much of the mathematics behind information theory with events of different probabilities were developed for the field of thermodynamics by Ludwig Boltzmann and J. Willard Gibbs. Connections between information-theoretic entropy and thermodynamic entropy, including the important contributions by Rolf Landauer in the 1960s, are explored in *Entropy in thermodynamics and information theory*.

In Shannon's revolutionary and groundbreaking paper, the work for which had been substantially completed at Bell Labs by the end of 1944, Shannon for the first time introduced the qualitative and quantitative model of communication as a statistical process underlying information theory, opening with the assertion that

> "The fundamental problem of communication is that of reproducing at one point, either exactly or approximately, a message selected at another point."

With it came the ideas of

- the information entropy and redundancy of a source, and its relevance through the source coding theorem;

- the mutual information, and the channel capacity of a noisy channel, including the promise of perfect loss-free communication given by the noisy-channel coding theorem;

- the practical result of the Shannon–Hartley law for the channel capacity of a Gaussian channel; as well as

- the bit—a new way of seeing the most fundamental unit of information.

2.6.3 Quantities of information

Main article: Quantities of information

Information theory is based on probability theory and statistics. Information theory often concerns itself with measures of information of the distributions associated with random variables. Important quantities of information are entropy, a measure of information in a single random variable, and mutual information, a measure of information in common between two random variables. The former quantity is a property of the probability distribution of a random variable and gives a limit on the rate at which data generated by independent samples with the given distribution can be reliably compressed. The latter is a property of the joint distribution of two random variables, and is the maximum rate of reliable communication across a noisy channel in the limit of long block lengths, when the channel statistics are determined by the joint distribution.

The choice of logarithmic base in the following formulae determines the unit of information entropy that is used. A common unit of information is the bit, based on the binary logarithm. Other units include the nat, which is based on the natural logarithm, and the hartley, which is based on the common logarithm.

In what follows, an expression of the form $p \log p$ is considered by convention to be equal to zero whenever $p = 0$. This is justified because $\lim_{p \to 0+} p \log p = 0$ for any logarithmic base.

Entropy

The **entropy**, H, of a discrete random variable X intuitively is a measure of the amount of *uncertainty* associated with the value of X when only its distribution is known. So, for example, if the distribution associated with a random variable was a constant distribution, (i.e. equal to some known value with probability 1), then entropy is minimal, and equal to 0. Furthermore, in the case of a distribution restricted to take on a finite number of values, entropy is

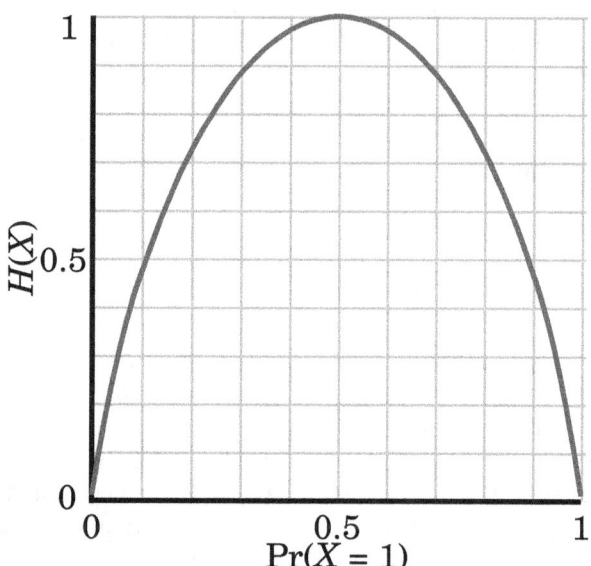

*Entropy of a Bernoulli trial as a function of success probability, often called the **binary entropy function**, $H_b(p)$. The entropy is maximized at 1 bit per trial when the two possible outcomes are equally probable, as in an unbiased coin toss.*

maximized with a uniform distribution over the values that the distribution takes on.

Suppose one transmits 1000 bits (0s and 1s). If the value of each these bits is known to the receiver (has a specific value with certainty) ahead of transmission, it is clear that no information is transmitted. If, however, each bit is independently equally likely to be 0 or 1, 1000 shannons of information (also often called bits, in the information theoretic sense) have been transmitted. Between these two extremes, information can be quantified as follows. If $\mathbb{X}$ is the set of all messages $\{x_1, ..., x_n\}$ that X could be, and $p(x)$ is the probability of some $x \in \mathbb{X}$, then the entropy, H, of X is defined:[8]

$$H(X) = \mathbb{E}_X[I(x)] = -\sum_{x \in \mathbb{X}} p(x) \log p(x).$$

(Here, $I(x)$ is the self-information, which is the entropy contribution of an individual message, and $\mathbb{E}_X$ is the expected value.) A property of entropy is that it is maximized when all the messages in the message space are equiprobable $p(x) = 1/n$,—i.e., most unpredictable—in which case $H(X) = \log n$.

The special case of information entropy for a random variable with two outcomes is the **binary entropy function**, usually taken to the logarithmic base 2, thus having the shannon (Sh) as unit:

2.6. INFORMATION THEORY

$$H_b(p) = -p\log_2 p - (1-p)\log_2(1-p).$$

Joint entropy

The **joint entropy** of two discrete random variables X and Y is merely the entropy of their pairing: (X, Y). This implies that if X and Y are independent, then their joint entropy is the sum of their individual entropies.

For example, if (X, Y) represents the position of a chess piece — X the row and Y the column, then the joint entropy of the row of the piece and the column of the piece will be the entropy of the position of the piece.

$$H(X,Y) = \mathbb{E}_{X,Y}[-\log p(x,y)] = -\sum_{x,y} p(x,y)\log p(x,y)$$

Despite similar notation, joint entropy should not be confused with **cross entropy**.

Conditional entropy (equivocation)

The **conditional entropy** or **conditional uncertainty** of X given random variable Y (also called the **equivocation** of X about Y) is the average conditional entropy over Y :[9]

$$H(X|Y) = \mathbb{E}_Y[H(X|y)] = -\sum_{y \in Y} p(y) \sum_{x \in X} p(x|y) \log p(x|y)$$

Because entropy can be conditioned on a random variable or on that random variable being a certain value, care should be taken not to confuse these two definitions of conditional entropy, the former of which is in more common use. A basic property of this form of conditional entropy is that:

$$H(X|Y) = H(X, Y) - H(Y).$$

Mutual information (transinformation)

Mutual information measures the amount of information that can be obtained about one random variable by observing another. It is important in communication where it can be used to maximize the amount of information shared between sent and received signals. The mutual information of X relative to Y is given by:

$$I(X;Y) = \mathbb{E}_{X,Y}[SI(x,y)] = \sum_{x,y} p(x,y) \log \frac{p(x,y)}{p(x)\,p(y)}$$

where SI (*S*pecific mutual *I*nformation) is the pointwise mutual information.

A basic property of the mutual information is that

$$I(X;Y) = H(X) - H(X|Y).$$

That is, knowing Y, we can save an average of $I(X;Y)$ bits in encoding X compared to not knowing Y.

Mutual information is symmetric:

$$I(X;Y) = I(Y;X) = H(X) + H(Y) - H(X,Y).$$

Mutual information can be expressed as the average Kullback–Leibler divergence (information gain) between the posterior probability distribution of X given the value of Y and the prior distribution on X:

$$I(X;Y) = \mathbb{E}_{p(y)}[D_{\mathrm{KL}}(p(X|Y=y) \| p(X))].$$

In other words, this is a measure of how much, on the average, the probability distribution on X will change if we are given the value of Y. This is often recalculated as the divergence from the product of the marginal distributions to the actual joint distribution:

$$I(X;Y) = D_{\mathrm{KL}}(p(X,Y) \| p(X)p(Y)).$$

Mutual information is closely related to the log-likelihood ratio test in the context of contingency tables and the multinomial distribution and to Pearson's χ^2 test: mutual information can be considered a statistic for assessing independence between a pair of variables, and has a well-specified asymptotic distribution.

Kullback–Leibler divergence (information gain)

The **Kullback–Leibler divergence** (or **information divergence**, **information gain**, or **relative entropy**) is a way of comparing two distributions: a "true" probability distribution $p(X)$, and an arbitrary probability distribution $q(X)$. If we compress data in a manner that assumes $q(X)$ is the distribution underlying some data, when, in reality, $p(X)$ is the correct distribution, the Kullback–Leibler divergence is the number of average additional bits per datum necessary for compression. It is thus defined

$$D_{\mathrm{KL}}(p(X)\|q(X)) = \sum_{x \in X} -p(x)\log q(x) - \sum_{x \in X} -p(x)\log p(x) = \sum_{x \in X} p(x$$

Although it is sometimes used as a 'distance metric', KL divergence is not a true metric since it is not symmetric and does not satisfy the triangle inequality (making it a semi-quasimetric).

Kullback–Leibler divergence of a prior from the truth

Another interpretation of KL divergence is this: suppose a number X is about to be drawn randomly from a discrete set with probability distribution $p(x)$. If Alice knows the true distribution $p(x)$, while Bob believes (has a prior) that the distribution is $q(x)$, then Bob will be more surprised than Alice, on average, upon seeing the value of X. The KL divergence is the (objective) expected value of Bob's (subjective) surprisal minus Alice's surprisal, measured in bits if the *log* is in base 2. In this way, the extent to which Bob's prior is "wrong" can be quantified in terms of how "unnecessarily surprised" it's expected to make him.

Other quantities

Other important information theoretic quantities include Rényi entropy (a generalization of entropy), differential entropy (a generalization of quantities of information to continuous distributions), and the conditional mutual information.

2.6.4 Coding theory

Main article: Coding theory

Coding theory is one of the most important and direct ap-

A picture showing scratches on the readable surface of a CD-R. Music and data CDs are coded using error correcting codes and thus can still be read even if they have minor scratches using error detection and correction.

plications of information theory. It can be subdivided into source coding theory and channel coding theory. Using a statistical description for data, information theory quantifies the number of bits needed to describe the data, which is the information entropy of the source.

- Data compression (source coding): There are two formulations for the compression problem:

1. lossless data compression: the data must be reconstructed exactly;

2. lossy data compression: allocates bits needed to reconstruct the data, within a specified fidelity level measured by a distortion function. This subset of Information theory is called rate–distortion theory.

- Error-correcting codes (channel coding): While data compression removes as much redundancy as possible, an error correcting code adds just the right kind of redundancy (i.e., error correction) needed to transmit the data efficiently and faithfully across a noisy channel.

This division of coding theory into compression and transmission is justified by the information transmission theorems, or source–channel separation theorems that justify the use of bits as the universal currency for information in many contexts. However, these theorems only hold in the situation where one transmitting user wishes to communicate to one receiving user. In scenarios with more than one transmitter (the multiple-access channel), more than one receiver (the broadcast channel) or intermediary "helpers" (the relay channel), or more general networks, compression followed by transmission may no longer be optimal. Network information theory refers to these multi-agent communication models.

Source theory

Any process that generates successive messages can be considered a **source** of information. A memoryless source is one in which each message is an independent identically distributed random variable, whereas the properties of ergodicity and stationarity impose less restrictive constraints. All such sources are stochastic. These terms are well studied in their own right outside information theory.

Rate Information **rate** is the average entropy per symbol. For memoryless sources, this is merely the entropy of each symbol, while, in the case of a stationary stochastic process, it is

$$r = \lim_{n \to \infty} H(X_n | X_{n-1}, X_{n-2}, X_{n-3}, \ldots);$$

that is, the conditional entropy of a symbol given all the previous symbols generated. For the more general case of

2.6. INFORMATION THEORY

a process that is not necessarily stationary, the *average rate* is

$$r = \lim_{n\to\infty} \frac{1}{n} H(X_1, X_2, \ldots X_n);$$

that is, the limit of the joint entropy per symbol. For stationary sources, these two expressions give the same result.[10]

It is common in information theory to speak of the "rate" or "entropy" of a language. This is appropriate, for example, when the source of information is English prose. The rate of a source of information is related to its redundancy and how well it can be compressed, the subject of **source coding**.

Channel capacity

Main article: Channel capacity

Communications over a channel—such as an ethernet cable—is the primary motivation of information theory. As anyone who's ever used a telephone (mobile or landline) knows, however, such channels often fail to produce exact reconstruction of a signal; noise, periods of silence, and other forms of signal corruption often degrade quality. How much information can one hope to communicate over a noisy (or otherwise imperfect) channel?

Consider the communications process over a discrete channel. A simple model of the process is shown below:

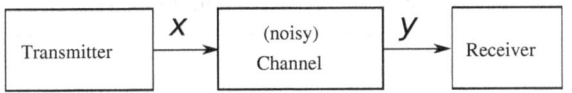

Here X represents the space of messages transmitted, and Y the space of messages received during a unit time over our channel. Let $p(y|x)$ be the conditional probability distribution function of Y given X. We will consider $p(y|x)$ to be an inherent fixed property of our communications channel (representing the nature of the **noise** of our channel). Then the joint distribution of X and Y is completely determined by our channel and by our choice of $f(x)$, the marginal distribution of messages we choose to send over the channel. Under these constraints, we would like to maximize the rate of information, or the **signal**, we can communicate over the channel. The appropriate measure for this is the mutual information, and this maximum mutual information is called the **channel capacity** and is given by:

$$C = \max_f I(X;Y).$$

This capacity has the following property related to communicating at information rate R (where R is usually bits per symbol). For any information rate $R < C$ and coding error $\varepsilon > 0$, for large enough N, there exists a code of length N and rate $\geq R$ and a decoding algorithm, such that the maximal probability of block error is $\leq \varepsilon$; that is, it is always possible to transmit with arbitrarily small block error. In addition, for any rate $R > C$, it is impossible to transmit with arbitrarily small block error.

Channel coding is concerned with finding such nearly optimal codes that can be used to transmit data over a noisy channel with a small coding error at a rate near the channel capacity.

Capacity of particular channel models

- A continuous-time analog communications channel subject to Gaussian noise — see Shannon–Hartley theorem.

- A binary symmetric channel (BSC) with crossover probability p is a binary input, binary output channel that flips the input bit with probability p. The BSC has a capacity of $1 - H_b(p)$ bits per channel use, where H_b is the binary entropy function to the base 2 logarithm:

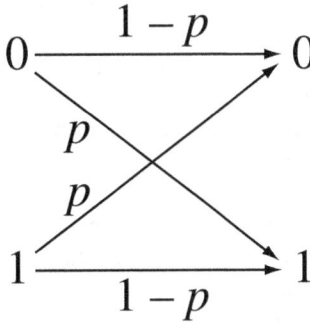

- A binary erasure channel (BEC) with erasure probability p is a binary input, ternary output channel. The possible channel outputs are 0, 1, and a third symbol 'e' called an erasure. The erasure represents complete loss of information about an input bit. The capacity of the BEC is $1 - p$ bits per channel use.

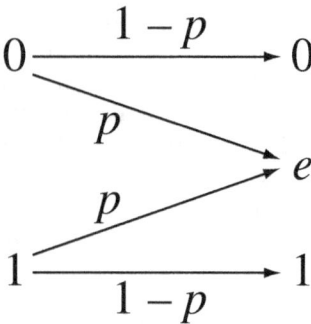

2.6.5 Applications to other fields

Intelligence uses and secrecy applications

Information theoretic concepts apply to cryptography and cryptanalysis. Turing's information unit, the ban, was used in the Ultra project, breaking the German Enigma machine code and hastening the end of World War II in Europe. Shannon himself defined an important concept now called the unicity distance. Based on the redundancy of the plaintext, it attempts to give a minimum amount of ciphertext necessary to ensure unique decipherability.

Information theory leads us to believe it is much more difficult to keep secrets than it might first appear. A brute force attack can break systems based on asymmetric key algorithms or on most commonly used methods of symmetric key algorithms (sometimes called secret key algorithms), such as block ciphers. The security of all such methods currently comes from the assumption that no known attack can break them in a practical amount of time.

Information theoretic security refers to methods such as the one-time pad that are not vulnerable to such brute force attacks. In such cases, the positive conditional mutual information between the plaintext and ciphertext (conditioned on the key) can ensure proper transmission, while the unconditional mutual information between the plaintext and ciphertext remains zero, resulting in absolutely secure communications. In other words, an eavesdropper would not be able to improve his or her guess of the plaintext by gaining knowledge of the ciphertext but not of the key. However, as in any other cryptographic system, care must be used to correctly apply even information-theoretically secure methods; the Venona project was able to crack the one-time pads of the Soviet Union due to their improper reuse of key material.

Pseudorandom number generation

Pseudorandom number generators are widely available in computer language libraries and application programs. They are, almost universally, unsuited to cryptographic use as they do not evade the deterministic nature of modern computer equipment and software. A class of improved random number generators is termed cryptographically secure pseudorandom number generators, but even they require random seeds external to the software to work as intended. These can be obtained via extractors, if done carefully. The measure of sufficient randomness in extractors is min-entropy, a value related to Shannon entropy through Rényi entropy; Rényi entropy is also used in evaluating randomness in cryptographic systems. Although related, the distinctions among these measures mean that a random variable with high Shannon entropy is not necessarily satisfactory for use in an extractor and so for cryptography uses.

Seismic exploration

One early commercial application of information theory was in the field of seismic oil exploration. Work in this field made it possible to strip off and separate the unwanted noise from the desired seismic signal. Information theory and digital signal processing offer a major improvement of resolution and image clarity over previous analog methods.[11]

Semiotics

Concepts from information theory such as redundancy and code control have been used by semioticians such as Umberto Eco and Rossi-Landi to explain ideology as a form of message transmission whereby a dominant social class emits its message by using signs that exhibit a high degree of redundancy such that only one message is decoded among a selection of competing ones.[12]

Miscellaneous applications

Information theory also has applications in gambling and investing, black holes, bioinformatics, and music.

2.6.6 See also

- Algorithmic probability
- Algorithmic information theory
- Bayesian inference
- Communication theory
- Constructor theory - a generalization of information theory that includes quantum information
- Inductive probability

2.6. INFORMATION THEORY

- Minimum message length
- Minimum description length
- List of important publications
- Philosophy of information

Applications

- Active networking
- Cryptanalysis
- Cryptography
- Cybernetics
- Entropy in thermodynamics and information theory
- Gambling
- Intelligence (information gathering)
- Seismic exploration

History

- Hartley, R.V.L.
- History of information theory
- Shannon, C.E.
- Timeline of information theory
- Yockey, H.P.

Theory

- Coding theory
- Detection theory
- Estimation theory
- Fisher information
- Information algebra
- Information asymmetry
- Information field theory
- Information geometry
- Information theory and measure theory
- Kolmogorov complexity
- Logic of information

- Network coding
- Philosophy of Information
- Quantum information science
- Semiotic information theory
- Source coding
- Unsolved Problems

Concepts

- Ban (unit)
- Channel capacity
- Channel (communications)
- Communication source
- Conditional entropy
- Covert channel
- Decoder
- Differential entropy
- Encoder
- Information entropy
- Joint entropy
- Kullback–Leibler divergence
- Mutual information
- Pointwise mutual information (PMI)
- Receiver (information theory)
- Redundancy
- Rényi entropy
- Self-information
- Unicity distance
- Variety

2.6.7 References

[1] F. Rieke, D. Warland, R Ruyter van Steveninck, W Bialek (1997). *Spikes: Exploring the Neural Code.* The MIT press. ISBN 978-0262681087.

[2] cf. Huelsenbeck, J. P., F. Ronquist, R. Nielsen and J. P. Bollback (2001) Bayesian inference of phylogeny and its impact on evolutionary biology, *Science* **294**:2310-2314

[3] Rando Allikmets, Wyeth W. Wasserman, Amy Hutchinson, Philip Smallwood, Jeremy Nathans, Peter K. Rogan, Thomas D. Schneider, Michael Dean (1998) Organization of the ABCR gene: analysis of promoter and splice junction sequences, *Gene* **215**:1, 111-122

[4] Burnham, K. P. and Anderson D. R. (2002) *Model Selection and Multimodel Inference: A Practical Information-Theoretic Approach, Second Edition* (Springer Science, New York) ISBN 978-0-387-95364-9.

[5] Jaynes, E. T. (1957) Information Theory and Statistical Mechanics, *Phys. Rev.* **106**:620

[6] Charles H. Bennett, Ming Li, and Bin Ma (2003) Chain Letters and Evolutionary Histories, *Scientific American* **288**:6, 76-81

[7] David R. Anderson (November 1, 2003). "Some background on why people in the empirical sciences may want to better understand the information-theoretic methods" (pdf). Retrieved 2010-06-23.

[8] Fazlollah M. Reza (1994) [1961]. *An Introduction to Information Theory.* Dover Publications, Inc., New York. ISBN 0-486-68210-2.

[9] Robert B. Ash (1990) [1965]. *Information Theory.* Dover Publications, Inc. ISBN 0-486-66521-6.

[10] Jerry D. Gibson (1998). *Digital Compression for Multimedia: Principles and Standards.* Morgan Kaufmann. ISBN 1-55860-369-7.

[11] The Corporation and Innovation, Haggerty, Patrick, Strategic Management Journal, Vol. 2, 97-118 (1981)

[12] Semiotics of Ideology, Noth, Winfried, Semiotica, Issue 148,(1981)

The classic work

- Shannon, C.E. (1948), "A Mathematical Theory of Communication", *Bell System Technical Journal*, 27, pp. 379–423 & 623–656, July & October, 1948. PDF.
  Notes and other formats.

- R.V.L. Hartley, "Transmission of Information", *Bell System Technical Journal*, July 1928

- Andrey Kolmogorov (1968), "Three approaches to the quantitative definition of information" in International Journal of Computer Mathematics.

Other journal articles

- J. L. Kelly, Jr., Saratoga.ny.us, "A New Interpretation of Information Rate" *Bell System Technical Journal*, Vol. 35, July 1956, pp. 917–26.

- R. Landauer, IEEE.org, "Information is Physical" *Proc. Workshop on Physics and Computation PhysComp'92* (IEEE Comp. Sci.Press, Los Alamitos, 1993) pp. 1–4.

- R. Landauer, IBM.com, "Irreversibility and Heat Generation in the Computing Process" *IBM J. Res. Develop.* Vol. 5, No. 3, 1961

- Timme, Nicholas; Alford, Wesley; Flecker, Benjamin; Beggs, John M. (2012). "Multivariate information measures: an experimentalist's perspective". *arXiv: 111.6857v5* (Cornell University) **5**. Retrieved 7 June 2015.

Textbooks on information theory

- Arndt, C. *Information Measures, Information and its Description in Science and Engineering* (Springer Series: Signals and Communication Technology), 2004, ISBN 978-3-540-40855-0

- Ash, RB. *Information Theory.* New York: Interscience, 1965. ISBN 0-470-03445-9. New York: Dover 1990. ISBN 0-486-66521-6

- Gallager, R. *Information Theory and Reliable Communication.* New York: John Wiley and Sons, 1968. ISBN 0-471-29048-3

- Goldman, S. *Information Theory.* New York: Prentice Hall, 1953. New York: Dover 1968 ISBN 0-486-62209-6, 2005 ISBN 0-486-44271-3

- Cover, TM, Thomas, JA. *Elements of information theory*, 1st Edition. New York: Wiley-Interscience, 1991. ISBN 0-471-06259-6.

  2nd Edition. New York: Wiley-Interscience, 2006. ISBN 0-471-24195-4.

- Csiszar, I, Korner, J. *Information Theory: Coding Theorems for Discrete Memoryless Systems* Akademiai Kiado: 2nd edition, 1997. ISBN 963-05-7440-3

- MacKay, DJC. *Information Theory, Inference, and Learning Algorithms* Cambridge: Cambridge University Press, 2003. ISBN 0-521-64298-1

- Mansuripur, M. *Introduction to Information Theory.* New York: Prentice Hall, 1987. ISBN 0-13-484668-0

- McEliece, R. *The Theory of Information and Coding".* Cambridge, 2002. ISBN 978-0521831857

- Pierce, JR. "An introduction to information theory: symbols, signals and noise". Dover (2nd Edition). 1961 (reprinted by Dover 1980).

- Reza, F. *An Introduction to Information Theory.* New York: McGraw-Hill 1961. New York: Dover 1994. ISBN 0-486-68210-2

- Shannon, CE. Warren Weaver. *The Mathematical Theory of Communication.* Univ of Illinois Press, 1949. ISBN 0-252-72548-4

- Stone, JV. Chapter 1 of book "Information Theory: A Tutorial Introduction", University of Sheffield, England, 2014. ISBN 978-0956372857.

- Yeung, RW. *A First Course in Information Theory* Kluwer Academic/Plenum Publishers, 2002. ISBN 0-306-46791-7.

- Yeung, RW. *Information Theory and Network Coding* Springer 2008, 2002. ISBN 978-0-387-79233-0

Other books

- Leon Brillouin, *Science and Information Theory*, Mineola, N.Y.: Dover, [1956, 1962] 2004. ISBN 0-486-43918-6

- James Gleick, *The Information: A History, a Theory, a Flood*, New York: Pantheon, 2011. ISBN 978-0-375-42372-7

- A. I. Khinchin, *Mathematical Foundations of Information Theory*, New York: Dover, 1957. ISBN 0-486-60434-9

- H. S. Leff and A. F. Rex, Editors, *Maxwell's Demon: Entropy, Information, Computing*, Princeton University Press, Princeton, New Jersey (1990). ISBN 0-691-08727-X

- Tom Siegfried, *The Bit and the Pendulum*, Wiley, 2000. ISBN 0-471-32174-5

- Charles Seife, *Decoding the Universe*, Viking, 2006. ISBN 0-670-03441-X

- Jeremy Campbell, *Grammatical Man*, Touchstone/Simon & Schuster, 1982, ISBN 0-671-44062-4

- Henri Theil, *Economics and Information Theory*, Rand McNally & Company - Chicago, 1967.

- Escolano, Suau, Bonev, *Information Theory in Computer Vision and Pattern Recognition*, Springer, 2009. ISBN 978-1-84882-296-2

2.6.8 External links

- Erill I. (2012), "A gentle introduction to information content in transcription factor binding sites" (University of Maryland, Baltimore County)

- Hazewinkel, Michiel, ed. (2001), "Information", *Encyclopedia of Mathematics*, Springer, ISBN 978-1-55608-010-4

- Lambert F. L. (1999), "Shuffled Cards, Messy Desks, and Disorderly Dorm Rooms - Examples of Entropy Increase? Nonsense!", *Journal of Chemical Education*

- Schneider T. D. (2014), "Information Theory Primer"

- Srinivasa, S., "A Review on Multivariate Mutual Information"

- IEEE Information Theory Society and ITSoc review articles

2.7 Coding theory

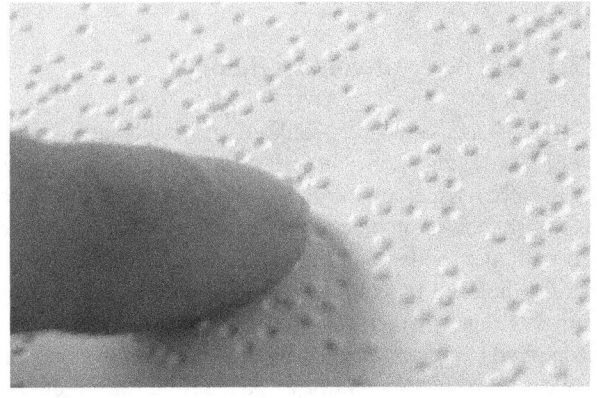

Braille, a code that uses data compression extensively to compensate for slower reading times.

Coding theory is the study of the properties of codes and their fitness for a specific application. Codes are used for data compression, cryptography, error-correction and more recently also for network coding. Codes are studied by various scientific disciplines—such as information theory, electrical engineering, mathematics, and computer science—for the purpose of designing efficient and reliable data transmission methods. This typically involves the removal of redundancy and the correction (or detection) of errors in the transmitted data.

There are four types of coding:[1]

1. Data compression (or, *source coding*)
2. Error correction (or *channel coding*)
3. Cryptographic coding
4. Line coding

Data compression and error correction may be studied in combination.

Source encoding attempts to compress the data from a source in order to transmit it more efficiently. This practice is found every day on the Internet where the common Zip data compression is used to reduce the network load and make files smaller.

The second, channel encoding, adds extra data bits to make the transmission of data more robust to disturbances present on the transmission channel. The ordinary user may not be aware of many applications using channel coding. A typical music CD uses the Reed-Solomon code to correct for scratches and dust. In this application the transmission channel is the CD itself. Cell phones also use coding techniques to correct for the fading and noise of high frequency radio transmission. Data modems, telephone transmissions, and NASA all employ channel coding techniques to get the bits through, for example the turbo code and LDPC codes.

2.7.1 History of coding theory

In 1948, Claude Shannon published "A Mathematical Theory of Communication", an article in two parts in the July and October issues of the *Bell System Technical Journal*. This work focuses on the problem of how best to encode the information a sender wants to transmit. In this fundamental work he used tools in probability theory, developed by Norbert Wiener, which were in their nascent stages of being applied to communication theory at that time. Shannon developed information entropy as a measure for the uncertainty in a message while essentially inventing the field of information theory.

The binary Golay code was developed in 1949. More specifically, it is an error-correcting code capable of correcting up to three errors in each 24-bit word, and detecting a fourth.

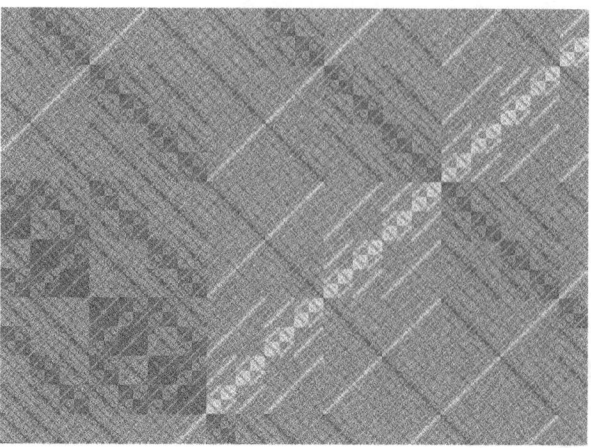

A two-dimensional visualisation of the Hamming distance

Richard Hamming won the Turing Award in 1968 for his work at Bell Labs in numerical methods, automatic coding systems, and error-detecting and error-correcting codes. He invented the concepts known as Hamming codes, Hamming windows, Hamming numbers, and Hamming distance.

2.7.2 Source coding

Main article: Data compression

The aim of source coding is to take the source data and make it smaller.

Definition

Data can be seen as a random variable $X : \Omega \to \mathcal{X}$, where $x \in \mathcal{X}$ appears with probability $\mathbb{P}[X = x]$.

Data are encoded by strings (words) over an alphabet Σ.

A code is a function

$C : \mathcal{X} \to \Sigma^*$ (or Σ^+ if the empty string is not part of the alphabet).

$C(x)$ is the code word associated with x.

Length of the code word is written as

$l(C(x))$.

Expected length of a code is

$l(C) = \sum_{x \in \mathcal{X}} l(C(x))\mathbb{P}[X = x]$

The concatenation of code words $C(x_1, ..., x_k) = C(x_1)C(x_2)...C(x_k)$.

The code word of the empty string is the empty string itself:

2.7. CODING THEORY

$C(\epsilon) = \epsilon$

Properties

1. $C : \mathcal{X} \to \Sigma^*$ is non-singular if injective.
2. $C : \mathcal{X}^* \to \Sigma^*$ is uniquely decodable if injective.
3. $C : \mathcal{X} \to \Sigma^*$ is instantaneous if $C(x_1)$ is not a prefix of $C(x_2)$ (and vice versa).

Principle

Entropy of a source is the measure of information. Basically, source codes try to reduce the redundancy present in the source, and represent the source with fewer bits that carry more information.

Data compression which explicitly tries to minimize the average length of messages according to a particular assumed probability model is called entropy encoding.

Various techniques used by source coding schemes try to achieve the limit of Entropy of the source. $C(x) \geq H(x)$, where $H(x)$ is entropy of source (bitrate), and $C(x)$ is the bitrate after compression. In particular, no source coding scheme can be better than the entropy of the source.

Example

Facsimile transmission uses a simple run length code. Source coding removes all data superfluous to the need of the transmitter, decreasing the bandwidth required for transmission.

2.7.3 Channel coding

Main article: Forward error correction

The purpose of channel coding theory is to find codes which transmit quickly, contain many valid code words and can correct or at least detect many errors. While not mutually exclusive, performance in these areas is a trade off. So, different codes are optimal for different applications. The needed properties of this code mainly depend on the probability of errors happening during transmission. In a typical CD, the impairment is mainly dust or scratches. Thus codes are used in an interleaved manner. The data is spread out over the disk.

Although not a very good code, a simple repeat code can serve as an understandable example. Suppose we take a block of data bits (representing sound) and send it three times. At the receiver we will examine the three repetitions bit by bit and take a majority vote. The twist on this is that we don't merely send the bits in order. We interleave them. The block of data bits is first divided into 4 smaller blocks. Then we cycle through the block and send one bit from the first, then the second, etc. This is done three times to spread the data out over the surface of the disk. In the context of the simple repeat code, this may not appear effective. However, there are more powerful codes known which are very effective at correcting the "burst" error of a scratch or a dust spot when this interleaving technique is used.

Other codes are more appropriate for different applications. Deep space communications are limited by the thermal noise of the receiver which is more of a continuous nature than a bursty nature. Likewise, narrowband modems are limited by the noise, present in the telephone network and also modeled better as a continuous disturbance. Cell phones are subject to rapid fading. The high frequencies used can cause rapid fading of the signal even if the receiver is moved a few inches. Again there are a class of channel codes that are designed to combat fading.

Linear codes

Main article: Linear code

The term **algebraic coding theory** denotes the sub-field of coding theory where the properties of codes are expressed in algebraic terms and then further researched.

Algebraic coding theory is basically divided into two major types of codes:

1. Linear block codes
2. Convolutional codes.

It analyzes the following three properties of a code – mainly:

- code word length
- total number of valid code words
- the minimum distance between two valid code words, using mainly the Hamming distance, sometimes also other distances like the Lee distance.

Linear block codes Main article: Block code

Linear block codes have the property of linearity, i.e. the sum of any two codewords is also a code word, and they are applied to the source bits in blocks, hence the name linear block codes. There are block codes that are not linear, but it is difficult to prove that a code is a good one without this property.[2]

Linear block codes are summarized by their symbol alphabets (e.g., binary or ternary) and parameters (*n,m,dmin*)[3] where

1. n is the length of the codeword, in symbols,
2. m is the number of source symbols that will be used for encoding at once,
3. *dmin* is the minimum hamming distance for the code.

There are many types of linear block codes, such as

1. Cyclic codes (e.g., Hamming codes)
2. Repetition codes
3. Parity codes
4. Polynomial codes (e.g., BCH codes)
5. Reed–Solomon codes
6. Algebraic geometric codes
7. Reed–Muller codes
8. Perfect codes.

Block codes are tied to the sphere packing problem, which has received some attention over the years. In two dimensions, it is easy to visualize. Take a bunch of pennies flat on the table and push them together. The result is a hexagon pattern like a bee's nest. But block codes rely on more dimensions which cannot easily be visualized. The powerful (24,12) Golay code used in deep space communications uses 24 dimensions. If used as a binary code (which it usually is) the dimensions refer to the length of the codeword as defined above.

The theory of coding uses the *N*-dimensional sphere model. For example, how many pennies can be packed into a circle on a tabletop, or in 3 dimensions, how many marbles can be packed into a globe. Other considerations enter the choice of a code. For example, hexagon packing into the constraint of a rectangular box will leave empty space at the corners. As the dimensions get larger, the percentage of empty space grows smaller. But at certain dimensions, the packing uses all the space and these codes are the so-called "perfect" codes. The only nontrivial and useful perfect codes are the distance-3 Hamming codes with parameters satisfying $(2^r - 1, 2^r - 1 - r, 3)$, and the [23,12,7] binary and [11,6,5] ternary Golay codes.[2][3]

Another code property is the number of neighbors that a single codeword may have.[4] Again, consider pennies as an example. First we pack the pennies in a rectangular grid. Each penny will have 4 near neighbors (and 4 at the corners which are farther away). In a hexagon, each penny will have 6 near neighbors. When we increase the dimensions, the number of near neighbors increases very rapidly. The result is the number of ways for noise to make the receiver choose a neighbor (hence an error) grows as well. This is a fundamental limitation of block codes, and indeed all codes. It may be harder to cause an error to a single neighbor, but the number of neighbors can be large enough so the total error probability actually suffers.[4]

Properties of linear block codes are used in many applications. For example, the syndrome-coset uniqueness property of linear block codes is used in trellis shaping,[5] one of the best known shaping codes. This same property is used in sensor networks for distributed source coding

Convolutional codes   Main article: Convolutional code

The idea behind a convolutional code is to make every codeword symbol be the weighted sum of the various input message symbols. This is like convolution used in LTI systems to find the output of a system, when you know the input and impulse response.

So we generally find the output of the system convolutional encoder, which is the convolution of the input bit, against the states of the convolution encoder, registers.

Fundamentally, convolutional codes do not offer more protection against noise than an equivalent block code. In many cases, they generally offer greater simplicity of implementation over a block code of equal power. The encoder is usually a simple circuit which has state memory and some feedback logic, normally XOR gates. The decoder can be implemented in software or firmware.

The Viterbi algorithm is the optimum algorithm used to decode convolutional codes. There are simplifications to reduce the computational load. They rely on searching only the most likely paths. Although not optimum, they have generally been found to give good results in the lower noise environments.

Convolutional codes are used in voiceband modems (V.32, V.17, V.34) and in GSM mobile phones, as well as satellite and military communication devices.

2.7.4 Cryptographical coding

Main article: Cryptography

Cryptography or cryptographic coding is the practice and study of techniques for secure communication in the presence of third parties (called adversaries).[6] More generally, it is about constructing and analyzing protocols that block adversaries;[7] various aspects in information security such as data confidentiality, data integrity, authentication, and non-repudiation[8] are central to modern cryptography. Modern cryptography exists at the intersection of the disciplines of mathematics, computer science, and electrical engineering. Applications of cryptography include ATM cards, computer passwords, and electronic commerce.

Cryptography prior to the modern age was effectively synonymous with *encryption*, the conversion of information from a readable state to apparent nonsense. The originator of an encrypted message shared the decoding technique needed to recover the original information only with intended recipients, thereby precluding unwanted persons from doing the same. Since World War I and the advent of the computer, the methods used to carry out cryptology have become increasingly complex and its application more widespread.

Modern cryptography is heavily based on mathematical theory and computer science practice; cryptographic algorithms are designed around computational hardness assumptions, making such algorithms hard to break in practice by any adversary. It is theoretically possible to break such a system, but it is infeasible to do so by any known practical means. These schemes are therefore termed computationally secure; theoretical advances, e.g., improvements in integer factorization algorithms, and faster computing technology require these solutions to be continually adapted. There exist information-theoretically secure schemes that provably cannot be broken even with unlimited computing power—an example is the one-time pad—but these schemes are more difficult to implement than the best theoretically breakable but computationally secure mechanisms.

2.7.5 Line coding

Main article: Line code

A line code (also called digital baseband modulation or digital baseband transmission method) is a code chosen for use within a communications system for baseband transmission purposes. Line coding is often used for digital data transport.

Line coding consists of representing the digital signal to be transported by an amplitude- and time-discrete signal that is optimally tuned for the specific properties of the physical channel (and of the receiving equipment). The waveform pattern of voltage or current used to represent the 1s and 0s of a digital data on a transmission link is called *line encoding*. The common types of line encoding are unipolar, polar, bipolar, and Manchester encoding.

2.7.6 Other applications of coding theory

Another concern of coding theory is designing codes that help synchronization. A code may be designed so that a phase shift can be easily detected and corrected and that multiple signals can be sent on the same channel.

Another application of codes, used in some mobile phone systems, is code-division multiple access (CDMA). Each phone is assigned a code sequence that is approximately uncorrelated with the codes of other phones. When transmitting, the code word is used to modulate the data bits representing the voice message. At the receiver, a demodulation process is performed to recover the data. The properties of this class of codes allow many users (with different codes) to use the same radio channel at the same time. To the receiver, the signals of other users will appear to the demodulator only as a low-level noise.

Another general class of codes are the automatic repeat-request (ARQ) codes. In these codes the sender adds redundancy to each message for error checking, usually by adding check bits. If the check bits are not consistent with the rest of the message when it arrives, the receiver will ask the sender to retransmit the message. All but the simplest wide area network protocols use ARQ. Common protocols include SDLC (IBM), TCP (Internet), X.25 (International) and many others. There is an extensive field of research on this topic because of the problem of matching a rejected packet against a new packet. Is it a new one or is it a retransmission? Typically numbering schemes are used, as in TCP."RFC793". *RFCs*. Internet Engineering Task Force (IETF). September 1981.

Group testing

Group testing uses codes in a different way. Consider a large group of items in which a very few are different in a particular way (e.g., defective products or infected test subjects). The idea of group testing is to determine which items are "different" by using as few tests as possible. The origin of the problem has its roots in the Second World War when the United States Army Air Forces needed to test its soldiers for syphilis. It originated from a ground-breaking paper by Robert Dorfman.

Analog coding

Information is encoded analogously in the neural networks of brains, in analog signal processing, and analog electronics. Aspects of analog coding include analog error correction,[9] analog data compression.[10] analog encryption[11]

2.7.7 Neural coding

Neural coding is a neuroscience-related field concerned with how sensory and other information is represented in the brain by networks of neurons. The main goal of studying neural coding is to characterize the relationship between the stimulus and the individual or ensemble neuronal responses and the relationship among electrical activity of the neurons in the ensemble.[12] It is thought that neurons can encode both digital and analog information,[13] and that neurons follow the principles of information theory and compress information,[14] and detect and correct[15] errors in the signals that are sent throughout the brain and wider nervous system.

2.7.8 See also

- Coding gain
- Covering code
- Error-correcting code
- Group testing
- Hamming distance, Hamming weight
- Information theory
- Lee distance
- Spatial coding and MIMO in multiple antenna research
    - Spatial diversity coding is spatial coding that transmits replicas of the information signal along different spatial paths, so as to increase the reliability of the data transmission.
    - Spatial interference cancellation coding
    - Spatial multiplex coding
- Timeline of information theory, data compression, and error correcting codes
- List of algebraic coding theory topics
- Folded Reed–Solomon codes
- ABNNR and AEL codes

2.7.9 Notes

[1] James Irvine, David Harle. "Data Communications and Networks". 2002. p. 18. section "2.4.4 Types of Coding". quote: "There are four types of coding"

[2] Terras, Audrey (1999). *Fourier Analysis on Finite Groups and Applications*. Cambridge University Press. ISBN 0-521-45718-1.

[3] Blahut, Richard E. (2003). *Algebraic Codes for Data Transmission*. Cambridge University Press. ISBN 0-521-55374-1.

[4] Christian Schlegel and Lance Pérez (2004). *Trellis and turbo coding*. Wiley-IEEE. p. 73. ISBN 978-0-471-22755-7.

[5] Forney, G.D., Jr. (March 1992). "Trellis shaping". *IEEE Transactions on Information Theory* **38** (2 Pt 2): 281–300. doi:10.1109/18.119687o.

[6] Rivest, Ronald L. (1990). "Cryptology". In J. Van Leeuwen. *Handbook of Theoretical Computer Science* **1**. Elsevier.

[7] Bellare, Mihir; Rogaway, Phillip (21 September 2005). "Introduction". *Introduction to Modern Cryptography*. p. 10.

[8] Menezes, A. J.; van Oorschot, P. C.; Vanstone, S. A. *Handbook of Applied Cryptography*. ISBN 0-8493-8523-7.

[9] Chen, Brian; Wornell, Gregory W. (July 1998). "Analog Error-Correcting Codes Based on Chaotic Dynamical Systems" (PDF). *IEEE Transactions on Communications* **46** (7): 881–890. doi:10.1109/26.701312. CiteSeerX: 10.1.1.30.4093.

[10] Hvala, Franc Novak Bojan; Klavžar, Sandi (1999). "On Analog Signature Analysis". *Proceedings of the conference on Design, automation and test in Europe*. ISBN 1-58113-121-6. CiteSeerX: 10.1.1.142.5853.

[11] Shujun Li, Chengqing Li, Kwok-Tung Lo, Guanrong Chen (April 2008). "Cryptanalyzing an Encryption Scheme Based on Blind Source Separation". *IEEE Transactions on Circuits and Systems I* **55** (4): 1055–63. doi:10.1109/TCSI.2008.916540.

[12] Brown EN, Kass RE, Mitra PP (May 2004). "Multiple neural spike train data analysis: state-of-the-art and future challenges". *Nat. Neurosci.* **7** (5): 456–61. doi:10.1038/nn1228. PMID 15114358.

[13] Thorpe, S.J. (1990). "Spike arrival times: A highly efficient coding scheme for neural networks" (PDF). In Eckmiller, R.; Hartmann, G.; Hauske, G. *Parallel processing in neural systems and computers* (PDF). North-Holland. pp. 91–94. ISBN 978-0-444-88390-2. Retrieved 30 June 2013.

[14] Gedeon, T.; Parker, A.E.; Dimitrov, A.G. (Spring 2002). "Information Distortion and Neural Coding". *Canadian Applied Mathematics Quarterly* **10** (1): 10. CiteSeerX: 10.1.1.5.6365.

2.8. PROGRAMMING LANGUAGE THEORY

[15] Stiber, M. (July 2005). "Spike timing precision and neural error correction: local behavior". *Neural Computation* **17** (7): 1577–1601. arXiv:q-bio/0501021. doi:10.1162/0899766053723069.

2.7.10 References

- Vera Pless (1982), *Introduction to the Theory of Error-Correcting Codes*, John Wiley & Sons, Inc., ISBN 0-471-08684-3.

- Elwyn R. Berlekamp (2014), *Algebraic Coding Theory*, World Scientific Publishing (revised edition), ISBN 978-9-81463-589-9.

- Randy Yates, *A Coding Theory Tutorial*.

2.8 Programming language theory

The lowercase Greek letter λ (lambda) is an unofficial symbol of the field of programming language theory. This usage derives from the lambda calculus, a computational model introduced by Alonzo Church in the 1930s and widely used by programming language researchers. It graces the cover of the classic text Structure and Interpretation of Computer Programs, *and the title of the so-called* Lambda Papers, *written by Gerald Jay Sussman and Guy Steele, the developers of the Scheme programming language.*

Programming language theory (**PLT**) is a branch of computer science that deals with the design, implementation, analysis, characterization, and classification of programming languages and their individual features. It falls within the discipline of computer science, both depending on and affecting mathematics, software engineering and linguistics. It is a well-recognized branch of computer science, and an active research area, with results published in numerous journals dedicated to PLT, as well as in general computer science and engineering publications.

2.8.1 History

In some ways, the history of programming language theory predates even the development of programming languages themselves. The lambda calculus, developed by Alonzo Church and Stephen Cole Kleene in the 1930s, is considered by some to be the world's first programming language, even though it was intended to *model* computation rather than being a means for programmers to *describe* algorithms to a computer system. Many modern functional programming languages have been described as providing a "thin veneer" over the lambda calculus,[1] and many are easily described in terms of it.

The first programming language to be invented was Plankalkül, which was designed by Konrad Zuse in the 1940s, but not publicly known until 1972 (and not implemented until 1998). The first widely known and successful programming language was Fortran, developed from 1954 to 1957 by a team of IBM researchers led by John Backus. The success of FORTRAN led to the formation of a committee of scientists to develop a "universal" computer language; the result of their effort was ALGOL 58. Separately, John McCarthy of MIT developed the Lisp programming language (based on the lambda calculus), the first language with origins in academia to be successful. With the success of these initial efforts, programming languages became an active topic of research in the 1960s and beyond.

Some other key events in the history of programming language theory since then:

1950s

- Noam Chomsky developed the Chomsky hierarchy in the field of linguistics; a discovery which has directly impacted programming language theory and other branches of computer science.

1960s

- The Simula language was developed by Ole-Johan Dahl and Kristen Nygaard; it is widely considered to be the first example of an object-oriented programming language; Simula also introduced the concept of coroutines.

- In 1964, Peter Landin is the first to realize Church's lambda calculus can be used to model programming languages. He introduces the SECD machine which "interprets" lambda expressions.

- In 1965, Landin introduces the J operator, essentially a form of continuation.

- In 1966, Landin introduces ISWIM, an abstract computer programming language in his article *The Next 700 Programming Languages*. It is influential in the design of languages leading to the Haskell programming language.

- In 1966, Corrado Böhm introduced the programming language CUCH (Curry-Church).[2]

- In 1967, Christopher Strachey publishes his influential set of lecture notes *Fundamental Concepts in Programming Languages*, introducing the terminology *R-values*, *L-values*, *parametric polymorphism*, and *ad hoc polymorphism*.

- In 1969, J. Roger Hindley publishes *The Principal Type-Scheme of an Object in Combinatory Logic*, later generalized into the Hindley–Milner type inference algorithm.

- In 1969, Tony Hoare introduces the Hoare logic, a form of axiomatic semantics.

- In 1969, William Alvin Howard observed that a "high-level" proof system, referred to as natural deduction, can be directly interpreted in its intuitionistic version as a typed variant of the model of computation known as lambda calculus. This became known as the Curry–Howard correspondence.

1970s

- In 1970, Dana Scott first publishes his work on denotational semantics.

- In 1972, Logic programming and Prolog were developed thus allowing computer programs to be expressed as mathematical logic.

- In 1974, John C. Reynolds discovers System F. It had already been discovered in 1971 by the mathematical logician Jean-Yves Girard.

- From 1975, Sussman and Steele develop the Scheme programming language, a Lisp dialect incorporating lexical scoping, a unified namespace, and elements from the Actor model including first-class continuations.

- Backus, at the 1977 ACM Turing Award lecture, assailed the current state of industrial languages and proposed a new class of programming languages now known as function-level programming languages.

- In 1977, Gordon Plotkin introduces Programming Computable Functions, an abstract typed functional language.

- In 1978, Robin Milner introduces the Hindley–Milner type inference algorithm for the ML programming language. Type theory became applied as a discipline to programming languages, this application has led to tremendous advances in type theory over the years.

1980s

- In 1981, Gordon Plotkin publishes his paper on structured operational semantics.

- In 1988, Gilles Kahn published his paper on natural semantics.

- A team of scientists at Xerox PARC led by Alan Kay develop Smalltalk, an object-oriented language widely known for its innovative development environment.

- There emerged process calculi, such as the Calculus of Communicating Systems of Robin Milner, and the Communicating sequential processes model of C. A. R. Hoare, as well as similar models of concurrency such as the Actor model of Carl Hewitt.

- In 1985, The release of Miranda sparks an academic interest in lazy-evaluated pure functional programming languages. A committee was formed to define an open standard resulting in the release of the Haskell 1.0 standard in 1990.

- Bertrand Meyer created the methodology Design by contract and incorporated it into the Eiffel programming language.

1990s

- Gregor Kiczales, Jim Des Rivieres and Daniel G. Bobrow published the book The Art of the Metaobject Protocol.

- Eugenio Moggi and Philip Wadler introduced the use of monads for structuring programs written in functional programming languages.

2.8.2 Sub-disciplines and related fields

There are several fields of study which either lie within programming language theory, or which have a profound influence on it; many of these have considerable overlap. In addition, PLT makes use of many other branches of mathematics, including computability theory, category theory, and set theory.

Formal semantics

Main article: Formal semantics of programming languages

Formal semantics is the formal specification of the behaviour of computer programs and programming languages. Three common approaches to describe the semantics or "meaning" of a computer program are denotational semantics, operational semantics and axiomatic semantics.

Type theory

Main article: Type theory

Type theory is the study of type systems; which are "a tractable syntactic method for proving the absence of certain program behaviors by classifying phrases according to the kinds of values they compute".[3] Many programming languages are distinguished by the characteristics of their type systems.

Program analysis and transformation

Main articles: Program analysis and Program transformation

Program analysis is the general problem of examining a program and determining key characteristics (such as the absence of classes of program errors). Program transformation is the process of transforming a program in one form (language) to another form.

Comparative programming language analysis

Comparative programming language analysis seeks to classify programming languages into different types based on their characteristics; broad categories of programming languages are often known as programming paradigms.

Generic and metaprogramming

Metaprogramming is the generation of higher-order programs which, when executed, produce programs (possibly in a different language, or in a subset of the original language) as a result.

Domain-specific languages

Domain-specific languages are languages constructed to efficiently solve problems in a particular problem domain.

Compiler construction

Main article: Compiler construction

Compiler theory is the theory of writing *compilers* (or more generally, *translators*); programs which translate a program written in one language into another form. The actions of a compiler are traditionally broken up into *syntax analysis* (scanning and parsing), *semantic analysis* (determining what a program should do), *optimization* (improving the performance of a program as indicated by some metric; typically execution speed) and *code generation* (generation and output of an equivalent program in some target language; often the instruction set of a CPU).

Run-time systems

Runtime systems refers to the development of programming language runtime environments and their components, including virtual machines, garbage collection, and foreign function interfaces.

2.8.3 Journals, publications, and conferences

Conferences are the primary venue for presenting research in programming languages. The most well known conferences include the Symposium on Principles of Programming Languages (POPL), Conference on Programming Language Design and Implementation (PLDI), the International Conference on Functional Programming (ICFP), and the International Conference on Object Oriented Programming, Systems, Languages and Applications (OOPSLA).

Notable journals that publish PLT research include the *ACM Transactions on Programming Languages and Systems* (TOPLAS), *Journal of Functional Programming* (JFP), *Journal of Functional and Logic Programming*, and *Higher-Order and Symbolic Computation*.

2.8.4 See also

- SIGPLAN
- Timeline of programming languages
- Very high-level programming language

2.8.5 References

[1] http://www.c2.com/cgi/wiki?ModelsOfComputation

[2] C. Böhm and W. Gross (1996). Introduction to the CUCH. In E. R. Caianiello (ed.), *Automata Theory*, p. 35-64/

[3] Benjamin C. Pierce. 2002. Types and Programming Languages. MIT Press, Cambridge, MA, USA.

2.8.6 Further reading

See also: Programming language § Further reading and Semantics of programming languages § Further reading

- Abadi, Martín and Cardelli, Luca. *A Theory of Objects*. Springer-Verlag.
- Michael J. C. Gordon. *Programming Language Theory and Its Implementation*. Prentice Hall.
- Gunter, Carl and Mitchell, John C. (eds.). *Theoretical Aspects of Object Oriented Programming Languages: Types, Semantics, and Language Design*. MIT Press.
- Harper, Robert. *Practical Foundations for Programming Languages*. Draft version.
- Knuth, Donald E. (2003). *Selected Papers on Computer Languages*. Stanford, California: Center for the Study of Language and Information.
- Mitchell, John C.. *Foundations for Programming Languages*.
- Mitchell, John C.. *Introduction to Programming Language Theory*.
- O'Hearn, Peter. W. and Tennent, Robert. D. (1997). *Algol-like Languages*. Progress in Theoretical Computer Science. Birkhauser, Boston.
- Pierce, Benjamin C. (2002). *Types and Programming Languages*. MIT Press.
- Pierce, Benjamin C. *Advanced Topics in Types and Programming Languages*.
- Pierce, Benjamin C. *et al.* (2010). *Software Foundations*.

2.8.7 External links

- Lambda the Ultimate, a community weblog for professional discussion and repository of documents on programming language theory.
- Great Works in Programming Languages. Collected by Benjamin C. Pierce (University of Pennsylvania).
- Classic Papers in Programming Languages and Logic. Collected by Karl Crary (Carnegie Mellon University).
- Programming Language Research. Directory by Mark Leone.
- Programming Language Theory Texts Online. At Utrecht University.
- λ-Calculus: Then & Now by Dana S. Scott for the ACM Turing Centenary Celebration
- Grand Challenges in Programming Languages. Panel session at POPL 2009.

2.9 Formal methods

In computer science, specifically software engineering and hardware engineering, **formal methods** are a particular kind of mathematically based techniques for the specification, development and verification of software and hardware systems.[1] The use of formal methods for software and hardware design is motivated by the expectation that, as in other engineering disciplines, performing appropriate mathematical analysis can contribute to the reliability and robustness of a design.[2]

Formal methods are best described as the application of a fairly broad variety of theoretical computer science fundamentals, in particular logic calculi, formal languages, automata theory, and program semantics, but also type systems and algebraic data types to problems in software and hardware specification and verification.[3]

2.9.1 Taxonomy

Formal methods can be used at a number of levels:

Level 0: Formal specification may be undertaken and then a program developed from this informally. This has been dubbed *formal methods lite*. This may be the most cost-effective option in many cases.

Level 1: Formal development and formal verification may be used to produce a program in a more formal manner. For example, proofs of properties or refinement from the specification to a program may be undertaken. This may be most appropriate in high-integrity systems involving safety or security.

Level 2: Theorem provers may be used to undertake fully formal machine-checked proofs. This can be very expensive and is only practically worthwhile if the cost of mistakes is extremely high (e.g., in critical parts of microprocessor design).

Further information on this is expanded below.

As with programming language semantics, styles of formal methods may be roughly classified as follows:

- Denotational semantics, in which the meaning of a system is expressed in the mathematical theory of domains. Proponents of such methods rely on the well-understood nature of domains to give meaning to the system; critics point out that not every system may be intuitively or naturally viewed as a function.

- Operational semantics, in which the meaning of a system is expressed as a sequence of actions of a (presumably) simpler computational model. Proponents of such methods point to the simplicity of their models as a means to expressive clarity; critics counter that the problem of semantics has just been delayed (who defines the semantics of the simpler model?).

- Axiomatic semantics, in which the meaning of the system is expressed in terms of preconditions and postconditions which are true before and after the system performs a task, respectively. Proponents note the connection to classical logic; critics note that such semantics never really describe what a system *does* (merely what is true before and afterwards).

Lightweight formal methods

Some practitioners believe that the formal methods community has overemphasized full formalization of a specification or design.[4][5] They contend that the expressiveness of the languages involved, as well as the complexity of the systems being modelled, make full formalization a difficult and expensive task. As an alternative, various *lightweight* formal methods, which emphasize partial specification and focused application, have been proposed. Examples of this lightweight approach to formal methods include the Alloy object modelling notation,[6] Denney's synthesis of some aspects of the Z notation with use case driven development,[7] and the CSK VDM Tools.[8]

2.9.2 Uses

Formal methods can be applied at various points through the development process.

Specification

Formal methods may be used to give a description of the system to be developed, at whatever level(s) of detail desired. This formal description can be used to guide further development activities (see following sections); additionally, it can be used to verify that the requirements for the system being developed have been completely and accurately specified.

The need for formal specification systems has been noted for years. In the ALGOL 58 report,[9] John Backus presented a formal notation for describing programming language syntax (later named Backus Normal Form then renamed Backus-Naur Form (BNF)[10]). Backus also wrote that a formal description of the meaning of syntactically valid ALGOL programs wasn't completed in time for inclusion in the report. "Therefore the formal treatment of the semantics of legal programs will be included in a subsequent paper." It never appeared.

Development

Once a formal specification has been produced, the specification may be used as a guide while the concrete system is developed during the design process (i.e., realized typically in software, but also potentially in hardware). For example:

- If the formal specification is in an operational semantics, the observed behavior of the concrete system can be compared with the behavior of the specification (which itself should be executable or simulateable). Additionally, the operational commands of the specification may be amenable to direct translation into executable code.

- If the formal specification is in an axiomatic semantics, the preconditions and postconditions of the specification may become assertions in the executable code.

Verification

Once a formal specification has been developed, the specification may be used as the basis for proving properties of the specification (and hopefully by inference the developed system).

Human-directed proof Sometimes, the motivation for proving the correctness of a system is not the obvious need for re-assurance of the correctness of the system, but a desire to understand the system better. Consequently, some proofs of correctness are produced in the style of mathematical proof: handwritten (or typeset) using natural language, using a level of informality common to such proofs. A "good" proof is one which is readable and understandable by other human readers.

Critics of such approaches point out that the ambiguity inherent in natural language allows errors to be undetected in such proofs; often, subtle errors can be present in the low-level details typically overlooked by such proofs. Additionally, the work involved in producing such a good proof requires a high level of mathematical sophistication and expertise.

Automated proof   In contrast, there is increasing interest in producing proofs of correctness of such systems by automated means. Automated techniques fall into three general categories:

- Automated theorem proving, in which a system attempts to produce a formal proof from scratch, given a description of the system, a set of logical axioms, and a set of inference rules.

- Model checking, in which a system verifies certain properties by means of an exhaustive search of all possible states that a system could enter during its execution.

- Abstract interpretation, in which a system verifies an over-approximation of a behavioural property of the program, using a fixpoint computation over a (possibly complete) lattice representing it.

Some automated theorem provers require guidance as to which properties are "interesting" enough to pursue, while others work without human intervention. Model checkers can quickly get bogged down in checking millions of uninteresting states if not given a sufficiently abstract model.

Proponents of such systems argue that the results have greater mathematical certainty than human-produced proofs, since all the tedious details have been algorithmically verified. The training required to use such systems is also less than that required to produce good mathematical proofs by hand, making the techniques accessible to a wider variety of practitioners.

Critics note that some of those systems are like oracles: they make a pronouncement of truth, yet give no explanation of that truth. There is also the problem of "verifying the verifier"; if the program which aids in the verification is itself unproven, there may be reason to doubt the soundness of the produced results. Some modern model checking tools produce a "proof log" detailing each step in their proof, making it possible to perform, given suitable tools, independent verification.

The main feature of the Abstract Interpretation approach is that it provides a sound analysis, i.e. no false negatives are returned. Moreover, it is efficiently scalable, by tuning the abstract domain representing the property to be analyzed, and by applying widening operators[11] to get fast convergence.

2.9.3 Applications

Formal methods are applied in different areas of hardware and software, including routers, Ethernet switches, routing protocols, and security applications. There are several examples in which FMs have been used to verify the functionality of the hardware and software used in DCs. IBM used ACL2, a theorem prover, in AMD x86 processor development process. Intel uses FMs to verify its hardware and firmware (permanent software programmed into a read-only memory). There are several other projects of NASA in which FMs are applied, such as Next Generation Air Transportation System, Unmanned Aircraft System integration in National Airspace System,[12] and Airborne Coordinated Conflict Resolution and Detection (ACCoRD).[13]

B-Method with AtelierB,[14] is used to develop safety automatisms for the various subways installed throughout the world by Alstom and Siemens, and also for Common Criteria certification and the development of system models by ATMEL and STMicroelectronics.

Formal verification has been frequently used in hardware by most of the well-known hardware vendors, such as IBM, Intel, and AMD. There are many areas of hardware, where Intel have used FMs to verify the working of the products, such as parameterized verification of cache coherent protocol,[15] Intel Core i7 processor execution engine validation [16] (using theorem proving, BDD's, and symbolic evaluation), optimization for Intel IA-64 architecture using HOL light theorem prover,[17] and verification of high performance dual-port gigabit Ethernet controller with a support for PCI express protocol and Intel advance management technology using Cadence.[18] Similarly, IBM has used formal methods in the verification of power gates,[19] registers,[20] and functional verification of the IBM Power7 microprocessor.[21]

2.9.4 Formal methods and notations

There are a variety of formal methods and notations available.

Specification languages

- Abstract State Machines (ASMs)

- A Computational Logic for Applicative Common Lisp (ACL2)
- ANSI/ISO C Specification Language (ACSL)
- Alloy
- Autonomic System Specification Language (ASSL)
- B-Method
- CADP
- Common Algebraic Specification Language (CASL)
- Java Modeling Language (JML)
- Knowledge Based Software Assistant (KBSA)
- Process calculi
  - CSP
  - LOTOS
  - π-calculus
- Actor model
- Esterel
- Lustre
- mCRL2
- Perfect Developer
- Petri nets
- Predicative programming
- RAISE
- Rebeca Modeling Language
- SPARK Ada
- Spec sharp (Spec#)
- Specification and Description Language
- TLA+
- USL
- VDM
  - VDM-SL
  - VDM++
- Z notation

Model checkers

- SPIN
- PAT is a powerful free model checker, simulator and refinement checker for concurrent systems and CSP extensions (e.g. shared variables, arrays, fairness).
- MALPAS Software Static Analysis Toolset is an industrial strength model checker used for Formal Proof of safety critical systems
- UPPAAL

2.9.5 See also

- Abstract interpretation
- Automated theorem proving
- Design by contract
- Formal methods people
- Formal specification
- Formal verification
- Formal system
- Model checking
- Software engineering
- Specification language

2.9.6 References

[1] R. W. Butler (2001-08-06). "What is Formal Methods?". Retrieved 2006-11-16.

[2] C. Michael Holloway. "Why Engineers Should Consider Formal Methods" (PDF). 16th Digital Avionics Systems Conference (27–30 October 1997). Retrieved 2006-11-16.

[3] Monin, pp.3-4

[4] Daniel Jackson and Jeannette Wing, "Lightweight Formal Methods", *IEEE Computer*, April 1996

[5] Vinu George and Rayford Vaughn, "Application of Lightweight Formal Methods in Requirement Engineering", *Crosstalk: The Journal of Defense Software Engineering*, January 2003

[6] Daniel Jackson, "Alloy: A Lightweight Object Modelling Notation", *ACM Transactions on Software Engineering and Methodology (TOSEM)*, Volume 11, Issue 2 (April 2002), pp. 256-290

[7] Richard Denney, *Succeeding with Use Cases: Working Smart to Deliver Quality*, Addison-Wesley Professional Publishing, 2005, ISBN 0-321-31643-6.

[8] Sten Agerholm and Peter G. Larsen, "A Lightweight Approach to Formal Methods", In *Proceedings of the International Workshop on Current Trends in Applied Formal Methods*, Boppard, Germany, Springer-Verlag, October 1998

[9] Backus, J.W. (1959). "The Syntax and Semantics of the Proposed International Algebraic Language of Zürich ACM-GAMM Conference". *Proceedings of the International Conference on Information Processing.* UNESCO.

[10] Knuth, Donald E. (1964), Backus Normal Form vs Backus Naur Form. *Communications of the ACM*, 7(12):735–736.

[11] A.Cortesi and M.Zanioli, Widening and Narrowing Operators for Abstract Interpretation. Computer Languages, Systems and Structures. Volume 37(1), pp. 24-42, Elsevier, ISSN: 1477-8424 (2011)

[12] Gheorghe, A. V., & Ancel, E. (2008, November). Unmanned aerial systems integration to National Airspace System. In Infrastructure Systems and Services: Building Networks for a Brighter Future (INFRA), 2008 First International Conference on (pp. 1-5). IEEE.

[13] Airborne Coordinated Conflict Resolution and Detection, http://shemesh.larc.nasa.gov/people/cam/ACCoRD/

[14] website : http://www.atelierb.eu/en/

[15] C. T. Chou, P. K. Mannava, S. Park, "A simple method for parameterized verification of cache coherence protocols," Formal Methods in Computer-Aided Design, pp. 382-398, 2004.

[16] Formal Verification in Intel® Core™ i7 Processor Execution Engine Validation, http://cps-vo.org/node/1371, accessed at Sep. 13, 2013.

[17] J. Grundy, "Verified optimizations for the Intel IA-64 architecture," In Theorem Proving in Higher Order Logics, Springer Berlin Heidelberg, 2004, pp. 215-232.

[18] E. Seligman, I. Yarom, "Best known methods for using Cadence Conformal LEC," at Intel.

[19] C. Eisner, A. Nahir, K. Yorav, "Functional verification of power gated designs by compositional reasoning," Computer Aided Verification Springer Berlin Heidelberg, pp. 433-445.

[20] P. C. Attie, H. Chockler, "Automatic verification of fault-tolerant register emulations," Electronic Notes in Theoretical Computer Science, vol. 149, no. 1, pp. 49-60.

[21] K. D. Schubert, W. Roesner, J. M. Ludden, J. Jackson, J. Buchert, V. Paruthi, B. Brock, "Functional verification of the IBM POWER7 microprocessor and POWER7 multiprocessor systems," IBM Journal of Research and Development, vol. 55, no 3.

This article is based on material taken from the Free On-line Dictionary of Computing prior to 1 November 2008 and incorporated under the "relicensing" terms of the GFDL, version 1.3 or later.

2.9.7 Further reading

- Jean François Monin and Michael G. Hinchey, *Understanding formal methods*, Springer, 2003, ISBN 1-85233-247-6.

- Jonathan P. Bowen and Michael G. Hinchey, *Formal Methods*. In Allen B. Tucker, Jr. (ed.), *Computer Science Handbook*, 2nd edition, Section XI, *Software Engineering*, Chapter 106, pages 106-1 – 106-25, Chapman & Hall / CRC Press, Association for Computing Machinery, 2004.

- Michael G. Hinchey, Jonathan P. Bowen, and Emil Vassev, *Formal Methods*. In Philip A. Laplante (ed.), *Encyclopedia of Software Engineering*, Taylor & Francis, 2010, pages 308–320.

2.9.8 External links

- Formal Methods Europe (FME)

- Formal method keyword on Microsoft Academic Search

- Foldoc:formal methods

- Evidence on Formal Methods uses and impact on Industry Supported by the DEPLOY project (EU FP7)

2.10 Artificial intelligence

"AI" redirects here. For other uses, see Ai and Artificial intelligence (disambiguation).

Artificial intelligence (**AI**) is the intelligence exhibited by machines or software. It is also the name of the academic field of study which studies how to create computers and computer software that are capable of intelligent behavior. Major AI researchers and textbooks define this field as "the study and design of intelligent agents",[1] in which an intelligent agent is a system that perceives its environment and takes actions that maximize its chances of success.[2] John McCarthy, who coined the term in 1955,[3] defines it as "the science and engineering of making intelligent machines".[4]

AI research is highly technical and specialized, and is deeply divided into subfields that often fail to communicate with each other.[5] Some of the division is due to social and cultural factors: subfields have grown up around particular institutions and the work of individual researchers. AI research is also divided by several technical issues. Some

2.10. ARTIFICIAL INTELLIGENCE

subfields focus on the solution of specific problems. Others focus on one of several possible approaches or on the use of a particular tool or towards the accomplishment of particular applications.

The central problems (or goals) of AI research include reasoning, knowledge, planning, learning, natural language processing (communication), perception and the ability to move and manipulate objects.[6] General intelligence is still among the field's long-term goals.[7] Currently popular approaches include statistical methods, computational intelligence and traditional symbolic AI. There are a large number of tools used in AI, including versions of search and mathematical optimization, logic, methods based on probability and economics, and many others. The AI field is interdisciplinary, in which a number of sciences and professions converge, including computer science, mathematics, psychology, linguistics, philosophy and neuroscience, as well as other specialized fields such as artificial psychology.

The field was founded on the claim that a central property of humans, human intelligence—the sapience of *Homo sapiens*—"can be so precisely described that a machine can be made to simulate it."[8] This raises philosophical issues about the nature of the mind and the ethics of creating artificial beings endowed with human-like intelligence, issues which have been addressed by myth, fiction and philosophy since antiquity.[9] Artificial intelligence has been the subject of tremendous optimism[10] but has also suffered stunning setbacks.[11] Today it has become an essential part of the technology industry, providing the heavy lifting for many of the most challenging problems in computer science.[12]

2.10.1 History

Main articles: History of artificial intelligence and Timeline of artificial intelligence

Thinking machines and artificial beings appear in Greek myths, such as Talos of Crete, the bronze robot of Hephaestus, and Pygmalion's Galatea.[13] Human likenesses believed to have intelligence were built in every major civilization: animated cult images were worshiped in Egypt and Greece[14] and humanoid automatons were built by Yan Shi, Hero of Alexandria and Al-Jazari.[15] It was also widely believed that artificial beings had been created by Jābir ibn Hayyān, Judah Loew and Paracelsus.[16] By the 19th and 20th centuries, artificial beings had become a common feature in fiction, as in Mary Shelley's *Frankenstein* or Karel Čapek's *R.U.R. (Rossum's Universal Robots)*.[17] Pamela McCorduck argues that all of these are some examples of an ancient urge, as she describes it, "to forge the gods".[9] Stories of these creatures and their fates discuss many of the same hopes, fears and ethical concerns that are presented by artificial intelligence.

Mechanical or "formal" reasoning has been developed by philosophers and mathematicians since antiquity. The study of logic led directly to the invention of the programmable digital electronic computer, based on the work of mathematician Alan Turing and others. Turing's theory of computation suggested that a machine, by shuffling symbols as simple as "0" and "1", could simulate any conceivable act of mathematical deduction.[18][19] This, along with concurrent discoveries in neurology, information theory and cybernetics, inspired a small group of researchers to begin to seriously consider the possibility of building an electronic brain.[20]

The field of AI research was founded at a conference on the campus of Dartmouth College in the summer of 1956.[21] The attendees, including John McCarthy, Marvin Minsky, Allen Newell, Arthur Samuel, and Herbert Simon, became the leaders of AI research for many decades.[22] They and their students wrote programs that were, to most people, simply astonishing:[23] computers were winning at checkers, solving word problems in algebra, proving logical theorems and speaking English.[24] By the middle of the 1960s, research in the U.S. was heavily funded by the Department of Defense[25] and laboratories had been established around the world.[26] AI's founders were profoundly optimistic about the future of the new field: Herbert Simon predicted that "machines will be capable, within twenty years, of doing any work a man can do" and Marvin Minsky agreed, writing that "within a generation ... the problem of creating 'artificial intelligence' will substantially be solved".[27]

They had failed to recognize the difficulty of some of the problems they faced.[28] In 1974, in response to the criticism of Sir James Lighthill[29] and ongoing pressure from the US Congress to fund more productive projects, both the U.S. and British governments cut off all undirected exploratory research in AI. The next few years would later be called an "AI winter",[30] a period when funding for AI projects was hard to find.

In the early 1980s, AI research was revived by the commercial success of expert systems,[31] a form of AI program that simulated the knowledge and analytical skills of one or more human experts. By 1985 the market for AI had reached over a billion dollars. At the same time, Japan's fifth generation computer project inspired the U.S and British governments to restore funding for academic research in the field.[32] However, beginning with the collapse of the Lisp Machine market in 1987, AI once again fell into disrepute, and a second, longer lasting AI winter began.[33]

In the 1990s and early 21st century, AI achieved its greatest successes, albeit somewhat behind the scenes. Artificial intelligence is used for logistics, data mining, medical diagnosis and many other areas throughout the technology industry.[12] The success was due to several factors: the increasing computational power of computers (see Moore's law), a greater emphasis on solving specific subproblems, the creation of new ties between AI and other fields working on similar problems, and a new commitment by researchers to solid mathematical methods and rigorous scientific standards.[34]

On 11 May 1997, Deep Blue became the first computer chess-playing system to beat a reigning world chess champion, Garry Kasparov.[35] In February 2011, in a *Jeopardy!* quiz show exhibition match, IBM's question answering system, Watson, defeated the two greatest Jeopardy champions, Brad Rutter and Ken Jennings, by a significant margin.[36] The Kinect, which provides a 3D body–motion interface for the Xbox 360 and the Xbox One, uses algorithms that emerged from lengthy AI research[37] as do intelligent personal assistants in smartphones.[38]

2.10.2 Research

Goals

The general problem of simulating (or creating) intelligence has been broken down into a number of specific subproblems. These consist of particular traits or capabilities that researchers would like an intelligent system to display. The traits described below have received the most attention.[6]

Deduction, reasoning, problem solving Early AI researchers developed algorithms that imitated the step-by-step reasoning that humans use when they solve puzzles or make logical deductions.[39] By the late 1980s and 1990s, AI research had also developed highly successful methods for dealing with uncertain or incomplete information, employing concepts from probability and economics.[40]

For difficult problems, most of these algorithms can require enormous computational resources – most experience a "combinatorial explosion": the amount of memory or computer time required becomes astronomical when the problem goes beyond a certain size. The search for more efficient problem-solving algorithms is a high priority for AI research.[41]

Human beings solve most of their problems using fast, intuitive judgements rather than the conscious, step-by-step deduction that early AI research was able to model.[42] AI has made some progress at imitating this kind of "sub-symbolic" problem solving: embodied agent approaches emphasize the importance of sensorimotor skills to higher reasoning; neural net research attempts to simulate the structures inside the brain that give rise to this skill; statistical approaches to AI mimic the probabilistic nature of the human ability to guess.

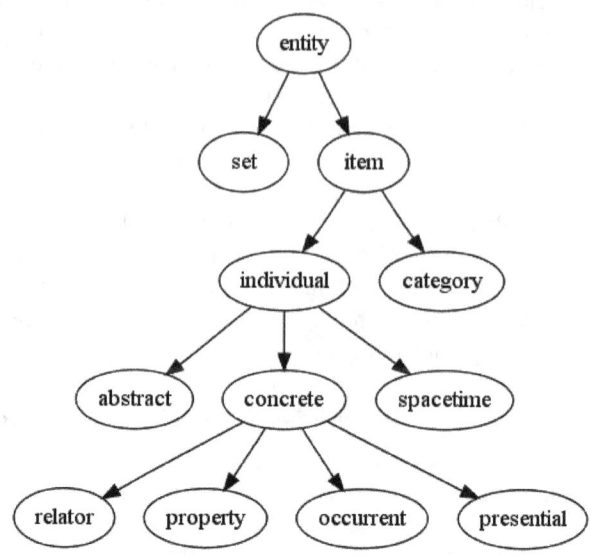

An ontology represents knowledge as a set of concepts within a domain and the relationships between those concepts.

Knowledge representation Main articles: Knowledge representation and Commonsense knowledge

Knowledge representation[43] and knowledge engineering[44] are central to AI research. Many of the problems machines are expected to solve will require extensive knowledge about the world. Among the things that AI needs to represent are: objects, properties, categories and relations between objects;[45] situations, events, states and time;[46] causes and effects;[47] knowledge about knowledge (what we know about what other people know);[48] and many other, less well researched domains. A representation of "what exists" is an ontology: the set of objects, relations, concepts and so on that the machine knows about. The most general are called upper ontologies, which attempt to provide a foundation for all other knowledge.[49]

Among the most difficult problems in knowledge representation are:

Default reasoning and the qualification problem Many of the things people know take the form of "working assumptions." For example, if a bird comes up in conversation, people typically picture an animal that is fist sized, sings, and flies. None of these things are true about all birds. John McCarthy identified this problem in 1969[50] as the qualification problem: for any commonsense rule that AI researchers care to represent, there tend to be a huge number of exceptions. Almost nothing is simply true or false in the way that abstract logic requires. AI research has explored a number of solutions to this problem.[51]

The breadth of commonsense knowledge The number of atomic facts that the average person knows is astronomical. Research projects that attempt to build a complete knowledge base of commonsense knowledge (e.g., Cyc) require enormous amounts of laborious ontological engineering—they must be built, by hand, one complicated concept at a time.[52] A major goal is to have the computer understand enough concepts to be able to learn by reading from sources like the internet, and thus be able to add to its own ontology.

The subsymbolic form of some commonsense knowledge Much of what people know is not represented as "facts" or "statements" that they could express verbally. For example, a chess master will avoid a particular chess position because it "feels too exposed"[53] or an art critic can take one look at a statue and instantly realize that it is a fake.[54] These are intuitions or tendencies that are represented in the brain non-consciously and sub-symbolically.[55] Knowledge like this informs, supports and provides a context for symbolic, conscious knowledge. As with the related problem of sub-symbolic reasoning, it is hoped that situated AI, computational intelligence, or statistical AI will provide ways to represent this kind of knowledge.[55]

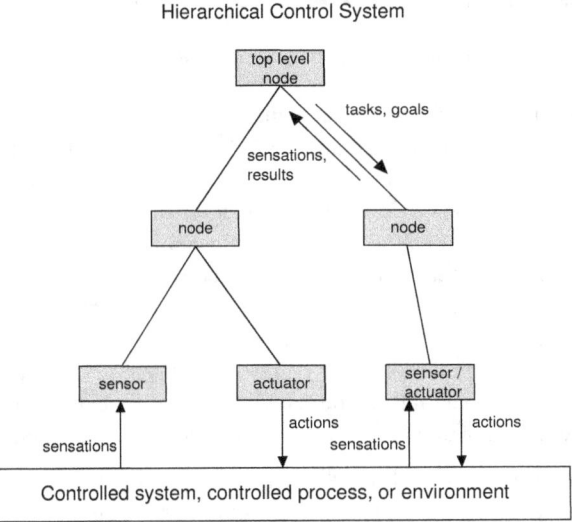

A hierarchical control system is a form of control system in which a set of devices and governing software is arranged in a hierarchy.

Planning   Main article: Automated planning and scheduling

Intelligent agents must be able to set goals and achieve them.[56] They need a way to visualize the future (they must have a representation of the state of the world and be able to make predictions about how their actions will change it) and be able to make choices that maximize the utility (or "value") of the available choices.[57]

In classical planning problems, the agent can assume that it is the only thing acting on the world and it can be certain what the consequences of its actions may be.[58] However, if the agent is not the only actor, it must periodically ascertain whether the world matches its predictions and it must change its plan as this becomes necessary, requiring the agent to reason under uncertainty.[59]

Multi-agent planning uses the cooperation and competition of many agents to achieve a given goal. Emergent behavior such as this is used by evolutionary algorithms and swarm intelligence.[60]

Learning   Main article: Machine learning

Machine learning is the study of computer algorithms that improve automatically through experience[61][62] and has been central to AI research since the field's inception.[63]

Unsupervised learning is the ability to find patterns in a stream of input. Supervised learning includes both classification and numerical regression. Classification is used to determine what category something belongs in, after seeing a number of examples of things from several categories. Regression is the attempt to produce a function that describes the relationship between inputs and outputs and predicts how the outputs should change as the inputs change. In reinforcement learning[64] the agent is rewarded for good responses and punished for bad ones. The agent uses this sequence of rewards and punishments to form a strategy for operating in its problem space. These three types of learning can be analyzed in terms of decision theory, using concepts like utility. The mathematical analysis of machine learning algorithms and their performance is a branch of theoretical computer science known as computational learning theory.[65]

Within developmental robotics, developmental learning approaches were elaborated for lifelong cumulative acquisition of repertoires of novel skills by a robot, through autonomous self-exploration and social interaction with human teachers, and using guidance mechanisms such as active learning, maturation, motor synergies, and imitation.[66][67][68][69]

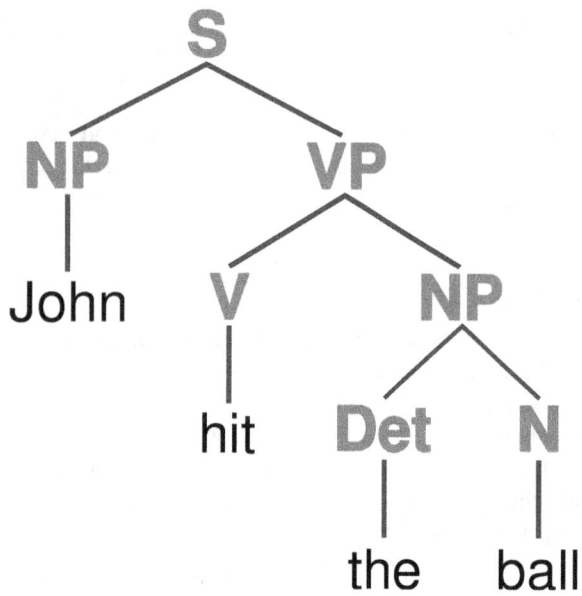

A parse tree represents the syntactic structure of a sentence according to some formal grammar.

Natural language processing (communication) Main article: Natural language processing

Natural language processing[70] gives machines the ability to read and understand the languages that humans speak. A sufficiently powerful natural language processing system would enable natural language user interfaces and the acquisition of knowledge directly from human-written sources, such as newswire texts. Some straightforward applications of natural language processing include information retrieval (or text mining), question answering[71] and machine translation.[72]

A common method of processing and extracting meaning from natural language is through semantic indexing. Increases in processing speeds and the drop in the cost of data storage makes indexing large volumes of abstractions of the user's input much more efficient.

Perception Main articles: Machine perception, Computer vision and Speech recognition

Machine perception[73] is the ability to use input from sensors (such as cameras, microphones, tactile sensors, sonar and others more exotic) to deduce aspects of the world. Computer vision[74] is the ability to analyze visual input. A few selected subproblems are speech recognition,[75] facial recognition and object recognition.[76]

Motion and manipulation Main article: Robotics

The field of robotics[77] is closely related to AI. Intelligence is required for robots to be able to handle such tasks as object manipulation[78] and navigation, with sub-problems of localization (knowing where you are, or finding out where other things are), mapping (learning what is around you, building a map of the environment), and motion planning (figuring out how to get there) or path planning (going from one point in space to another point, which may involve compliant motion – where the robot moves while maintaining physical contact with an object).[79][80]

Long-term goals Among the long-term goals in the research pertaining to artificial intelligence are: (1) Social intelligence, (2) Creativity, and (3) General intelligence.

Social intelligence Main article: Affective computing
Affective computing is the study and development of

Kismet, a robot with rudimentary social skills[81]

systems and devices that can recognize, interpret, process, and simulate human affects.[82][83] It is an interdisciplinary field spanning computer sciences, psychology, and cognitive science.[84] While the origins of the field may be traced as far back as to early philosophical inquiries into emotion,[85] the more modern branch of computer science originated with Rosalind Picard's 1995 paper[86] on affective computing.[87][88] A motivation for the research is the ability to simulate empathy. The machine should interpret the emotional state of humans and adapt its behaviour to them, giving an appropriate response for those emotions.

Emotion and social skills[89] play two roles for an intelligent agent. First, it must be able to predict the actions of others, by understanding their motives and emotional states. (This involves elements of game theory, decision theory, as well as the ability to model human emotions and the perceptual skills to detect emotions.) Also, in an effort to facilitate human-computer interaction, an intelligent machine might want to be able to *display* emotions—even if it does not actually experience them itself—in order to appear sensitive to the emotional dynamics of human interaction.

Creativity   Main article: Computational creativity

A sub-field of AI addresses creativity both theoretically (from a philosophical and psychological perspective) and practically (via specific implementations of systems that generate outputs that can be considered creative, or systems that identify and assess creativity). Related areas of computational research are Artificial intuition and Artificial thinking.

General intelligence   Main articles: Artificial general intelligence and AI-complete

Many researchers think that their work will eventually be incorporated into a machine with *general* intelligence (known as strong AI), combining all the skills above and exceeding human abilities at most or all of them.[7] A few believe that anthropomorphic features like artificial consciousness or an artificial brain may be required for such a project.[90][91]

Many of the problems above may require general intelligence to be considered solved. For example, even a straightforward, specific task like machine translation requires that the machine read and write in both languages (NLP), follow the author's argument (reason), know what is being talked about (knowledge), and faithfully reproduce the author's intention (social intelligence). A problem like machine translation is considered "AI-complete". In order to solve this particular problem, you must solve all the problems.[92]

Approaches

There is no established unifying theory or paradigm that guides AI research. Researchers disagree about many issues.[93] A few of the most long standing questions that have remained unanswered are these: should artificial intelligence simulate natural intelligence by studying psychology or neurology? Or is human biology as irrelevant to AI research as bird biology is to aeronautical engineering?[94] Can intelligent behavior be described using simple, elegant principles (such as logic or optimization)? Or does it necessarily require solving a large number of completely unrelated problems?[95] Can intelligence be reproduced using high-level symbols, similar to words and ideas? Or does it require "sub-symbolic" processing?[96] John Haugeland, who coined the term GOFAI (Good Old-Fashioned Artificial Intelligence), also proposed that AI should more properly be referred to as synthetic intelligence,[97] a term which has since been adopted by some non-GOFAI researchers.[98][99]

Cybernetics and brain simulation   Main articles: Cybernetics and Computational neuroscience

In the 1940s and 1950s, a number of researchers explored the connection between neurology, information theory, and cybernetics. Some of them built machines that used electronic networks to exhibit rudimentary intelligence, such as W. Grey Walter's turtles and the Johns Hopkins Beast. Many of these researchers gathered for meetings of the Teleological Society at Princeton University and the Ratio Club in England.[20] By 1960, this approach was largely abandoned, although elements of it would be revived in the 1980s.

Symbolic   Main article: Symbolic AI

When access to digital computers became possible in the middle 1950s, AI research began to explore the possibility that human intelligence could be reduced to symbol manipulation. The research was centered in three institutions: Carnegie Mellon University, Stanford and MIT, and each one developed its own style of research. John Haugeland named these approaches to AI "good old fashioned AI" or "GOFAI".[100] During the 1960s, symbolic approaches had achieved great success at simulating high-level thinking in small demonstration programs. Approaches based on cybernetics or neural networks were abandoned or pushed into the background.[101] Researchers in the 1960s and the 1970s were convinced that symbolic approaches would eventually succeed in creating a machine with artificial general intelligence and considered this the goal of their field.

Cognitive simulation   Economist Herbert Simon and Allen Newell studied human problem-solving skills and attempted to formalize them, and their work laid the foundations of the field of artificial intelligence, as well as cognitive science, operations research and management science. Their research team used the results of psychological experiments to develop programs that simulated the techniques that people used to solve problems. This tradition, centered at Carnegie Mellon University would eventually culminate in the development of the Soar architecture in the middle 1980s.[102][103]

Logic-based   Unlike Newell and Simon, John McCarthy felt that machines did not need to simulate human thought, but should instead try to find the essence of abstract reasoning and problem solving, regardless of whether people used the same algorithms.[94] His laboratory at Stanford (SAIL) focused on using formal logic to solve a wide variety of problems, including knowledge representation, planning and learning.[104] Logic was also the focus of the work at the University of Edinburgh and elsewhere in Europe which led to the development of the programming language Prolog and the science of logic programming.[105]

"Anti-logic" or "scruffy" Researchers at MIT (such as Marvin Minsky and Seymour Papert)[106] found that solving difficult problems in vision and natural language processing required ad-hoc solutions – they argued that there was no simple and general principle (like logic) that would capture all the aspects of intelligent behavior. Roger Schank described their "anti-logic" approaches as "scruffy" (as opposed to the "neat" paradigms at CMU and Stanford).[95] Commonsense knowledge bases (such as Doug Lenat's Cyc) are an example of "scruffy" AI, since they must be built by hand, one complicated concept at a time.[107]

Knowledge-based When computers with large memories became available around 1970, researchers from all three traditions began to build knowledge into AI applications.[108] This "knowledge revolution" led to the development and deployment of expert systems (introduced by Edward Feigenbaum), the first truly successful form of AI software.[31] The knowledge revolution was also driven by the realization that enormous amounts of knowledge would be required by many simple AI applications.

Sub-symbolic By the 1980s progress in symbolic AI seemed to stall and many believed that symbolic systems would never be able to imitate all the processes of human cognition, especially perception, robotics, learning and pattern recognition. A number of researchers began to look into "sub-symbolic" approaches to specific AI problems.[96]

Bottom-up, embodied, situated, behavior-based or nouvelle AI
Researchers from the related field of robotics, such as Rodney Brooks, rejected symbolic AI and focused on the basic engineering problems that would allow robots to move and survive.[109] Their work revived the non-symbolic viewpoint of the early cybernetics researchers of the 1950s and reintroduced the use of control theory in AI. This coincided with the development of the embodied mind thesis in the related field of cognitive science: the idea that aspects of the body (such as movement, perception and visualization) are required for higher intelligence.

Computational intelligence and soft computing
Interest in neural networks and "connectionism" was revived by David Rumelhart and others in the middle 1980s.[110] Neural networks are an example of soft computing --- they are solutions to problems which cannot be solved with complete logical certainty, and where an approximate solution is often enough. Other soft computing approaches to AI include fuzzy systems, evolutionary computation and many statistical tools. The application of soft computing to AI is studied collectively by the emerging discipline of computational intelligence.[111]

Statistical In the 1990s, AI researchers developed sophisticated mathematical tools to solve specific subproblems. These tools are truly scientific, in the sense that their results are both measurable and verifiable, and they have been responsible for many of AI's recent successes. The shared mathematical language has also permitted a high level of collaboration with more established fields (like mathematics, economics or operations research). Stuart Russell and Peter Norvig describe this movement as nothing less than a "revolution" and "the victory of the neats."[34] Critics argue that these techniques (with few exceptions[112]) are too focused on particular problems and have failed to address the long-term goal of general intelligence.[113] There is an ongoing debate about the relevance and validity of statistical approaches in AI, exemplified in part by exchanges between Peter Norvig and Noam Chomsky.[114][115]

Integrating the approaches

Intelligent agent paradigm An intelligent agent is a system that perceives its environment and takes actions which maximize its chances of success. The simplest intelligent agents are programs that solve specific problems. More complicated agents include human beings and organizations of human beings (such as firms). The paradigm gives researchers license to study isolated problems and find solutions that are both verifiable and useful, without agreeing on one single approach. An agent that solves a specific problem can use any approach that works – some agents are symbolic and logical, some are sub-symbolic neural networks and others may use new approaches. The paradigm also gives researchers a common language to communicate with other fields—such as decision theory and economics—that also use concepts of abstract agents. The intelligent agent paradigm became widely accepted during the 1990s.[2]

Agent architectures and cognitive architectures

Researchers have designed systems to build intelligent systems out of interacting intelligent agents in a multi-agent system.[116] A system with both symbolic and sub-symbolic components is a hybrid intelligent system, and the study of such systems is artificial intelligence systems integration. A hierarchical control system provides a bridge between sub-symbolic AI at its lowest, reactive levels and traditional symbolic AI at its highest levels, where relaxed time constraints permit planning and world modelling.[117] Rodney Brooks' subsumption architecture was an early proposal for such a hierarchical system.[118]

Tools

In the course of 50 years of research, AI has developed a large number of tools to solve the most difficult problems in computer science. A few of the most general of these methods are discussed below.

Search and optimization Main articles: Search algorithm, Mathematical optimization and Evolutionary computation

Many problems in AI can be solved in theory by intelligently searching through many possible solutions:[119] Reasoning can be reduced to performing a search. For example, logical proof can be viewed as searching for a path that leads from premises to conclusions, where each step is the application of an inference rule.[120] Planning algorithms search through trees of goals and subgoals, attempting to find a path to a target goal, a process called means-ends analysis.[121] Robotics algorithms for moving limbs and grasping objects use local searches in configuration space.[78] Many learning algorithms use search algorithms based on optimization.

Simple exhaustive searches[122] are rarely sufficient for most real world problems: the search space (the number of places to search) quickly grows to astronomical numbers. The result is a search that is too slow or never completes. The solution, for many problems, is to use "heuristics" or "rules of thumb" that eliminate choices that are unlikely to lead to the goal (called "pruning the search tree"). Heuristics supply the program with a "best guess" for the path on which the solution lies.[123] Heuristics limit the search for solutions into a smaller sample size.[79]

A very different kind of search came to prominence in the 1990s, based on the mathematical theory of optimization. For many problems, it is possible to begin the search with some form of a guess and then refine the guess incrementally until no more refinements can be made. These algorithms can be visualized as blind hill climbing: we begin the search at a random point on the landscape, and then, by jumps or steps, we keep moving our guess uphill, until we reach the top. Other optimization algorithms are simulated annealing, beam search and random optimization.[124]

Evolutionary computation uses a form of optimization search. For example, they may begin with a population of organisms (the guesses) and then allow them to mutate and recombine, selecting only the fittest to survive each generation (refining the guesses). Forms of evolutionary computation include swarm intelligence algorithms (such as ant colony or particle swarm optimization)[125] and evolutionary algorithms (such as genetic algorithms, gene expression programming, and genetic programming).[126]

Logic Main articles: Logic programming and Automated reasoning

Logic[127] is used for knowledge representation and problem solving, but it can be applied to other problems as well. For example, the satplan algorithm uses logic for planning[128] and inductive logic programming is a method for learning.[129]

Several different forms of logic are used in AI research. Propositional or sentential logic[130] is the logic of statements which can be true or false. First-order logic[131] also allows the use of quantifiers and predicates, and can express facts about objects, their properties, and their relations with each other. Fuzzy logic,[132] is a version of first-order logic which allows the truth of a statement to be represented as a value between 0 and 1, rather than simply True (1) or False (0). Fuzzy systems can be used for uncertain reasoning and have been widely used in modern industrial and consumer product control systems. Subjective logic[133] models uncertainty in a different and more explicit manner than fuzzy-logic: a given binomial opinion satisfies belief + disbelief + uncertainty = 1 within a Beta distribution. By this method, ignorance can be distinguished from probabilistic statements that an agent makes with high confidence.

Default logics, non-monotonic logics and circumscription[51] are forms of logic designed to help with default reasoning and the qualification problem. Several extensions of logic have been designed to handle specific domains of knowledge, such as: description logics;[45] situation calculus, event calculus and fluent calculus (for representing events and time);[46] causal calculus;[47] belief calculus; and modal logics.[48]

Probabilistic methods for uncertain reasoning Main articles: Bayesian network, Hidden Markov model, Kalman filter, Decision theory and Utility theory

Many problems in AI (in reasoning, planning, learning, perception and robotics) require the agent to operate with incomplete or uncertain information. AI researchers have devised a number of powerful tools to solve these problems using methods from probability theory and economics.[134]

Bayesian networks[135] are a very general tool that can be used for a large number of problems: reasoning (using the Bayesian inference algorithm),[136] learning (using the expectation-maximization algorithm),[137] planning (using decision networks)[138] and perception (using dynamic Bayesian networks).[139] Probabilistic algorithms can also be used for filtering, prediction, smoothing and finding explanations for streams of data, helping perception systems to analyze processes that occur over time (e.g., hidden Markov models or Kalman filters).[139]

A key concept from the science of economics is "utility": a measure of how valuable something is to an intelligent agent. Precise mathematical tools have been developed that analyze how an agent can make choices and plan, using decision theory, decision analysis,[140] and information value theory.[57] These tools include models such as Markov decision processes,[141] dynamic decision networks,[139] game theory and mechanism design.[142]

Classifiers and statistical learning methods Main articles: Classifier (mathematics), Statistical classification and Machine learning

The simplest AI applications can be divided into two types: classifiers ("if shiny then diamond") and controllers ("if shiny then pick up"). Controllers do, however, also classify conditions before inferring actions, and therefore classification forms a central part of many AI systems. Classifiers are functions that use pattern matching to determine a closest match. They can be tuned according to examples, making them very attractive for use in AI. These examples are known as observations or patterns. In supervised learning, each pattern belongs to a certain predefined class. A class can be seen as a decision that has to be made. All the observations combined with their class labels are known as a data set. When a new observation is received, that observation is classified based on previous experience.[143]

A classifier can be trained in various ways; there are many statistical and machine learning approaches. The most widely used classifiers are the neural network,[144] kernel methods such as the support vector machine,[145] k-nearest neighbor algorithm,[146] Gaussian mixture model,[147] naive Bayes classifier,[148] and decision tree.[149] The performance of these classifiers have been compared over a wide range of tasks. Classifier performance depends greatly on the characteristics of the data to be classified. There is no single classifier that works best on all given problems; this is also referred to as the "no free lunch" theorem. Determining a suitable classifier for a given problem is still more an art than science.[150]

Neural networks Main articles: Artificial neural network and Connectionism

The study of artificial neural networks[144] began in the

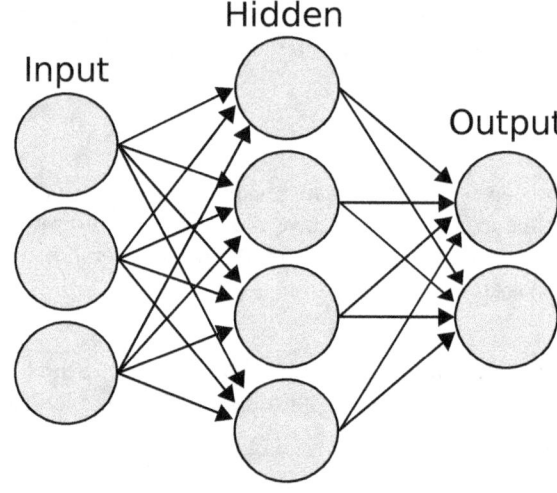

A neural network is an interconnected group of nodes, akin to the vast network of neurons in the human brain.

decade before the field of AI research was founded, in the work of Walter Pitts and Warren McCullough. Other important early researchers were Frank Rosenblatt, who invented the perceptron and Paul Werbos who developed the backpropagation algorithm.[151]

The main categories of networks are acyclic or feedforward neural networks (where the signal passes in only one direction) and recurrent neural networks (which allow feedback). Among the most popular feedforward networks are perceptrons, multi-layer perceptrons and radial basis networks.[152] Among recurrent networks, the most famous is the Hopfield net, a form of attractor network, which was first described by John Hopfield in 1982.[153] Neural networks can be applied to the problem of intelligent control (for robotics) or learning, using such techniques as Hebbian learning and competitive learning.[154]

Hierarchical temporal memory is an approach that models some of the structural and algorithmic properties of the neocortex.[155] The term "deep learning" gained traction in the mid-2000s after a publication by Geoffrey

2.10. ARTIFICIAL INTELLIGENCE

Hinton and Ruslan Salakhutdinov showed how a many-layered feedforward neural network could be effectively pre-trained one layer at a time, treating each layer in turn as an unsupervised restricted Boltzmann machine, then using supervised backpropagation for fine-tuning.[156]

Control theory Main article: Intelligent control

Control theory, the grandchild of cybernetics, has many important applications, especially in robotics.[157]

Languages Main article: List of programming languages for artificial intelligence

AI researchers have developed several specialized languages for AI research, including Lisp[158] and Prolog.[159]

Evaluating progress

Main article: Progress in artificial intelligence

In 1950, Alan Turing proposed a general procedure to test the intelligence of an agent now known as the Turing test. This procedure allows almost all the major problems of artificial intelligence to be tested. However, it is a very difficult challenge and at present all agents fail.[160]

Artificial intelligence can also be evaluated on specific problems such as small problems in chemistry, hand-writing recognition and game-playing. Such tests have been termed subject matter expert Turing tests. Smaller problems provide more achievable goals and there are an ever-increasing number of positive results.[161]

One classification for outcomes of an AI test is:[162]

1. Optimal: it is not possible to perform better.
2. Strong super-human: performs better than all humans.
3. Super-human: performs better than most humans.
4. Sub-human: performs worse than most humans.

For example, performance at draughts (i.e. checkers) is optimal,[163] performance at chess is super-human and nearing strong super-human (see computer chess: computers versus human) and performance at many everyday tasks (such as recognizing a face or crossing a room without bumping into something) is sub-human.

A quite different approach measures machine intelligence through tests which are developed from *mathematical* definitions of intelligence. Examples of these kinds of tests start in the late nineties devising intelligence tests using notions from Kolmogorov complexity and data compression.[164] Two major advantages of mathematical definitions are their applicability to nonhuman intelligences and their absence of a requirement for human testers.

A derivative of the Turing test is the Completely Automated Public Turing test to tell Computers and Humans Apart (CAPTCHA). as the name implies, this helps to determine that a user is an actual person and not a computer posing as a human. In contrast to the standard Turing test, CAPTCHA administered by a machine and targeted to a human as opposed to being administered by a human and targeted to a machine. A computer asks a user to complete a simple test then generates a grade for that test. Computers are unable to solve the problem, so correct solutions are deemed to be the result of a person taking the test. A common type of CAPTCHA is the test that requires the typing of distorted letters, numbers or symbols that appear in an image undecipherable by a computer.[165]

2.10.3 Applications

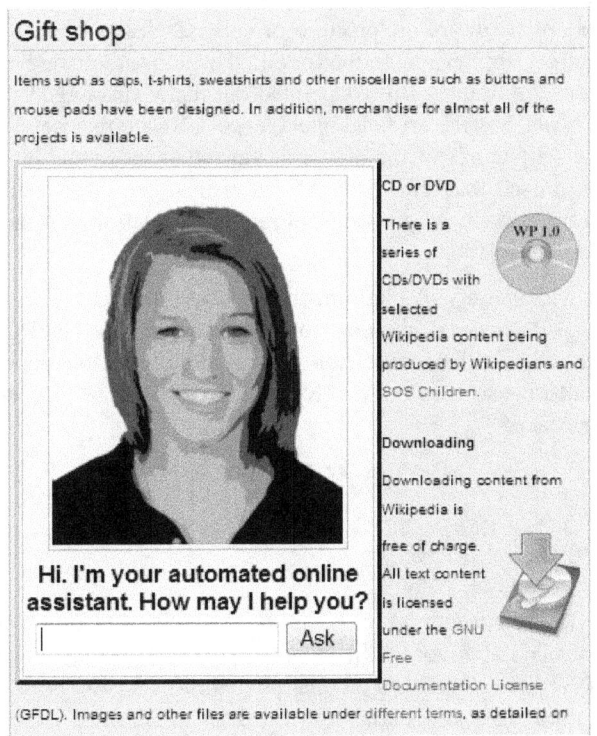

An automated online assistant providing customer service on a web page – one of many very primitive applications of artificial intelligence.

Main article: Applications of artificial intelligence

Artificial intelligence techniques are pervasive and are too numerous to list. Frequently, when a technique reaches mainstream use, it is no considered artificial intelligence; this phenomenon is described as the AI effect.[166] An area that artificial intelligence has contributed greatly to is intrusion detection.[167]

Competitions and prizes

Main article: Competitions and prizes in artificial intelligence

There are a number of competitions and prizes to promote research in artificial intelligence. The main areas promoted are: general machine intelligence, conversational behavior, data-mining, robotic cars, robot soccer and games.

Platforms

A platform (or "computing platform") is defined as "some sort of hardware architecture or software framework (including application frameworks), that allows software to run." As Rodney Brooks pointed out many years ago,[168] it is not just the artificial intelligence software that defines the AI features of the platform, but rather the actual platform itself that affects the AI that results, i.e., there needs to be work in AI problems on real-world platforms rather than in isolation.

A wide variety of platforms has allowed different aspects of AI to develop, ranging from expert systems, albeit PC-based but still an entire real-world system, to various robot platforms such as the widely available Roomba with open interface.[169]

Toys

AIBO, the first robotic pet, grew out of Sony's Computer Science Laboratory (CSL). Famed engineer Toshitada Doi is credited as AIBO's original progenitor: in 1994 he had started work on robots with artificial intelligence expert Masahiro Fujita, at CSL. Doi's friend, the artist Hajime Sorayama, was enlisted to create the initial designs for the AIBO's body. Those designs are now part of the permanent collections of Museum of Modern Art and the Smithsonian Institution, with later versions of AIBO being used in studies in Carnegie Mellon University. In 2006, AIBO was added into Carnegie Mellon University's "Robot Hall of Fame".

2.10.4 Philosophy and ethics

Main articles: Philosophy of artificial intelligence and Ethics of artificial intelligence

There are three philosophical questions related to AI:

1. Is artificial general intelligence possible? Can a machine solve any problem that a human being can solve using intelligence? Or are there hard limits to what a machine can accomplish?

2. Are intelligent machines dangerous? How can we ensure that machines behave ethically and that they are used ethically?

3. Can a machine have a mind, consciousness and mental states in exactly the same sense that human beings do? Can it a machine be sentient, and thus deserve certain rights? Can a machine intentionally cause harm?

The limits of artificial general intelligence

Main articles: philosophy of AI, Turing test, Physical symbol systems hypothesis, Dreyfus' critique of AI, The Emperor's New Mind and AI effect

Can a machine be intelligent? Can it "think"?

Turing's "polite convention" We need not decide if a machine can "think"; we need only decide if a machine can act as intelligently as a human being. This approach to the philosophical problems associated with artificial intelligence forms the basis of the Turing test.[160]

The Dartmouth proposal "Every aspect of learning or any other feature of intelligence can be so precisely described that a machine can be made to simulate it." This conjecture was printed in the proposal for the Dartmouth Conference of 1956, and represents the position of most working AI researchers.[170]

Newell and Simon's physical symbol system hypothesis "A physical symbol system has the necessary and sufficient means of general intelligent action." Newell and Simon argue that intelligence consists of formal operations on symbols.[171] Hubert Dreyfus argued that, on the contrary, human expertise depends on unconscious instinct rather than conscious symbol manipulation and on having a "feel" for the situation rather than explicit symbolic knowledge. (See Dreyfus' critique of AI.)[172][173]

Gödelian arguments Gödel himself,[174] John Lucas (in 1961) and Roger Penrose (in a more detailed argument from 1989 onwards) argued that humans are not reducible to Turing machines.[175] The detailed arguments are complex, but in essence they derive from Kurt Gödel's 1931 proof in his first incompleteness theorem that it is always possible to create statements that a formal system could not prove. A human being, however, can (with some thought) see the truth of these "Gödel statements". Any Turing program designed to search for these statements can have its methods reduced to a formal system, and so will always have a "Gödel statement" derivable from its program which it can never discover. However, if humans are indeed capable of understanding mathematical truth, it doesn't seem possible that we could be limited in the same way. This is quite a general result, if accepted, since it can be shown that hardware neural nets, and computers based on random processes (e.g. annealing approaches) and quantum computers based on entangled qubits (so long as they involve no new physics) can all be reduced to Turing machines. All they do is reduce the complexity of the tasks, not permit new types of problems to be solved. Roger Penrose speculates that there may be new physics involved in our brain, perhaps at the intersection of gravity and quantum mechanics at the Planck scale. This argument, if accepted does not rule out the possibility of true artificial intelligence, but means it has to be biological in basis or based on new physical principles. The argument has been followed up by many counter arguments, and then Roger Penrose has replied to those with counter counter examples, and it is now an intricate complex debate.[176] For details see Philosophy of artificial intelligence: Lucas, Penrose and Gödel

The artificial brain argument The brain can be simulated by machines and because brains are intelligent, simulated brains must also be intelligent; thus machines can be intelligent. Hans Moravec, Ray Kurzweil and others have argued that it is technologically feasible to copy the brain directly into hardware and software, and that such a simulation will be essentially identical to the original.[91]

The AI effect Machines are *already* intelligent, but observers have failed to recognize it. When Deep Blue beat Gary Kasparov in chess, the machine was acting intelligently. However, onlookers commonly discount the behavior of an artificial intelligence program by arguing that it is not "real" intelligence after all; thus "real" intelligence is whatever intelligent behavior people can do that machines still can not. This is known as the AI Effect: "AI is whatever hasn't been done yet."

Intelligent behaviour and machine ethics

As a minimum, an AI system must be able to reproduce aspects of human intelligence. This raises the issue of how ethically the machine should behave towards both humans and other AI agents. This issue was addressed by Wendell Wallach in his book titled *Moral Machines* in which he introduced the concept of artificial moral agents (AMA).[177] For Wallach, AMAs have become a part of the research landscape of artificial intelligence as guided by its two central questions which he identifies as "Does Humanity Want Computers Making Moral Decisions"[178] and "Can (Ro)bots Really Be Moral".[179] For Wallach the question is not centered on the issue of *whether* machines can demonstrate the equivalent of moral behavior in contrast to the *constraints* which society may place on the development of AMAs.[180]

Machine ethics   Main article: Machine ethics

The field of machine ethics is concerned with giving machines ethical principles, or a procedure for discovering a way to resolve the ethical dilemmas they might encounter, enabling them to function in an ethically responsible manner through their own ethical decision making.[181] The field was delineated in the AAAI Fall 2005 Symposium on Machine Ethics: "Past research concerning the relationship between technology and ethics has largely focused on responsible and irresponsible use of technology by human beings, with a few people being interested in how human beings ought to treat machines. In all cases, only human beings have engaged in ethical reasoning. The time has come for adding an ethical dimension to at least some machines. Recognition of the ethical ramifications of behavior involving machines, as well as recent and potential developments in machine autonomy, necessitate this. In contrast to computer hacking, software property issues, privacy issues and other topics normally ascribed to computer ethics, machine ethics is concerned with the behavior of machines towards human users and other machines. Research in machine ethics is key to alleviating concerns with autonomous systems — it could be argued that the notion of autonomous machines without such a dimension is at the root of all fear concerning machine intelligence. Further, investigation of machine ethics could enable the discovery of problems with current ethical theories, advancing our thinking about Ethics."[182] Machine ethics is sometimes referred to as machine morality, computational ethics or computational morality. A variety of perspectives of this nascent field can be found in the collected edition "Machine Ethics" [181] that stems from the AAAI Fall 2005 Symposium on Machine Ethics.[182]

Malevolent and friendly AI   Main article: Friendly AI

Political scientist Charles T. Rubin believes that AI can be neither designed nor guaranteed to be benevolent.[183] He argues that "any sufficiently advanced benevolence may be indistinguishable from malevolence." Humans should not assume machines or robots would treat us favorably, because there is no *a priori* reason to believe that they would be sympathetic to our system of morality, which has evolved along with our particular biology (which AIs would not share). Hyper-intelligent software may not necessarily decide to support the continued existence of mankind, and would be extremely difficult to stop. This topic has also recently begun to be discussed in academic publications as a real source of risks to civilization, humans, and planet Earth.

Physicist Stephen Hawking, Microsoft founder Bill Gates and SpaceX founder Elon Musk have expressed concerns about the possibility that AI could evolve to the point that humans could not control it, with Hawking theorizing that this could "spell the end of the human race".[184]

One proposal to deal with this is to ensure that the first generally intelligent AI is 'Friendly AI', and will then be able to control subsequently developed AIs. Some question whether this kind of check could really remain in place.

Leading AI researcher Rodney Brooks writes, "I think it is a mistake to be worrying about us developing malevolent AI anytime in the next few hundred years. I think the worry stems from a fundamental error in not distinguishing the difference between the very real recent advances in a particular aspect of AI, and the enormity and complexity of building sentient volitional intelligence."[185]

Devaluation of humanity   Main article: Computer Power and Human Reason

Joseph Weizenbaum wrote that AI applications can not, by definition, successfully simulate genuine human empathy and that the use of AI technology in fields such as customer service or psychotherapy[186] was deeply misguided. Weizenbaum was also bothered that AI researchers (and some philosophers) were willing to view the human mind as nothing more than a computer program (a position now known as computationalism). To Weizenbaum these points suggest that AI research devalues human life.[187]

Decrease in demand for human labor   Martin Ford, author of *The Lights in the Tunnel: Automation, Accelerating Technology and the Economy of the Future*,[188] and others argue that specialized artificial intelligence applications, robotics and other forms of automation will ultimately result in significant unemployment as machines begin to match and exceed the capability of workers to perform most routine and repetitive jobs. Ford predicts that many knowledge-based occupations—and in particular entry level jobs—will be increasingly susceptible to automation via expert systems, machine learning[189] and other AI-enhanced applications. AI-based applications may also be used to amplify the capabilities of low-wage offshore workers, making it more feasible to outsource knowledge work.[190]

Machine consciousness, sentience and mind

Main article: Artificial consciousness

If an AI system replicates all key aspects of human intelligence, will that system also be sentient – will it have a mind which has conscious experiences? This question is closely related to the philosophical problem as to the nature of human consciousness, generally referred to as the hard problem of consciousness.

Consciousness   Main articles: Hard problem of consciousness and Theory of mind

There are no objective criteria for knowing whether an intelligent agent is sentient – that it has conscious experiences. We assume that other people do because we do and they tell us that they do, but this is only a subjective determination. The lack of any hard criteria is known as the "hard problem" in the theory of consciousness. The problem applies not only to other people but to the higher animals and, by extension, to AI agents.

Computationalism   Main articles: Computationalism and Functionalism (philosophy of mind)

Are human intelligence, consciousness and mind products of information processing? Is the brain essentially a computer?

Computationalism is the idea that "the human mind or the human brain (or both) is an information processing system and that thinking is a form of computing". AI, or implementing machines with human intelligence was founded on the claim that "a central property of humans, intelligence can be so precisely described that a machine can be made to simulate it". A program can then be derived from this human computer and implemented into an artificial one to create efficient artificial intelligence. This program would act upon a set of outputs that result from set inputs of the internal memory of the computer, that is, the machine can only act with what it has implemented in it to start with. A long term goal for AI researchers is to provide machines with a deep understanding of the many abilities of a human being to replicate a general intelligence or STRONG AI, defined as a machine surpassing human abilities to perform the skills implanted in it, a scary thought to many, who fear losing control of such a powerful machine. Obstacles for researchers are mainly time contstraints. That is, AI scientists cannot establish much of a database for commonsense knowledge because it must be ontologically crafted into the machine which takes up a tremendous amount of time. To combat this, AI research looks to have the machine able to understand enough concepts in order to add to its own ontology, but how can it do this when machine ethics is primarily concerned with behavior of machines towards humans or other machines, limiting the extent of developing AI. In order to function like a common human AI must also display, "the ability to solve subsymbolic commonsense knowledge tasks such as how artists can tell statues are fake or how chess masters don't move certain spots to avoid exposure," but by developing machines who can do it all AI research is faced with the difficulty of potentially putting a lot of people out of work, while on the economy side of things businesses would boom from efficiency, thus forcing AI into a bottleneck trying to developing self improving machines.

Strong AI hypothesis   Main article: Chinese room

Searle's strong AI hypothesis states that "The appropriately programmed computer with the right inputs and outputs would thereby have a mind in exactly the same sense human beings have minds."[191] John Searle counters this assertion with his Chinese room argument, which asks us to look *inside* the computer and try to find where the "mind" might be.[192]

Robot rights   Main article: Robot rights

Mary Shelley's *Frankenstein* considers a key issue in the ethics of artificial intelligence: if a machine can be created that has intelligence, could it also *feel*? If it can feel, does it have the same rights as a human? The idea also appears in modern science fiction, such as the film *A.I.: Artificial Intelligence*, in which humanoid machines have the ability to feel emotions. This issue, now known as "robot rights", is currently being considered by, for example, California's Institute for the Future, although many critics believe that the discussion is premature.[193] The subject is profoundly discussed in the 2010 documentary film *Plug & Pray*.[194]

Superintelligence

Main article: Superintelligence

Are there limits to how intelligent machines – or human-machine hybrids – can be? A superintelligence, hyperintelligence, or superhuman intelligence is a hypothetical agent that would possess intelligence far surpassing that of the brightest and most gifted human mind. "Superintelligence" may also refer to the form or degree of intelligence possessed by such an agent.

Technological singularity   Main articles: Technological singularity and Moore's law

If research into Strong AI produced sufficiently intelligent software, it might be able to reprogram and improve itself. The improved software would be even better at improving itself, leading to recursive self-improvement.[195] The new intelligence could thus increase exponentially and dramatically surpass humans. Science fiction writer Vernor Vinge named this scenario "singularity".[196] Technological singularity is when accelerating progress in technologies will cause a runaway effect wherein artificial intelligence will exceed human intellectual capacity and control, thus radically changing or even ending civilization. Because the capabilities of such an intelligence may be impossible to comprehend, the technological singularity is an occurrence beyond which events are unpredictable or even unfathomable.[196]

Ray Kurzweil has used Moore's law (which describes the relentless exponential improvement in digital technology) to calculate that desktop computers will have the same processing power as human brains by the year 2029, and predicts that the singularity will occur in 2045.[196]

Transhumanism   Main article: Transhumanism

You awake one morning to find your brain has another lobe functioning. Invisible, this auxiliary lobe answers your questions with information beyond the realm of your own memory, suggests plausible courses of action, and asks questions that help bring out relevant facts. You quickly come to rely on the new lobe so much that you stop wondering how it works. You just

use it. This is the dream of artificial intelligence.
—*BYTE*, April 1985[197]

Robot designer Hans Moravec, cyberneticist Kevin Warwick and inventor Ray Kurzweil have predicted that humans and machines will merge in the future into cyborgs that are more capable and powerful than either.[198] This idea, called transhumanism, which has roots in Aldous Huxley and Robert Ettinger, has been illustrated in fiction as well, for example in the manga *Ghost in the Shell* and the science-fiction series *Dune*.

In the 1980s artist Hajime Sorayama's Sexy Robots series were painted and published in Japan depicting the actual organic human form with lifelike muscular metallic skins and later "the Gynoids" book followed that was used by or influenced movie makers including George Lucas and other creatives. Sorayama never considered these organic robots to be real part of nature but always unnatural product of the human mind, a fantasy existing in the mind even when realized in actual form.

Edward Fredkin argues that "artificial intelligence is the next stage in evolution", an idea first proposed by Samuel Butler's "Darwin among the Machines" (1863), and expanded upon by George Dyson in his book of the same name in 1998.[199]

2.10.5 In fiction

Main article: Artificial intelligence in fiction

The implications of artificial intelligence have been a persistent theme in science fiction. Early stories typically revolved around intelligent robots. The word "robot" itself was coined by Karel Čapek in his 1921 play *R.U.R.*, the title standing for "Rossum's Universal Robots". Later, the SF writer Isaac Asimov developed the three laws of robotics which he subsequently explored in a long series of robot stories. These laws have since gained some traction in genuine AI research.

Other influential fictional intelligences include HAL, the computer in charge of the spaceship in *2001: A Space Odyssey*, released as both a film and a book in 1968 and written by Arthur C. Clarke.

Since then, AI has become firmly rooted in popular culture.

2.10.6 See also

Main article: Outline of artificial intelligence

- AI takeover
- *Artificial Intelligence* (journal)
- Artificial intelligence (video games)
- Artificial stupidity
- Nick Bostrom
- Computer Go
- Effective altruism
- Existential risk
- Existential risk of artificial general intelligence
- Future of Humanity Institute
- Human Cognome Project
- List of artificial intelligence projects
- List of artificial intelligence researchers
- List of emerging technologies
- List of important artificial intelligence publications
- List of machine learning algorithms
- List of scientific journals
- Machine ethics
- Machine learning
- Never-Ending Language Learning
- *Our Final Invention*
- Outline of artificial intelligence
- Outline of human intelligence
- Philosophy of mind
- Simulated reality
- Superintelligence
- Symbolic artificial intelligence

2.10.7 Notes

[1] Definition of AI as the study of intelligent agents:

- Poole, Mackworth & Goebel 1998, p. 1, which provides the version that is used in this article. Note that they use the term "computational intelligence" as a synonym for artificial intelligence.
- Russell & Norvig (2003) (who prefer the term "rational agent") and write "The whole-agent view is now widely accepted in the field" (Russell & Norvig 2003, p. 55).
- Nilsson 1998
- Legg & Hutter 2007.

[2] The intelligent agent paradigm:

- Russell & Norvig 2003, pp. 27, 32–58, 968–972
- Poole, Mackworth & Goebel 1998, pp. 7–21
- Luger & Stubblefield 2004, pp. 235–240
- Hutter 2005, pp. 125–126

The definition used in this article, in terms of goals, actions, perception and environment, is due to Russell & Norvig (2003). Other definitions also include knowledge and learning as additional criteria.

[3] Although there is some controversy on this point (see Crevier (1993, p. 50)), McCarthy states unequivocally "I came up with the term" in a clnet interview. (Skillings 2006) McCarthy first used the term in the proposal for the Dartmouth conference, which appeared in 1955. (McCarthy et al. 1955)

[4] McCarthy's definition of AI:

- McCarthy 2007

[5] Pamela McCorduck (2004, pp. 424) writes of "the rough shattering of AI in subfields—vision, natural language, decision theory, genetic algorithms, robotics ... and these with own sub-subfield—that would hardly have anything to say to each other."

[6] This list of intelligent traits is based on the topics covered by the major AI textbooks, including:

- Russell & Norvig 2003
- Luger & Stubblefield 2004
- Poole, Mackworth & Goebel 1998
- Nilsson 1998

[7] General intelligence (strong AI) is discussed in popular introductions to AI:

- Kurzweil 1999 and Kurzweil 2005

[8] See the Dartmouth proposal, under Philosophy, below.

[9] This is a central idea of Pamela McCorduck's *Machines Who Think*. She writes: "I like to think of artificial intelligence as the scientific apotheosis of a venerable cultural tradition." (McCorduck 2004, p. 34) "Artificial intelligence in one form or another is an idea that has pervaded Western intellectual history, a dream in urgent need of being realized." (McCorduck 2004, p. xviii) "Our history is full of attempts—nutty, eerie, comical, earnest, legendary and real—to make artificial intelligences, to reproduce what is the essential us—bypassing the ordinary means. Back and forth between myth and reality, our imaginations supplying what our workshops couldn't, we have engaged for a long time in this odd form of self-reproduction." (McCorduck 2004, p. 3) She traces the desire back to its Hellenistic roots and calls it the urge to "forge the Gods." (McCorduck 2004, pp. 340–400)

[10] The optimism referred to includes the predictions of early AI researchers (see optimism in the history of AI) as well as the ideas of modern transhumanists such as Ray Kurzweil.

[11] The "setbacks" referred to include the ALPAC report of 1966, the abandonment of perceptrons in 1970, the Lighthill Report of 1973 and the collapse of the Lisp machine market in 1987.

[12] AI applications widely used behind the scenes:

- Russell & Norvig 2003, p. 28
- Kurzweil 2005, p. 265
- NRC 1999, pp. 216–222

[13] AI in myth:

- McCorduck 2004, pp. 4–5
- Russell & Norvig 2003, p. 939

[14] Cult images as artificial intelligence:

- Crevier (1993, p. 1) (statue of Amun)
- McCorduck (2004, pp. 6–9)

These were the first machines to be believed to have true intelligence and consciousness. Hermes Trismegistus expressed the common belief that with these statues, craftsman had reproduced "the true nature of the gods", their *sensus* and *spiritus*. McCorduck makes the connection between sacred automatons and Mosaic law (developed around the same time), which expressly forbids the worship of robots (McCorduck 2004, pp. 6–9)

[15] Humanoid automata:
Yan Shi:

- Needham 1986, p. 53

Hero of Alexandria:

- McCorduck 2004, p. 6

Al-Jazari:

- "A Thirteenth Century Programmable Robot". Shef.ac.uk. Retrieved 25 April 2009.

Wolfgang von Kempelen:

- McCorduck 2004, p. 17

[16] Artificial beings:
Jābir ibn Hayyān's Takwin:

- O'Connor 1994

Judah Loew's Golem:

- McCorduck 2004, pp. 15–16
- Buchanan 2005, p. 50

Paracelsus' Homunculus:

- McCorduck 2004, pp. 13–14

[17] AI in early science fiction.

- McCorduck 2004, pp. 17–25

[18] This insight, that digital computers can simulate any process of formal reasoning, is known as the Church–Turing thesis.

[19] Formal reasoning:

- Berlinski, David (2000). *The Advent of the Algorithm*. Harcourt Books. ISBN 0-15-601391-6. OCLC 46890682.

[20] AI's immediate precursors:

- McCorduck 2004, pp. 51–107
- Crevier 1993, pp. 27–32
- Russell & Norvig 2003, pp. 15, 940
- Moravec 1988, p. 3

See also Cybernetics and early neural networks (in History of artificial intelligence). Among the researchers who laid the foundations of AI were Alan Turing, John von Neumann, Norbert Wiener, Claude Shannon, Warren McCullough, Walter Pitts and Donald Hebb.

[21] Dartmouth conference:

- McCorduck 2004, pp. 111–136
- Crevier 1993, pp. 47–49, who writes "the conference is generally recognized as the official birthdate of the new science."
- Russell & Norvig 2003, p. 17, who call the conference "the birth of artificial intelligence."
- NRC 1999, pp. 200–201

[22] Hegemony of the Dartmouth conference attendees:

- Russell & Norvig 2003, p. 17, who write "for the next 20 years the field would be dominated by these people and their students."
- McCorduck 2004, pp. 129–130

[23] Russell and Norvig write "it was astonishing whenever a computer did anything kind of smartish." Russell & Norvig 2003, p. 18

[24] "Golden years" of AI (successful symbolic reasoning programs 1956–1973):

- McCorduck 2004, pp. 243–252
- Crevier 1993, pp. 52–107
- Moravec 1988, p. 9
- Russell & Norvig 2003, pp. 18–21

The programs described are Arthur Samuel's checkers program for the IBM 701, Daniel Bobrow's STUDENT, Newell and Simon's Logic Theorist and Terry Winograd's SHRDLU.

[25] DARPA pours money into undirected pure research into AI during the 1960s:

- McCorduck 2004, pp. 131
- Crevier 1993, pp. 51, 64–65
- NRC 1999, pp. 204–205

[26] AI in England:

- Howe 1994

[27] Optimism of early AI:

- Herbert Simon quote: Simon 1965, p. 96 quoted in Crevier 1993, p. 109.
- Marvin Minsky quote: Minsky 1967, p. 2 quoted in Crevier 1993, p. 109.

[28] See The problems (in History of artificial intelligence)

[29] Lighthill 1973.

[30] First AI Winter, Mansfield Amendment, Lighthill report

- Crevier 1993, pp. 115–117
- Russell & Norvig 2003, p. 22
- NRC 1999, pp. 212–213
- Howe 1994

[31] Expert systems:

- ACM 1998, I.2.1
- Russell & Norvig 2003, pp. 22–24
- Luger & Stubblefield 2004, pp. 227–331
- Nilsson 1998, chpt. 17.4
- McCorduck 2004, pp. 327–335, 434–435
- Crevier 1993, pp. 145–62, 197–203

[32] Boom of the 1980s: rise of expert systems, Fifth Generation Project, Alvey, MCC, SCI:

- McCorduck 2004, pp. 426–441
- Crevier 1993, pp. 161–162,197–203, 211, 240
- Russell & Norvig 2003, p. 24
- NRC 1999, pp. 210–211

[33] Second AI winter:

- McCorduck 2004, pp. 430–435
- Crevier 1993, pp. 209–210
- NRC 1999, pp. 214–216

[34] Formal methods are now preferred ("Victory of the neats"):

- Russell & Norvig 2003, pp. 25–26
- McCorduck 2004, pp. 486–487

[35] McCorduck 2004, pp. 480–483

[36] Markoff 2011.

[37] Administrator. "Kinect's AI breakthrough explained". *i-programmer.info*.

[38] http://readwrite.com/2013/01/15/virtual-personal-assistants-the-future-of-your-smartphone-infographic

[39] Problem solving, puzzle solving, game playing and deduction:

- Russell & Norvig 2003, chpt. 3–9,
- Poole, Mackworth & Goebel 1998, chpt. 2,3,7,9,
- Luger & Stubblefield 2004, chpt. 3,4,6,8,
- Nilsson 1998, chpt. 7–12

[40] Uncertain reasoning:

- Russell & Norvig 2003, pp. 452–644,
- Poole, Mackworth & Goebel 1998, pp. 345–395,
- Luger & Stubblefield 2004, pp. 333–381,
- Nilsson 1998, chpt. 19

[41] Intractability and efficiency and the combinatorial explosion:

- Russell & Norvig 2003, pp. 9, 21–22

[42] Psychological evidence of sub-symbolic reasoning:

- Wason & Shapiro (1966) showed that people do poorly on completely abstract problems, but if the problem is restated to allow the use of intuitive social intelligence, performance dramatically improves. (See Wason selection task)
- Kahneman, Slovic & Tversky (1982) have shown that people are terrible at elementary problems that involve uncertain reasoning. (See list of cognitive biases for several examples).
- Lakoff & Núñez (2000) have controversially argued that even our skills at mathematics depend on knowledge and skills that come from "the body", i.e. sensorimotor and perceptual skills. (See Where Mathematics Comes From)

[43] Knowledge representation:

- ACM 1998, I.2.4,
- Russell & Norvig 2003, pp. 320–363,
- Poole, Mackworth & Goebel 1998, pp. 23–46, 69–81, 169–196, 235–277, 281–298, 319–345,
- Luger & Stubblefield 2004, pp. 227–243,
- Nilsson 1998, chpt. 18

[44] Knowledge engineering:

- Russell & Norvig 2003, pp. 260–266,
- Poole, Mackworth & Goebel 1998, pp. 199–233,
- Nilsson 1998, chpt. ~17.1–17.4

[45] Representing categories and relations: Semantic networks, description logics, inheritance (including frames and scripts):

- Russell & Norvig 2003, pp. 349–354,
- Poole, Mackworth & Goebel 1998, pp. 174–177,
- Luger & Stubblefield 2004, pp. 248–258,
- Nilsson 1998, chpt. 18.3

[46] Representing events and time:Situation calculus, event calculus, fluent calculus (including solving the frame problem):

- Russell & Norvig 2003, pp. 328–341,
- Poole, Mackworth & Goebel 1998, pp. 281–298,
- Nilsson 1998, chpt. 18.2

[47] Causal calculus:

- Poole, Mackworth & Goebel 1998, pp. 335–337

[48] Representing knowledge about knowledge: Belief calculus, modal logics:

- Russell & Norvig 2003, pp. 341–344,
- Poole, Mackworth & Goebel 1998, pp. 275–277

[49] Ontology:

- Russell & Norvig 2003, pp. 320–328

[50] Qualification problem:

- McCarthy & Hayes 1969
- Russell & Norvig 2003

While McCarthy was primarily concerned with issues in the logical representation of actions, Russell & Norvig 2003 apply the term to the more general issue of default reasoning in the vast network of assumptions underlying all our commonsense knowledge.

[51] Default reasoning and default logic, non-monotonic logics, circumscription, closed world assumption, abduction (Poole *et al.* places abduction under "default reasoning". Luger *et al.* places this under "uncertain reasoning"):

- Russell & Norvig 2003, pp. 354–360,
- Poole, Mackworth & Goebel 1998, pp. 248–256, 323–335,
- Luger & Stubblefield 2004, pp. 335–363,
- Nilsson 1998, ~18.3.3

[52] Breadth of commonsense knowledge:

- Russell & Norvig 2003, p. 21,
- Crevier 1993, pp. 113–114,
- Moravec 1988, p. 13,
- Lenat & Guha 1989 (Introduction)

[53] Dreyfus & Dreyfus 1986

[54] Gladwell 2005

[55] Expert knowledge as embodied intuition:

- Dreyfus & Dreyfus 1986 (Hubert Dreyfus is a philosopher and critic of AI who was among the first to argue that most useful human knowledge was encoded subsymbolically. See Dreyfus' critique of AI)
- Gladwell 2005 (Gladwell's *Blink* is a popular introduction to sub-symbolic reasoning and knowledge.)
- Hawkins & Blakeslee 2005 (Hawkins argues that subsymbolic knowledge should be the primary focus of AI research.)

[56] Planning:

- ACM 1998, ~I.2.8,
- Russell & Norvig 2003, pp. 375–459,
- Poole, Mackworth & Goebel 1998, pp. 281–316,
- Luger & Stubblefield 2004, pp. 314–329,
- Nilsson 1998, chpt. 10.1–2, 22

[57] Information value theory:

- Russell & Norvig 2003, pp. 600–604

[58] Classical planning:

- Russell & Norvig 2003, pp. 375–430,
- Poole, Mackworth & Goebel 1998, pp. 281–315,
- Luger & Stubblefield 2004, pp. 314–329,
- Nilsson 1998, chpt. 10.1–2, 22

[59] Planning and acting in non-deterministic domains: conditional planning, execution monitoring, replanning and continuous planning:

- Russell & Norvig 2003, pp. 430–449

[60] Multi-agent planning and emergent behavior:

- Russell & Norvig 2003, pp. 449–455

[61] This is a form of Tom Mitchell's widely quoted definition of machine learning: "A computer program is set to learn from an experience E with respect to some task T and some performance measure P if its performance on T as measured by P improves with experience E."

[62] Learning:

- ACM 1998, I.2.6,
- Russell & Norvig 2003, pp. 649–788,
- Poole, Mackworth & Goebel 1998, pp. 397–438,
- Luger & Stubblefield 2004, pp. 385–542,
- Nilsson 1998, chpt. 3.3, 10.3, 17.5, 20

[63] Alan Turing discussed the centrality of learning as early as 1950, in his classic paper "Computing Machinery and Intelligence".(Turing 1950) In 1956, at the original Dartmouth AI summer conference, Ray Solomonoff wrote a report on unsupervised probabilistic machine learning: "An Inductive Inference Machine".(Solomonoff 1956)

[64] Reinforcement learning:

- Russell & Norvig 2003, pp. 763–788
- Luger & Stubblefield 2004, pp. 442–449

[65] Computational learning theory:

- **CITATION IN PROGRESS.**

[66] Weng et al. 2001.

[67] Lungarella et al. 2003.

[68] Asada et al. 2009.

[69] Oudeyer 2010.

[70] Natural language processing:

- ACM 1998, I.2.7
- Russell & Norvig 2003, pp. 790–831
- Poole, Mackworth & Goebel 1998, pp. 91–104
- Luger & Stubblefield 2004, pp. 591–632

[71] "Versatile question answering systems: seeing in synthesis", Mittal et al., IJIIDS, 5(2), 119-142, 2011

[72] Applications of natural language processing, including information retrieval (i.e. text mining) and machine translation:

- Russell & Norvig 2003, pp. 840–857,
- Luger & Stubblefield 2004, pp. 623–630

[73] Machine perception:

- Russell & Norvig 2003, pp. 537–581, 863–898

2.10. ARTIFICIAL INTELLIGENCE

- Nilsson 1998, ~chpt. 6

[74] Computer vision:
- ACM 1998, I.2.10
- Russell & Norvig 2003, pp. 863–898
- Nilsson 1998, chpt. 6

[75] Speech recognition:
- ACM 1998, ~I.2.7
- Russell & Norvig 2003, pp. 568–578

[76] Object recognition:
- Russell & Norvig 2003, pp. 885–892

[77] Robotics:
- ACM 1998, I.2.9,
- Russell & Norvig 2003, pp. 901–942,
- Poole, Mackworth & Goebel 1998, pp. 443–460

[78] Moving and configuration space:
- Russell & Norvig 2003, pp. 916–932

[79] Tecuci 2012.

[80] Robotic mapping (localization, etc):
- Russell & Norvig 2003, pp. 908–915

[81] *Kismet*.

[82] Thro 1993.

[83] Edelson 1991.

[84] Tao & Tan 2005.

[85] James 1884.

[86] Picard 1995.

[87] Kleine-Cosack 2006: "The introduction of emotion to computer science was done by Pickard (sic) who created the field of affective computing."

[88] Diamond 2003: "Rosalind Picard, a genial MIT professor, is the field's godmother; her 1997 book, Affective Computing, triggered an explosion of interest in the emotional side of computers and their users."

[89] Emotion and affective computing:
- Minsky 2006

[90] Gerald Edelman, Igor Aleksander and others have argued that artificial consciousness is required for strong AI. (Aleksander 1995; Edelman 2007)

[91] Artificial brain arguments: AI requires a simulation of the operation of the human brain

- Russell & Norvig 2003, p. 957
- Crevier 1993, pp. 271 and 279

A few of the people who make some form of the argument:
- Moravec 1988
- Kurzweil 2005, p. 262
- Hawkins & Blakeslee 2005

The most extreme form of this argument (the brain replacement scenario) was put forward by Clark Glymour in the mid-1970s and was touched on by Zenon Pylyshyn and John Searle in 1980.

[92] AI complete: Shapiro 1992, p. 9

[93] Nils Nilsson writes: "Simply put, there is wide disagreement in the field about what AI is all about" (Nilsson 1983, p. 10).

[94] Biological intelligence vs. intelligence in general:
- Russell & Norvig 2003, pp. 2–3, who make the analogy with aeronautical engineering.
- McCorduck 2004, pp. 100–101, who writes that there are "two major branches of artificial intelligence: one aimed at producing intelligent behavior regardless of how it was accomplioshed, and the other aimed at modeling intelligent processes found in nature, particularly human ones."
- Kolata 1982, a paper in *Science*, which describes McCarthy's indifference to biological models. Kolata quotes McCarthy as writing: "This is AI, so we don't care if it's psychologically real". McCarthy recently reiterated his position at the AI@50 conference where he said "Artificial intelligence is not, by definition, simulation of human intelligence" (Maker 2006).

[95] Neats vs. scruffies:
- McCorduck 2004, pp. 421–424, 486–489
- Crevier 1993, pp. 168
- Nilsson 1983, pp. 10–11

[96] Symbolic vs. sub-symbolic AI:
- Nilsson (1998, p. 7), who uses the term "sub-symbolic".

[97] Haugeland 1985, p. 255.

[98] Law 1994.

[99] Bach 2008.

[100] Haugeland 1985, pp. 112–117

[101] The most dramatic case of sub-symbolic AI being pushed into the background was the devastating critique of perceptrons by Marvin Minsky and Seymour Papert in 1969. See History of AI, AI winter, or Frank Rosenblatt.

[102] Cognitive simulation, Newell and Simon, AI at CMU (then called Carnegie Tech):

- McCorduck 2004, pp. 139–179, 245–250, 322–323 (EPAM)
- Crevier 1993, pp. 145–149

[103] Soar (history):

- McCorduck 2004, pp. 450–451
- Crevier 1993, pp. 258–263

[104] McCarthy and AI research at SAIL and SRI International:

- McCorduck 2004, pp. 251–259
- Crevier 1993

[105] AI research at Edinburgh and in France, birth of Prolog:

- Crevier 1993, pp. 193–196
- Howe 1994

[106] AI at MIT under Marvin Minsky in the 1960s :

- McCorduck 2004, pp. 259–305
- Crevier 1993, pp. 83–102, 163–176
- Russell & Norvig 2003, p. 19

[107] Cyc:

- McCorduck 2004, p. 489, who calls it "a determinedly scruffy enterprise"
- Crevier 1993, pp. 239–243
- Russell & Norvig 2003, p. 363–365
- Lenat & Guha 1989

[108] Knowledge revolution:

- McCorduck 2004, pp. 266–276, 298–300, 314, 421
- Russell & Norvig 2003, pp. 22–23

[109] Embodied approaches to AI:

- McCorduck 2004, pp. 454–462
- Brooks 1990
- Moravec 1988

[110] Revival of connectionism:

- Crevier 1993, pp. 214–215
- Russell & Norvig 2003, p. 25

[111] Computational intelligence

- IEEE Computational Intelligence Society

[112] Hutter 2012.

[113] Langley 2011.

[114] Katz 2012.

[115] Norvig 2012.

[116] Agent architectures, hybrid intelligent systems:

- Russell & Norvig (2003, pp. 27, 932, 970–972)
- Nilsson (1998, chpt. 25)

[117] Hierarchical control system:

- Albus 2002

[118] Subsumption architecture:

- CITATION IN PROGRESS.

[119] Search algorithms:

- Russell & Norvig 2003, pp. 59–189
- Poole, Mackworth & Goebel 1998, pp. 113–163
- Luger & Stubblefield 2004, pp. 79–164, 193–219
- Nilsson 1998, chpt. 7–12

[120] Forward chaining, backward chaining, Horn clauses, and logical deduction as search:

- Russell & Norvig 2003, pp. 217–225, 280–294
- Poole, Mackworth & Goebel 1998, pp. ~46–52
- Luger & Stubblefield 2004, pp. 62–73
- Nilsson 1998, chpt. 4.2, 7.2

[121] State space search and planning:

- Russell & Norvig 2003, pp. 382–387
- Poole, Mackworth & Goebel 1998, pp. 298–305
- Nilsson 1998, chpt. 10.1–2

[122] Uninformed searches (breadth first search, depth first search and general state space search):

- Russell & Norvig 2003, pp. 59–93
- Poole, Mackworth & Goebel 1998, pp. 113–132
- Luger & Stubblefield 2004, pp. 79–121
- Nilsson 1998, chpt. 8

[123] Heuristic or informed searches (e.g., greedy best first and A*):

- Russell & Norvig 2003, pp. 94–109,
- Poole, Mackworth & Goebel 1998, pp. pp. 132–147,
- Luger & Stubblefield 2004, pp. 133–150,
- Nilsson 1998, chpt. 9

[124] Optimization searches:

- Russell & Norvig 2003, pp. 110–116,120–129
- Poole, Mackworth & Goebel 1998, pp. 56–163
- Luger & Stubblefield 2004, pp. 127–133

[125] Artificial life and society based learning:

2.10. ARTIFICIAL INTELLIGENCE

- Luger & Stubblefield 2004, pp. 530–541

[126] Genetic programming and genetic algorithms:
- Luger & Stubblefield 2004, pp. 509–530,
- Nilsson 1998, chpt. 4.2,
- Holland 1975,
- Koza 1992,
- Poli, Langdon & McPhee 2008.

[127] Logic:
- ACM 1998, ~I.2.3,
- Russell & Norvig 2003, pp. 194–310,
- Luger & Stubblefield 2004, pp. 35–77,
- Nilsson 1998, chpt. 13–16

[128] Satplan:
- Russell & Norvig 2003, pp. 402–407,
- Poole, Mackworth & Goebel 1998, pp. 300–301,
- Nilsson 1998, chpt. 21

[129] Explanation based learning, relevance based learning, inductive logic programming, case based reasoning:
- Russell & Norvig 2003, pp. 678–710,
- Poole, Mackworth & Goebel 1998, pp. 414–416,
- Luger & Stubblefield 2004, pp. ~422–442,
- Nilsson 1998, chpt. 10.3, 17.5

[130] Propositional logic:
- Russell & Norvig 2003, pp. 204–233,
- Luger & Stubblefield 2004, pp. 45–50
- Nilsson 1998, chpt. 13

[131] First-order logic and features such as equality:
- ACM 1998, ~I.2.4,
- Russell & Norvig 2003, pp. 240–310,
- Poole, Mackworth & Goebel 1998, pp. 268–275,
- Luger & Stubblefield 2004, pp. 50–62,
- Nilsson 1998, chpt. 15

[132] Fuzzy logic:
- Russell & Norvig 2003, pp. 526–527

[133] Subjective logic:
- **CITATION IN PROGRESS.**

[134] Stochastic methods for uncertain reasoning:
- ACM 1998, ~I.2.3,
- Russell & Norvig 2003, pp. 462–644,
- Poole, Mackworth & Goebel 1998, pp. 345–395,
- Luger & Stubblefield 2004, pp. 165–191, 333–381,
- Nilsson 1998, chpt. 19

[135] Bayesian networks:
- Russell & Norvig 2003, pp. 492–523,
- Poole, Mackworth & Goebel 1998, pp. 361–381,
- Luger & Stubblefield 2004, pp. ~182–190, ~363–379,
- Nilsson 1998, chpt. 19.3–4

[136] Bayesian inference algorithm:
- Russell & Norvig 2003, pp. 504–519,
- Poole, Mackworth & Goebel 1998, pp. 361–381,
- Luger & Stubblefield 2004, pp. ~363–379,
- Nilsson 1998, chpt. 19.4 & 7

[137] Bayesian learning and the expectation-maximization algorithm:
- Russell & Norvig 2003, pp. 712–724,
- Poole, Mackworth & Goebel 1998, pp. 424–433,
- Nilsson 1998, chpt. 20

[138] Bayesian decision theory and Bayesian decision networks:
- Russell & Norvig 2003, pp. 597–600

[139] Stochastic temporal models:
- Russell & Norvig 2003, pp. 537–581

Dynamic Bayesian networks:
- Russell & Norvig 2003, pp. 551–557

Hidden Markov model:
- (Russell & Norvig 2003, pp. 549–551)

Kalman filters:
- Russell & Norvig 2003, pp. 551–557

[140] decision theory and decision analysis:
- Russell & Norvig 2003, pp. 584–597,
- Poole, Mackworth & Goebel 1998, pp. 381–394

[141] Markov decision processes and dynamic decision networks:
- Russell & Norvig 2003, pp. 613–631

[142] Game theory and mechanism design:
- Russell & Norvig 2003, pp. 631–643

[143] Statistical learning methods and classifiers:
- Russell & Norvig 2003, pp. 712–754,
- Luger & Stubblefield 2004, pp. 453–541

[144] Neural networks and connectionism:

- Russell & Norvig 2003, pp. 736–748,
- Poole, Mackworth & Goebel 1998, pp. 408–414,
- Luger & Stubblefield 2004, pp. 453–505,
- Nilsson 1998, chpt. 3

[145] kernel methods such as the support vector machine:

- Russell & Norvig 2003, pp. 749–752

[146] K-nearest neighbor algorithm:

- Russell & Norvig 2003, pp. 733–736

[147] Gaussian mixture model:

- Russell & Norvig 2003, pp. 725–727

[148] Naive Bayes classifier:

- Russell & Norvig 2003, pp. 718

[149] Decision tree:

- Russell & Norvig 2003, pp. 653–664,
- Poole, Mackworth & Goebel 1998, pp. 403–408,
- Luger & Stubblefield 2004, pp. 408–417

[150] Classifier performance:

- van der Walt & Bernard 2006

[151] Backpropagation:

- Russell & Norvig 2003, pp. 744–748,
- Luger & Stubblefield 2004, pp. 467–474,
- Nilsson 1998, chpt. 3.3

[152] Feedforward neural networks, perceptrons and radial basis networks:

- Russell & Norvig 2003, pp. 739–748, 758
- Luger & Stubblefield 2004, pp. 458–467

[153] Recurrent neural networks, Hopfield nets:

- Russell & Norvig 2003, p. 758
- Luger & Stubblefield 2004, pp. 474–505

[154] Competitive learning, Hebbian coincidence learning, Hopfield networks and attractor networks:

- Luger & Stubblefield 2004, pp. 474–505

[155] Hierarchical temporal memory:

- Hawkins & Blakeslee 2005

[156] Hinton 2007.

[157] Control theory:

- ACM 1998, ~I.2.8,
- Russell & Norvig 2003, pp. 926–932

[158] Lisp:

- Luger & Stubblefield 2004, pp. 723–821
- Crevier 1993, pp. 59–62,
- Russell & Norvig 2003, p. 18

[159] Prolog:

- Poole, Mackworth & Goebel 1998, pp. 477–491,
- Luger & Stubblefield 2004, pp. 641–676, 575–581

[160] The Turing test:
Turing's original publication:

- Turing 1950

Historical influence and philosophical implications:

- Haugeland 1985, pp. 6–9
- Crevier 1993, p. 24
- McCorduck 2004, pp. 70–71
- Russell & Norvig 2003, pp. 2–3 and 948

[161] Subject matter expert Turing test:

- **CITATION IN PROGRESS.**

[162] Rajani 2011.

[163] Game AI:

- **CITATION IN PROGRESS.**

[164] Mathematical definitions of intelligence:

- Hernandez-Orallo 2000
- Dowe & Hajek 1997
- Hernandez-Orallo & Dowe 2010

[165] O'Brien & Marakas 2011.

[166] *CNN* 2006.

[167] Intrusion detection:

- Kumar & Kumar 2012

[168] Brooks 1991.

[169] "Hacking Roomba". *hackingroomba.com*.

[170] Dartmouth proposal:

- McCarthy et al. 1955 (the original proposal)
- Crevier 1993, p. 49 (historical significance)

[171] The physical symbol systems hypothesis:

- Newell & Simon 1976, p. 116
- McCorduck 2004, p. 153
- Russell & Norvig 2003, p. 18

2.10. ARTIFICIAL INTELLIGENCE

[172] Dreyfus criticized the necessary condition of the physical symbol system hypothesis, which he called the "psychological assumption": "The mind can be viewed as a device operating on bits of information according to formal rules". (Dreyfus 1992, p. 156)

[173] Dreyfus' critique of artificial intelligence:

- Dreyfus 1972, Dreyfus & Dreyfus 1986
- Crevier 1993, pp. 120–132
- McCorduck 2004, pp. 211–239
- Russell & Norvig 2003, pp. 950–952,

[174] Gödel 1951: in this lecture, Kurt Gödel uses the incompleteness theorem to arrive at the following disjunction: (a) the human mind is not a consistent finite machine, or (b) there exist Diophantine equations for which it cannot decide whether solutions exist. Gödel finds (b) implausible, and thus seems to have believed the human mind was not equivalent to a finite machine, i.e., its power exceeded that of any finite machine. He recognized that this was only a conjecture, since one could never disprove (b). Yet he considered the disjunctive conclusion to be a "certain fact".

[175] The Mathematical Objection:

- Russell & Norvig 2003, p. 949
- McCorduck 2004, pp. 448–449

Making the Mathematical Objection:

- Lucas 1961
- Penrose 1989

Refuting Mathematical Objection:

- Turing 1950 under "(2) The Mathematical Objection"
- Hofstadter 1979

Background:

- Gödel 1931, Church 1936, Kleene 1935, Turing 1937

[176] Beyond the Doubting of a Shadow, A Reply to Commentaries on Shadows of the Mind, Roger Penrose 1996 The links to the original articles he responds to there are easily found in the Wayback machine: Can Physics Provide a Theory of Consciousness? Barnard J. Bars, Penrose's Gödelian Argument etc.

[177] Wendell Wallach (2010). *Moral Machines*, Oxford University Press.

[178] Wallach, pp 37–54.

[179] Wallach, pp 55–73.

[180] Wallach, Introduction chapter.

[181] Michael Anderson and Susan Leigh Anderson (2011), Machine Ethics, Cambridge University Press.

[182] "Machine Ethics". *aaai.org*.

[183] Rubin, Charles (Spring 2003). "Artificial Intelligence and Human Nature". *The New Atlantis* **1**: 88–100.

[184] Rawlinson, Kevin. "Microsoft's Bill Gates insists AI is a threat". BBC News. Retrieved 30 January 2015.

[185] Brooks, Rodney (10 November 2014). "artificial intelligence is a tool, not a threat".

[186] In the early 1970s, Kenneth Colby presented a version of Weizenbaum's ELIZA known as DOCTOR which he promoted as a serious therapeutic tool. (Crevier 1993, pp. 132–144)

[187] Joseph Weizenbaum's critique of AI:

- Weizenbaum 1976
- Crevier 1993, pp. 132–144
- McCorduck 2004, pp. 356–373
- Russell & Norvig 2003, p. 961

Weizenbaum (the AI researcher who developed the first chatterbot program, ELIZA) argued in 1976 that the misuse of artificial intelligence has the potential to devalue human life.

[188] Ford, Martin R. (2009), *The Lights in the Tunnel: Automation, Accelerating Technology and the Economy of the Future*, Acculant Publishing, ISBN 978-1448659814. *(e-book available free online.)*

[189] "Machine Learning: A job killer?". *econfuture - Robots, AI and Unemployment - Future Economics and Technology*.

[190] AI could decrease the demand for human labor:

- Russell & Norvig 2003, pp. 960–961
- Ford, Martin (2009). *The Lights in the Tunnel: Automation, Accelerating Technology and the Economy of the Future*. Acculant Publishing. ISBN 978-1-4486-5981-4.

[191] This version is from Searle (1999), and is also quoted in Dennett 1991, p. 435. Searle's original formulation was "The appropriately programmed computer really is a mind, in the sense that computers given the right programs can be literally said to understand and have other cognitive states." (Searle 1980, p. 1). Strong AI is defined similarly by Russell & Norvig (2003, p. 947): "The assertion that machines could possibly act intelligently (or, perhaps better, act as if they were intelligent) is called the 'weak AI' hypothesis by philosophers, and the assertion that machines that do so are actually thinking (as opposed to simulating thinking) is called the 'strong AI' hypothesis."

[192] Searle's Chinese room argument:

- Searle 1980. Searle's original presentation of the thought experiment.

- Searle 1999.

Discussion:

- Russell & Norvig 2003, pp. 958–960
- McCorduck 2004, pp. 443–445
- Crevier 1993, pp. 269–271

[193] Robot rights:

- Russell & Norvig 2003, p. 964
- *BBC News* 2006

Prematurity of:

- Henderson 2007

In fiction:

- McCorduck (2004, p. 190-25) discusses *Frankenstein* and identifies the key ethical issues as scientific hubris and the suffering of the monster, i.e. robot rights.

[194] maschafilm. "Content: Plug & Pray Film - Artificial Intelligence - Robots -". *plugandpray-film.de*.

[195] Omohundro, Steve (2008). *The Nature of Self-Improving Artificial Intelligence.* presented and distributed at the 2007 Singularity Summit, San Francisco, CA.

[196] Technological singularity:

- Vinge 1993
- Kurzweil 2005
- Russell & Norvig 2003, p. 963

[197] Lemmons, Phil (April 1985). "Artificial Intelligence". *BYTE*. p. 125. Retrieved 14 February 2015.

[198] Transhumanism:

- Moravec 1988
- Kurzweil 2005
- Russell & Norvig 2003, p. 963

[199] AI as evolution:

- Edward Fredkin is quoted in McCorduck (2004, p. 401).
- Butler 1863
- Dyson 1998

2.10.8 References

AI textbooks

- Hutter, Marcus (2005). *Universal Artificial Intelligence*. Berlin: Springer. ISBN 978-3-540-22139-5.
- Luger, George; Stubblefield, William (2004). *Artificial Intelligence: Structures and Strategies for Complex Problem Solving* (5th ed.). Benjamin/Cummings. ISBN 0-8053-4780-1.
- Neapolitan, Richard; Jiang, Xia (2012). *Contemporary Artificial Intelligence.* Chapman & Hall/CRC. ISBN 978-1-4398-4469-4.
- Nilsson, Nils (1998). *Artificial Intelligence: A New Synthesis.* Morgan Kaufmann. ISBN 978-1-55860-467-4.
- Russell, Stuart J.; Norvig, Peter (2003), *Artificial Intelligence: A Modern Approach* (2nd ed.), Upper Saddle River, New Jersey: Prentice Hall, ISBN 0-13-790395-2.
- Poole, David; Mackworth, Alan; Goebel, Randy (1998). *Computational Intelligence: A Logical Approach*. New York: Oxford University Press. ISBN 0-19-510270-3.
- Winston, Patrick Henry (1984). *Artificial Intelligence.* Reading, MA: Addison-Wesley. ISBN 0-201-08259-4.
- Rich, Elaine (1983). *Artificial Intelligence.* McGraw-Hill. ISBN 0-07-052261-8.

History of AI

- Crevier, Daniel (1993), *AI: The Tumultuous Search for Artificial Intelligence*, New York, NY: BasicBooks, ISBN 0-465-02997-3.
- McCorduck, Pamela (2004), *Machines Who Think* (2nd ed.), Natick, MA: A. K. Peters, Ltd., ISBN 1-56881-205-1.
- Nilsson, Nils (2010). *The Quest for Artificial Intelligence: A History of Ideas and Achievements.* New York: Cambridge University Press. ISBN 978-0-521-12293-1.

Other sources

- Asada, M.; Hosoda, K.; Kuniyoshi, Y.; Ishiguro, H.; Inui, T.; Yoshikawa, Y.; Ogino, M.;

- Yoshida, C. (2009). "Cognitive developmental robotics: a survey" (PDF). *IEEE Transactions on Autonomous Mental Development* **1** (1): 12–34. doi:10.1109/tamd.2009.2021702.

- "ACM Computing Classification System: Artificial intelligence". ACM. 1998. Retrieved 30 August 2007.

- Albus, J. S. (2002). "4-D/RCS: A Reference Model Architecture for Intelligent Unmanned Ground Vehicles" (PDF). In Gerhart, G.; Gunderson, R.; Shoemaker, C. *Proceedings of the SPIE AeroSense Session on Unmanned Ground Vehicle Technology* **3693**. pp. 11–20. Archived from the original (PDF) on 25 July 2004.

- Aleksander, Igor (1995). *Artificial Neuroconsciousness: An Update*. IWANN. Archived from the original on 2 March 1997. BibTex Archived 2 March 1997 at the Wayback Machine.

- Bach, Joscha (2008). "Seven Principles of Synthetic Intelligence". In Wang, Pei; Goertzel, Ben; Franklin, Stan. *Artificial General Intelligence, 2008: Proceedings of the First AGI Conference*. IOS Press. pp. 63–74. ISBN 978-1-58603-833-5.

- "Robots could demand legal rights". *BBC News*. 21 December 2006. Retrieved 3 February 2011.

- Brooks, Rodney (1990). "Elephants Don't Play Chess" (PDF). *Robotics and Autonomous Systems* **6**: 3–15. doi:10.1016/S0921-8890(05)80025-9. Archived (PDF) from the original on 9 August 2007.

- Brooks, R. A. (1991). "How to build complete creatures rather than isolated cognitive simulators". In VanLehn, K. *Architectures for Intelligence*. Hillsdale, NJ: Lawrence Erlbaum Associates. pp. 225–239.

- Buchanan, Bruce G. (2005). "A (Very) Brief History of Artificial Intelligence" (PDF). *AI Magazine*: 53–60. Archived (PDF) from the original on 26 September 2007.

- Butler, Samuel (13 June 1863). "Darwin among the Machines". Letters to the Editor. *The Press* (Christchurch, New Zealand). Retrieved 16 October 2014 – via Victoria University of Wellington.

- "AI set to exceed human brain power". *CNN*. 26 July 2006. Archived from the original on 19 February 2008.

- Dennett, Daniel (1991). *Consciousness Explained*. The Penguin Press. ISBN 0-7139-9037-6.

- Diamond, David (December 2003). "The Love Machine; Building computers that care". Wired. Archived from the original on 18 May 2008.

- Dowe, D. L.; Hajek, A. R. (1997). "A computational extension to the Turing Test". *Proceedings of the 4th Conference of the Australasian Cognitive Science Society*.

- Dreyfus, Hubert (1972). *What Computers Can't Do*. New York: MIT Press. ISBN 0-06-011082-1.

- Dreyfus, Hubert; Dreyfus, Stuart (1986). *Mind over Machine: The Power of Human Intuition and Expertise in the Era of the Computer*. Oxford, UK: Blackwell. ISBN 0-02-908060-6.

- Dreyfus, Hubert (1992). *What Computers* Still *Can't Do*. New York: MIT Press. ISBN 0-262-54067-3.

- Dyson, George (1998). *Darwin among the Machines*. Allan Lane Science. ISBN 0-7382-0030-1.

- Edelman, Gerald (23 November 2007). "Gerald Edelman – Neural Darwinism and Brain-based Devices". Talking Robots.

- Edelson, Edward (1991). *The Nervous System*. New York: Chelsea House. ISBN 978-0-7910-0464-7.

- Fearn, Nicholas (2007). *The Latest Answers to the Oldest Questions: A Philosophical Adventure with the World's Greatest Thinkers*. New York: Grove Press. ISBN 0-8021-1839-9.

- Gladwell, Malcolm (2005). *Blink*. New York: Little, Brown and Co. ISBN 0-316-17232-4.

- Gödel, Kurt (1951). *Some basic theorems on the foundations of mathematics and their implications*. Gibbs Lecture. In
Feferman, Solomon, ed. (1995). *Kurt Gödel: Collected Works, Vol. III: Unpublished Essays and Lectures*. Oxford University Press. pp. 304–23. ISBN 978-0-19-514722-3.

- Haugeland, John (1985). *Artificial Intelligence: The Very Idea*. Cambridge, Mass.: MIT Press. ISBN 0-262-08153-9.

- Hawkins, Jeff; Blakeslee, Sandra (2005). *On Intelligence*. New York, NY: Owl Books. ISBN 0-8050-7853-3.

- Henderson, Mark (24 April 2007). "Human rights for robots? We're getting carried away". *The Times Online* (London).

- Hernandez-Orallo, Jose (2000). "Beyond the Turing Test". *Journal of Logic, Language and Information* **9** (4): 447–466. doi:10.1023/A:1008367325700.

- Hernandez-Orallo, J.; Dowe, D. L. (2010). "Measuring Universal Intelligence: Towards an Anytime Intelligence Test". *Artificial Intelligence Journal* **174** (18): 1508–1539. doi:10.1016/j.artint.2010.09.006.

- Hinton, G. E. (2007). "Learning multiple layers of representation". *Trends in Cognitive Sciences* **11**: 428–434. doi:10.1016/j.tics.2007.09.004.

- Hofstadter, Douglas (1979). *Gödel, Escher, Bach: an Eternal Golden Braid*. New York, NY: Vintage Books. ISBN 0-394-74502-7.

- Holland, John H. (1975). *Adaptation in Natural and Artificial Systems*. University of Michigan Press. ISBN 0-262-58111-6.

- Howe, J. (November 1994). "Artificial Intelligence at Edinburgh University: a Perspective". Retrieved 30 August 2007.

- Hutter, M. (2012). "One Decade of Universal Artificial Intelligence". *Theoretical Foundations of Artificial General Intelligence*. Atlantis Thinking Machines **4**. doi:10.2991/978-94-91216-62-6_5. ISBN 978-94-91216-61-9.

- James, William (1884). "What is Emotion". *Mind* **9**: 188–205. doi:10.1093/mind/os-IX.34.188. Cited by Tao & Tan 2005.

- Kahneman, Daniel; Slovic, D.; Tversky, Amos (1982). *Judgment under uncertainty: Heuristics and biases*. New York: Cambridge University Press. ISBN 0-521-28414-7.

- Katz, Yarden (1 November 2012). "Noam Chomsky on Where Artificial Intelligence Went Wrong". *The Atlantic*. Retrieved 26 October 2014.

- "Kismet". MIT Artificial Intelligence Laboratory, Humanoid Robotics Group. Retrieved 25 October 2014.

- Koza, John R. (1992). *Genetic Programming (On the Programming of Computers by Means of Natural Selection)*. MIT Press. ISBN 0-262-11170-5.

- Kleine-Cosack, Christian (October 2006). "Recognition and Simulation of Emotions" (PDF). Archived from the original (PDF) on 28 May 2008.

- Kolata, G. (1982). "How can computers get common sense?". *Science* **217** (4566): 1237–1238. doi:10.1126/science.217.4566.1237. PMID 17837639.

- Kumar, Gulshan; Kumar, Krishan (2012). "The Use of Artificial-Intelligence-Based Ensembles for Intrusion Detection: A Review". *Applied Computational Intelligence and Soft Computing* **2012**: 1–20. doi:10.1155/2012/850160.

- Kurzweil, Ray (1999). *The Age of Spiritual Machines*. Penguin Books. ISBN 0-670-88217-8.

- Kurzweil, Ray (2005). *The Singularity is Near*. Penguin Books. ISBN 0-670-03384-7.

- Lakoff, George; Núñez, Rafael E. (2000). *Where Mathematics Comes From: How the Embodied Mind Brings Mathematics into Being*. Basic Books. ISBN 0-465-03771-2.

- Langley, Pat (2011). "The changing science of machine learning". *Machine Learning* **82** (3): 275–279. doi:10.1007/s10994-011-5242-y.

- Law, Diane (June 1994). *Searle, Subsymbolic Functionalism and Synthetic Intelligence* (Technical report). University of Texas at Austin. p. AI94-222. CiteSeerX: 10.1.1.38.8384.

- Legg, Shane; Hutter, Marcus (15 June 2007). *A Collection of Definitions of Intelligence* (Technical report). IDSIA. arXiv:0706.3639. 07-07.

- Lenat, Douglas; Guha, R. V. (1989). *Building Large Knowledge-Based Systems*. Addison-Wesley. ISBN 0-201-51752-3.

- Lighthill, James (1973). "Artificial Intelligence: A General Survey". *Artificial Intelligence: a paper symposium*. Science Research Council.

- Lucas, John (1961). "Minds, Machines and Gödel". In Anderson, A.R. *Minds and Machines*. Archived from the original on 19 August 2007. Retrieved 30 August 2007.

- Lungarella, M.; Metta, G.; Pfeifer, R.; Sandini, G. (2003). "Developmental robotics: a survey". *Connection Science* **15**: 151–190. doi:10.1080/09540090310001655110. CiteSeerX: 10.1.1.83.7615.

- Mahmud, Ashik (June 2015), "Post/Human Beings & Techno-salvation: Exploring Artificial Intelligence in Selected Science Fictions", *Socrates Journal*, doi:10.7910/DVN/VAELLN, retrieved 2015-06-26

- Maker, Meg Houston (2006). "AI@50: AI Past, Present, Future". Dartmouth College. Archived from the original on 8 October 2008. Retrieved 16 October 2008.

- Markoff, John (16 February 2011). "Computer Wins on 'Jeopardy!': Trivial, It's Not". *The New York Times*. Retrieved 25 October 2014.

- McCarthy, John; Minsky, Marvin; Rochester, Nathan; Shannon, Claude (1955). "A Proposal for the Dartmouth Summer Research Project on Artificial Intelligence". Archived from the original on 26 August 2007. Retrieved 30 August 2007..

- McCarthy, John; Hayes, P. J. (1969). "Some philosophical problems from the standpoint of artificial intelligence". *Machine Intelligence* 4: 463–502. Archived from the original on 10 August 2007. Retrieved 30 August 2007.

- McCarthy, John (12 November 2007). "What Is Artificial Intelligence?".

- Minsky, Marvin (1967). *Computation: Finite and Infinite Machines*. Englewood Cliffs, N.J.: Prentice-Hall. ISBN 0-13-165449-7.

- Minsky, Marvin (2006). *The Emotion Machine*. New York, NY: Simon & Schusterl. ISBN 0-7432-7663-9.

- Moravec, Hans (1988). *Mind Children*. Harvard University Press. ISBN 0-674-57616-0.

- Norvig, Peter (25 June 2012). "On Chomsky and the Two Cultures of Statistical Learning". Peter Norvig. Archived from the original on 19 October 2014.

- NRC (United States National Research Council) (1999). "Developments in Artificial Intelligence". *Funding a Revolution: Government Support for Computing Research*. National Academy Press.

- Needham, Joseph (1986). *Science and Civilization in China: Volume 2*. Caves Books Ltd.

- Newell, Allen; Simon, H. A. (1976). "Computer Science as Empirical Inquiry: Symbols and Search". *Communications of the ACM* 19 (3): 113–126. doi:10.1145/360018.360022..

- Nilsson, Nils (1983). "Artificial Intelligence Prepares for 2001" (PDF). *AI Magazine* 1 (1). Presidential Address to the Association for the Advancement of Artificial Intelligence.

- O'Brien, James; Marakas, George (2011). *Management Information Systems* (10th ed.). McGraw-Hill/Irwin. ISBN 978-0-07-337681-3.

- O'Connor, Kathleen Malone (1994). "The alchemical creation of life (takwin) and other concepts of Genesis in medieval Islam". University of Pennsylvania.

- Oudeyer, P-Y. (2010). "On the impact of robotics in behavioral and cognitive sciences: from insect navigation to human cognitive development" (PDF). *IEEE Transactions on Autonomous Mental Development* 2 (1): 2–16. doi:10.1109/tamd.2009.2039057.

- Penrose, Roger (1989). *The Emperor's New Mind: Concerning Computer, Minds and The Laws of Physics*. Oxford University Press. ISBN 0-19-851973-7.

- Picard, Rosalind (1995). *Affective Computing* (PDF) (Technical report). MIT. 321. Lay summary – *Abstract*.

- Poli, R.; Langdon, W. B.; McPhee, N. F. (2008). *A Field Guide to Genetic Programming*. Lulu.com. ISBN 978-1-4092-0073-4 – via gp-field-guide.org.uk.

- Rajani, Sandeep (2011). "Artificial Intelligence – Man or Machine" (PDF). *International Journal of Information Technology and Knowledge Management* 4 (1): 173–176.

- Searle, John (1980). "Minds, Brains and Programs". *Behavioral and Brain Sciences* 3 (3): 417–457. doi:10.1017/S0140525X00005756.

- Searle, John (1999). *Mind, language and society*. New York, NY: Basic Books. ISBN 0-465-04521-9. OCLC 231867665 43689264.

- Shapiro, Stuart C. (1992). "Artificial Intelligence". In Shapiro, Stuart C. *Encyclopedia of Artificial Intelligence* (PDF) (2nd ed.). New York: John Wiley. pp. 54–57. ISBN 0-471-50306-1.

- Simon, H. A. (1965). *The Shape of Automation for Men and Management*. New York: Harper & Row.

- Skillings, Jonathan (3 July 2006). "Getting Machines to Think Like Us". *cnet*. Retrieved 3 February 2011.

- Solomonoff, Ray (1956). *An Inductive Inference Machine* (PDF). Dartmouth Summer Research Conference on Artificial Intelligence – via std.com, pdf scanned copy of the original. Later published as Solomonoff, Ray (1957). "An Inductive Inference Machine". *IRE Convention Record*. Section on Information Theory, part 2. pp. 56–62.

- Tao, Jianhua; Tan, Tieniu (2005). *Affective Computing and Intelligent Interaction*. Affective Computing: A Review. LNCS 3784. Springer. pp. 981–995. doi:10.1007/11573548.

- Tecuci, Gheorghe (March–April 2012). "Artificial Intelligence". *Wiley Interdisciplinary Reviews: Computational Statistics* (Wiley) 4 (2): 168–180. doi:10.1002/wics.200.

- Thro, Ellen (1993). *Robotics: The Marriage of Computers and Machines*. New York: Facts on File. ISBN 978-0-8160-2628-9.

- Turing, Alan (October 1950), "Computing Machinery and Intelligence", *Mind* **LIX** (236): 433–460, doi:10.1093/mind/LIX.236.433, ISSN 0026-4423, retrieved 2008-08-18.

- van der Walt, Christiaan; Bernard, Etienne (2006). "Data characteristics that determine classifier performance" (PDF). Retrieved 5 August 2009.

- Vinge, Vernor (1993). "The Coming Technological Singularity: How to Survive in the Post-Human Era".

- Wason, P. C.; Shapiro, D. (1966). "Reasoning". In Foss, B. M. *New horizons in psychology*. Harmondsworth: Penguin.

- Weizenbaum, Joseph (1976). *Computer Power and Human Reason*. San Francisco: W.H. Freeman & Company. ISBN 0-7167-0464-1.

- Weng, J.; McClelland; Pentland, A.; Sporns, O.; Stockman, I.; Sur, M.; Thelen, E. (2001). "Autonomous mental development by robots and animals" (PDF). *Science* **291**: 599–600. doi:10.1126/science.291.5504.599 – via msu.edu.

2.10.9 Further reading

- TechCast Article Series, John Sagi, Framing Consciousness

- Boden, Margaret, Mind As Machine, Oxford University Press, 2006

- Johnston, John (2008) "The Allure of Machinic Life: Cybernetics, Artificial Life, and the New AI", MIT Press

- Myers, Courtney Boyd ed. (2009). The AI Report. Forbes June 2009

- Serenko, Alexander (2010). "The development of an AI journal ranking based on the revealed preference approach" (PDF). *Journal of Informetrics* **4** (4): 447–459. doi:10.1016/j.joi.2010.04.001.

- Serenko, Alexander; Michael Dohan (2011). "Comparing the expert survey and citation impact journal ranking methods: Example from the field of Artificial Intelligence" (PDF). *Journal of Informetrics* **5** (4): 629–649. doi:10.1016/j.joi.2011.06.002.

- Sun, R. & Bookman, L. (eds.), *Computational Architectures: Integrating Neural and Symbolic Processes*. Kluwer Academic Publishers, Needham, MA. 1994.

- Tom Simonite (29 December 2014). "2014 in Computing: Breakthroughs in Artificial Intelligence". *MIT Technology Review*.

2.10.10 External links

- What Is AI? – An introduction to artificial intelligence by AI founder John McCarthy.

- The Handbook of Artificial Intelligence Volume I by Avron Barr and Edward A. Feigenbaum (Stanford University)

- Artificial Intelligence entry in the *Internet Encyclopedia of Philosophy*

- Logic and Artificial Intelligence entry by Richmond Thomason in the *Stanford Encyclopedia of Philosophy*

- AI at DMOZ

- AITopics – A large directory of links and other resources maintained by the Association for the Advancement of Artificial Intelligence, the leading organization of academic AI researchers.

2.11 Computer architecture

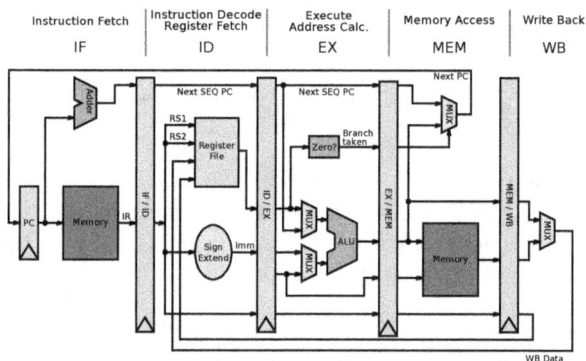

Pipelined implementation of MIPS architecture. Pipelining is a key concept in computer architecture.

In computer engineering and computer science,[1] **computer architecture** is a set of rules and methods that describe the functionality, organization and implementation of computer systems. Some definitions of architecture define it as describing the capabilities and programming model of a computer but not a particular implementation.[2]

In other descriptions computer architecture involves instruction set architecture design, microarchitecture design, logic design, and implementation.[3]

2.11.1 History

The first documented computer architecture was in the correspondence between Charles Babbage and Ada Lovelace, describing the analytical engine. Two other early and important examples were:

- John von Neumann's 1945 paper, First Draft of a Report on the EDVAC, which described an organization of logical elements; and

- Alan Turing's more detailed *Proposed Electronic Calculator* for the Automatic Computing Engine, also 1945 and which cited von Neumann's paper.[4]

The term "architecture" in computer literature can be traced to the work of Lyle R. Johnson, Mohammad Usman Khan and Frederick P. Brooks, Jr., members in 1959 of the Machine Organization department in IBM's main research center. Johnson had the opportunity to write a proprietary research communication about the Stretch, an IBM-developed supercomputer for Los Alamos Scientific Laboratory. To describe the level of detail for discussing the luxuriously embellished computer, he noted that his description of formats, instruction types, hardware parameters, and speed enhancements were at the level of "system architecture" – a term that seemed more useful than "machine organization."

Subsequently, Brooks, a Stretch designer, started Chapter 2 of a book (Planning a Computer System: Project Stretch, ed. W. Buchholz, 1962) by writing,

> Computer architecture, like other architecture, is the art of determining the needs of the user of a structure and then designing to meet those needs as effectively as possible within economic and technological constraints.

Brooks went on to help develop the IBM System/360 (now called the IBM zSeries) line of computers, in which "architecture" became a noun defining "what the user needs to know". Later, computer users came to use the term in many less-explicit ways.

The earliest computer architectures were designed on paper and then directly built into the final hardware form.[5] Later, computer architecture prototypes were physically built in the form of a Transistor–Transistor Logic (TTL) computer—such as the prototypes of the 6800 and the PA-RISC—tested, and tweaked, before committing to the final hardware form. As of the 1990s, new computer architectures are typically "built", tested, and tweaked—inside some other computer architecture in a computer architecture simulator; or inside a FPGA as a soft microprocessor; or both—before committing to the final hardware form.

2.11.2 Subcategories

The discipline of computer architecture has three main subcategories:[6]

1. *Instruction Set Architecture*, or ISA. The ISA defines the machine code that a processor reads and acts upon as well as the word size, memory address modes, processor registers, and data formats.

2. *Microarchitecture*, or *computer organization* describes how a particular processor will implement the ISA.[7] The size of a computer's CPU cache for instance, is an organizational issue that generally has nothing to do with the ISA.

3. *System Design* includes all of the other hardware components within a computing system. These include:

    (a) Data processing other than the CPU, such as direct memory access (DMA)

    (b) Other issues such as virtualization, multiprocessing and software features.

Some architects at companies such as Intel and AMD use finer distinctions:

- Macroarchitecture: architectural layers more abstract than microarchitecture

- Instruction Set Architecture (ISA): as above but without:

    - Assembly ISA: a smart assembler may convert an abstract assembly language common to a group of machines into slightly different machine language for different implementations

- Programmer Visible Macroarchitecture: higher level language tools such as compilers may define a consistent interface or contract to programmers using them, abstracting differences between underlying ISA, UISA, and microarchitectures. E.g. the C, C++, or Java standards define different Programmer Visible Macroarchitecture.

- UISA (Microcode Instruction Set Architecture)—a family of machines with different hardware level microarchitectures may share a common microcode architecture, and hence a UISA.

- Pin Architecture: The hardware functions that a microprocessor should provide to a hardware platform, e.g., the x86 pins A20M, FERR/IGNNE or FLUSH. Also, messages that the processor should emit so that external caches can be invalidated (emptied). Pin architecture functions are more flexible than ISA functions because external hardware can adapt to new encodings, or change from a pin to a message. The term "architecture" fits, because the functions must be provided for compatible systems, even if the detailed method changes.

2.11.3 The Roles

Definition

The purpose is to design a computer that maximizes performance while keeping power consumption in check, costs low relative to the amount of expected performance, and is also very reliable. For this, many aspects are to be considered which includes Instruction Set Design, Functional Organization, Logic Design, and Implementation. The implementation involves Integrated Circuit Design, Packaging, Power, and Cooling. Optimization of the design requires familiarity with Compilers, Operating Systems to Logic Design and Packaging.

Instruction set architecture

Main article: Instruction set architecture

An instruction set architecture (ISA) is the interface between the computer's software and hardware and also can be viewed as the programmer's view of the machine. Computers do not understand high level languages which have few, if any, language elements that translate directly into a machine's native opcodes. A processor only understands instructions encoded in some numerical fashion, usually as binary numbers. Software tools, such as compilers, translate high level languages, such as C, into instructions.

Besides instructions, the ISA defines items in the computer that are available to a program—e.g. data types, registers, addressing modes, and memory. Instructions locate operands with Register indexes (or names) and memory addressing modes.

The ISA of a computer is usually described in a small book or pamphlet, which describes how the instructions are encoded. Also, it may define short (vaguely) mnemonic names for the instructions. The names can be recognized by a software development tool called an assembler. An assembler is a computer program that translates a human-readable form of the ISA into a computer-readable form. Disassemblers are also widely available, usually in debuggers, software programs to isolate and correct malfunctions in binary computer programs.

ISAs vary in quality and completeness. A good ISA compromises between programmer convenience (more operations can be better), cost of the computer to interpret the instructions (cheaper is better), speed of the computer (faster is better), and size of the code (smaller is better). For example, a single-instruction ISA is possible, inexpensive, and fast, (e.g., subtract and jump if zero. It was actually used in the SSEM), but it was not convenient or helpful to make programs small. Memory organization defines how instructions interact with the memory, and also how different parts of memory interact with each other.

During design emulation software can run programs written in a proposed instruction set. Modern emulators running tests may measure time, energy consumption, and compiled code size to determine if a particular instruction set architecture is meeting its goals.

Computer organization

Main article: Microarchitecture

Computer organization helps optimize performance-based products. For example, software engineers need to know the processing ability of processors. They may need to optimize software in order to gain the most performance at the least expense. This can require quite detailed analysis of the computer organization. For example, in a multimedia decoder, the designers might need to arrange for most data to be processed in the fastest data path.

Computer organization also helps plan the selection of a processor for a particular project. Multimedia projects may need very rapid data access, while supervisory software may need fast interrupts. Sometimes certain tasks need additional components as well. For example, a computer capable of virtualization needs virtual memory hardware so that the memory of different simulated computers can be kept separated. Computer organization and features also affect power consumption and processor cost.

Implementation

Once an instruction set and micro-architecture are described, a practical machine must be designed. This de-

2.11. COMPUTER ARCHITECTURE

sign process is called the *implementation*. Implementation is usually not considered architectural definition, but rather hardware design engineering. Implementation can be further broken down into several (not fully distinct) steps:

- **Logic Implementation** designs the blocks defined in the micro-architecture at (primarily) the register-transfer level and logic gate level.

- **Circuit Implementation** does transistor-level designs of basic elements (gates, multiplexers, latches etc.) as well as of some larger blocks (ALUs, caches etc.) that may be implemented at this level, or even (partly) at the physical level, for performance reasons.

- **Physical Implementation** draws physical circuits. The different circuit components are placed in a chip floorplan or on a board and the wires connecting them are routed.

- **Design Validation** tests the computer as a whole to see if it works in all situations and all timings. Once implementation starts, the first design validations are simulations using logic emulators. However, this is usually too slow to run realistic programs. So, after making corrections, prototypes are constructed using Field-Programmable Gate-Arrays (FPGAs). Many hobby projects stop at this stage. The final step is to test prototype integrated circuits. Integrated circuits may require several redesigns to fix problems.

For CPUs, the entire implementation process is often called CPU design.

2.11.4 Design goals

The exact form of a computer system depends on the constraints and goals. Computer architectures usually trade off standards, power versus performance, cost, memory capacity, latency (latency is the amount of time that it takes for information from one node to travel to the source) and throughput. Sometimes other considerations, such as features, size, weight, reliability, and expandability are also factors.

The most common scheme does an in depth power analysis and figures out how to keep power consumption low, while maintaining adequate performance.

Performance

Modern computer performance is often described in IPC (instructions per cycle). This measures the efficiency of the architecture at any clock speed. Since a faster clock can make a faster computer, this is a useful, widely applicable measurement. Historic computers had IPC counts as low as 0.1 (See instructions per second). Simple modern processors easily reach near 1. Superscalar processors may reach three to five by executing several instructions per clock cycle. Multicore and vector processing CPUs can multiply this further by acting on a lot of data per instruction, which have several CPUs executing in parallel.

Counting machine language instructions would be misleading because they can do varying amounts of work in different ISAs. The "instruction" in the standard measurements is not a count of the ISA's actual machine language instructions, but a historical unit of measurement, usually based on the speed of the VAX computer architecture.

Historically, many people measured a computer's speed by the clock rate (usually in MHz or GHz). This refers to the cycles per second of the main clock of the CPU. However, this metric is somewhat misleading, as a machine with a higher clock rate may not necessarily have greater performance. As a result, manufacturers have moved away from clock speed as a measure of performance.

Other factors influence speed, such as the mix of functional units, bus speeds, available memory, and the type and order of instructions in the programs being run.

In a typical home computer, the simplest, most reliable way to speed performance is usually to add random access memory (RAM). More RAM increases the likelihood that needed data or a program is in RAM—so the system is less likely to need to move memory data from the disk. The disk is often ten thousand times slower than RAM because it has mechanical parts that must move to access its data.

There are two main types of speed: latency and throughput. Latency is the time between the start of a process and its completion. Throughput is the amount of work done per unit time. Interrupt latency is the guaranteed maximum response time of the system to an electronic event (*e.g.* when the disk drive finishes moving some data).

Performance is affected by a very wide range of design choices — for example, pipelining a processor usually makes latency worse (slower) but makes throughput better. Computers that control machinery usually need low interrupt latencies. These computers operate in a real-time environment and fail if an operation is not completed in a specified amount of time. For example, computer-controlled anti-lock brakes must begin braking within a predictable, short time after the brake pedal is sensed.

The performance of a computer can be measured using other metrics, depending upon its application domain. A system may be CPU bound (as in numerical calculation), I/O bound (as in a web hosted application) or memory bound (as in video editing). Power consumption has become important in servers, laptops, and mobile devices.

Benchmarking tries to take all these factors into account by measuring the time a computer takes to run through a series of test programs. Although benchmarking shows strengths, it may not help one to choose a computer. Often the measured machines split on different measures. For example, one system might handle scientific applications quickly, while another might render popular video games more smoothly. Furthermore, designers may target and add special features to their products, through hardware or software, that permit a specific benchmark to execute quickly but don't offer similar advantages to general tasks.

Power consumption

Main article: low-power electronics

Power consumption is another measurement that is important in modern computers. Power efficiency can often be traded for speed or lower cost. The typical measurement in this case is MIPS/W (millions of instructions per second per watt).

Modern circuits have less power per transistor as the number of transistors per chip grows. Therefore, power efficiency has increased in importance. Recent processor designs such as Intel's Haswell (microarchitecture), put more emphasis on increasing power efficiency. Also, in the world of embedded computing, power efficiency has long been and remains an important goal next to throughput and latency.

Shifts in consumer demand

Increases in publicly-released clock-speeds have relatively grown slowly over the past few years, with respect to vast leaps in power consumption reduction and miniaturization demand. Compared to the exponential growth within the same preceding time frame, processing speeds have steady increased between 3 GHz (2006)–4 GHz (2014). A strong demand fueled by mobile technology has shifted focus into improving processing to achieve longer battery life and reductions in size. Significant reductions in power consumption, as much as 50% reported by Intel in their release of the Haswell (microarchitecture); where they dropped their target down to 10-20 watts vs 30-40 watts in the previous model. In addition, overall performance has improved through leveraging multi-core parallelism operations that can accomplish more responsive and efficient 'system-wide' through-put with less single-core cycles. By dividing the work among multiple cores, system architectures are achieving much greater 'perceived performance' without the requiring 8-10 GHz processors.

2.11.5 See also

- Comparison of CPU architectures
- Computer hardware
- CPU design
- Floating point
- Harvard architecture
- Influence of the IBM PC on the personal computer market
- Orthogonal instruction set
- Software architecture
- von Neumann architecture

2.11.6 Notes

- John L. Hennessy and David Patterson (2006). *Computer Architecture: A Quantitative Approach* (Fourth ed.). Morgan Kaufmann. ISBN 978-0-12-370490-0.

- Barton, Robert S., "Functional Design of Computers", *Communications of the ACM* 4(9): 405 (1961).

- Barton, Robert S., "A New Approach to the Functional Design of a Digital Computer", *Proceedings of the Western Joint Computer Conference*, May 1961, pp. 393–396. About the design of the Burroughs B5000 computer.

- Bell, C. Gordon; and Newell, Allen (1971). "Computer Structures: Readings and Examples", McGraw-Hill.

- Blaauw, G.A., and Brooks, F.P., Jr., "The Structure of System/360, Part I-Outline of the Logical Structure", *IBM Systems Journal*, vol. 3, no. 2, pp. 119–135, 1964.

- Tanenbaum, Andrew S. (1979). *Structured Computer Organization*. Englewood Cliffs, New Jersey: Prentice-Hall. ISBN 0-13-148521-0.

2.11.7 References

[1] *Curriculum Guidelines for Undergraduate Degree Programs in Computer Engineering* (PDF). Association for Computing Machinery. 2004. p. 60. Computer architecture is a key component of computer engineering and the practicing computer engineer should have a practical understanding of this topic...

[2] Clements, Alan. *Principles of Computer Hardware* (Fourth ed.). p. 1. Architecture describes the internal organization of a computer in an abstract way; that is, it defines the capabilities of the computer and its programming model. You can have two computers that have been constructed in different ways with different technologies but with the same architecture.

[3] Hennessy, John; Patterson, David. *Computer Architecture: A Quantitative Approach* (Fifth ed.). p. 11. This task has many aspects, including instruction set design, functional organization, logic design, and implementation.

[4] Reproduced in B. J. Copeland (Ed.), "Alan Turing's Automatic Computing Engine", OUP, 2005, pp. 369-454.

[5] ACE underwent seven paper designs in one year, before a prototype was initiated in 1948. [B. J. Copeland (Ed.), "Alan Turing's Automatic Computing Engine", OUP, 2005, p. 57]

[6] John L. Hennessy and David A. Patterson. *Computer Architecture: A Quantitative Approach* (Third ed.). Morgan Kaufmann Publishers.

[7] Laplante, Phillip A. (2001). *Dictionary of Computer Science, Engineering, and Technology.* CRC Press. pp. 94–95. ISBN 0-8493-2691-5.

The motherboard used in a typical personal computer. The result of computer engineering efforts.

2.11.8 External links

- ISCA: Proceedings of the International Symposium on Computer Architecture
- Micro: IEEE/ACM International Symposium on Microarchitecture
- HPCA: International Symposium on High Performance Computer Architecture
- ASPLOS: International Conference on Architectural Support for Programming Languages and Operating Systems
- ACM Transactions on Computer Systems
- ACM Transactions on Architecture and Code Optimization
- IEEE Transactions on Computers
- The von Neumann Architecture of Computer Systems

2.12 Computer engineering

"Hardware engineering" redirects here. For engineering of other types of hardware, see Mechanical engineering.

Computer engineering is a discipline that integrates several fields of electrical engineering and computer science required to develop computer hardware and software.[1] Computer engineers usually have training in electronic engineering (or electrical engineering), software design, and hardware-software integration instead of only software engineering or electronic engineering. Computer engineers are involved in many hardware and software aspects of computing, from the design of individual microcontrollers, microprocessors, personal computers, and supercomputers, to circuit design. This field of engineering not only focuses on how computer systems themselves work, but also how they integrate into the larger picture.[2]

Usual tasks involving computer engineers include writing software and firmware for embedded microcontrollers, designing VLSI chips, designing analog sensors, designing mixed signal circuit boards, and designing operating systems. Computer engineers are also suited for robotics research, which relies heavily on using digital systems to control and monitor electrical systems like motors, communications, and sensors.

In many institutions, computer engineering students are allowed to choose areas of in-depth study in their junior and senior year, because the full breadth of knowledge used in the design and application of computers is beyond the scope of an undergraduate degree. Other institutions may require engineering students to complete one year of General Engineering before declaring computer engineering as their primary focus.[3][4][5]

2.12.1 History

The first computer engineering degree program in the United States was established at Case Western Reserve University in 1972. As of October 2004, there were 170 ABET-accredited computer engineering programs in the US.[6] In Europe, accreditation of computer engineering schools is done by a variety of agencies part of the EQANIE network. Due to increasing job requirements for engineers who can concurrently design hardware, software, firmware, and manage all forms of computer systems used in industry, some tertiary institutions around the world offer a bachelor's degree generally called computer engineering. Both computer engineering and electronic engineering programs include analog and digital circuit design in their curriculum. As with most engineering disciplines, having a sound knowledge of mathematics and science is necessary for computer engineers.

2.12.2 Work

There are two major specialties in computer engineering: software and hardware.

Computer software engineering

Main article: Software engineering

Computer software engineers develop, design, and test software. Some software engineers design, construct, and maintain computer programs for companies. Some set up networks such as "intranets" for companies. Others make or install new software or upgrade computer systems. Computer software engineers can also work in application design. This involves designing or coding new programs and applications to meet the needs of a business or individual. Computer software engineers can also work as freelancers and sell their software products/applications to an enterprise/individual.[7]

Computer hardware engineering

Most computer hardware engineers research, develop, design, and test various computer equipment. This can range from circuit boards and microprocessors to routers. Some update existing computer equipment to be more efficient and work with newer software. Most computer hardware engineers work in research laboratories and high-tech manufacturing firms. Some also work for the federal government. According to BLS, 95% of computer hardware engineers work in metropolitan areas. They generally work full-time. Approximately 33% of their work requires more than 40 hours a week. The median salary for employed qualified computer hardware engineers (2012) was $100,920 per year or $48.52 per hour. Computer hardware engineers held 83,300 jobs in 2012.[8]

2.12.3 Specialty areas

There are many specialty areas in the field of computer engineering.

Coding, cryptography, and information protection

Main article: Information security

Computer engineers work in Coding, Cryptography, and Information Protection to develop new methods for protecting various information, such as digital images and music, fragmentation, copyright infringement and other forms of tampering. Examples include work on wireless communications, multi-antenna systems, optical transmission, and digital watermarking.[9]

Communications and wireless networks

Main articles: Communications networks and Wireless network

Those focusing on communications and wireless networks, work advancements in telecommunications systems and networks (especially wireless networks), modulation and error-control coding, and information theory. High-speed network design, interference suppression and modulation, design and analysis of fault-tolerant system, and storage and transmission schemes are all a part of this specialty.[9]

Compilers and operating systems

Main articles: Compiler and Operating system

This specialty focuses on compilers and operating systems design and development. Engineers in this field develop new operating system architecture, program analysis techniques, and new techniques to assure quality. Examples of work in this field includes post-link-time code transformation algorithm development and new operating system development.[9]

Computational science and engineering

Main article: Computational science and engineering

Computational Science and Engineering is a relatively new discipline. According to the Sloan Career Cornerstone Center, individuals working in this area, "computational methods are applied to formulate and solve complex mathematical problems in engineering and the physical and the social sciences. Examples include aircraft design, the plasma processing of nanometer features on semiconductor wafers, VLSI circuit design, radar detection systems, ion transport through biological channels, and much more".[9]

Computer networks, mobile computing, and distributed systems

Main articles: Computer network, Mobile computing and Distributed computing

In this specialty, engineers build integrated environments for computing, communications, and information access. Examples include shared-channel wireless networks, adaptive resource management in various systems, and improving the quality of service in mobile and ATM environments. Some other examples include work on wireless network systems and fast Ethernet cluster wired systems.[9]

Computer systems: architecture, parallel processing, and dependability

Main articles: Computer architecture, Parallel processing and Dependability

Engineers working in computer systems work on research projects that allow for reliable, secure, and high-performance computer systems. Projects such as designing processors for multi-threading and parallel processing are included in this field. Other examples of work in this field include development of new theories, algorithms, and other tools that add performance to computer systems.[9]

Computer vision and robotics

Main articles: Computer vision and Robotics

In this specialty, computer engineers focus on developing visual sensing technology to sense an environment, representation of an environment, and manipulation of the environment. The gathered three-dimensional information is then implemented to perform a variety of tasks. These include, improved human modeling, image communication, and human-computer interfaces, as well as devices such as special-purpose cameras with versatile vision sensors.[9]

Embedded systems

Examples of devices that use embedded systems.

Main article: Embedded systems

Individuals working in this area design technology for enhancing the speed, reliability, and performance of systems. Embedded systems are found in many devices from a small FM radio to the space shuttle. According to the Sloan Cornerstone Career Center, ongoing developments in embedded systems include "automated vehicles and equipment to conduct search and rescue, automated transportation systems, and human-robot coordination to repair equipment in space."[9]

Integrated circuits, VLSI design, testing and CAD

Main articles: Integrated circuit and Very-large-scale integration

This specialty of computer engineering requires adequate knowledge of electronics and electrical systems. Engineers working in this area work on enhancing the speed, reliability, and energy efficiency of next-generation very-large-scale integrated (VLSI) circuits and microsystems. An example of this specialty is work done on reducing the power consumption of VLSI algorithms and architecture.[9]

Signal, image and speech processing

Main articles: Signal processing, Image processing and Speech processing

Computer engineers in this area develop improvements in human–computer interaction, including speech recognition and synthesis, medical and scientific imaging, or communications systems. Other work in this area includes computer vision development such as recognition of human facial features.[9]

2.12.4 Education

Most entry-level computer engineering jobs require at least a bachelor's degree in computer engineering. Sometimes a degree in electronic engineering is accepted, due to the similarity of the two fields. Because hardware engineers commonly work with computer software systems, a background in computer programming usually is needed. According to BLS, "a computer engineering major is similar to electrical engineering but with some computer science courses added to the curriculum".[8] Some large firms or specialized jobs require a master's degree. It is also important for computer engineers to keep up with rapid advances in technology. Therefore, many continue learning throughout their careers.

2.12.5 Job outlook in the United States

Computer software engineering

According to the U.S. Bureau of Labor Statistics (BLS), "computer applications software engineers and computer systems software engineers are projected to be among the faster than average growing occupations from 2012 to 2022".[7] BLS reports an expected growth of 22% for software developers from 2012 to 2022 [10] (down from the 30% 2010 to 2020 estimate).[11] In addition, growing concerns over cyber security add up to put computer software engineering high above the average rate of increase for all fields. However, some of the work will be outsourced in foreign countries. Due to this, job growth will not be as fast as during the last decade, as jobs that would have gone to computer software engineers in the United States would instead go to computer software engineers in countries such as India.[7]

Computer hardware engineering

According to the BLS, "employment of computer hardware engineers is expected to only increase 7% from 2012 to 2022 ("Slower than average" in their own words when compared to other occupations)[12] and is down from 9 percent in the BLS 2010 to 2020 estimate." Today, computer hardware is somehow equal to Electronic and Computer Engineering (ECE) and has divided to many subcategories, the most significant of them is Embedded system design.[8]

2.12.6 Similar occupations and field

- Computer programming
- Electrical engineering
- Software development
- Systems analyst

2.12.7 References

[1] IEEE Computer Society; ACM (December 12, 2004). *Computer Engineering 2004: Curriculum Guidelines for Undergraduate Degree Programs in Computer Engineering* (PDF). p. iii. Retrieved December 17, 2012. Computer System engineering has traditionally been viewed as a combination of both electronic engineering (EE) and computer science (CS).

[2] Trinity College Dublin. "What is Computer System Engineering". Retrieved April 21, 2006., "Computer engineers need not only to understand how computer systems themselves work, but also how they integrate into the larger picture. Consider the car. A modern car contains many separate computer systems for controlling such things as the engine timing, the brakes and the air bags. To be able to design and implement such a car, the computer engineer needs a broad theoretical understanding of all these various subsystems & how they interact.

[3] "Changing Majors @ Clemson". Clemson University. Retrieved September 20, 2011.

[4] "Declaring a College of Engineering Major". University of Arkansas. Retrieved September 20, 2011.

[5] "Degree Requirements". Carnegie Mellon University. Retrieved September 20, 2011.

[6] IEEE Computer Society; ACM (December 12, 2004). *Computer Engineering 2004: Curriculum Guidelines for Undergraduate Degree Programs in Computer Engineering* (PDF). p. 7. Retrieved April 21, 2006. In the United States, the first computer engineering program accredited by ABET (formerly the Accreditation Board for Engineering and Technology) was at Case Western Reserve University in 1972. As of October 2004, ABET has accredited over 170 computer engineering or similarly named programs.

[7] "Computer Software Engineer". Bureau of Labor Statistics. March 19, 2010. Archived from the original on July 26, 2013. Retrieved July 20, 2012.

[8] "Computer Hardware Engineers". Bureau of Labor Statistics. January 8, 2014. Retrieved July 20, 2012.

[9] "Computer Engineering Overview" (PDF). Sloan Career Cornerstone Center. Retrieved July 20, 2012.

[10] http://www.bls.gov/ooh/computer-and-information-technology/software-developers.htm Retrieved 10/01/2014

[11] "Software Developers". Bureau of Labor Statistics. January 8, 2014. Retrieved July 21, 2012.

[12] http://www.bls.gov/ooh/architecture-and-engineering/computer-hardware-engineers.htm Retrieved 10/01/2014

2.13 Computer performance

Computer performance is characterized by the amount of useful work accomplished by a computer system or computer network compared to the time and resources used. Depending on the context, high computer performance may involve one or more of the following:

- Short response time for a given piece of work
- High throughput (rate of processing work)
- Low utilization of computing resource(s)
- High availability of the computing system or application
- Fast (or highly compact) data compression and decompression
- High bandwidth
- Short data transmission time

2.13.1 Technical and non-technical definitions

The performance of any computer system can be evaluated in measurable, technical terms, using one or more of the metrics listed above. This way the performance can be

- Compared relative to other systems or the same system before/after changes
- In absolute terms, e.g. for fulfilling a contractual obligation

Whilst the above definition relates to a scientific, technical approach, the following definition given by Arnold Allen would be useful for a non-technical audience:

The word performance *in computer performance means the same thing that performance means in other contexts, that is, it means "How well is the computer doing the work it is supposed to do?"*[1]

As an aspect of software quality

Computer software performance, particularly software application response time, is an aspect of software quality that is important in human–computer interactions.

2.13.2 Performance engineering

Performance engineering within systems engineering, encompasses the set of roles, skills, activities, practices, tools, and deliverables applied at every phase of the systems development life cycle which ensures that a solution will be designed, implemented, and operationally supported to meet the performance requirements defined for the solution.

Performance engineering continuously deals with trade-offs between types of performance. Occasionally a CPU designer can find a way to make a CPU with better overall performance by improving one of the aspects of performance, presented below, without sacrificing the CPU's performance in other areas. For example, building the CPU out of better, faster transistors.

However, sometimes pushing one type of performance to an extreme leads to a CPU with worse overall performance, because other important aspects were sacrificed to get one impressive-looking number, for example, the chip's clock rate (see the megahertz myth).

Application performance engineering

Main article: Application performance engineering

Application Performance Engineering (APE) is a specific methodology within performance engineering designed to meet the challenges associated with application performance in increasingly distributed mobile, cloud and terrestrial IT environments. It includes the roles, skills, activities, practices, tools and deliverables applied at every phase of the application lifecycle that ensure an application will be designed, implemented and operationally supported to meet non-functional performance requirements.

2.13.3 Aspects of performance

Computer performance metrics (things to measure) include availability, response time, channel capacity, latency, completion time, service time, bandwidth, throughput, relative efficiency, scalability, performance per watt, compression ratio, instruction path length and speed up. CPU benchmarks are available.[2]

Availability

Main article: Availability

Availability of a system is typically measured as a factor of its reliability - as reliability increases, so does availability (that is, less downtime). Availability of a system may also be increased by the strategy of focusing on increasing testability and maintainability and not on reliability. Improving maintainability is generally easier than reliability. Maintainability estimates (Repair rates) are also generally more accurate. However, because the uncertainties in the reliability estimates are in most cases very large, it is likely to dominate the availability (prediction uncertainty) problem, even while maintainability levels are very high.

Response time

Main article: Response time (technology)

Response time is the total amount of time it takes to respond to a request for service. In computing, that service can be any unit of work from a simple disk IO to loading a complex web page. The response time is the sum of three numbers:[3]

- Service time - How long it takes to do the work requested.

- Wait time - How long the request has to wait for requests queued ahead of it before it gets to run.

- Transmission time – How long it takes to move the request to the computer doing the work and the response back to the requestor.

Processing speed

Main articles: Instructions per second and FLOPS

Most consumers pick a computer architecture (normally Intel IA32 architecture) to be able to run a large base of pre-existing, pre-compiled software. Being relatively uninformed on computer benchmarks, some of them pick a particular CPU based on operating frequency (see megahertz myth).

Some system designers building parallel computers pick CPUs based on the speed per dollar.

Channel capacity

Main article: Channel capacity

Channel capacity is the tightest upper bound on the rate of information that can be reliably transmitted over a communications channel. By the noisy-channel coding theorem, the channel capacity of a given channel is the limiting information rate (in units of information per unit time) that can be achieved with arbitrarily small error probability.[4][5]

Information theory, developed by Claude E. Shannon during World War II, defines the notion of channel capacity and provides a mathematical model by which one can compute it. The key result states that the capacity of the channel, as defined above, is given by the maximum of the mutual information between the input and output of the channel, where the maximization is with respect to the input distribution.[6]

Latency

Main article: Latency (engineering)

Latency is a time delay between the cause and the effect of some physical change in the system being observed. Latency is a result of the limited velocity with which any physical interaction can take place. This velocity is always lower or equal to speed of light. Therefore, every physical system that has spatial dimensions different from zero will experience some sort of latency.

The precise definition of latency depends on the system being observed and the nature of stimulation. In communications, the lower limit of latency is determined by the medium being used for communications. In reliable two-way communication systems, latency limits the maximum rate that information can be transmitted, as there is often a limit on the amount of information that is "in-flight" at any one moment. In the field of human-machine interaction, perceptible latency (delay between what the user commands and when the computer provides the results) has a strong effect on user satisfaction and usability.

Computers run sets of instructions called a process. In operating systems, the execution of the process can be postponed if other processes are also executing. In addition, the operating system can schedule when to perform the action that the process is commanding. For example, suppose a process commands that a computer card's voltage output be set high-low-high-low and so on at a rate of 1000 Hz. The operating system may choose to adjust the scheduling of each transition (high-low or low-high) based on an internal clock. The latency is the delay between the process instruction commanding the transition and the hardware actually transitioning the voltage from high to low or low to high.

System designers building real-time computing systems want to guarantee worst-case response. That is easier to do when the CPU has low interrupt latency and when it has deterministic response.

Bandwidth

Main article: Bandwidth (computing)

In computer networking, bandwidth is a measurement of bit-rate of available or consumed data communication resources, expressed in bits per second or multiples of it (bit/s, kbit/s, Mbit/s, Gbit/s, etc.).

Bandwidth sometimes defines the net bit rate (aka. peak bit rate, information rate, or physical layer useful bit rate), channel capacity, or the maximum throughput of a logical or physical communication path in a digital communication system. For example, bandwidth tests measure the maximum throughput of a computer network. The reason for this usage is that according to Hartley's law, the maximum data rate of a physical communication link is proportional to its bandwidth in hertz, which is sometimes called frequency bandwidth, spectral bandwidth, RF bandwidth, signal bandwidth or analog bandwidth.

Throughput

Main article: Throughput

In general terms, throughput is the rate of production or the rate at which something can be processed.

In communication networks, throughput is essentially synonymous to digital bandwidth consumption. In wireless networks or cellular systems, the system spectral efficiency in bit/s/Hz/area unit, bit/s/Hz/site or bit/s/Hz/cell, is the maximum system throughput (aggregate throughput) divided by the analog bandwidth and some measure of the system coverage area.

In integrated circuits, often a block in a data flow diagram has a single input and a single output, and operate on discrete packets of information. Examples of such blocks are FFT modules or binary multipliers. Because the units of throughput are the reciprocal of the unit for propagation delay, which is 'seconds per message' or 'seconds per output', throughput can be used to relate a computational device performing a dedicated function such as an ASIC or embedded processor to a communications channel, simplifying system analysis.

Relative efficiency

Main article: Relative efficiency

Scalability

Main article: Scalability

Scalability is the ability of a system, network, or process to handle a growing amount of work in a capable manner or its ability to be enlarged to accommodate that growth

Power consumption

The amount of electricity used by the computer. This becomes especially important for systems with limited power sources such as solar, batteries, human power.

Performance per watt Main article: Performance per watt

System designers building parallel computers, such as Google's hardware, pick CPUs based on their speed per watt of power, because the cost of powering the CPU outweighs the cost of the CPU itself.[7]

Compression ratio

Main article: Data compression

Compression is useful because it helps reduce resource usage, such as data storage space or transmission capacity. Because compressed data must be decompressed to use, this extra processing imposes computational or other costs through decompression; this situation is far from being a free lunch. Data compression is subject to a space–time complexity trade-off.

Size and weight

This is an important performance feature of mobile systems, from the smart phones you keep in your pocket to the portable embedded systems in a spacecraft.

Environmental impact

Further information: Green computing

The effect of a computer or computers on the environment, during manufacturing and recycling as well as during use. Measurements are taken with the objectives of reducing waste, reducing hazardous materials, and minimizing a computer's ecological footprint.

2.13.4 Benchmarks

Main article: Benchmark (computing)

Because there are so many programs to test a CPU on all aspects of performance, benchmarks were developed.

The most famous benchmarks are the SPECint and SPECfp benchmarks developed by Standard Performance Evaluation Corporation and the ConsumerMark benchmark developed by the Embedded Microprocessor Benchmark Consortium EEMBC.

2.13.5 Software performance testing

Main article: Software performance testing

In software engineering, performance testing is in general testing performed to determine how a system performs in terms of responsiveness and stability under a particular workload. It can also serve to investigate, measure, validate or verify other quality attributes of the system, such as scalability, reliability and resource usage.

Performance testing is a subset of performance engineering, an emerging computer science practice which strives to build performance into the implementation, design and architecture of a system.

Profiling (performance analysis)

Main article: Profiling (computer programming)

In software engineering, profiling ("program profiling", "software profiling") is a form of dynamic program analysis that measures, for example, the space (memory) or time complexity of a program, the usage of particular instructions, or frequency and duration of function calls. The most common use of profiling information is to aid program optimization.

Profiling is achieved by instrumenting either the program source code or its binary executable form using a tool called a *profiler* (or *code profiler*). A number of different techniques may be used by profilers, such as event-based, statistical, instrumented, and simulation methods.

2.13.6 Performance tuning

Main article: Performance tuning

Performance tuning is the improvement of system performance. This is typically a computer application, but the same methods can be applied to economic markets, bureaucracies or other complex systems. The motivation for such activity is called a performance problem, which can be real or anticipated. Most systems will respond to increased load with some degree of decreasing performance. A system's ability to accept a higher load is called scalability, and modifying a system to handle a higher load is synonymous to performance tuning.

Systematic tuning follows these steps:

1. Assess the problem and establish numeric values that categorize acceptable behavior.
2. Measure the performance of the system before modification.
3. Identify the part of the system that is critical for improving the performance. This is called the bottleneck.
4. Modify that part of the system to remove the bottleneck.
5. Measure the performance of the system after modification.
6. If the modification makes the performance better, adopt it. If the modification makes the performance worse, put it back to the way it was.

2.13.7 Perceived performance

Main article: Perceived performance

Perceived performance, in computer engineering, refers to how quickly a software feature appears to perform its task. The concept applies mainly to user acceptance aspects.

2.13. COMPUTER PERFORMANCE

The amount of time an application takes to start up, or a file to download, is not made faster by showing a startup screen (see Splash screen) or a file progress dialog box. However, it satisfies some human needs: it appears faster to the user as well as providing a visual cue to let them know the system is handling their request.

In most cases, increasing real performance increases perceived performance, but when real performance cannot be increased due to physical limitations, techniques can be used to increase perceived performance at the cost of marginally decreasing real performance.

2.13.8 Performance Equation

The total amount of time (**t**) required to execute a particular benchmark program is

$t = N * C/f$, or equivalently

$P = I * f/N$ [8]

where

- **P** = 1/t is "the performance" in terms of time-to-execute
- **N** is the number of instructions actually executed (the instruction path length). The code density of the instruction set strongly affects N. The value of N can either be determined **exactly** by using an instruction set simulator (if available) or by estimation—itself based partly on estimated or actual frequency distribution of input variables and by examining generated machine code from an HLL compiler. It cannot be determined from the number of lines of HLL source code. N is not affected by other processes running on the same processor. The significant point here is that hardware normally does not keep track of (or at least make easily available) a value of N for executed programs. The value can therefore only be accurately determined by instruction set simulation, which is rarely practiced.
- **f** is the clock frequency in cycles per second.
- **C** = $1/I$ is the average cycles per instruction (CPI) for this benchmark.
- **I** = $1/C$ is the average instructions per cycle (IPC) for this benchmark.

Even on one machine, a different compiler or the same compiler with different compiler optimization switches can change N and CPI—the benchmark executes faster if the new compiler can improve N or C without making the other worse, but often there is a trade-off between them—is it better, for example, to use a few complicated instructions that take a long time to execute, or to use instructions that execute very quickly, although it takes more of them to execute the benchmark?

A CPU designer is often required to implement a particular instruction set, and so cannot change N. Sometimes a designer focuses on improving performance by making significant improvements in f (with techniques such as deeper pipelines and faster caches), while (hopefully) not sacrificing too much C—leading to a speed-demon CPU design. Sometimes a designer focuses on improving performance by making significant improvements in CPI (with techniques such as out-of-order execution, superscalar CPUs, larger caches, caches with improved hit rates, improved branch prediction, speculative execution, etc.), while (hopefully) not sacrificing too much clock frequency—leading to a brainiac CPU design.[9] For a given instruction set (and therefore fixed N) and semiconductor process, the maximum single-thread performance (1/t) requires a balance between brainiac techniques and speedracer techniques.[8]

2.13.9 See also

- Algorithmic efficiency
- Computer performance by orders of magnitude
- Network performance
- Optimization (computer science)
- RAM update rate
- Complete instruction set

2.13.10 References

[1] Computer Performance Analysis with Mathematica by Arnold O. Allen, Academic Press, 1994. *$1.1 Introduction, pg 1.*

[2] *Measuring Program Similarity: Experiments with SPEC CPU Benchmark Suites*, CiteSeerX: 10.1.1.123.501

[3] Wescott, Bob (2013). *The Every Computer Performance Book, Chapter 3: Useful laws.* CreateSpace. ISBN 1482657759.

[4] Saleem Bhatti. "Channel capacity". *Lecture notes for M.Sc. Data Communication Networks and Distributed Systems D51 -- Basic Communications and Networks.*

[5] Jim Lesurf. "Signals look like noise!". *Information and Measurement, 2nd ed.*

[6] Thomas M. Cover, Joy A. Thomas (2006). *Elements of Information Theory*. John Wiley & Sons, New York.

[7]

[8] Paul DeMone. "The Incredible Shrinking CPU". 2004.

[9] "Brainiacs, Speed Demons, and Farewell" by Linley Gwennap 1999

2.14 Computer graphics (computer science)

This article is about the scientific discipline of computer graphics. For other uses see Computer graphics (disambiguation).
Computer graphics is a sub-field of computer science

A modern rendering of the Utah teapot, an iconic model in 3D computer graphics created by Martin Newell in 1975.

which studies methods for digitally synthesizing and manipulating visual content. Although the term often refers to the study of three-dimensional computer graphics, it also encompasses two-dimensional graphics and image processing.

2.14.1 Overview

Computer graphics studies the manipulation of visual and geometric information using computational techniques. It focuses on the *mathematical* and *computational* foundations of image generation and processing rather than purely aesthetic issues. Computer graphics is often differentiated from the field of visualization, although the two fields have many similarities.

Connected studies include:

- Applied mathematics

- Computational geometry
- Computational topology
- Computer vision
- Image processing
- Information visualization
- Scientific visualization

Applications of computer graphics include:

- Digital art
- Special effects
- Video games
- Visual effects

2.14.2 History

One of the first displays of computer animation was *Futureworld* (1976), which included an animation of a human face and hand — produced by Ed Catmull and Fred Parke at the University of Utah. Swedish inventor Håkan Lans applied for the first patent on color graphics in 1979.[1]

There are several international conferences and journals where the most significant results in computer graphics are published. Among them are the SIGGRAPH and Eurographics conferences and the Association for Computing Machinery (ACM) Transactions on Graphics journal. The joint Eurographics and ACM SIGGRAPH symposium series features the major venues for the more specialized sub-fields: Symposium on Geometry Processing,[2] Symposium on Rendering, and Symposium on Computer Animation.[3] As in the rest of computer science, conference publications in computer graphics are generally more significant than journal publications (and subsequently have lower acceptance rates).[4][5][6][7]

2.14.3 Subfields in computer graphics

A broad classification of major subfields in computer graphics might be:

1. Geometry: studies ways to represent and process surfaces

2. Animation: studies with ways to represent and manipulate motion

3. Rendering: studies algorithms to reproduce light transport

2.14. COMPUTER GRAPHICS (COMPUTER SCIENCE)

4. Imaging: studies image acquisition or image editing

5. Topology: studies the behaviour of spaces and surfaces.

Geometry

Successive approximations of a surface computed using quadric error metrics.

The subfield of geometry studies the representation of three-dimensional objects in a discrete digital setting. Because the appearance of an object depends largely on its exterior, boundary representations are most commonly used. Two dimensional surfaces are a good representation for most objects, though they may be non-manifold. Since surfaces are not finite, discrete digital approximations are used. Polygonal meshes (and to a lesser extent subdivision surfaces) are by far the most common representation, although point-based representations have become more popular recently (see for instance the Symposium on Point-Based Graphics).[8] These representations are *Lagrangian*, meaning the spatial locations of the samples are independent. Recently, *Eulerian* surface descriptions (i.e., where spatial samples are fixed) such as level sets have been developed into a useful representation for deforming surfaces which undergo many topological changes (with fluids being the most notable example).[9]

Geometry Subfields

- Implicit surface modeling - an older subfield which examines the use of algebraic surfaces, constructive solid geometry, etc., for surface representation.

- Digital geometry processing - surface reconstruction, simplification, fairing, mesh repair, parameterization, remeshing, mesh generation, surface compression, and surface editing all fall under this heading.[10][11][12]

- Discrete differential geometry - a nascent field which defines geometric quantities for the discrete surfaces used in computer graphics.[13]

- Point-based graphics - a recent field which focuses on points as the fundamental representation of surfaces.

- Subdivision surfaces

- Out-of-core mesh processing - another recent field which focuses on mesh datasets that do not fit in main memory.

Animation

The subfield of animation studies descriptions for surfaces (and other phenomena) that move or deform over time. Historically, most work in this field has focused on parametric and data-driven models, but recently physical simulation has become more popular as computers have become more powerful computationally.

Subfields

- Performance capture

- Character animation

- Physical simulation (e.g. cloth modeling, animation of fluid dynamics, etc.)

Rendering

Indirect diffuse scattering simulated using path tracing and irradiance caching.

Rendering generates images from a model. Rendering may simulate light transport to create realistic images or it may create images that have a particular artistic style in non-photorealistic rendering. The two basic operations in realistic rendering are transport (how much light passes from one place to another) and scattering (how surfaces interact with light). See Rendering (computer graphics) for more information.

Transport

Transport describes how illumination in a scene gets from one place to another. Visibility is a major component of light transport.

Scattering

Models of *scattering* and *shading* are used to describe the appearance of a surface. In graphics these problems are often studied within the context of rendering since they can substantially affect the design of rendering algorithms. Shading can be broken down into two orthogonal issues, which are often studied independently:

1. **scattering** - how light interacts with the surface *at a given point*
2. **shading** - how material properties vary across the surface

The former problem refers to scattering, i.e., the relationship between incoming and outgoing illumination at a given point. Descriptions of scattering are usually given in terms of a bidirectional scattering distribution function or BSDF. The latter issue addresses how different types of scattering are distributed across the surface (i.e., which scattering function applies where). Descriptions of this kind are typically expressed with a program called a shader. (Note that there is some confusion since the word "shader" is sometimes used for programs that describe local *geometric* variation.)

Other subfields

- physically based rendering - concerned with generating images according to the laws of geometric optics
- real time rendering - focuses on rendering for interactive applications, typically using specialized hardware like GPUs
- non-photorealistic rendering
- relighting - recent area concerned with quickly re-rendering scenes

2.14.4 Notable researchers in computer graphics

- Jim Blinn
- Jack E. Bresenham
- Loren Carpenter
- Edwin Catmull
- Robert L. Cook
- Paul Debevec
- Ron Fedkiw
- James D. Foley
- David Forsyth
- Henry Fuchs
- Pat Hanrahan
- David R. Hedgley, Jr.
- Jim Kajiya
- Takeo Kanade
- Kenneth Knowlton
- Marc Levoy
- James O'Brien
- Ken Perlin
- Matt Pharr
- Przemyslaw Prusinkiewicz
- William Reeves
- James Sethian
- Ivan Sutherland
- Greg Turk
- Andries van Dam
- Henrik Wann Jensen
- Lance Williams

2.14.5 See also

- 3D computer graphics
- Cloth modeling
- Computer facial animation
- Digital geometry
- Digital image editing
- Geometry processing

- Graphics processing unit (GPU)
- Painter's algorithm
- SIGGRAPH
- Stanford Bunny
- Utah Teapot

2.14.6 References

[1] US patent 4303986, Lans, Håkan, "Data processing system and apparatus for color graphics display", issued 1981-12-01

[2] "geometryprocessing.org". geometryprocessing.org. Retrieved 2014-05-01.

[3]

[4] "Best Practices Memo". Cra.org. Retrieved 2014-05-01.

[5] "Choosing a venue: conference or journal?". People.csail.mit.edu. Retrieved 2014-05-01.

[6] "Graphics/vision publications acceptance rates statistics". Vrlab.epfl.ch. Retrieved 2014-05-01.

[7] An extensive history of computer graphics can be found at this page.

[8] "Point Based Graphics 2007 - PBG07". Graphics.ethz.ch. Retrieved 2014-05-01.

[9] "Ron Fedkiw". Graphics.stanford.edu. Retrieved 2014-05-01.

[10]

[11] CS 598: Digital Geometry Processing (Fall 2004)

[12] "Digital Geometry Processing". Cs.ubc.ca. Retrieved 2014-05-01.

[13] "Discrete Differential Geometry". Ddg.cs.columbia.edu. Retrieved 2014-05-01.

2.14.7 Further reading

- Foley *et al*. *Computer Graphics: Principles and Practice*.
- Shirley. *Fundamentals of Computer Graphics*.
- Watt. *3D Computer Graphics*.

2.14.8 External links

- A Critical History of Computer Graphics and Animation
- *History of Computer Graphics* series of articles

University groups

- Computer Graphics Usability and Visualization Group at Simon Fraser University
- Computer Graphics Group at The University of Hong Kong
- Media Technology Research Centre at the University of Bath
- Berkeley Computer Animation and Modeling Group
- Berkeley Computer Graphics
- Bristol University Computer Graphics Group
- C^2G^2 at Columbia University
- Center for Visual Information Technology, IIIT Hyderabad
- Caltech Multi-Res Modeling Group
- Carnegie Mellon Graphics Lab
- Center for Graphics and Geometric Computing at Technion Israel Institute of Technology, Haifa, Israel
- Computer Graphics Department at Max-Planck-Institut fur Informatik
- Computer Graphics Department at Haute Ecole Albert Jacquard
- Computer Graphics Group at Brown
- Computer Graphics Group at RWTH Aachen University
- Computer Graphics at Harvard
- Computer Graphics and Immersive Technologies Laboratory at USC
- Graphics Lab of Institute for Creative Technologies at USC
- Computer Graphics Laboratory at Korea Advanced Institute of Science and Technology (KAIST)
- Computer Graphics Group at PUC-Rio
- Computer Graphics Group at University of Bonn
- Computer Graphics Group at University of Virginia
- Computer Graphics Laboratory at University of Tokyo
- Computer Graphics Laboratory at UT Austin
- Computer Graphics Laboratory at ETH Zurich

- Computer Graphics / Geometric Design Group at Rice
- Computer Graphics and User Interfaces Lab at Columbia University
- High Performance Computer Graphics Lab at Purdue University
- Computer Graphics and Visualization Lab at Purdue University
- Computer Graphics and Visualization Lab at University of Utah
- Computer Graphics and Visualization Lab at University of Wisconsin
- Cornell University Program of Computer Graphics
- Dynamic Graphics Project at University of Toronto
- Geometric Modeling and Industrial Geometry Group at Technische Universitat Wien
- The Institute of Computer Graphics and Algorithms at Technische Universitat Wien
- Graphics and Image Analysis at UNC
- Graphics and Geometric Computing Group at Tsinghua University
- Graphics@Illinois
- GRAIL at University of Washington
- GRAVIR at iMAGIS
- GVIL at University of Maryland, College Park
- GVU Center at Georgia Tech
- IDAV Visualization and Graphics Research Group at UC Davis
- IMAGINE Research Group at Universidad de los Andes, Bogotá, Colombia
- Imager Laboratory at University of British Columbia
- MIT Computer Graphics Group
- MRL at NYU
- Princeton Graphics and Geometry Group
- Stanford Computer Graphics Laboratory
- UCSD Computer Graphics Laboratory
- Vision Research Center at Vanderbilt
- INI-GraphicsNet international network

Industry

Industrial labs doing "blue sky" graphics research include:

- Adobe Advanced Technology Labs
- MERL
- Microsoft Research - Graphics
- Nvidia Research

Major film studios notable for graphics research include:

- ILM
- PDI/Dreamworks Animation
- Pixar

2.15 Computer security

Computer security, also known as **cybersecurity** or **IT security**, is the protection of information systems from theft or damage to the hardware, the software, and to the information on them, as well as from disruption or misdirection of the services they provide.[1] It includes controlling physical access to the hardware, as well as protecting against harm that may come via network access, data and code injection,[2] and due to malpractice by operators, whether intentional, accidental, or due to them being tricked into deviating from secure procedures.[3]

The field is of growing importance due to the increasing reliance of computer systems in most societies.[4] Computer systems now include a very wide variety of "smart" devices, including smartphones, televisions and tiny devices as part of the Internet of Things - and networks include not only the Internet and private data networks, but also Bluetooth, Wi-Fi and other wireless networks.

Computer security covers all the processes and mechanisms by which digital equipment, information and services are protected from unintended or unauthorized access, change or destruction and the process of applying security measures to ensure confidentiality, integrity, and availability of data both in transit and at rest.[5]

2.15.1 Vulnerabilities and attacks

Main article: Vulnerability (computing)

2.15. COMPUTER SECURITY

A vulnerability is a system susceptibility or flaw, and many vulnerabilities are documented in the Common Vulnerabilities and Exposures (CVE) database and vulnerability management is the cyclical practice of identifying, classifying, remediating, and mitigating vulnerabilities as they are discovered. An *exploitable* vulnerability is one for which at least one working attack or "exploit" exists.

To secure a computer system, it is important to understand the attacks that can be made against it, and these threats can typically be classified into one of the categories below:

Backdoors

A backdoor in a computer system, a cryptosystem or an algorithm, is any secret method of bypassing normal authentication or security controls. They may exist for a number of reasons, including by original design or from poor configuration. They may also have been added later by an authorized party to allow some legitimate access, or by an attacker for malicious reasons; but regardless of the motives for their existence, they create a vulnerability.

Denial-of-service attack

Main article: Denial-of-service attack

Denial of service attacks are designed to make a machine or network resource unavailable to its intended users. Attackers can deny service to individual victims, such as by deliberately entering a wrong password enough consecutive times to cause the victim account to be locked, or they may overload the capabilities of a machine or network and block all users at once. While a network attack from a single IP address can be blocked by adding a new firewall rule, many forms of Distributed denial of service (DDoS) attacks are possible, where the attack comes from a large number of points - and defending is much more difficult. Such attacks can originate from the zombie computers of a botnet, but a range of other techniques are possible including reflection and amplification attacks, where innocent systems are fooled into sending traffic to the victim.

Direct-access attacks

An unauthorized user gaining physical access to a computer is often able to directly download data from it. They may also compromise security by making operating system modifications, installing software worms, keyloggers, or covert listening devices. Even when the system is protected by standard security measures, these may be able to be by passed by booting another operating system or tool

Common consumer devices that can be used to transfer data surreptitiously.

from a CD-ROM or other bootable media. Disk encryption and Trusted Platform Module are designed to prevent these attacks.

Eavesdropping

Eavesdropping is the act of surreptitiously listening to a private conversation, typically between hosts on a network. For instance, programs such as Carnivore and NarusInsight have been used by the FBI and NSA to eavesdrop on the systems of internet service providers. Even machines that operate as a closed system (i.e., with no contact to the outside world) can be eavesdropped upon via monitoring the faint electro-magnetic transmissions generated by the hardware; TEMPEST is a specification by the NSA referring to these attacks.

Spoofing

Spoofing of user identity describes a situation in which one person or program successfully masquerades as another by falsifying data.

Tampering

Tampering describes a malicious modification of products. So-called "Evil Maid" attacks and security services planting of surveillance capability into routers[6] are examples.

Privilege escalation

Privilege escalation describes a situation where an attacker with some level of restricted access is able to, without authorization, elevate their privileges or access level. So for example a standard computer user may be able to fool the system into giving them access to restricted data; or even to "become root" and have full unrestricted access to a system.

Social engineering and trojans

Main article: Social engineering (security)
See also: Category:Cryptographic attacks

Social engineering aims to convince a user to disclose secrets such as passwords, card numbers, etc. by, for example, impersonating a bank, a contractor, or a customer.[7]

2.15.2 Systems at risk

Computer security is critical in almost any industry which uses computers.[8]

Financial systems

Web sites that accept or store credit card numbers and bank account information are prominent hacking targets, because of the potential for immediate financial gain from transferring money, making purchases, or selling the information on the black market. In-store payment systems and ATMs have also been tampered with in order to gather customer account data and PINs.

Utilities and industrial equipment

Computers control functions at many utilities, including coordination of telecommunications, the power grid, nuclear power plants, and valve opening and closing in water and gas networks. The Internet is a potential attack vector for such machines if connected, but the Stuxnet worm demonstrated that even equipment controlled by computers not connected to the Internet can be vulnerable to physical damage caused by malicious commands sent to industrial equipment (in that case uranium enrichment centrifuges) which are infected via removable media. In 2014, the Computer Emergency Readiness Team, a division of the Department of Homeland Security, investigated 79 hacking incidents at energy companies.[9]

Aviation

The aviation industry is very reliant on a series of complex system which could be attacked.[10] A simple power outage at one airport can cause repercussions worldwide,[11] much of the system relies on radio transmissions which could be disrupted,[12] and controlling aircraft over oceans is especially dangerous because radar surveillance only extends 175 to 225 miles offshore.[13] There is also potential for attack from within an aircraft.[14]

The consequences of a successful attack range from loss of confidentiality to loss of system integrity, which may lead to more serious concerns such as exfiltration of data, network and air traffic control outages, which in turn can lead to airport closures, loss of aircraft, loss of passenger life, damages on the ground and to transportation infrastructure. A successful attack on a military aviation system that controls munitions could have even more serious consequences.

Consumer devices

Desktop computers and laptops are commonly infected with malware either to gather passwords or financial account information, or to construct a botnet to attack another target. Smart phones, tablet computers, smart watches, and other mobile devices such as Quantified Self devices like activity trackers have also become targets and many of these have sensors such as cameras, microphones, GPS receivers, compasses, and accelerometers which could be exploited, and may collect personal information, including sensitive health information. Wifi, Bluetooth, and cell phone network on any of these devices could be used as attack vectors, and sensors might be remotely activated after a successful breach.[15]

Home automation devices such as the Nest thermostat are also potential targets. [15]

Large corporations

Large corporations are common targets. In many cases this is aimed at financial gain through identity theft and involves data breaches such as the loss of millions of clients' credit card details by Home Depot,[16] Staples,[17] and Target Corporation.[18]

Not all attacks are financially motivated however; for example security firm HBGary Federal suffered a serious series of attacks in 2011 from hacktivist goup Anonymous in retaliation for the firm's CEO claiming to have infiltrated their group, [19][20] and Sony Pictures was attacked in 2014 where the motive appears to have been to embarrass with data leaks, and cripple the company by wiping workstations and servers.[21][22]

Automobiles

If access is gained to a car's internal controller area network, it is possible to disable the brakes and turn the steering wheel.[23] Computerized engine timing, cruise control, anti-lock brakes, seat belt tensioners, door locks, airbags and advanced driver assistance systems make these disruptions possible, and self-driving cars go even further. Connected cars may use wifi and bluetooth to communicate with onboard consumer devices, and the cell phone network to contact concierge and emergency assistance services or get navigational or entertainment information; each of these networks is a potential entry point for malware or an attacker.[23] Researchers in 2011 were even able to use a malicious compact disc in a car's stereo system as a successful attack vector,[24] and cars with built-in voice recognition or remote assistance features have onboard microphones which could be used for eavesdropping.

A 2015 report by U.S. Senator Edward Markey criticized manufacturers' security measures as inadequate, and also highlighted privacy concerns about driving, location, and diagnostic data being collected, which is vulnerable to abuse by both manufacturers and hackers.[25]

Government

Government and military computer systems are commonly attacked by activists[26][27][28][29] and foreign powers.[30][31][32][33] Local and regional government infrastructure such as traffic light controls, police and intelligence agency communications, personnel records and financial systems are also potential targets as they are now all largely computerized.

2.15.3 Impact of security breaches

Serious financial damage has been caused by security breaches, but because there is no standard model for estimating the cost of an incident, the only data available is that which is made public by the organizations involved. "Several computer security consulting firms produce estimates of total worldwide losses attributable to virus and worm attacks and to hostile digital acts in general. The 2003 loss estimates by these firms range from $13 billion (worms and viruses only) to $226 billion (for all forms of covert attacks). The reliability of these estimates is often challenged; the underlying methodology is basically anecdotal."[34]

However, reasonable estimates of the financial cost of security breaches can actually help organizations make rational investment decisions. According to the classic Gordon-Loeb Model analyzing the optimal investment level in information security, one can conclude that the amount a firm spends to protect information should generally be only a small fraction of the expected loss (i.e., the expected value of the loss resulting from a cyber/information security breach).[35]

2.15.4 Attacker motivation

As with physical security, the motivations for breaches of computer security vary between attackers. Some are thrill-seekers or vandals, others are activists; or criminals looking for financial gain. State-sponsored attackers are now common and well resourced, but started with amateurs such as Markus Hess who hacked for the KGB, as recounted by Clifford Stoll, in *The Cuckoo's Egg*.

A standard part of threat modelling for any particular system is to identify what might motivate an attack on that system, and who might be motivated to breach it. The level and detail of precautions will vary depending on the system to be secured. A home personal computer, bank and classified military network all face very different threats, even when the underlying technologies in use are similar.

2.15.5 Computer protection (countermeasures)

In computer security a countermeasure is an action, device, procedure, or technique that reduces a threat, a vulnerability, or an attack by eliminating or preventing it, by minimizing the harm it can cause, or by discovering and reporting it so that corrective action can be taken.[36][37][38]

Some common countermeasures are listed in the following sections:

Security measures

A state of computer "security" is the conceptual ideal, attained by the use of the three processes: threat prevention, detection, and response. These processes are based on various policies and system components, which include the following:

- User account access controls and cryptography can protect systems files and data, respectively.

- Firewalls are by far the most common prevention systems from a network security perspective as they can (if properly configured) shield access to internal network services, and block certain kinds of attacks through packet filtering. Firewalls can be both hardware- or software-based.

- Intrusion Detection System (IDS) products are designed to detect network attacks in-progress and assist in post-attack forensics, while audit trails and logs serve a similar function for individual systems.

- "Response" is necessarily defined by the assessed security requirements of an individual system and may cover the range from simple upgrade of protections to notification of legal authorities, counter-attacks, and the like. In some special cases, a complete destruction of the compromised system is favored, as it may happen that not all the compromised resources are detected.

Today, computer security comprises mainly "preventive" measures, like firewalls or an exit procedure. A firewall can be defined as a way of filtering network data between a host or a network and another network, such as the Internet, and can be implemented as software running on the machine, hooking into the network stack (or, in the case of most UNIX-based operating systems such as Linux, built into the operating system kernel) to provide real time filtering and blocking. Another implementation is a so-called physical firewall which consists of a separate machine filtering network traffic. Firewalls are common amongst machines that are permanently connected to the Internet.

However, relatively few organisations maintain computer systems with effective detection systems, and fewer still have organised response mechanisms in place. As result, as Reuters points out: "Companies for the first time report they are losing more through electronic theft of data than physical stealing of assets".[39] The primary obstacle to effective eradication of cyber crime could be traced to excessive reliance on firewalls and other automated "detection" systems. Yet it is basic evidence gathering by using packet capture appliances that puts criminals behind bars.

Reducing vulnerabilities

While formal verification of the correctness of computer systems is possible,[40][41] it is not yet common. Operating systems formally verified include seL4,[42] and SYSGO's PikeOS[43][44] - but these make up a very small percentage of the market.

Cryptography properly implemented is now virtually impossible to directly break. Breaking them requires some non-cryptographic input, such as a stolen key, stolen plaintext (at either end of the transmission), or some other extra cryptanalytic information.

Two factor authentication is a method for mitigating unauthorized access to a system or sensitive information. It requires "something you know"; a password or PIN, and "something you have"; a card, dongle, cellphone, or other piece of hardware. This increases security as an unauthorized person needs both of these to gain access.

Social engineering and direct computer access (physical) attacks can only be prevented by non-computer means, which can be difficult to enforce, relative to the sensitivity of the information. Even in a highly disciplined environment, such as in military organizations, social engineering attacks can still be difficult to foresee and prevent.

It is possible to reduce an attacker's chances by keeping systems up to date with security patches and updates, using a security scanner or/and hiring competent people responsible for security. The effects of data loss/damage can be reduced by careful backing up and insurance.

Security by design

Main article: Secure by design

Security by design, or alternately secure by design, means that the software has been designed from the ground up to be secure. In this case, security is considered as a main feature.

Some of the techniques in this approach include:

- The principle of least privilege, where each part of the system has only the privileges that are needed for its function. That way even if an attacker gains access to that part, they have only limited access to the whole system.

- Automated theorem proving to prove the correctness of crucial software subsystems.

- Code reviews and unit testing, approaches to make modules more secure where formal correctness proofs are not possible.

- Defense in depth, where the design is such that more than one subsystem needs to be violated to compromise the integrity of the system and the information it holds.

- Default secure settings, and design to "fail secure" rather than "fail insecure" (see fail-safe for the equivalent in safety engineering). Ideally, a secure system should require a deliberate, conscious, knowledgeable and free decision on the part of legitimate authorities in order to make it insecure.

- Audit trails tracking system activity, so that when a security breach occurs, the mechanism and extent of the breach can be determined. Storing audit trails remotely, where they can only be appended to, can keep intruders from covering their tracks.

- Full disclosure of all vulnerabilities, to ensure that the "window of vulnerability" is kept as short as possible when bugs are discovered.

Security architecture

The Open Security Architecture organization defines IT security architecture as "the design artifacts that describe how the security controls (security countermeasures) are positioned, and how they relate to the overall information technology architecture. These controls serve the purpose to maintain the system's quality attributes: confidentiality, integrity, availability, accountability and assurance services".[45]

Techopedia defines security architecture as "a unified security design that addresses the necessities and potential risks involved in a certain scenario or environment. It also specifies when and where to apply security controls. The design process is generally reproducible." The key attributes of security architecture are:[46]

- the relationship of different components and how they depend on each other.
- the determination of controls based on risk assessment, good practice, finances, and legal matters.
- the standardization of controls.

Hardware protection mechanisms

See also: Computer security compromised by hardware failure

While hardware may be a source of insecurity, such as with microchip vulnerabilities maliciously introduced during the manufacturing process,[47][48] hardware-based or assisted computer security also offers an alternative to software-only computer security. Using devices and methods such as dongles, trusted platform modules, intrusion-aware cases, drive locks, disabling USB ports, and mobile-enabled access may be considered more secure due to the physical access (or sophisticated backdoor access) required in order to be compromised. Each of these is covered in more detail below.

- USB dongles are typically used in software licensing schemes to unlock software capabilities,[49] but they can also be seen as a way to prevent unauthorized access to a computer or other device's software. The dongle, or key, essentially creates a secure encrypted tunnel between the software application and the key. The principle is that an encryption scheme on the dongle, such as Advanced Encryption Standard (AES) provides a stronger measure of security, since it is harder to hack and replicate the dongle than to simply copy the native software to another machine and use it. Another security application for dongles is to use them for accessing web-based content such as cloud software or Virtual Private Networks (VPNs).[50] In addition, a USB dongle can be configured to lock or unlock a computer.[51]

- Trusted platform modules (TPMs) secure devices by integrating cryptographic capabilities onto access devices, through the use of microprocessors, or so-called computers-on-a-chip. TPMs used in conjunction with server-side software offer a way to detect and authenticate hardware devices, preventing unauthorized network and data access.[52]

- Computer case intrusion detection refers to a push-button switch which is triggered when a computer case is opened. The firmware or BIOS is programmed to show an alert to the operator when the computer is booted up the next time.

- Drive locks are essentially software tools to encrypt hard drives, making them inaccessible to thieves.[53] Tools exist specifically for encrypting external drives as well.[54]

- Disabling USB ports is a security option for preventing unauthorized and malicious access to an otherwise secure computer. Infected USB dongles connected to a network from a computer inside the firewall are considered by Network World as the most common hardware threat facing computer networks.[55]

- Mobile-enabled access devices are growing in popularity due to the ubiquitous nature of cell phones. Built-in capabilities such as Bluetooth, the newer Bluetooth low energy (LE), Near field communication (NFC) on non-iOS devices and biometric validation such as thumb print readers, as well as QR code reader software designed for mobile devices, offer new, secure ways for mobile phones to connect to access control systems. These control systems provide computer security and can also be used for controlling access to secure buildings.[56]

Secure operating systems

Main article: Security-focused operating system

One use of the term "computer security" refers to technology that is used to implement secure operating systems. Much of this technology is based on science developed in the 1980s and used to produce what may be some of the most impenetrable operating systems ever. Though still valid, the technology is in limited use today, primarily because it imposes some changes to system management and also because it is not widely understood. Such ultra-strong secure operating systems are based on operating system kernel technology that can guarantee that certain security policies are absolutely enforced in an operating environment. An example of such a Computer security policy is the Bell-LaPadula model. The strategy is based on a coupling of special microprocessor hardware features, often involving the memory management unit, to a special correctly implemented operating system kernel. This forms the foundation for a secure operating system which, if certain critical parts are designed and implemented correctly, can ensure the absolute impossibility of penetration by hostile elements. This capability is enabled because the configuration not only imposes a security policy, but in theory completely protects itself from corruption. Ordinary operating systems, on the other hand, lack the features that assure this maximal level of security. The design methodology to produce such secure systems is precise, deterministic and logical.

Systems designed with such methodology represent the state of the art of computer security although products using such security are not widely known. In sharp contrast to most kinds of software, they meet specifications with verifiable certainty comparable to specifications for size, weight and power. Secure operating systems designed this way are used primarily to protect national security information, military secrets, and the data of international financial institutions. These are very powerful security tools and very few secure operating systems have been certified at the highest level (Orange Book A-1) to operate over the range of "Top Secret" to "unclassified" (including Honeywell SCOMP, USAF SACDIN, NSA Blacker and Boeing MLS LAN). The assurance of security depends not only on the soundness of the design strategy, but also on the assurance of correctness of the implementation, and therefore there are degrees of security strength defined for COMPUSEC. The Common Criteria quantifies security strength of products in terms of two components, security functionality and assurance level (such as EAL levels), and these are specified in a Protection Profile for requirements and a Security Target for product descriptions. None of these ultra-high assurance secure general purpose operating systems have been produced for decades or certified under Common Criteria.

In USA parlance, the term High Assurance usually suggests the system has the right security functions that are implemented robustly enough to protect DoD and DoE classified information. Medium assurance suggests it can protect less valuable information, such as income tax information. Secure operating systems designed to meet medium robustness levels of security functionality and assurance have seen wider use within both government and commercial markets. Medium robust systems may provide the same security functions as high assurance secure operating systems but do so at a lower assurance level (such as Common Criteria levels EAL4 or EAL5). Lower levels mean we can be less certain that the security functions are implemented flawlessly, and therefore less dependable. These systems are found in use on web servers, guards, database servers, and management hosts and are used not only to protect the data stored on these systems but also to provide a high level of protection for network connections and routing services.

Secure coding

Main article: Secure coding

If the operating environment is not based on a secure operating system capable of maintaining a domain for its own execution, and capable of protecting application code from malicious subversion, and capable of protecting the system from subverted code, then high degrees of security are understandably not possible. While such secure operating systems are possible and have been implemented, most commercial systems fall in a 'low security' category because they rely on features not supported by secure operating systems (like portability, and others). In low security operating environments, applications must be relied on to participate in their own protection. There are 'best effort' secure coding practices that can be followed to make an application more resistant to malicious subversion.

In commercial environments, the majority of software subversion vulnerabilities result from a few known kinds of coding defects. Common software defects include buffer overflows, format string vulnerabilities, integer overflow, and code/command injection. These defects can be used to cause the target system to execute putative data. However, the "data" contain executable instructions, allowing the attacker to gain control of the processor.

Some common languages such as C and C++ are vulnerable to all of these defects (see Seacord, "*Secure Coding in C and C++*").[57] Other languages, such as Java, are more resistant to some of these defects, but are still prone to code/command injection and other software defects which facilitate subversion.

2.15. COMPUTER SECURITY

Another bad coding practice occurs when an object is deleted during normal operation yet the program neglects to update any of the associated memory pointers, potentially causing system instability when that location is referenced again. This is called dangling pointer, and the first known exploit for this particular problem was presented in July 2007. Before this publication the problem was known but considered to be academic and not practically exploitable.[58]

Unfortunately, there is no theoretical model of "secure coding" practices, nor is one practically achievable, insofar as the code (ideally, read-only) and data (generally read/write) generally tends to have some form of defect.

Capabilities and access control lists

Main articles: Access control list and Capability (computers)

Within computer systems, two of many security models capable of enforcing privilege separation are access control lists (ACLs) and capability-based security. Using ACLs to confine programs has been proven to be insecure in many situations, such as if the host computer can be tricked into indirectly allowing restricted file access, an issue known as the confused deputy problem. It has also been shown that the promise of ACLs of giving access to an object to only one person can never be guaranteed in practice. Both of these problems are resolved by capabilities. This does not mean practical flaws exist in all ACL-based systems, but only that the designers of certain utilities must take responsibility to ensure that they do not introduce flaws.

Capabilities have been mostly restricted to research operating systems, while commercial OSs still use ACLs. Capabilities can, however, also be implemented at the language level, leading to a style of programming that is essentially a refinement of standard object-oriented design. An open source project in the area is the E language.

The most secure computers are those not connected to the Internet and shielded from any interference. In the real world, the most secure systems are operating systems where security is not an add-on.

Response to breaches

Responding forcefully to attempted security breaches (in the manner that one would for attempted physical security breaches) is often very difficult for a variety of reasons:

- Identifying attackers is difficult, as they are often in a different jurisdiction to the systems they attempt to breach, and operate through proxies, temporary anonymous dial-up accounts, wireless connections, and other anonymising procedures which make backtracing difficult and are often located in yet another jurisdiction. If they successfully breach security, they are often able to delete logs to cover their tracks.

- The sheer number of attempted attacks is so large that organisations cannot spend time pursuing each attacker (a typical home user with a permanent (e.g., cable modem) connection will be attacked at least several times per day, so more attractive targets could be presumed to see many more). Note however, that most of the sheer bulk of these attacks are made by automated vulnerability scanners and computer worms.

- Law enforcement officers are often unfamiliar with information technology, and so lack the skills and interest in pursuing attackers. There are also budgetary constraints. It has been argued that the high cost of technology, such as DNA testing, and improved forensics mean less money for other kinds of law enforcement, so the overall rate of criminals not getting dealt with goes up as the cost of the technology increases. In addition, the identification of attackers across a network may require logs from various points in the network and in many countries, the release of these records to law enforcement (with the exception of being voluntarily surrendered by a network administrator or a system administrator) requires a search warrant and, depending on the circumstances, the legal proceedings required can be drawn out to the point where the records are either regularly destroyed, or the information is no longer relevant.

2.15.6 Notable computer security attacks and breaches

Some illustrative examples of different types of computer security breaches are given below.

Robert Morris and the first computer worm

Main article: Morris worm

In 1988, only 60,000 computers were connected to the Internet, and most were mainframes, minicomputers and professional workstations. On November 2, 1988, many started to slow down, because they were running a malicious code that demanded processor time and that spread itself to other computers - the first internet "computer worm".[59] The software was traced back to 23-year-old Cornell University graduate student Robert Tappan Morris, Jr. who said 'he wanted to count how many machines were connected to the Internet'.[59]

Rome Laboratory

In 1994, over a hundred intrusions were made by unidentified crackers into the Rome Laboratory, the US Air Force's main command and research facility. Using trojan horses, hackers were able to obtain unrestricted access to Rome's networking systems and remove traces of their activities. The intruders were able to obtain classified files, such as air tasking order systems data and furthermore able to penetrate connected networks of National Aeronautics and Space Administration's Goddard Space Flight Center, Wright-Patterson Air Force Base, some Defense contractors, and other private sector organizations, by posing as a trusted Rome center user.[60]

TJX loses 45.7m customer credit card details

In early 2007, American apparel and home goods company TJX announced that it was the victim of an unauthorized computer systems intrusion[61] and that the hackers had accessed a system that stored data on credit card, debit card, check, and merchandise return transactions.[62]

Stuxnet attack

The computer worm known as Stuxnet reportedly ruined almost one-fifth of Iran's nuclear centrifuges[63] by disrupting industrial programmable logic controllers (PLCs) in a targeted attack generally believed to have been launched by Israel and the United States[64][65][66][67] although neither has publicly acknowledged this.

Global surveillance disclosures

Main article: Global surveillance disclosures (2013–present)

In early 2013, massive breaches of computer security by the NSA were revealed, including deliberately inserting a backdoor in a NIST standard for encryption[68] and tapping the links between Google's data centres.[69] These were disclosed by NSA contractor Edward Snowden.[70]

Target and Home Depot breaches

In 2013 and 2014, a Russian/Ukrainian hacking ring known as "Rescator" broke into Target Corporation computers in 2013, stealing roughly 40 million credit cards,[71] and then Home Depot computers in 2014, stealing between 53 and 56 million credit card numbers.[72] Warnings were delivered at both corporations, but ignored; physical security breaches using self checkout machines are believed to have played a large role. "The malware utilized is absolutely unsophisticated and uninteresting," says Jim Walter, director of threat intelligence operations at security technology company McAfee - meaning that the heists could have easily been stopped by existing antivirus software had administrators responded to the warnings. The size of the thefts has resulted in major attention from state and Federal United States authorities and the investigation is ongoing.

2.15.7 Legal issues and global regulation

Conflict of laws in cyberspace has become a major cause of concern for computer security community. Some of the main challenges and complaints about the antivirus industry are the lack of global web regulations, a global base of common rules to judge, and eventually punish, cyber crimes and cyber criminals. There is no global cyber law and cybersecurity treaty that can be invoked for enforcing global cybersecurity issues.

International legal issues of cyber attacks are complicated in nature. Even if an antivirus firm locates the cyber criminal behind the creation of a particular virus or piece of malware or form of cyber attack, often the local authorities cannot take action due to lack of laws under which to prosecute.[73][74] Authorship attribution for cyber crimes and cyber attacks is a major problem for all law enforcement agencies.

"[Computer viruses] switch from one country to another, from one jurisdiction to another — moving around the world, using the fact that we don't have the capability to globally police operations like this. So the Internet is as if someone [had] given free plane tickets to all the online criminals of the world."[73] Use of dynamic DNS, fast flux and bullet proof servers have added own complexities to this situation.

2.15.8 Government

The role of the government is to make regulations to force companies and organizations to protect their systems, infrastructure and information from any cyber attacks, but also to protect its own national infrastructure such as the national power-grid.

The question of whether the government should intervene or not in the regulation of the cyberspace is a very polemical one. Indeed, for as long as it has existed and by definition, the cyberspace is a virtual space free of any government intervention. Where everyone agree that an improvement on cybersecurity is more than vital, is the government the best actor to solve this issue? Many government officials and experts think that the government should step in and that there is a crucial need for regulation, mainly due to the failure of the private sector to solve efficiently the cybersecurity problem. R. Clarke said during a panel discussion at the RSA Security Conference in San Francisco, he believes that the "industry only responds when you threaten regulation. If industry doesn't respond (to the threat), you have to follow through."[75] On the other hand, executives from the private sector agree that improvements are necessary but think that the government intervention would affect their ability to innovate efficiently.

2.15.9 Actions and teams in the US

Legislation

The 1986 18 U.S.C. § 1030, more commonly known as the Computer Fraud and Abuse Act is the key legislation. It prohibits unauthorized access or damage of "protected computers" as defined in 18 U.S.C. § 1030(e)(2).

Although various other measures have been proposed, such as the "Cybersecurity Act of 2010 - S. 773" in 2009, the "International Cybercrime Reporting and Cooperation Act - H.R.4962"[76] and "Protecting Cyberspace as a National Asset Act of 2010 - S.3480"[77] in 2010 - none of these has succeeded.

Executive order 13636 *Improving Critical Infrastructure Cybersecurity* was signed February 12, 2013.

Agencies

Homeland Security The Department of Homeland Security has a dedicated division responsible for the response system, risk management program and requirements for cybersecurity in the United States called the National Cyber Security Division.[78][79] The division is home to US-CERT operations and the National Cyber Alert System.[79] The National Cybersecurity and Communications Integration Center brings together government organizations responsible for protecting computer networks and networked infrastructure.[80]

FBI The third priority of the Federal Bureau of Investigation (FBI) is to: *"Protect the United States against cyber-based attacks and high-technology crimes"*,[81] and they, along with the National White Collar Crime Center (NW3C), and the Bureau of Justice Assistance (BJA) are part of the multi-agency task force, The Internet Crime Complaint Center, also known as IC3.[82]

In addition to its own specific duties, the FBI participates alongside non-profit organizations such as InfraGard.[83][84]

Department of Justice In the criminal division of the United States Department of Justice operates a section called the Computer Crime and Intellectual Property Section. The CCIPS is in charge of investigating computer crime and intellectual property crime and is specialized in the search and seizure of digital evidence in computers and networks.[85]

USCYBERCOM The United States Cyber Command, also known as USCYBERCOM, is tasked with the defense of specified Department of Defense information networks and *"ensure US/Allied freedom of action in cyberspace and deny the same to our adversaries."*[86] It has no role in the protection of civilian networks.[87][88]

FCC

The U.S. Federal Communications Commission's role in cybersecurity is to strengthen the protection of critical communications infrastructure, to assist in maintaining the reliability of networks during disasters, to aid in swift recovery after, and to ensure that first responders have access to effective communications services.[89]

Computer Emergency Readiness Team

Computer Emergency Response Team is a name given to expert groups that handle computer security incidents. In the US, two distinct organization exist, although they do work closely together.

- US-CERT: part of the National Cyber Security Division of the United States Department of Homeland Security.[90]

- CERT/CC: created by the Defense Advanced Research Projects Agency (DARPA) and run by the Software Engineering Institute (SEI).

2.15.10 International actions

Many different teams and organisations exist, including:

- The Forum of Incident Response and Security Teams (FIRST) is the global association of CSIRTs.[91] The

US-CERT, AT&T, Apple, Cisco, McAfee, Microsoft are all members of this international team.[92]

- The Council of Europe helps protect societies worldwide from the threat of cybercrime through the Convention on Cybercrime.[93]

- The purpose of the Messaging Anti-Abuse Working Group (MAAWG) is to bring the messaging industry together to work collaboratively and to successfully address the various forms of messaging abuse, such as spam, viruses, denial-of-service attacks and other messaging exploitations.[94] France Telecom, Facebook, AT&T, Apple, Cisco, Sprint are some of the members of the MAAWG.[94]

- ENISA : The European Network and Information Security Agency (ENISA) is an agency of the European Union with the objective to improve network and information security in the European Union.

Germany

Berlin starts National Cyber Defense Initiative On June 16, 2011, the German Minister for Home Affairs, officially opened the new German NCAZ (National Center for Cyber Defense) Nationales Cyber-Abwehrzentrum, which is located in Bonn. The NCAZ closely cooperates with BSI (Federal Office for Information Security) Bundesamt für Sicherheit in der Informationstechnik, BKA (Federal Police Organisation) Bundeskriminalamt (Deutschland), BND (Federal Intelligence Service) Bundesnachrichtendienst, MAD (Military Intelligence Service) Amt für den Militärischen Abschirmdienst and other national organisations in Germany taking care of national security aspects. According to the Minister the primary task of the new organisation founded on February 23, 2011, is to detect and prevent attacks against the national infrastructure and mentioned incidents like Stuxnet.

South Korea

Following cyberattacks in the first half of 2013, when government, news-media, television station, and bank websites were compromised, the national government committed to the training of 5,000 new cybersecurity experts by 2017. The South Korean government blamed its northern counterpart for these attacks, as well as incidents that occurred in 2009, 2011,[95] and 2012, but Pyongyang denies the accusations.[96]

India

Some provisions for cybersecurity have been incorporated into rules framed under the Information Technology Act 2000.

The National Cyber Security Policy 2013 is a policy framework by Department of Electronics and Information Technology (DeitY) which aims to protect the public and private infrastructure from cyber attacks, and safeguard "information, such as personal information (of web users), financial and banking information and sovereign data".

The Indian Companies Act 2013 has also introduced cyber law and cyber security obligations on the part of Indian directors.

Canada

On October 3, 2010, Public Safety Canada unveiled Canada's Cyber Security Strategy, following a Speech from the Throne commitment to boost the security of Canadian cyberspace.[97][98] The aim of the strategy is to strengthen Canada's "cyber systems and critical infrastructure sectors, support economic growth and protect Canadians as they connect to each other and to the world."[99] Three main pillars define the strategy: securing government systems, partnering to secure vital cyber systems outside the federal government, and helping Canadians to be secure online.[99] The strategy involves multiple departments and agencies across the Government of Canada.[100] The Cyber Incident Management Framework for Canada outlines these responsibilities, and provides a plan for coordinated response between government and other partners in the event of a cyber incident.[101] The Action Plan 2010-2015 for Canada's Cyber Security Strategy outlines the ongoing implementation of the strategy.[102]

Public Safety Canada's Canadian Cyber Incident Response Centre (CCIRC) is responsible for mitigating and responding to threats to Canada's critical infrastructure and cyber systems. The CCIRC provides support to mitigate cyber threats, technical support to respond and recover from targeted cyber attacks, and provides online tools for members of Canada's critical infrastructure sectors.[103] The CCIRC posts regular cyber security bulletins on the Public Safety Canada website.[104] The CCIRC also operates an online reporting tool where individuals and organizations can report a cyber incident.[105] Canada's Cyber Security Strategy is part of a larger, integrated approach to critical infrastructure protection, and functions as a counterpart document to the National Strategy and Action Plan for Critical Infrastructure.[100]

On September 27, 2010, Public Safety Canada partnered with STOP.THINK.CONNECT, a coalition of non-profit, private sector, and government organizations dedicated to informing the general public on how to protect themselves online.[106] On February 4, 2014, the Government of Canada launched the Cyber Security Cooperation Program.[107] The program is a $1.5 million five-year initiative aimed at improving Canada's cyber systems through grants and contributions to projects in support of this objective.[108] Public Safety Canada aims to begin an evaluation of Canada's Cyber Security Strategy in early 2015.[100] Public Safety Canada administers and routinely updates the GetCyberSafe portal for Canadian citizens, and carries out Cyber Security Awareness Month during October.[109]

2.15.11 National teams

Here are the main computer emergency response teams around the world. Every country have their own team to protect network security. February 27, 2014, the Chinese network security and information technology leadership team is established. The leadership team will focus on national security and long-term development, co-ordination of major issues related to network security and information technology economic, political, cultural, social, and military and other fields of research to develop network security and information technology strategy, planning and major macroeconomic policy promote national network security and information technology law, and constantly enhance security capabilities.

Europe

CSIRTs in Europe collaborate in the TERENA task force TF-CSIRT. TERENA's Trusted Introducer service provides an accreditation and certification scheme for CSIRTs in Europe. A full list of known CSIRTs in Europe is available from the Trusted Introducer website.

Other countries

- CERT Brazil, member of FIRST (Forum for Incident Response and Security Teams)

- CARNet CERT, Croatia, member of FIRST

- AE CERT, United Arab Emirates

- SingCERT, Singapore

- CERT-LEXSI, France, Canada, Singapore

2.15.12 Modern warfare

Main article: Cyberwarfare

Cybersecurity is becoming increasingly important as more information and technology is being made available on cyberspace. There is growing concern among governments that cyberspace will become the next theatre of warfare. As Mark Clayton from the *Christian Science Monitor* described in an article titled "The New Cyber Arms Race":

> In the future, wars will not just be fought by soldiers with guns or with planes that drop bombs. They will also be fought with the click of a mouse a half a world away that unleashes carefully weaponized computer programs that disrupt or destroy critical industries like utilities, transportation, communications, and energy. Such attacks could also disable military networks that control the movement of troops, the path of jet fighters, the command and control of warships.[110]

This has led to new terms such as *cyberwarfare* and *cyberterrorism*. More and more critical infrastructure is being controlled via computer programs that, while increasing efficiency, exposes new vulnerabilities. The test will be to see if governments and corporations that control critical systems such as energy, communications and other information will be able to prevent attacks before they occur. As Jay Cross, the chief scientist of the Internet Time Group, remarked, "Connectedness begets vulnerability."[110]

2.15.13 The cyber security job market

Cyber Security is a fast-growing[111] field of IT concerned with reducing organizations' risk of hack or data breach. Commercial, government and non-governmental organizations all employ cybersecurity professionals. However, the use of the term "cybersecurity" is more prevalent in government job descriptions.[112]

Typical cybersecurity job titles and descriptions include:[113]

Security Analyst Analyzes and assesses vulnerabilities in the infrastructure (software, hardware, networks), investigates available tools and countermeasures to remedy the detected vulnerabilities, and recommends solutions and best practices. Analyzes and assesses damage to the data/infrastructure as a result of security incidents, examines available recovery tools and processes, and recommends solutions. Tests for compliance with security policies and procedures. May assist in the creation, implementation, and/or management of security solutions.

Security Engineer

Performs security monitoring, security and data/logs analysis, and forensic analysis, to detect security incidents, and mounts incident response. Investigates and utilizes new technologies and processes to enhance security capabilities and implement improvements. May also review code or perform other security engineering methodologies.

Security Architect

Designs a security system or major components of a security system, and may head a security design team building a new security system.

Security Administrator

Installs and manages organization-wide security systems. May also take on some of the tasks of a security analyst in smaller organizations.

Chief Information Security Officer

A high-level management position responsible for the entire information security division/staff. The position may include hands-on technical work.

Security Consultant/Specialist/Intelligence

Broad titles that encompass any one or all of the other roles/titles, tasked with protecting computers, networks, software, data, and/or information systems against viruses, worms, spyware, malware, intrusion detection, unauthorized access, denial-of-service attacks, and an ever increasing list of attacks by hackers acting as individuals or as part of organized crime or foreign governments.

Student programs are also available to people interested in beginning a career in cybersecurity.[114][115] Meanwhile, a flexible and effective option for information security professionals of all experience levels to keep studying is online security training, including webcasts.[116][117][118]

2.15.14 Terminology

The following terms used with regards to engineering secure systems are explained below.

- Access authorization restricts access to a computer to group of users through the use of authentication systems. These systems can protect either the whole computer – such as through an interactive login screen – or individual services, such as an FTP server. There are many methods for identifying and authenticating users, such as passwords, identification cards, and, more recently, smart cards and biometric systems.

- Anti-virus software consists of computer programs that attempt to identify, thwart and eliminate computer viruses and other malicious software (malware).

- Applications with known security flaws should not be run. Either leave it turned off until it can be patched or otherwise fixed, or delete it and replace it with some other application. Publicly known flaws are the main entry used by worms to automatically break into a system and then spread to other systems connected to it. The security website Secunia provides a search tool for unpatched known flaws in popular products.

- Authentication techniques can be used to ensure that communication end-points are who they say they are.

- Automated theorem proving and other verification tools can enable critical algorithms and code used in secure systems to be mathematically proven to meet their specifications.

- Backups are a way of securing information; they are another copy of all the important computer files kept in another location. These files are kept on hard disks, CD-Rs, CD-RWs, tapes and more recently on the cloud. Suggested locations for backups are a fireproof, waterproof, and heat proof safe, or in a separate, off-site location than that in which the original files are contained. Some individuals and companies also keep their backups in safe deposit boxes inside bank vaults. There is also a fourth option, which involves using one of the file hosting services that backs up files over the Internet for both business and individuals, known as the cloud.

  - Backups are also important for reasons other than security. Natural disasters, such as earthquakes, hurricanes, or tornadoes, may strike the building where the computer is located. The building can be on fire, or an explosion may occur. There needs to be a recent backup at an alternate secure location, in case of such kind of disaster. Further, it is recommended that the alternate location be placed where the same disaster would not affect both locations. Examples of alternate disaster recovery sites being compromised by the same disaster that affected the primary site include having had a primary site in World Trade Center I and the recovery site in 7 World Trade Center, both of which were destroyed in the 9/11 attack, and

2.15. COMPUTER SECURITY

having one's primary site and recovery site in the same coastal region, which leads to both being vulnerable to hurricane damage (for example, primary site in New Orleans and recovery site in Jefferson Parish, both of which were hit by Hurricane Katrina in 2005). The backup media should be moved between the geographic sites in a secure manner, in order to prevent them from being stolen.

- Capability and access control list techniques can be used to ensure privilege separation and mandatory access control. This section discusses their use.

- Chain of trust techniques can be used to attempt to ensure that all software loaded has been certified as authentic by the system's designers.

- Confidentiality is the nondisclosure of information except to another authorized person.[119]

- Cryptographic techniques can be used to defend data in transit between systems, reducing the probability that data exchanged between systems can be intercepted or modified.

- Cyberwarfare is an Internet-based conflict that involves politically motivated attacks on information and information systems. Such attacks can, for example, disable official websites and networks, disrupt or disable essential services, steal or alter classified data, and criple financial systems.

- Data integrity is the accuracy and consistency of stored data, indicated by an absence of any alteration in data between two updates of a data record.[120]

This is secret stuff, PSE do not...
⮕ **5a0 (k$hQ% ...**
⮕ **This is secret stuff, PSE do not...**

Cryptographic techniques involve transforming information, scrambling it so it becomes unreadable during transmission. The intended recipient can unscramble the message; ideally, eavesdroppers cannot.

- Encryption is used to protect the message from the eyes of others. Cryptographically secure ciphers are designed to make any practical attempt of breaking infeasible. Symmetric-key ciphers are suitable for bulk encryption using shared keys, and public-key encryption using digital certificates can provide a practical solution for the problem of securely communicating when no key is shared in advance.

- Endpoint security software helps networks to prevent exfiltration (data theft) and virus infection at network entry points made vulnerable by the prevalence of potentially infected portable computing devices, such as laptops and mobile devices, and external storage devices, such as USB drives.[121]

- Firewalls are an important method for control and security on the Internet and other networks. A network firewall can be a communications processor, typically a router, or a dedicated server, along with firewall software. A firewall serves as a gatekeeper system that protects a company's intranets and other computer networks from intrusion by providing a filter and safe transfer point for access to and from the Internet and other networks. It screens all network traffic for proper passwords or other security codes and only allows authorized transmission in and out of the network. Firewalls can deter, but not completely prevent, unauthorized access (hacking) into computer networks; they can also provide some protection from online intrusion.

- Honey pots are computers that are either intentionally or unintentionally left vulnerable to attack by crackers. They can be used to catch crackers or fix vulnerabilities.

- Intrusion-detection systems can scan a network for people that are on the network but who should not be there or are doing things that they should not be doing, for example trying a lot of passwords to gain access to the network.

- A microkernel is the near-minimum amount of software that can provide the mechanisms to implement an operating system. It is used solely to provide very low-level, very precisely defined machine code upon which an operating system can be developed. A simple example is the early '90s GEMSOS (Gemini Computers), which provided extremely low-level machine code, such as "segment" management, atop which an operating system could be built. The theory (in the case of "segments") was that—rather than have the operating system itself worry about mandatory access separation by means of military-style labeling—it is safer if a low-level, independently scrutinized module can be charged **solely** with the management of individually labeled segments, be they memory "segments" or file system "segments" or executable text "segments." If software below the visibility of the operating system is (as in this case) charged with labeling, there is no theoretically viable means for a clever hacker to subvert the labeling scheme, since the operating system *per se* does **not** provide mechanisms for interfering with labeling: the operating system is, essentially, a client (an "application," arguably) atop the microkernel and, as such, subject to its restrictions.

- Pinging The ping application can be used by potential crackers to find if an IP address is reachable. If a cracker finds a computer, they can try a port scan to detect and attack services on that computer.

- Social engineering awareness keeps employees aware of the dangers of social engineering and/or having a policy in place to prevent social engineering can reduce successful breaches of the network and servers.

2.15.15 Scholars

- Salvatore J. Stolfo
- Ross J. Anderson
- Annie Anton
- Adam Back
- Daniel J. Bernstein
- Matt Blaze
- Stefan Brands
- L. Jean Camp
- Lance Cottrell
- Lorrie Cranor
- Dorothy E. Denning
- Peter J. Denning
- Cynthia Dwork
- Deborah Estrin
- Joan Feigenbaum
- Ian Goldberg
- Shafi Goldwasser
- Lawrence A. Gordon
- Peter Gutmann
- Paul Kocher
- Monica S. Lam
- Butler Lampson
- Brian LaMacchia
- Carl Landwehr
- Kevin Mitnick
- Peter G. Neumann
- Susan Nycum
- Roger R. Schell
- Bruce Schneier
- Dawn Song
- Gene Spafford
- Joseph Steinberg
- Willis Ware
- Moti Yung

2.15.16 See also

- Attack tree
- CAPTCHA
- CERT
- CertiVox
- Cloud computing security
- Comparison of antivirus software
- Computer insecurity
- Computer security model
- Content security
- Countermeasure (computer)
- Cyber security standards
- Dancing pigs
- Data loss prevention products
- Data security
- Differentiated security
- Disk encryption
- Exploit (computer security)
- Fault tolerance
- Human-computer interaction (security)
- Identity Based Security
- Identity management

2.15. COMPUTER SECURITY

- Identity theft
- Information Leak Prevention
- Information Security Awareness
- Internet privacy
- ISO/IEC 15408
- IT risk
- List of Computer Security Certifications
- Mobile security
- Network security
- Network Security Toolkit
- Next-Generation Firewall
- Open security
- OWASP
- Penetration test
- Physical information security
- Presumed security
- Privacy software
- Proactive Cyber Defence
- Risk cybernetics
- Sandbox (computer security)
- Separation of protection and security
- Software Defined Perimeter
- Cyber Insurance

2.15.17 Further reading

- Chwan-Hwa (John) Wu and J. David Irwin, *Introduction to Computer Networks and Cybersecurity* (Boca Raton: CRC Press, 2013), ISBN 978-1466572133.
- Newton Lee, *Counterterrorism and Cybersecurity: Total Information Awareness (Second Edition)* (Switzerland: Springer International Publishing, 2015), ISBN 978-3-319-17243-9.
- P. W. Singer and Allan Friedman, *Cybersecurity and Cyberwar: What Everyone Needs to Know* (Oxford: Oxford University Press, 2014), ISBN 978-0199918119.
- Peter Kim, *The Hacker Playbook: Practical Guide To Penetration Testing* (Seattle: CreateSpace Independent Publishing Platform, 2014), ISBN 978-1494932633.

2.15.18 References

[1] Gasser, Morrie (1988). *Building a Secure Computer System* (PDF). Van Nostrand Reinhold. p. 3. ISBN 0-442-23022-2. Retrieved 6 September 2015.

[2] "Definition of computer security". *Encyclopedia*. Ziff Davis, PCMag. Retrieved 6 September 2015.

[3] Rouse, Margaret. "Social engineering definition". TechTarget. Retrieved 6 September 2015.

[4] "Reliance spells end of road for ICT amateurs", May 07, 2013, The Australian

[5] http://www.evolllution.com/opinions/cybersecurity-understanding-online-threat/

[6] Gallagher, Sean (May 14, 2014). "Photos of an NSA "upgrade" factory show Cisco router getting implant". Ars Technica. Retrieved August 3, 2014.

[7] Arcos Sergio. "Social Engineering" (PDF).

[8] J. C. Willemssen, "FAA Computer Security". GAO/T-AIMD-00-330. Presented at Committee on Science, House of Representatives, 2000.

[9] Pagliery, Jose. "Hackers attacked the U.S. energy grid 79 times this year". *CNN Money*. Cable News Network. Retrieved 16 April 2015.

[10] P. G. Neumann, "Computer Security in Aviation," presented at International Conference on Aviation Safety and Security in the 21st Century, White House Commission on Safety and Security, 1997.

[11] J. Zellan, Aviation Security. Hauppauge, NY: Nova Science, 2003, pp. 65–70.

[12] http://www.securityweek.com/air-traffic-control-systems-vulnerabilities-could-make-unfriendly-skies-black

[13] http://www.npr.org/blogs/alltechconsidered/2014/08/04/337794061/hacker-says-he-can-break-into-airplane-systems-using-in-flight-wi-fi

[14] http://www.reuters.com/article/2014/08/04/us-cybersecurity-hackers-airplanes-idUSKBN0G40WQ20140804

[15] http://www.npr.org/blogs/alltechconsidered/2014/08/06/338334508/is-your-watch-or-thermostat-a-spy-cyber-security-firms-are-on-it

[16] Melvin Backman (18 September 2014). "Home Depot: 56 million cards exposed in breach". CNNMoney.

[17] "Staples: Breach may have affected 1.16 million customers' cards". Fortune.com. December 19, 2014. Retrieved 2014-12-21.

[18] "Target security breach affects up to 40M cards". *Associated Press via Milwaukee Journal Sentinel*. 19 December 2013. Retrieved 21 December 2013.

[19] Bright, Peter (February 15, 2011). "Anonymous speaks: the inside story of the HBGary hack". Arstechnica.com. Retrieved March 29, 2011.

[20] Anderson, Nate (February 9, 2011). "How one man tracked down Anonymous—and paid a heavy price". Arstechnica.com. Retrieved March 29, 2011.

[21] Palilery, Jose (December 24, 2014). "What caused Sony hack: What we know now". CNN Money. Retrieved January 4, 2015.

[22] James Cook (December 16, 2014). "Sony Hackers Have Over 100 Terabytes Of Documents. Only Released 200 Gigabytes So Far". *Business Insider*. Retrieved December 18, 2014.

[23] http://www.vox.com/2015/1/18/7629603/car-hacking-dangers

[24] http://www.autosec.org/pubs/cars-usenixsec2011.pdf

[25] http://www.markey.senate.gov/imo/media/doc/2015-02-06_MarkeyReport-Tracking_Hacking_CarSecurity%202.pdf

[26] "Internet strikes back: Anonymous' Operation Megaupload explained". *RT*. January 20, 2012. Archived from the original on May 5, 2013. Retrieved May 5, 2013.

[27] "Gary McKinnon profile: Autistic 'hacker' who started writing computer programs at 14". *The Daily Telegraph* (London). 23 January 2009.

[28] "Gary McKinnon extradition ruling due by 16 October". BBC News. September 6, 2012. Retrieved September 25, 2012.

[29] Law Lords Department (30 July 2008). "House of Lords - Mckinnon V Government of The United States of America and Another". Publications.parliament.uk. Retrieved 30 January 2010. 15. ... alleged to total over $700,000

[30] "NSA Accessed Mexican President's Email", October 20, 2013, Jens Glüsing, Laura Poitras, Marcel Rosenbach and Holger Stark, spiegel.de

[31] Sanders, Sam (4 June 2015). "Massive Data Breach Puts 4 Million Federal Employees' Records At Risk". *NPR*. Retrieved 5 June 2015.

[32] Liptak, Kevin (4 June 2015). "U.S. government hacked; feds think China is the culprit". *CNN*. Retrieved 5 June 2015.

[33] Sean Gallagher. "Encryption "would not have helped" at OPM, says DHS official".

[34] Cashell, B., Jackson, W. D., Jickling, M., & Webel, B. (2004). The Economic Impact of Cyber-Attacks. Congressional Research Service, Government and Finance Division. Washington DC: The Library of Congress.

[35] Gordon, Lawrence; Loeb, Martin (November 2002). "The Economics of Information Security Investment". *ACM Transactions on Information and System Security* **5** (4): 438–457. doi:10.1145/581271.581274.

[36] RFC 2828 Internet Security Glossary

[37] CNSS Instruction No. 4009 dated 26 April 2010

[38] InfosecToday Glossary

[39] "Firms lose more to electronic than physical theft". Reuters.

[40] Harrison, J. (2003). "Formal verification at Intel". pp. 45–54. doi:10.1109/LICS.2003.1210044.

[41] Formal verification of a real-time hardware design. Portal.acm.org (1983-06-27). Retrieved on April 30, 2011.

[42] "Abstract Formal Specification of the seL4/ARMv6 API" (PDF). Retrieved May 19, 2015.

[43] Christoph Baumann, Bernhard Beckert, Holger Blasum, and Thorsten Bormer Ingredients of Operating System Correctness? Lessons Learned in the Formal Verification of PikeOS

[44] "Getting it Right" by Jack Ganssle

[45] Definitions: IT Security Architecture. SecurityArchitecture.org, Jan, 2006

[46] Jannsen, Cory. "Security Architecture". *Techopedia*. Janalta Interactive Inc. Retrieved 9 October 2014.

[47] *The Hacker in Your Hardware: The Next Security Threat* August 4, 2010 Scientific American

[48] Waksman, Adam; Sethumadhavan, Simha (2010), "Tamper Evident Microprocessors" (PDF), *Proceedings of the IEEE Symposium on Security and Privacy* (Oakland, California)

[49] "Sentinel HASP HL". E-Spin. Retrieved 2014-03-20.

[50] "Token-based authentication". SafeNet.com. Retrieved 2014-03-20.

[51] "Lock and protect your Windows PC". TheWindowsClub.com. Retrieved 2014-03-20.

[52] James Greene (2012). "Intel Trusted Execution Technology: White Paper" (PDF). Intel Corporation. Retrieved 2013-12-18.

[53] "SafeNet ProtectDrive 8.4". SCMagazine.com. 2008-10-04. Retrieved 2014-03-20.

[54] "Secure Hard Drives: Lock Down Your Data". PCMag.com. 2009-05-11.

[55] "Top 10 vulnerabilities inside the network". Network World. 2010-11-08. Retrieved 2014-03-20.

[56] "Forget IDs, use your phone as credentials". Fox Business Network. 2013-11-04. Retrieved 2014-03-20.

2.15. COMPUTER SECURITY

[57] "Secure Coding in C and C++, Second Edition". Cert.org. Retrieved 2013-09-25.

[58] New hacking technique exploits common programming error. SearchSecurity.com, July 2007

[59] Jonathan Zittrain, 'The Future of The Internet', Penguin Books, 2008

[60] Information Security. United States Department of Defense, 1986

[61] "THE TJX COMPANIES, INC. VICTIMIZED BY COMPUTER SYSTEMS INTRUSION; PROVIDES INFORMATION TO HELP PROTECT CUSTOMERS" (Press release). The TJX Companies, Inc. 2007-01-17. Retrieved 2009-12-12.

[62] Largest Customer Info Breach Grows. MyFox Twin Cities, 29 March 2007.

[63] "The Stuxnet Attack On Iran's Nuclear Plant Was 'Far More Dangerous' Than Previously Thought". Business Insider. 20 November 2013.

[64] Reals, Tucker (24 September 2010). "Stuxnet Worm a U.S. Cyber-Attack on Iran Nukes?". CBS News.

[65] Kim Zetter (17 February 2011). "Cyberwar Issues Likely to Be Addressed Only After a Catastrophe". Wired. Retrieved 18 February 2011.

[66] Chris Carroll (18 October 2011). "Cone of silence surrounds U.S. cyberwarfare". Stars and Stripes. Retrieved 30 October 2011.

[67] John Bumgarner (27 April 2010). "Computers as Weapons of War" (PDF). IO Journal. Retrieved 30 October 2011.

[68] "Can You Trust NIST?".

[69] "New Snowden Leak: NSA Tapped Google, Yahoo Data Centers", Oct 31, 2013, Lorenzo Franceschi-Bicchierai, mashable.com

[70] Seipel, Hubert. "Transcript: ARD interview with Edward Snowden". *La Foundation Courage*. Retrieved 11 June 2014.

[71] "Missed Alarms and 40 Million Stolen Credit Card Numbers: How Target Blew It"

[72] "Home Depot says 53 million emails stolen"

[73] "Mikko Hypponen: Fighting viruses, defending the net". TED.

[74] "Mikko Hypponen - Behind Enemy Lines". Hack In The Box Security Conference.

[75] Kirby, Carrie (June 24, 2011). "Former White House aide backs some Net regulation / Clarke says government, industry deserve 'F' in cybersecurity". *The San Francisco Chronicle*.

[76] "Text of H.R.4962 as Introduced in House: International Cybercrime Reporting and Cooperation Act - U.S. Congress". OpenCongress. Retrieved 2013-09-25.

[77] Archived July 4, 2015 at the Wayback Machine

[78] "National Cyber Security Division". U.S. Department of Homeland Security. Retrieved June 14, 2008.

[79] "FAQ: Cyber Security R&D Center". U.S. Department of Homeland Security S&T Directorate. Retrieved June 14, 2008.

[80] AFP-JiJi, "U.S. boots up cybersecurity center", October 31, 2009.

[81] "Federal Bureau of Investigation - Priorities". Federal Bureau of Investigation.

[82] Internet Crime Complaint Center

[83] "Infragard, Official Site". *Infragard*. Retrieved 10 September 2010.

[84] "Robert S. Mueller, III -- InfraGard Interview at the 2005 InfraGard Conference". *Infragard (Official Site) -- "Media Room"*. Retrieved 9 December 2009.

[85] "CCIPS".

[86] U.S. Department of Defense, Cyber Command Fact Sheet, May 21, 2010 http://www.stratcom.mil/factsheets/Cyber_Command/

[87] "Speech:". Defense.gov. Retrieved 2010-07-10.

[88] Shachtman, Noah. "Military's Cyber Commander Swears: "No Role" in Civilian Networks", The Brookings Institution, 23 September 2010.

[89] "FCC Cybersecurity". FCC.

[90] Verton, Dan (January 28, 2004). "DHS launches national cyber alert system". *Computerworld* (IDG). Retrieved 2008-06-15.

[91] "FIRST website".

[92] "First members".

[93] "European council".

[94] "MAAWG".

[95] "South Korea seeks global support in cyber attack probe". *BBC Monitoring Asia Pacific*. 7 March 2011.

[96] Kwanwoo Jun (23 September 2013). "Seoul Puts a Price on Cyberdefense". *Wall Street Journal*. Dow Jones & Company, Inc. Retrieved 24 September 2013.

[97] (Press Release) "Government of Canada Launches Canada's Cyber Security Strategy". *Market Wired*. 3 October 2010. Retrieved 1 November 2014.

[98] "Canada's Cyber Security Strategy".

[99] "Canada's Cyber Security Strategy". *Public Safety Canada*. Government of Canada. Retrieved 1 November 2014.

[100] "Action Plan 2010-2015 for Canada's Cyber Security Strategy". *Public Safety Canada*. Government of Canada. Retrieved 3 November 2014.

[101] "Cyber Incident Management Framework For Canada". *Public Safety Canada*. Government of Canada. Retrieved 3 November 2014.

[102] "Action Plan 2010-2015 for Canada's Cyber Security Strategy". *Public Safety Canada*. Government of Canada. Retrieved 1 November 2014.

[103] "Canadian Cyber Incident Response Centre". *Public Safety Canada*. Retrieved 1 November 2014.

[104] "Cyber Security Bulletins". *Public Safety Canada*. Retrieved 1 November 2014.

[105] "Report a Cyber Security Incident". *Public Safety Canada*. Government of Canada. Retrieved 3 November 2014.

[106] "Government of Canada Launches Cyber Security Awareness Month With New Public Awareness Partnership". *Market Wired* (Government of Canada). 27 September 2012. Retrieved 3 November 2014.

[107] "Cyber Security Cooperation Program". *Public Safety Canada*. Retrieved 1 November 2014.

[108] "Cyber Security Cooperation Program". *Public Safety Canada*.

[109] "GetCyberSafe". *Get Cyber Safe*. Government of Canada. Retrieved 3 November 2014.

[110] Clayton, Mark. "The new cyber arms race". *The Christian Science Monitor*. Retrieved 16 April 2015.

[111] "The Growth of Cybersecurity Jobs". Mar 2014. Retrieved 24 April 2014.

[112] de Silva, Richard (11 Oct 2011). "Government vs. Commerce: The Cyber Security Industry and You (Part One)". Defence IQ. Retrieved 24 Apr 2014.

[113] "Department of Computer Science". Retrieved April 30, 2013.

[114] "(Information for) Students". NICCS (US National Initiative for Cybercareers and Studies). Retrieved 24 April 2014.

[115] "Current Job Opportunities at DHS". U.S. Department of Homeland Security. Retrieved 2013-05-05.

[116] "Cybersecurity Training & Exercises". U.S. Department of Homeland Security. Retrieved 2015-01-09.

[117] "Cyber Security Awareness Free Training and Webcasts". MS-ISAC (Multi-State Information Sharing & Analysis Center. Retrieved 9 January 2015.

[118] "Security Training Courses". LearnQuest. Retrieved 2015-01-09.

[119] "Confidentiality". Retrieved 2011-10-31.

[120] "Data Integrity". Retrieved 2011-10-31.

[121] "Endpoint Security". Retrieved 2014-03-15.

2.15.19 External links

- Computer security at DMOZ

2.16 Cryptography

"Secret code" redirects here. For the Aya Kamiki album, see Secret Code.
"Cryptology" redirects here. For the David S. Ware album, see Cryptology (album).

Cryptography or **cryptology**; from Greek κρυπτός *kryp-*

German Lorenz cipher machine, used in World War II to encrypt very-high-level general staff messages

tós, "hidden, secret"; and γράφειν *graphein*, "writing", or -λογία *-logia*, "study", respectively[1] is the practice and study of techniques for secure communication in the presence of third parties (called adversaries).[2] More generally, it is about constructing and analyzing protocols that block adversaries;[3] various aspects in information security such as data confidentiality, data integrity, authentication, and non-repudiation[4] are central to modern cryptography. Modern cryptography exists at the intersection of the disciplines of mathematics, computer science, and electrical engineering. Applications of cryptography include ATM cards, computer passwords, and electronic commerce.

Cryptography prior to the modern age was effectively synonymous with *encryption*, the conversion of information from a readable state to apparent nonsense. The originator of an encrypted message shared the decoding technique needed to recover the original information only with intended recipients, thereby precluding unwanted persons from doing the same. Since World War I and the advent of the computer, the methods used to carry out cryptology have become increasingly complex and its application more widespread.

Modern cryptography is heavily based on mathematical theory and computer science practice; cryptographic algorithms are designed around computational hardness assumptions, making such algorithms hard to break in practice by any adversary. It is theoretically possible to break such a system, but it is infeasible to do so by any known practical means. These schemes are therefore termed computationally secure; theoretical advances, e.g., improvements in integer factorization algorithms, and faster computing technology require these solutions to be continually adapted. There exist information-theoretically secure schemes that provably cannot be broken even with unlimited computing power—an example is the one-time pad—but these schemes are more difficult to implement than the best theoretically breakable but computationally secure mechanisms.

The growth of cryptographic technology has raised a number of legal issues in the information age. Cryptography's potential for use as a tool for espionage and sedition has led many governments to classify it as a weapon and to limit or even prohibit its use and export.[5] In some jurisdictions where the use of cryptography is legal, laws permit investigators to compel the disclosure of encryption keys for documents relevant to an investigation.[6] Cryptography also plays a major role in digital rights management and piracy of digital media.[7]

2.16.1 Terminology

Until modern times, cryptography referred almost exclusively to *encryption*, which is the process of converting ordinary information (called plaintext) into unintelligible text (called ciphertext).[8] Decryption is the reverse, in other words, moving from the unintelligible ciphertext back to plaintext. A *cipher* (or *cypher*) is a pair of algorithms that create the encryption and the reversing decryption. The detailed operation of a cipher is controlled both by the algorithm and in each instance by a "key". This is a secret (ideally known only to the communicants), usually a short string of characters, which is needed to decrypt the ciphertext. Formally, a "cryptosystem" is the ordered list of elements of finite possible plaintexts, finite possible cyphertexts, finite possible keys, and the encryption and decryption algorithms which correspond to each key. Keys are important both formally and in actual practice, as ciphers without variable keys can be trivially broken with only the knowledge of the cipher used and are therefore useless (or even counter-productive) for most purposes. Historically, ciphers were often used directly for encryption or decryption without additional procedures such as authentication or integrity checks.

In colloquial use, the term "code" is often used to mean any method of encryption or concealment of meaning. However, in cryptography, *code* has a more specific meaning. It means the replacement of a unit of plaintext (i.e., a meaningful word or phrase) with a code word (for example, "wallaby" replaces "attack at dawn"). Codes are no longer used in serious cryptography—except incidentally for such things as unit designations (e.g., Bronco Flight or Operation Overlord)—since properly chosen ciphers are both more practical and more secure than even the best codes and also are better adapted to computers.

Cryptanalysis is the term used for the study of methods for obtaining the meaning of encrypted information without access to the key normally required to do so; i.e., it is the study of how to crack encryption algorithms or their implementations.

Some use the terms *cryptography* and *cryptology* interchangeably in English, while others (including US military practice generally) use *cryptography* to refer specifically to the use and practice of cryptographic techniques and *cryptology* to refer to the combined study of cryptography and cryptanalysis.[9][10] English is more flexible than several other languages in which *cryptology* (done by cryptologists) is always used in the second sense above. RFC 2828 advises that steganography is sometimes included in cryptology.[11]

The study of characteristics of languages that have some application in cryptography or cryptology (e.g. frequency data, letter combinations, universal patterns, etc.) is called cryptolinguistics.

2.16.2 History of cryptography and cryptanalysis

Main article: History of cryptography

Before the modern era, cryptography was concerned solely with message confidentiality (i.e., encryption)—conversion of messages from a comprehensible form into an incomprehensible one and back again at the other end, rendering it unreadable by interceptors or eavesdroppers without secret knowledge (namely the key needed for decryption of that message). Encryption attempted to ensure secrecy in communications, such as those of spies, military leaders, and diplomats. In recent decades, the field has expanded beyond confidentiality concerns to include techniques for message integrity checking, sender/receiver identity authentication, digital signatures, interactive proofs and secure computation, among others.

Classic cryptography

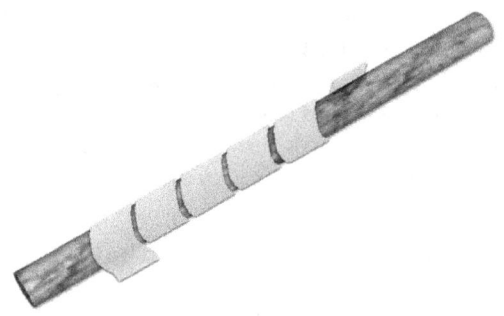

Reconstructed ancient Greek scytale, *an early cipher device*

The earliest forms of secret writing required little more than writing implements since most people could not read. More literacy, or literate opponents, required actual cryptography. The main classical cipher types are transposition ciphers, which rearrange the order of letters in a message (e.g., 'hello world' becomes 'ehlo owrdl' in a trivially simple rearrangement scheme), and substitution ciphers, which systematically replace letters or groups of letters with other letters or groups of letters (e.g., 'fly at once' becomes 'gmz bu podf' by replacing each letter with the one following it in the Latin alphabet). Simple versions of either have never offered much confidentiality from enterprising opponents. An early substitution cipher was the Caesar cipher, in which each letter in the plaintext was replaced by a letter some fixed number of positions further down the alphabet. Suetonius reports that Julius Caesar used it with a shift of three to communicate with his generals. Atbash is an example of an early Hebrew cipher. The earliest known use of cryptography is some carved ciphertext on stone in Egypt (ca 1900 BCE), but this may have been done for the amusement of literate observers rather than as a way of concealing information.

The Greeks of Classical times are said to have known of ciphers (e.g., the scytale transposition cipher claimed to have been used by the Spartan military).[12] Steganography (i.e., hiding even the existence of a message so as to keep it confidential) was also first developed in ancient times. An early example, from Herodotus, was a message tattooed on a slave's shaved head and concealed under the regrown hair.[8] More modern examples of steganography include the use of invisible ink, microdots, and digital watermarks to conceal information.

In India, the 2000-year old Kamasutra of Vātsyāyana speaks of two different kinds of ciphers called Kautiliyam and Mulavediya. In the Kautiliyam, the cipher letter substitutions are based on phonetic relations, such as vowels becoming consonants. In the Mulavediya, the cipher alphabet consists of pairing letters and using the reciprocal ones.[8]

First page of a book by Al-Kindi which discusses encryption of messages

Ciphertexts produced by a classical cipher (and some modern ciphers) always reveal statistical information about the plaintext, which can often be used to break them. After the discovery of frequency analysis, perhaps by the Arab mathematician and polymath Al-Kindi (also known as *Alkindus*) in the 9th century,[13] nearly all such ciphers became more or less readily breakable by any informed attacker. Such classical ciphers still enjoy popularity today, though mostly as puzzles (see cryptogram). Al-Kindi wrote a book on cryptography entitled *Risalah fi Istikhraj al-Mu'amma* (*Manuscript for the Deciphering Cryptographic Messages*), which described the first known use frequency analysis cryptanalysis techniques.[13][14]

Essentially all ciphers remained vulnerable to cryptanalysis using the frequency analysis technique until the development of the polyalphabetic cipher, most clearly by Leon Battista Alberti around the year 1467, though there is some indication that it was already known to Al-Kindi.[14] Alberti's innovation was to use different ciphers (i.e., substitution alphabets) for various parts of a message (perhaps

2.16. CRYPTOGRAPHY

16th-century book-shaped French cipher machine, with arms of Henri II of France

Enciphered letter from Gabriel de Luetz d'Aramon, French Ambassador to the Ottoman Empire, after 1546, with partial decipherment

for each successive plaintext letter at the limit). He also invented what was probably the first automatic cipher device, a wheel which implemented a partial realization of his invention. In the polyalphabetic Vigenère cipher, encryption uses a *key word*, which controls letter substitution depending on which letter of the key word is used. In the mid-19th century Charles Babbage showed that the Vigenère cipher was vulnerable to Kasiski examination, but this was first published about ten years later by Friedrich Kasiski.[15]

Although frequency analysis can be a powerful and general technique against many ciphers, encryption has still often been effective in practice, as many a would-be cryptanalyst was unaware of the technique. Breaking a message without using frequency analysis essentially required knowledge of the cipher used and perhaps of the key involved, thus making espionage, bribery, burglary, defection, etc., more attractive approaches to the cryptanalytically uninformed. It was finally explicitly recognized in the 19th century that secrecy of a cipher's algorithm is not a sensible nor practical safeguard of message security; in fact, it was further realized that any adequate cryptographic scheme (including ci-

phers) should remain secure even if the adversary fully understands the cipher algorithm itself. Security of the key used should alone be sufficient for a good cipher to maintain confidentiality under an attack. This fundamental principle was first explicitly stated in 1883 by Auguste Kerckhoffs and is generally called Kerckhoffs's Principle; alternatively and more bluntly, it was restated by Claude Shannon, the inventor of information theory and the fundamentals of theoretical cryptography, as *Shannon's Maxim*—'the enemy knows the system'.

Different physical devices and aids have been used to assist with ciphers. One of the earliest may have been the scytale of ancient Greece, a rod supposedly used by the Spartans as an aid for a transposition cipher (see image above). In medieval times, other aids were invented such as the cipher grille, which was also used for a kind of steganography. With the invention of polyalphabetic ciphers came more sophisticated aids such as Alberti's own cipher disk, Johannes Trithemius' tabula recta scheme, and Thomas Jefferson's multi cylinder (not publicly known, and reinvented independently by Bazeries around 1900). Many mechanical encryption/decryption devices were invented early in the 20th century, and several patented, among them rotor machines—famously including the Enigma machine used by the German government and military from the late 1920s and during World War II.[16] The ciphers implemented by better quality examples of these machine designs brought about a substantial increase in cryptanalytic difficulty after WWI.[17]

Computer era

Cryptanalysis of the new mechanical devices proved to be both difficult and laborious. In the United Kingdom, cryptanalytic efforts at Bletchley Park during WWII spurred the development of more efficient means for carrying out repetitious tasks. This culminated in the development of the Colossus, the world's first fully electronic, digital, programmable computer, which assisted in the decryption of ciphers generated by the German Army's Lorenz SZ40/42 machine.

Just as the development of digital computers and electronics helped in cryptanalysis, it made possible much more complex ciphers. Furthermore, computers allowed for the encryption of any kind of data representable in any binary format, unlike classical ciphers which only encrypted written language texts; this was new and significant. Computer use has thus supplanted linguistic cryptography, both for cipher design and cryptanalysis. Many computer ciphers can be characterized by their operation on binary bit sequences (sometimes in groups or blocks), unlike classical and mechanical schemes, which generally manipulate traditional characters (i.e., letters and digits) directly. However, computers have also assisted cryptanalysis, which has compensated to some extent for increased cipher complexity. Nonetheless, good modern ciphers have stayed ahead of cryptanalysis; it is typically the case that use of a quality cipher is very efficient (i.e., fast and requiring few resources, such as memory or CPU capability), while breaking it requires an effort many orders of magnitude larger, and vastly larger than that required for any classical cipher, making cryptanalysis so inefficient and impractical as to be effectively impossible.

Extensive open academic research into cryptography is relatively recent; it began only in the mid-1970s. In recent times, IBM personnel designed the algorithm that became the Federal (i.e., US) Data Encryption Standard; Whitfield Diffie and Martin Hellman published their key agreement algorithm;[18] and the RSA algorithm was published in Martin Gardner's *Scientific American* column. Since then, cryptography has become a widely used tool in communications, computer networks, and computer security generally. Some modern cryptographic techniques can only keep their keys secret if certain mathematical problems are intractable, such as the integer factorization or the discrete logarithm problems, so there are deep connections with abstract mathematics. There are very few cryptosystems that are proven to be unconditionally secure. The one-time pad is one. There are a few important ones that are proven secure under certain unproven assumptions. For example, the infeasibility of factoring extremely large integers is the basis for believing that RSA is secure, and some other systems, but even there, the proof is usually lost due to practical considerations. There are systems similar to RSA, such as one by Michael O. Rabin that is provably secure provided factoring n = pq is impossible, but the more practical system RSA has never been proved secure in this sense. The discrete logarithm problem is the basis for believing some other cryptosystems are secure, and again, there are related, less practical systems that are provably secure relative to the discrete log problem.[19]

As well as being aware of cryptographic history, cryptographic algorithm and system designers must also sensibly consider probable future developments while working on their designs. For instance, continuous improvements in computer processing power have increased the scope of brute-force attacks, so when specifying key lengths, the required key lengths are similarly advancing.[20] The potential effects of quantum computing are already being considered by some cryptographic system designers; the announced imminence of small implementations of these machines may be making the need for this preemptive caution rather more than merely speculative.[4]

Essentially, prior to the early 20th century, cryptography was chiefly concerned with linguistic and lexicographic patterns. Since then the emphasis has shifted, and cryptography now makes extensive use of mathematics, including aspects of information theory, computational complexity, statistics, combinatorics, abstract algebra, number theory, and finite mathematics generally. Cryptography is also a branch of engineering, but an unusual one since it deals with active, intelligent, and malevolent opposition (see cryptographic engineering and security engineering); other kinds of engineering (e.g., civil or chemical engineering) need deal only with neutral natural forces. There is also active research examining the relationship between cryptographic problems and quantum physics (see quantum cryptography and quantum computer).

2.16.3 Modern cryptography

The modern field of cryptography can be divided into several areas of study. The chief ones are discussed here; see Topics in Cryptography for more.

Symmetric-key cryptography

Main article: Symmetric-key algorithm
Symmetric-key cryptography refers to encryption methods

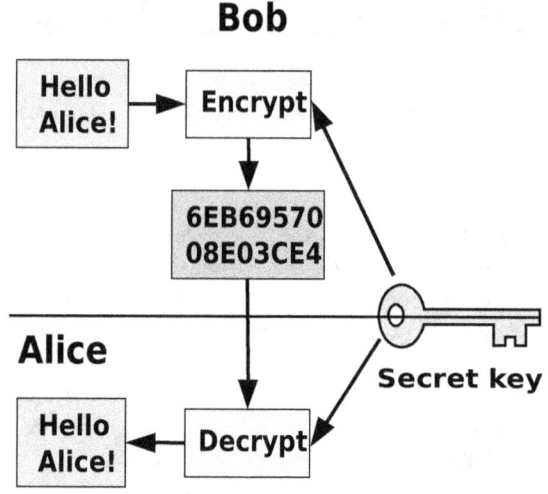

Symmetric-key cryptography, where a single key is used for encryption and decryption

in which both the sender and receiver share the same key (or, less commonly, in which their keys are different, but related in an easily computable way). This was the only kind of encryption publicly known until June 1976.[18]

Symmetric key ciphers are implemented as either block ciphers or stream ciphers. A block cipher enciphers input in

2.16. CRYPTOGRAPHY

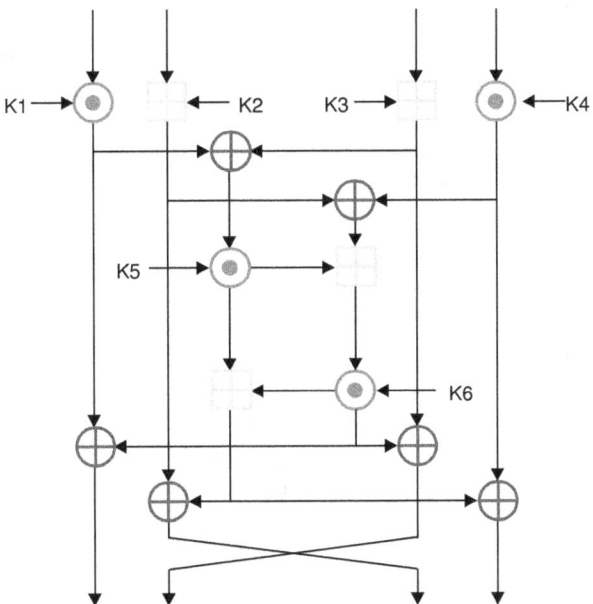

One round (out of 8.5) of the IDEA cipher, used in some versions of PGP for high-speed encryption of, for instance, e-mail

blocks of plaintext as opposed to individual characters, the input form used by a stream cipher.

The Data Encryption Standard (DES) and the Advanced Encryption Standard (AES) are block cipher designs which have been designated cryptography standards by the US government (though DES's designation was finally withdrawn after the AES was adopted).[21] Despite its deprecation as an official standard, DES (especially its still-approved and much more secure triple-DES variant) remains quite popular; it is used across a wide range of applications, from ATM encryption[22] to e-mail privacy[23] and secure remote access.[24] Many other block ciphers have been designed and released, with considerable variation in quality. Many have been thoroughly broken, such as FEAL.[4][25]

Stream ciphers, in contrast to the 'block' type, create an arbitrarily long stream of key material, which is combined with the plaintext bit-by-bit or character-by-character, somewhat like the one-time pad. In a stream cipher, the output stream is created based on a hidden internal state which changes as the cipher operates. That internal state is initially set up using the secret key material. RC4 is a widely used stream cipher; see Category:Stream ciphers.[4] Block ciphers can be used as stream ciphers; see Block cipher modes of operation.

Cryptographic hash functions are a third type of cryptographic algorithm. They take a message of any length as input, and output a short, fixed length hash which can be used in (for example) a digital signature. For good hash functions, an attacker cannot find two messages that produce the same hash. MD4 is a long-used hash function which is now broken; MD5, a strengthened variant of MD4, is also widely used but broken in practice. The US National Security Agency developed the Secure Hash Algorithm series of MD5-like hash functions: SHA-0 was a flawed algorithm that the agency withdrew; SHA-1 is widely deployed and more secure than MD5, but cryptanalysts have identified attacks against it; the SHA-2 family improves on SHA-1, but it isn't yet widely deployed; and the US standards authority thought it "prudent" from a security perspective to develop a new standard to "significantly improve the robustness of NIST's overall hash algorithm toolkit."[26] Thus, a hash function design competition was meant to select a new U.S. national standard, to be called SHA-3, by 2012. The competition ended on October 2, 2012 when the NIST announced that Keccak would be the new SHA-3 hash algorithm.[27]

Message authentication codes (MACs) are much like cryptographic hash functions, except that a secret key can be used to authenticate the hash value upon receipt;[4] this additional complication blocks an attack scheme against bare digest algorithms, and so has been thought worth the effort.

Public-key cryptography

Main article: Public-key cryptography

Symmetric-key cryptosystems use the same key for en-

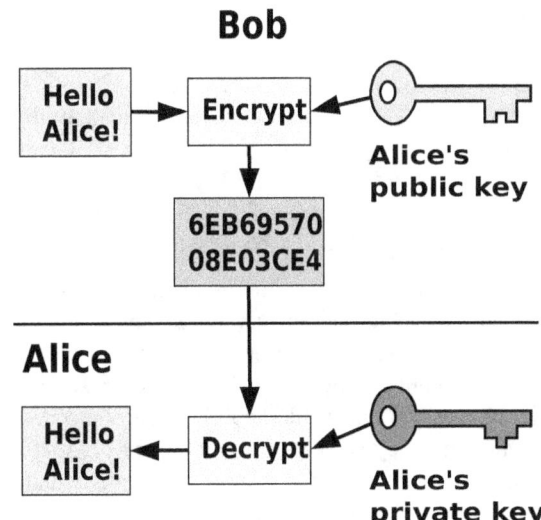

Public-key cryptography, where different keys are used for encryption and decryption

cryption and decryption of a message, though a message or group of messages may have a different key than others. A significant disadvantage of symmetric ciphers is the key management necessary to use them securely. Each distinct pair of communicating parties must, ideally, share a different key, and perhaps each ciphertext exchanged as well. The number of keys required increases as the square of the number of network members, which very quickly requires complex key management schemes to keep them all consistent and secret. The difficulty of securely establishing a secret key between two communicating parties, when a secure channel does not already exist between them, also presents a chicken-and-egg problem which is a considerable practical obstacle for cryptography users in the real world.

Whitfield Diffie and Martin Hellman, authors of the first published paper on public-key cryptography

In a groundbreaking 1976 paper, Whitfield Diffie and Martin Hellman proposed the notion of *public-key* (also, more generally, called *asymmetric key*) cryptography in which two different but mathematically related keys are used— a *public* key and a *private* key.[28] A public key system is so constructed that calculation of one key (the 'private key') is computationally infeasible from the other (the 'public key'), even though they are necessarily related. Instead, both keys are generated secretly, as an interrelated pair.[29] The historian David Kahn described public-key cryptography as "the most revolutionary new concept in the field since polyalphabetic substitution emerged in the Renaissance".[30]

In public-key cryptosystems, the public key may be freely distributed, while its paired private key must remain secret. In a public-key encryption system, the *public key* is used for encryption, while the *private* or *secret key* is used for decryption. While Diffie and Hellman could not find such a system, they showed that public-key cryptography was indeed possible by presenting the Diffie–Hellman key exchange protocol, a solution that is now widely used in secure communications to allow two parties to secretly agree on a shared encryption key.[18]

Diffie and Hellman's publication sparked widespread academic efforts in finding a practical public-key encryption system. This race was finally won in 1978 by Ronald Rivest, Adi Shamir, and Len Adleman, whose solution has since become known as the RSA algorithm.[31]

The Diffie–Hellman and RSA algorithms, in addition to being the first publicly known examples of high quality public-key algorithms, have been among the most widely used. Others include the Cramer–Shoup cryptosystem, ElGamal encryption, and various elliptic curve techniques. See Category:Asymmetric-key cryptosystems.

To much surprise, a document published in 1997 by the Government Communications Headquarters (GCHQ), a British intelligence organization, revealed that cryptographers at GCHQ had anticipated several academic developments.[32] Reportedly, around 1970, James H. Ellis had conceived the principles of asymmetric key cryptography. In 1973, Clifford Cocks invented a solution that essentially resembles the RSA algorithm.[32][33] And in 1974, Malcolm J. Williamson is claimed to have developed the Diffie–Hellman key exchange.[34]

Padlock icon from the Firefox Web browser, which indicates that TLS, a public-key cryptography system, is in use.

Public-key cryptography can also be used for implementing digital signature schemes. A digital signature is reminiscent of an ordinary signature; they both have the characteristic of being easy for a user to produce, but difficult for anyone else to forge. Digital signatures can also be permanently tied to the content of the message being signed; they cannot then be 'moved' from one document to another, for any attempt will be detectable. In digital signature schemes, there are two algorithms: one for *signing*, in which a secret key is used to process the message (or a hash of the message, or both), and one for *verification*, in which the matching public key is used with the message to check the validity of the signature. RSA and DSA are two of the most popular digital signature schemes. Digital signatures are central to the operation of public key infrastructures and many network security schemes (e.g., SSL/TLS, many VPNs, etc.).[25]

Public-key algorithms are most often based on the computational complexity of "hard" problems, often from number theory. For example, the hardness of RSA is related to the integer factorization problem, while Diffie–Hellman and DSA are related to the discrete logarithm problem. More recently, *elliptic curve cryptography* has developed, a system in which security is based on number theoretic problems involving elliptic curves. Because of the difficulty of the underlying problems, most public-key algorithms involve operations such as modular multiplication and exponentiation, which are much more computationally expensive than the techniques used in most block ciphers, especially with typical key sizes. As a result, public-key cryptosystems are commonly hybrid cryptosystems, in which a fast high-quality symmetric-key encryption algorithm is used for the message itself, while the relevant symmetric key is sent with the message, but encrypted using a public-key algorithm. Similarly, hybrid signature schemes are often used, in which a cryptographic hash function is computed, and only the resulting hash is digitally signed.[4]

Cryptanalysis

Main article: Cryptanalysis

The goal of cryptanalysis is to find some weakness or insecurity in a cryptographic scheme, thus permitting its subversion or evasion.

It is a common misconception that every encryption method can be broken. In connection with his WWII work at Bell Labs, Claude Shannon proved that the one-time pad cipher is unbreakable, provided the key material is truly random, never reused, kept secret from all possible attackers, and of equal or greater length than the message.[35] Most ciphers, apart from the one-time pad, can be broken with enough computational effort by brute force attack, but the amount of effort needed may be exponentially dependent on the key size, as compared to the effort needed to make use of the cipher. In such cases, effective security could be achieved if it is proven that the effort required (i.e., "work factor", in Shannon's terms) is beyond the ability of any adversary. This means it must be shown that no efficient method (as opposed to the time-consuming brute force method) can be found to break the cipher. Since no such proof has been found to date, the one-time-pad remains the only theoretically unbreakable cipher.

There are a wide variety of cryptanalytic attacks, and they can be classified in any of several ways. A common distinction turns on what an attacker knows and what capabilities are available. In a ciphertext-only attack, the cryptanalyst has access only to the ciphertext (good modern cryptosystems are usually effectively immune to ciphertext-only attacks). In a known-plaintext attack, the cryptanalyst has access to a ciphertext and its corresponding plaintext (or to many such pairs). In a chosen-plaintext attack, the cryptanalyst may choose a plaintext and learn its corresponding ciphertext (perhaps many times); an example is gardening, used by the British during WWII. Finally, in a chosen-ciphertext attack, the cryptanalyst may be able to *choose* ciphertexts and learn their corresponding plaintexts.[4] Also important, often overwhelmingly so, are mistakes (generally in the design or use of one of the protocols involved; see Cryptanalysis of the Enigma for some historical examples of this).

Variants of the Enigma machine, used by Germany's military and civil authorities from the late 1920s through World War II, implemented a complex electro-mechanical polyalphabetic cipher. Breaking and reading of the Enigma cipher at Poland's Cipher Bureau, for 7 years before the war, and subsequent decryption at Bletchley Park, was important to Allied victory.[8]

Poznań monument (center) to Polish cryptologists whose breaking of Germany's Enigma machine ciphers, beginning in 1932, altered the course of World War II

Cryptanalysis of symmetric-key ciphers typically involves looking for attacks against the block ciphers or stream ciphers that are more efficient than any attack that could be against a perfect cipher. For example, a simple brute force attack against DES requires one known plaintext and 2^{55} decryptions, trying approximately half of the possible keys, to reach a point at which chances are better than even that the key sought will have been found. But this may not be enough assurance; a linear cryptanalysis attack against DES requires 2^{43} known plaintexts and approximately 2^{43} DES operations.[36] This is a considerable improvement on brute force attacks.

Public-key algorithms are based on the computational difficulty of various problems. The most famous of these is integer factorization (e.g., the RSA algorithm is based on a problem related to integer factoring), but the discrete logarithm problem is also important. Much public-key cryptanalysis concerns numerical algorithms for solving these computational problems, or some of them, efficiently (i.e., in a practical time). For instance, the best known algorithms for solving the elliptic curve-based version of discrete logarithm are much more time-consuming than the best known algorithms for factoring, at least for problems of more or less equivalent size. Thus, other things being equal, to achieve an equivalent strength of attack resistance, factoring-based encryption techniques must use larger keys than elliptic curve techniques. For this reason, public-key cryptosystems based on elliptic curves have become popular since their invention in the mid-1990s.

While pure cryptanalysis uses weaknesses in the algorithms themselves, other attacks on cryptosystems are based on actual use of the algorithms in real devices, and are called *side-channel attacks*. If a cryptanalyst has access to, for example, the amount of time the device took to encrypt a number of plaintexts or report an error in a password or PIN character, he may be able to use a timing attack to break a cipher that is otherwise resistant to analysis. An attacker might also study the pattern and length of messages to derive valuable information; this is known as traffic analysis[37] and can be quite useful to an alert adversary. Poor administration of a cryptosystem, such as permitting too short keys, will make any system vulnerable, regardless of other virtues. And, of course, social engineering, and other attacks against the personnel who work with cryptosystems or the messages they handle (e.g., bribery, extortion, blackmail, espionage, torture, ...) may be the most productive attacks of all.

Cryptographic primitives

Much of the theoretical work in cryptography concerns cryptographic *primitives*—algorithms with basic cryptographic properties—and their relationship to other cryptographic problems. More complicated cryptographic tools are then built from these basic primitives. These primitives provide fundamental properties, which are used to develop more complex tools called *cryptosystems* or *cryptographic protocols*, which guarantee one or more high-level security properties. Note however, that the distinction between cryptographic *primitives* and cryptosystems, is quite arbitrary; for example, the RSA algorithm is sometimes considered a cryptosystem, and sometimes a primitive. Typical examples of cryptographic primitives include pseudorandom functions, one-way functions, etc.

Cryptosystems

One or more cryptographic primitives are often used to develop a more complex algorithm, called a cryptographic system, or *cryptosystem*. Cryptosystems (e.g., El-Gamal encryption) are designed to provide particular functionality (e.g., public key encryption) while guaranteeing certain security properties (e.g., chosen-plaintext attack (CPA) security in the random oracle model). Cryptosystems use the properties of the underlying cryptographic primitives to support the system's security properties. Of course, as the distinction between primitives and cryptosystems is somewhat arbitrary, a sophisticated cryptosystem can be derived from a combination of several more primitive cryptosystems. In many cases, the cryptosystem's structure involves back and forth communication among two or more parties in space (e.g., between the sender of a secure message and its receiver) or across time (e.g., cryptographically protected backup data). Such cryptosystems are sometimes called *cryptographic protocols*.

Some widely known cryptosystems include RSA encryption, Schnorr signature, El-Gamal encryption, PGP, etc. More complex cryptosystems include electronic cash[38] systems, signcryption systems, etc. Some more 'theoretical' cryptosystems include interactive proof systems,[39] (like zero-knowledge proofs),[40] systems for secret sharing,[41][42] etc.

Until recently, most security properties of most cryptosystems were demonstrated using empirical techniques or using ad hoc reasoning. Recently, there has been considerable effort to develop formal techniques for establishing the security of cryptosystems; this has been generally called *provable security*. The general idea of provable security is to give arguments about the computational difficulty needed to compromise some security aspect of the cryptosystem (i.e., to any adversary).

The study of how best to implement and integrate cryptography in software applications is itself a distinct field (see Cryptographic engineering and Security engineering).

2.16.4 Legal issues

See also: Cryptography laws in different nations

Prohibitions

Cryptography has long been of interest to intelligence gathering and law enforcement agencies. Secret communications may be criminal or even treasonous. Because of its facilitation of privacy, and the diminution of privacy attendant on its prohibition, cryptography is also of considerable interest to civil rights supporters. Accordingly, there has been a history of controversial legal issues surrounding cryptography, especially since the advent of inexpensive computers has made widespread access to high quality cryptography possible.

In some countries, even the domestic use of cryptography is, or has been, restricted. Until 1999, France significantly restricted the use of cryptography domestically, though it has since relaxed many of these rules. In China and Iran, a license is still required to use cryptography.[5] Many countries have tight restrictions on the use of cryptography. Among the more restrictive are laws in Belarus, Kazakhstan, Mongolia, Pakistan, Singapore, Tunisia, and Vietnam.[43]

In the United States, cryptography is legal for domestic use, but there has been much conflict over legal issues related to cryptography. One particularly important issue has been the export of cryptography and cryptographic software and hardware. Probably because of the importance of cryptanalysis in World War II and an expectation that cryptography would continue to be important for national security, many Western governments have, at some point, strictly regulated export of cryptography. After World War II, it was illegal in the US to sell or distribute encryption technology overseas; in fact, encryption was designated as auxiliary military equipment and put on the United States Munitions List.[44] Until the development of the personal computer, asymmetric key algorithms (i.e., public key techniques), and the Internet, this was not especially problematic. However, as the Internet grew and computers became more widely available, high-quality encryption techniques became well known around the globe.

Export controls

Main article: Export of cryptography

In the 1990s, there were several challenges to US export regulation of cryptography. After the source code for Philip Zimmermann's Pretty Good Privacy (PGP) encryption program found its way onto the Internet in June 1991, a complaint by RSA Security (then called RSA Data Security, Inc.) resulted in a lengthy criminal investigation of Zimmermann by the US Customs Service and the FBI, though no charges were ever filed.[45][46] Daniel J. Bernstein, then a graduate student at UC Berkeley, brought a lawsuit against the US government challenging some aspects of the restrictions based on free speech grounds. The 1995 case Bernstein v. United States ultimately resulted in a 1999 decision that printed source code for cryptographic algorithms and systems was protected as free speech by the United States Constitution.[47]

In 1996, thirty-nine countries signed the Wassenaar Arrangement, an arms control treaty that deals with the export of arms and "dual-use" technologies such as cryptography. The treaty stipulated that the use of cryptography with short key-lengths (56-bit for symmetric encryption, 512-bit for RSA) would no longer be export-controlled.[48] Cryptography exports from the US became less strictly regulated as a consequence of a major relaxation in 2000;[49] there are no longer very many restrictions on key sizes in US-exported mass-market software. Since this relaxation in US export restrictions, and because most personal computers connected to the Internet include US-sourced web browsers such as Firefox or Internet Explorer, almost every Internet user worldwide has potential access to quality cryptography via their browsers (e.g., via Transport Layer Security). The Mozilla Thunderbird and Microsoft Outlook E-mail client programs similarly can transmit and receive emails via TLS, and can send and receive email encrypted with S/MIME. Many Internet users don't realize that their basic application software contains such extensive cryptosystems. These browsers and email programs are so ubiquitous that even governments whose intent is to regulate civilian use of cryptography generally don't find it practical to do much to control distribution or use of cryptography of this quality, so even when such laws are in force, actual enforcement is often effectively impossible.

NSA involvement

See also: Clipper chip

Another contentious issue connected to cryptography in the United States is the influence of the National Security Agency on cipher development and policy. The NSA was involved with the design of DES during its development at IBM and its consideration by the National Bureau of Standards as a possible Federal Standard for cryptography.[50] DES was designed to be resistant to differential cryptanalysis,[51] a powerful and general cryptanalytic technique known to the NSA and IBM, that became publicly known only when it was rediscovered in the late 1980s.[52] According to Steven Levy, IBM discovered differential cryptanalysis,[46] but kept the technique secret at the NSA's request. The technique became publicly known only when Biham and Shamir re-discovered and announced it some years later. The entire affair illustrates the difficulty of determining what resources and knowledge an attacker might actually have.

Another instance of the NSA's involvement was the 1993 Clipper chip affair, an encryption microchip intended to be part of the Capstone cryptography-control initiative. Clipper was widely criticized by cryptographers for two reasons. The cipher algorithm (called Skipjack) was then classified (declassified in 1998, long after the Clipper initiative lapsed). The classified cipher caused concerns that the NSA had deliberately made the cipher weak in order to assist its intelligence efforts. The whole initiative was also criticized based on its violation of Kerckhoffs's Principle, as the scheme included a special escrow key held by the government for use by law enforcement, for example in wiretaps.[46]

Digital rights management

Main article: Digital rights management

Cryptography is central to digital rights management (DRM), a group of techniques for technologically controlling use of copyrighted material, being widely implemented and deployed at the behest of some copyright holders. In 1998, U.S. President Bill Clinton signed the Digital Millennium Copyright Act (DMCA), which criminalized all production, dissemination, and use of certain cryptanalytic techniques and technology (now known or later discovered); specifically, those that could be used to circumvent DRM technological schemes.[53] This had a noticeable impact on the cryptography research community since an argument can be made that *any* cryptanalytic research violated, or might violate, the DMCA. Similar statutes have since been enacted in several countries and regions, including the implementation in the EU Copyright Directive. Similar restrictions are called for by treaties signed by World Intellectual Property Organization member-states.

The United States Department of Justice and FBI have not enforced the DMCA as rigorously as had been feared by some, but the law, nonetheless, remains a controversial one. Niels Ferguson, a well-respected cryptography researcher, has publicly stated that he will not release some of his research into an Intel security design for fear of prosecution under the DMCA.[54] Both Alan Cox (longtime number 2 in Linux kernel development) and Edward Felten (and some of his students at Princeton) have encountered problems related to the Act. Dmitry Sklyarov was arrested during a visit to the US from Russia, and jailed for five months pending trial for alleged violations of the DMCA arising from work he had done in Russia, where the work was legal. In 2007, the cryptographic keys responsible for Blu-ray and HD DVD content scrambling were discovered and released onto the Internet. In both cases, the MPAA sent out numerous DMCA takedown notices, and there was a massive Internet backlash[7] triggered by the perceived impact of such notices on fair use and free speech.

Forced disclosure of encryption keys

Main article: Key disclosure law

In the United Kingdom, the Regulation of Investigatory Powers Act gives UK police the powers to force suspects to decrypt files or hand over passwords that protect encryption keys. Failure to comply is an offense in its own right, punishable on conviction by a two-year jail sentence or up to five years in cases involving national security.[6] Successful prosecutions have occurred under the Act; the first, in 2009,[55] resulted in a term of 13 months' imprisonment.[56] Similar forced disclosure laws in Australia, Finland, France, and India compel individual suspects under investigation to hand over encryption keys or passwords during a criminal investigation.

In the United States, the federal criminal case of United States v. Fricosu addressed whether a search warrant can compel a person to reveal an encryption passphrase or password.[57] The Electronic Frontier Foundation (EFF) argued that this is a violation of the protection from self-incrimination given by the Fifth Amendment.[58] In 2012, the court ruled that under the All Writs Act, the defendant was required to produce an unencrypted hard drive for the court.[59]

In many jurisdictions, the legal status of forced disclosure remains unclear.

2.16.5 See also

- List of cryptographers
- Encyclopedia of Cryptography and Security
- List of important publications in cryptography
- List of multiple discoveries (see "RSA")
- List of unsolved problems in computer science
- Outline of cryptography
- Global surveillance
- Strong cryptography
- A Syllabical and Steganographical table - first cryptography chart

2.16.6 References

[1] Liddell, Henry George; Scott, Robert; Jones, Henry Stuart; McKenzie, Roderick (1984). *A Greek-English Lexicon*. Oxford University Press.

[2] Rivest, Ronald L. (1990). "Cryptology". In J. Van Leeuwen. *Handbook of Theoretical Computer Science* **1**. Elsevier.

[3] Bellare, Mihir; Rogaway, Phillip (21 September 2005). "Introduction". *Introduction to Modern Cryptography*. p. 10.

[4] Menezes, A. J.; van Oorschot, P. C.; Vanstone, S. A. *Handbook of Applied Cryptography*. ISBN 0-8493-8523-7.

[5] "Overview per country". *Crypto Law Survey*. February 2013. Retrieved 26 March 2015.

[6] "UK Data Encryption Disclosure Law Takes Effect". *PC World*. 1 October 2007. Retrieved 26 March 2015.

[7] Doctorow, Cory (2 May 2007). "Digg users revolt over AACS key". *Boing Boing*. Retrieved 26 March 2015.

[8] Kahn, David (1967). *The Codebreakers*. ISBN 0-684-83130-9.

[9] Oded Goldreich, *Foundations of Cryptography, Volume 1: Basic Tools*, Cambridge University Press, 2001, ISBN 0-521-79172-3

[10] "Cryptology (definition)". *Merriam-Webster's Collegiate Dictionary* (11th ed.). Merriam-Webster. Retrieved 26 March 2015.

[11] "RFC 2828 - Internet Security Glossary". *Internet Engineering Task Force*. May 2000. Retrieved 26 March 2015.

[12] Íãshchenko, V. V. (2002). *Cryptography: an introduction*. AMS Bookstore. p. 6. ISBN 0-8218-2986-6.

[13] Singh, Simon (2000). *The Code Book*. New York: Anchor Books. pp. 14–20. ISBN 9780385495325.

[14] Al-Kadi, Ibrahim A. (April 1992). "The origins of cryptology: The Arab contributions". *Cryptologia* **16** (2): 97–126.

[15] Schrödel, Tobias (October 2008). "Breaking Short Vigenère Ciphers". *Cryptologia* **32** (4): 334–337. doi:10.1080/01611190802336097.

[16] Hakim, Joy (1995). *A History of US: War, Peace and all that Jazz*. New York: Oxford University Press. ISBN 0-19-509514-6.

[17] Gannon, James (2001). *Stealing Secrets, Telling Lies: How Spies and Codebreakers Helped Shape the Twentieth Century*. Washington, D.C.: Brassey's. ISBN 1-57488-367-4.

[18] Diffie, Whitfield; Hellman, Martin (November 1976). "New Directions in Cryptography" (pdf). *IEEE Transactions on Information Theory*. IT-22: 644–654.

[19] *Cryptography: Theory and Practice*, Third Edition (Discrete Mathematics and Its Applications), 2005, by Douglas R. Stinson, Chapman and Hall/CRC

[20] Blaze, Matt; Diffie, Whitefield; Rivest, Ronald L.; Schneier, Bruce; Shimomura, Tsutomu; Thompson, Eric; Wiener, Michael (January 1996). "Minimal key lengths for symmetric ciphers to provide adequate commercial security". Fortify. Retrieved 26 March 2015.

[21] "FIPS PUB 197: The official Advanced Encryption Standard" (PDF). *Computer Security Resource Center*. National Institute of Standards and Technology. Retrieved 26 March 2015.

[22] "NCUA letter to credit unions" (PDF). *National Credit Union Administration*. July 2004. Retrieved 26 March 2015.

[23] "RFC 2440 - Open PGP Message Format". *Internet Engineering Task Force*. November 1998. Retrieved 26 March 2015.

[24] Golen, Pawel (19 July 2002). "SSH". *WindowSecurity*. Retrieved 26 March 2015.

[25] Schneier, Bruce (1996). *Applied Cryptography* (2nd ed.). Wiley. ISBN 0-471-11709-9.

[26] "Notices". *Federal Register* **72** (212). 2 November 2007. Archived 28 February 2008 at the Wayback Machine

[27] "NIST Selects Winner of Secure Hash Algorithm (SHA-3) Competition". *Tech Beat*. National Institute of Standards and Technology. October 2, 2012. Retrieved 26 March 2015.

[28] Diffie, Whitfield; Hellman, Martin (8 June 1976). "Multi-user cryptographic techniques". *AFIPS Proceedings* **45**: 109–112.

[29] Ralph Merkle was working on similar ideas at the time and encountered publication delays, and Hellman has suggested that the term used should be Diffie–Hellman–Merkle aysmmetric key cryptography.

[30] Kahn, David (Fall 1979). "Cryptology Goes Public". *Foreign Affairs* **58** (1): 153.

[31] Rivest, Ronald L.; Shamir, A.; Adleman, L. (1978). "A Method for Obtaining Digital Signatures and Public-Key Cryptosystems". *Communications of the ACM* (Association for Computing Machinery) **21** (2): 120–126.
Archived November 16, 2001 at the Wayback Machine
Previously released as an MIT "Technical Memo" in April 1977, and published in Martin Gardner's *Scientific American* Mathematical recreations column

[32] Wayner, Peter (24 December 1997). "British Document Outlines Early Encryption Discovery". *New York Times*. Retrieved 26 March 2015.

[33] Cocks, Clifford (20 November 1973). "A Note on 'Non-Secret Encryption'" (PDF). *CESG Research Report*.

[34] Singh, Simon (1999). *The Code Book*. Doubleday. pp. 279–292.

[35] Shannon, Claude; Weaver, Warren (1963). *The Mathematical Theory of Communication*. University of Illinois Press. ISBN 0-252-72548-4.

[36] Junod, Pascal (2001). "On the Complexity of Matsui's Attack" (PDF). *Selected Areas in Cryptography*.

[37] Song, Dawn; Wagner, David A.; Tian, Xuqing (2001). "Timing Analysis of Keystrokes and Timing Attacks on SSH" (PDF). *Tenth USENIX Security Symposium*.

[38] Brands, S. (1994). "Untraceable Off-line Cash in Wallets with Observers". *Advances in Cryptology—Proceedings of CRYPTO* (Springer-Verlag).

[39] Babai, László (1985). "Trading group theory for randomness". *Proceedings of the Seventeenth Annual Symposium on the Theory of Computing* (Association for Computing Machinery).

[40] Goldwasser, S.; Micali, S.; Rackoff, C. (1989). "The Knowledge Complexity of Interactive Proof Systems". *SIAM Journal on Computing* **18** (1): 186–208.

[41] Blakley, G. (June 1979). "Safeguarding cryptographic keys". *Proceedings of AFIPS 1979* **48**: 313–317.

[42] Shamir, A. (1979). "How to share a secret". *Communications of the ACM* (Association for Computing Machinery) **22**: 612–613.

[43] "6.5.1 WHAT ARE THE CRYPTOGRAPHIC POLICIES OF SOME COUNTRIES?". RSA Laboratories. Retrieved 26 March 2015.

[44] Rosenoer, Jonathan (1995). "CRYPTOGRAPHY & SPEECH". *CyberLaw*. Archived December 1, 2005 at the Wayback Machine

[45] "Case Closed on Zimmermann PGP Investigation". *IEEE Computer Society's Technical Committee on Security and Privacy*. 14 February 1996. Retrieved 26 March 2015.

[46] Levy, Steven (2001). *Crypto: How the Code Rebels Beat the Government—Saving Privacy in the Digital Age*. Penguin Books. p. 56. ISBN 0-14-024432-8. OCLC 244148644 48066852 48846639.

[47] "Bernstein v USDOJ". *Electronic Privacy Information Center*. United States Court of Appeals for the Ninth Circuit. 6 May 1999. Retrieved 26 March 2015.

[48] "DUAL-USE LIST - CATEGORY 5 – PART 2 – "INFORMATION SECURITY"" (DOC). *Wassenaar Arrangement*. Retrieved 26 March 2015.

[49] "6.4 UNITED STATES CRYPTOGRAPHY EXPORT/IMPORT LAWS". *RSA Laboratories*. Retrieved 26 March 2015.

[50] Schneier, Bruce (15 June 2000). "The Data Encryption Standard (DES)". *Crypto-Gram*. Retrieved 26 March 2015.

[51] Coppersmith, D. (May 1994). "The Data Encryption Standard (DES) and its strength against attacks" (PDF). *IBM Journal of Research and Development* **38** (3): 243. doi:10.1147/rd.383.0243. Retrieved 26 March 2015.

[52] Biham, E.; Shamir, A. (1991). "Differential cryptanalysis of DES-like cryptosystems" (PDF). *Journal of Cryptology* (Springer-Verlag) **4** (1): 3–72. Retrieved 26 March 2015.

[53] "The Digital Millennium Copyright Act of 1998" (PDF). *United States Copyright Office*. Retrieved 26 March 2015.

[54] Ferguson, Niels (15 August 2001). "Censorship in action: why I don't publish my HDCP results". Archived December 1, 2001 at the Wayback Machine

[55] Williams, Christopher (11 August 2009). "Two convicted for refusal to decrypt data". *The Register*. Retrieved 26 March 2015.

[56] Williams, Christopher (24 November 2009). "UK jails schizophrenic for refusal to decrypt files". *The Register*. Retrieved 26 March 2015.

[57] Ingold, John (January 4, 2012). "Password case reframes Fifth Amendment rights in context of digital world". *The Denver Post*. Retrieved 26 March 2015.

[58] Leyden, John (13 July 2011). "US court test for rights not to hand over crypto keys". *The Register*. Retrieved 26 March 2015.

[59] "ORDER GRANTING APPLICATION UNDER THE ALL WRITS ACT REQUIRING DEFENDANT FRICOSU TO ASSIST IN THE EXECUTION OF PREVIOUSLY ISSUED SEARCH WARRANTS" (PDF). United States District Court for the District of Colorado. Retrieved 26 March 2015.

2.16.7 Further reading

Further information: Books on cryptography

- Becket, B (1988). *Introduction to Cryptology*. Blackwell Scientific Publications. ISBN 0-632-01836-4. OCLC 16832704. Excellent coverage of many classical ciphers and cryptography concepts and of the "modern" DES and RSA systems.

- *Cryptography and Mathematics* by Bernhard Esslinger, 200 pages, part of the free open-source package CrypTool, PDF download at the Wayback Machine (archived July 22, 2011). CrypTool is the most widespread e-learning program about cryptography and cryptanalysis, open source.

- *In Code: A Mathematical Journey* by Sarah Flannery (with David Flannery). Popular account of Sarah's award-winning project on public-key cryptography, co-written with her father.

- James Gannon, *Stealing Secrets, Telling Lies: How Spies and Codebreakers Helped Shape the Twentieth Century*, Washington, D.C., Brassey's, 2001, ISBN 1-57488-367-4.

- Oded Goldreich, Foundations of Cryptography, in two volumes, Cambridge University Press, 2001 and 2004.

- *Introduction to Modern Cryptography* by Jonathan Katz and Yehuda Lindell.

- *Alvin's Secret Code* by Clifford B. Hicks (children's novel that introduces some basic cryptography and cryptanalysis).

- Ibrahim A. Al-Kadi, "The Origins of Cryptology: the Arab Contributions," Cryptologia, vol. 16, no. 2 (April 1992), pp. 97–126.

- Christof Paar, Jan Pelzl, Understanding Cryptography, A Textbook for Students and Practitioners. Springer, 2009. (Slides, online cryptography lectures and other information are available on the companion web site.) Very accessible introduction to practical cryptography for non-mathematicians.

- *Introduction to Modern Cryptography* by Phillip Rogaway and Mihir Bellare, a mathematical introduction to theoretical cryptography including reduction-based security proofs. PDF download.

- Johann-Christoph Woltag, 'Coded Communications (Encryption)' in Rüdiger Wolfrum (ed) Max Planck Encyclopedia of Public International Law (Oxford University Press 2009). *"Max Planck Encyclopedia of Public International Law"., giving an overview of international law issues regarding cryptography.

- Jonathan Arbib & John Dwyer, Discrete Mathematics for Cryptography, 1st Edition ISBN 978-1-907934-01-8.

- Stallings, William (March 2013). *Cryptography and Network Security: Principles and Practice* (6th ed.). Prentice Hall. ISBN 978-0133354690.

2.16.8 External links

- The dictionary definition of cryptography at Wiktionary

- Media related to Cryptography at Wikimedia Commons

-
- Cryptography on *In Our Time* at the BBC. (listen now)

- Crypto Glossary and Dictionary of Technical Cryptography

- NSA's CryptoKids.

- Overview and Applications of Cryptology by the CrypTool Team; PDF; 3.8 MB—July 2008

- A Course in Cryptography by Raphael Pass & Abhi Shelat - offered at Cornell in the form of lecture notes.

- Cryptocorner.com by Chuck Easttom - A generalized resource on all aspects of cryptology.

- For more on the use of cryptographic elements in fiction, see: Dooley, John F., William and Marilyn Ingersoll Professor of Computer Science, Knox College (23 August 2012). "Cryptology in Fiction".

- The George Fabyan Collection at the Library of Congress has early editions of works of seventeenth-century English literature, publications relating to cryptography.

2.17 Distributed computing

"Distributed Information Processing" redirects here. For the computer company, see DIP Research.

Distributed computing is a field of computer science that studies distributed systems. A *distributed system* is a software system in which components located on networked computers communicate and coordinate their actions by passing messages.[1] The components interact with each other in order to achieve a common goal. Three significant characteristics of distributed systems are: concurrency of components, lack of a global clock, and independent failure of components.[1] Examples of distributed systems vary from SOA-based systems to massively multiplayer online games to peer-to-peer applications.

A computer program that runs in a distributed system is called a **distributed program**, and distributed programming is the process of writing such programs.[2] There are many alternatives for the message passing mechanism, including RPC-like connectors and message queues.

A goal and challenge pursued by some computer scientists and practitioners in distributed systems is location transparency; however, this goal has fallen out of favour in industry, as distributed systems are different from conventional non-distributed systems, and the differences, such as network partitions, partial system failures, and partial upgrades, cannot simply be "papered over" by attempts at "transparency" - see CAP theorem.

Distributed computing also refers to the use of distributed systems to solve computational problems. In *distributed computing*, a problem is divided into many tasks, each of which is solved by one or more computers,[3] which communicate with each other by message passing.[4]

2.17.1 Introduction

The word *distributed* in terms such as "distributed system", "distributed programming", and "distributed algorithm" originally referred to computer networks where individual computers were physically distributed within some geographical area.[5] The terms are nowadays used in a much wider sense, even referring to autonomous processes that run on the same physical computer and interact with each other by message passing.[4] While there is no single definition of a distributed system,[6] the following defining properties are commonly used:

- There are several autonomous computational entities, each of which has its own local memory.[7]

- The entities communicate with each other by message passing.[8]

In this article, the computational entities are called *computers* or *nodes*.

A distributed system may have a common goal, such as solving a large computational problem.[9] Alternatively, each computer may have its own user with individual needs, and the purpose of the distributed system is to coordinate the use of shared resources or provide communication services to the users.[10]

Other typical properties of distributed systems include the following:

- The system has to tolerate failures in individual computers.[11]

- The structure of the system (network topology, network latency, number of computers) is not known in advance, the system may consist of different kinds of computers and network links, and the system may change during the execution of a distributed program.[12]

- Each computer has only a limited, incomplete view of the system. Each computer may know only one part of the input.[13]

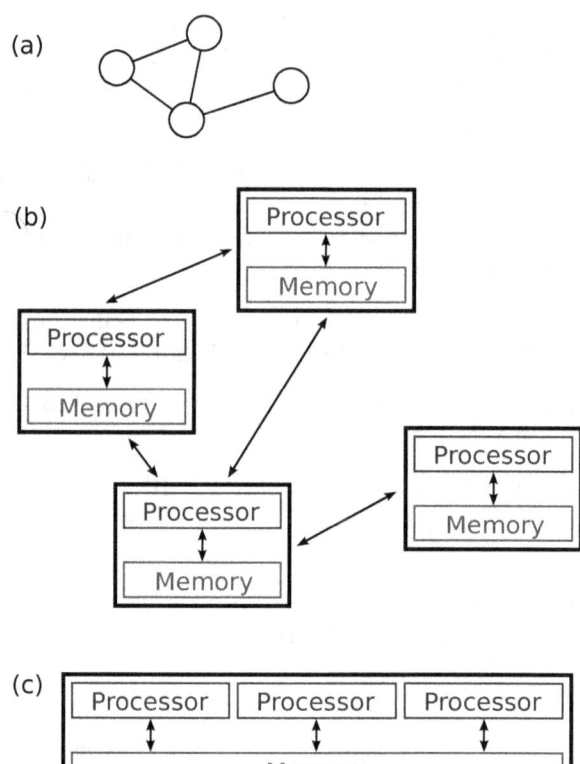

(a)–(b) A distributed system.
(c) A parallel system.

Architecture

Client/Server System : The Client-server architecture is a way to provide a service from a central source. There is a single server that provides a service, and many clients that communicate with the server to consume its products. In this architecture, clients and servers have different jobs. The server's job is to respond to service requests from clients, while a client's job is to use the data provided in response in order to perform some tasks.

Peer-to-Peer System : The term peer-to-peer is used to describe distributed systems in which labour is divided among all the components of the system. All the computers send and receive data, and they all contribute some processing power and memory to a distributed computation. As a distributed system increases in size, its capacity of computational resources increases.

2.17.2 Parallel and distributed computing

Distributed systems are groups of networked computers, which have the same goal for their work. The terms "concurrent computing", "parallel computing", and "distributed computing" have a lot of overlap, and no clear distinction exists between them.[14] The same system may be characterized both as "parallel" and "distributed"; the processors in a typical distributed system run concurrently in parallel.[15] Parallel computing may be seen as a particular tightly coupled form of distributed computing,[16] and distributed computing may be seen as a loosely coupled form of parallel computing.[6] Nevertheless, it is possible to roughly classify concurrent systems as "parallel" or "distributed" using the following criteria:

- In parallel computing, all processors may have access to a shared memory to exchange information between processors.[17]

- In distributed computing, each processor has its own private memory (distributed memory). Information is exchanged by passing messages between the processors.[18]

The figure on the right illustrates the difference between distributed and parallel systems. Figure (a) is a schematic view of a typical distributed system; as usual, the system is represented as a network topology in which each node is a computer and each line connecting the nodes is a communication link. Figure (b) shows the same distributed system in more detail: each computer has its own local memory, and information can be exchanged only by passing messages from one node to another by using the available communication links. Figure (c) shows a parallel system in which each processor has a direct access to a shared memory.

The situation is further complicated by the traditional uses of the terms parallel and distributed *algorithm* that do not quite match the above definitions of parallel and distributed *systems*; see the section Theoretical foundations below for more detailed discussion. Nevertheless, as a rule of thumb, high-performance parallel computation in a shared-memory multiprocessor uses parallel algorithms while the coordination of a large-scale distributed system uses distributed algorithms.

2.17.3 History

The use of concurrent processes that communicate by message-passing has its roots in operating system architectures studied in the 1960s.[19] The first widespread distributed systems were local-area networks such as Ethernet, which was invented in the 1970s.[20]

ARPANET, the predecessor of the Internet, was introduced in the late 1960s, and ARPANET e-mail was invented in the early 1970s. E-mail became the most successful application of ARPANET,[21] and it is probably the earliest example of a large-scale distributed application. In addition to ARPANET, and its successor, the Internet, other early worldwide computer networks included Usenet and FidoNet from 1980s, both of which were used to support distributed discussion systems.

The study of distributed computing became its own branch of computer science in the late 1970s and early 1980s. The first conference in the field, Symposium on Principles of Distributed Computing (PODC), dates back to 1982, and its European counterpart International Symposium on Distributed Computing (DISC) was first held in 1985.

2.17.4 Applications

Reasons for using distributed systems and distributed computing may include:

1. The very nature of an application may *require* the use of a communication network that connects several computers: for example, data produced in one physical location and required in another location.

2. There are many cases in which the use of a single computer would be possible in principle, but the use of a distributed system is *beneficial* for practical reasons. For example, it may be more cost-efficient to obtain the desired level of performance by using a cluster of several low-end computers, in comparison with a single high-end computer. A distributed system can provide more reliability than a non-distributed system, as there is no single point of failure. Moreover, a distributed system may be easier to expand and manage than a monolithic uniprocessor system.[22]

Ghaemi *et al.* define a **distributed query** as a query "that selects data from databases located at multiple sites in a network" and offer as an SQL example:

SELECT ename, dname
FROM   company.emp   e,   company.dept@sales.goods d
WHERE e.deptno = d.deptno[23]

2.17.5 Examples

Examples of distributed systems and applications of distributed computing include the following:[24]

- Telecommunication networks:
    - Telephone networks and cellular networks
    - Computer networks such as the Internet

- Wireless sensor networks
- Routing algorithms
- Network applications:
  - World wide web and peer-to-peer networks
  - Massively multiplayer online games and virtual reality communities
  - Distributed databases and distributed database management systems
  - Network file systems
  - Distributed information processing systems such as banking systems and airline reservation systems
- Real-time process control:
  - Aircraft control systems
  - Industrial control systems
- Parallel computation:
  - Scientific computing, including cluster computing and grid computing and various volunteer computing projects; see the list of distributed computing projects
  - Distributed rendering in computer graphics

2.17.6 Theoretical foundations

Main article: Distributed algorithm

Models

Many tasks that we would like to automate by using a computer are of question–answer type: we would like to ask a question and the computer should produce an answer. In theoretical computer science, such tasks are called computational problems. Formally, a computational problem consists of *instances* together with a *solution* for each instance. Instances are questions that we can ask, and solutions are desired answers to these questions.

Theoretical computer science seeks to understand which computational problems can be solved by using a computer (computability theory) and how efficiently (computational complexity theory). Traditionally, it is said that a problem can be solved by using a computer if we can design an algorithm that produces a correct solution for any given instance. Such an algorithm can be implemented as a computer program that runs on a general-purpose computer: the program reads a problem instance from input, performs some computation, and produces the solution as output. Formalisms such as random access machines or universal Turing machines can be used as abstract models of a sequential general-purpose computer executing such an algorithm.

The field of concurrent and distributed computing studies similar questions in the case of either multiple computers, or a computer that executes a network of interacting processes: which computational problems can be solved in such a network and how efficiently? However, it is not at all obvious what is meant by "solving a problem" in the case of a concurrent or distributed system: for example, what is the task of the algorithm designer, and what is the concurrent or distributed equivalent of a sequential general-purpose computer?

The discussion below focuses on the case of multiple computers, although many of the issues are the same for concurrent processes running on a single computer.

Three viewpoints are commonly used:

Parallel algorithms in shared-memory model

- All processors have access to a shared memory. The algorithm designer chooses the program executed by each processor.
- One theoretical model is the parallel random access machines (PRAM) that are used.[25] However, the classical PRAM model assumes synchronous access to the shared memory.
- Shared-memory programs can be extended to distributed systems if the underlying operating system encapsulates the communication between nodes and virtually unifies the memory across all individual systems.
- A model that is closer to the behavior of real-world multiprocessor machines and takes into account the use of machine instructions, such as Compare-and-swap (CAS), is that of *asynchronous shared memory*. There is a wide body of work on this model, a summary of which can be found in the literature.[26][27]

Parallel algorithms in message-passing model

- The algorithm designer chooses the structure of the network, as well as the program executed by each computer.
- Models such as Boolean circuits and sorting networks are used.[28] A Boolean circuit can be seen as a computer network: each gate is a computer that runs an extremely simple computer program. Similarly, a sorting network can be seen as a computer network: each comparator is a computer.

2.17. DISTRIBUTED COMPUTING

Distributed algorithms in message-passing model

- The algorithm designer only chooses the computer program. All computers run the same program. The system must work correctly regardless of the structure of the network.

- A commonly used model is a graph with one finite-state machine per node.

In the case of distributed algorithms, computational problems are typically related to graphs. Often the graph that describes the structure of the computer network *is* the problem instance. This is illustrated in the following example.

An example

Consider the computational problem of finding a coloring of a given graph G. Different fields might take the following approaches:

Centralized algorithms

- The graph G is encoded as a string, and the string is given as input to a computer. The computer program finds a coloring of the graph, encodes the coloring as a string, and outputs the result.

Parallel algorithms

- Again, the graph G is encoded as a string. However, multiple computers can access the same string in parallel. Each computer might focus on one part of the graph and produce a coloring for that part.

- The main focus is on high-performance computation that exploits the processing power of multiple computers in parallel.

Distributed algorithms

- The graph G is the structure of the computer network. There is one computer for each node of G and one communication link for each edge of G. Initially, each computer only knows about its immediate neighbors in the graph G; the computers must exchange messages with each other to discover more about the structure of G. Each computer must produce its own color as output.

- The main focus is on coordinating the operation of an arbitrary distributed system.

While the field of parallel algorithms has a different focus than the field of distributed algorithms, there is a lot of interaction between the two fields. For example, the Cole–Vishkin algorithm for graph coloring[29] was originally presented as a parallel algorithm, but the same technique can also be used directly as a distributed algorithm.

Moreover, a parallel algorithm can be implemented either in a parallel system (using shared memory) or in a distributed system (using message passing).[30] The traditional boundary between parallel and distributed algorithms (choose a suitable network vs. run in any given network) does not lie in the same place as the boundary between parallel and distributed systems (shared memory vs. message passing).

Complexity measures

In parallel algorithms, yet another resource in addition to time and space is the number of computers. Indeed, often there is a trade-off between the running time and the number of computers: the problem can be solved faster if there are more computers running in parallel (see speedup). If a decision problem can be solved in polylogarithmic time by using a polynomial number of processors, then the problem is said to be in the class NC.[31] The class NC can be defined equally well by using the PRAM formalism or Boolean circuits – PRAM machines can simulate Boolean circuits efficiently and vice versa.[32]

In the analysis of distributed algorithms, more attention is usually paid on communication operations than computational steps. Perhaps the simplest model of distributed computing is a synchronous system where all nodes operate in a lockstep fashion. During each *communication round*, all nodes in parallel (1) receive the latest messages from their neighbours, (2) perform arbitrary local computation, and (3) send new messages to their neighbours. In such systems, a central complexity measure is the number of synchronous communication rounds required to complete the task.[33]

This complexity measure is closely related to the diameter of the network. Let D be the diameter of the network. On the one hand, any computable problem can be solved trivially in a synchronous distributed system in approximately $2D$ communication rounds: simply gather all information in one location (D rounds), solve the problem, and inform each node about the solution (D rounds).

On the other hand, if the running time of the algorithm is much smaller than D communication rounds, then the nodes in the network must produce their output without having the possibility to obtain information about distant parts of the network. In other words, the nodes must make globally consistent decisions based on information that is available in their *local neighbourhood*. Many distributed algorithms are known with the running time much smaller than D rounds, and understanding which problems can be solved by such algorithms is one of the central research questions of the field.[34]

Other commonly used measures are the total number of bits transmitted in the network (cf. communication complexity).

Other problems

Traditional computational problems take the perspective that we ask a question, a computer (or a distributed system) processes the question for a while, and then produces an answer and stops. However, there are also problems where we do not want the system to ever stop. Examples of such problems include the dining philosophers problem and other similar mutual exclusion problems. In these problems, the distributed system is supposed to continuously coordinate the use of shared resources so that no conflicts or deadlocks occur.

There are also fundamental challenges that are unique to distributed computing. The first example is challenges that are related to *fault-tolerance*. Examples of related problems include consensus problems,[35] Byzantine fault tolerance,[36] and self-stabilisation.[37]

A lot of research is also focused on understanding the *asynchronous* nature of distributed systems:

- Synchronizers can be used to run synchronous algorithms in asynchronous systems.[38]
- Logical clocks provide a causal happened-before ordering of events.[39]
- Clock synchronization algorithms provide globally consistent physical time stamps.[40]

Properties of distributed systems

So far the focus has been on *designing* a distributed system that solves a given problem. A complementary research problem is *studying* the properties of a given distributed system.

The halting problem is an analogous example from the field of centralised computation: we are given a computer program and the task is to decide whether it halts or runs forever. The halting problem is undecidable in the general case, and naturally understanding the behaviour of a computer network is at least as hard as understanding the behaviour of one computer.

However, there are many interesting special cases that are decidable. In particular, it is possible to reason about the behaviour of a network of finite-state machines. One example is telling whether a given network of interacting (asynchronous and non-deterministic) finite-state machines can reach a deadlock. This problem is PSPACE-complete,[41] i.e., it is decidable, but it is not likely that there is an efficient (centralised, parallel or distributed) algorithm that solves the problem in the case of large networks.

2.17.7 Coordinator election

Coordinator election (sometimes called **leader election**) is the process of designating a single process as the organizer of some task distributed among several computers (nodes). Before the task is begun, all network nodes are either unaware which node will serve as the "coordinator" (or leader) of the task, or unable to communicate with the current coordinator. After a coordinator election algorithm has been run, however, each node throughout the network recognizes a particular, unique node as the task coordinator.

The network nodes communicate among themselves in order to decide which of them will get into the "coordinator" state. For that, they need some method in order to break the symmetry among them. For example, if each node has unique and comparable identities, then the nodes can compare their identities, and decide that the node with the highest identity is the coordinator.

The definition of this problem is often attributed to LeLann, who formalized it as a method to create a new token in a token ring network in which the token has been lost.

Coordinator election algorithms are designed to be economical in terms of total bytes transmitted, and time. The algorithm suggested by Gallager, Humblet, and Spira [42] for general undirected graphs has had a strong impact on the design of distributed algorithms in general, and won the Dijkstra Prize for an influential paper in distributed computing.

Many other algorithms were suggested for different kind of network graphs, such as undirected rings, unidirectional rings, complete graphs, grids, directed Euler graphs, and others. A general method that decouples the issue of the graph family from the design of the coordinator election algorithm was suggested by Korach, Kutten, and Moran.[43]

In order to perform coordination, distributed systems employ the concept of coordinators. The coordinator election problem is to choose a process from among a group of processes on different processors in a distributed system to act as the central coordinator. Several central coordinator election algorithms exist.[44]

Bully algorithm

When using the Bully algorithm, any process sends a message to the current coordinator. If there is no response within a given time limit, the process tries to elect itself as leader.

Chang and Roberts algorithm

The Chang and Roberts algorithm (or "Ring Algorithm") is a ring-based election algorithm used to find a process with the largest unique identification number.

2.17.8 Architectures

Various hardware and software architectures are used for distributed computing. At a lower level, it is necessary to interconnect multiple CPUs with some sort of network, regardless of whether that network is printed onto a circuit board or made up of loosely coupled devices and cables. At a higher level, it is necessary to interconnect processes running on those CPUs with some sort of communication system.

Distributed programming typically falls into one of several basic architectures or categories: client–server, 3-tier architecture, *n*-tier architecture, distributed objects, loose coupling, or tight coupling.

- Client–server: Smart client code contacts the server for data then formats and displays it to the user. Input at the client is committed back to the server when it represents a permanent change.

- 3-tier architecture: Three tier systems move the client intelligence to a middle tier so that stateless clients can be used. This simplifies application deployment. Most web applications are 3-Tier.

- *n*-tier architecture: *n*-tier refers typically to web applications which further forward their requests to other enterprise services. This type of application is the one most responsible for the success of application servers.

- highly coupled (clustered): refers typically to a cluster of machines that closely work together, running a shared process in parallel. The task is subdivided in parts that are made individually by each one and then put back together to make the final result.

- Peer-to-peer: an architecture where there is no special machine or machines that provide a service or manage the network resources. Instead all responsibilities are uniformly divided among all machines, known as peers. Peers can serve both as clients and servers.

- Space based: refers to an infrastructure that creates the illusion (virtualization) of one single address-space. Data are transparently replicated according to application needs. Decoupling in time, space and reference is achieved.

Another basic aspect of distributed computing architecture is the method of communicating and coordinating work among concurrent processes. Through various message passing protocols, processes may communicate directly with one another, typically in a master/slave relationship. Alternatively, a "database-centric" architecture can enable distributed computing to be done without any form of direct inter-process communication, by utilizing a shared database.[45]

2.17.9 See also

- AppScale
- BOINC
- Code mobility
- Decentralized computing
- Distributed algorithmic mechanism design
- Distributed cache
- Distributed operating system
- Edsger W. Dijkstra Prize in Distributed Computing
- Folding@home
- Inferno
- Jungle computing
- Layered queueing network
- Library Oriented Architecture - LOA
- List of distributed computing conferences
- List of important publications in concurrent, parallel, and distributed computing
- Parallel distributed processing
- Parallel programming model
- Plan 9 from Bell Labs

2.17.10 Notes

[1] Coulouris, George; Jean Dollimore; Tim Kindberg; Gordon Blair (2011). *Distributed Systems: Concepts and Design (5th Edition)*. Boston: Addison-Wesley. ISBN 0-132-14301-1.

[2] Andrews (2000). Dolev (2000). Ghosh (2007), p. 10.

[3] Godfrey (2002).

[4] Andrews (2000), p. 291–292. Dolev (2000), p. 5.

[5] Lynch (1996), p. 1.

[6] Ghosh (2007), p. 10.

[7] Andrews (2000), p. 8–9, 291. Dolev (2000), p. 5. Ghosh (2007), p. 3. Lynch (1996), p. xix, 1. Peleg (2000), p. xv.

[8] Andrews (2000), p. 291. Ghosh (2007), p. 3. Peleg (2000), p. 4.

[9] Ghosh (2007), p. 3–4. Peleg (2000), p. 1.

[10] Ghosh (2007), p. 4. Peleg (2000), p. 2.

[11] Ghosh (2007), p. 4, 8. Lynch (1996), p. 2–3. Peleg (2000), p. 4.

[12] Lynch (1996), p. 2. Peleg (2000), p. 1.

[13] Ghosh (2007), p. 7. Lynch (1996), p. xix, 2. Peleg (2000), p. 4.

[14] Ghosh (2007), p. 10. Keidar (2008).

[15] Lynch (1996), p. xix, 1–2. Peleg (2000), p. 1.

[16] Peleg (2000), p. 1.

[17] Papadimitriou (1994), Chapter 15. Keidar (2008).

[18] See references in Introduction.

[19] Andrews (2000), p. 348.

[20] Andrews (2000), p. 32.

[21] Peter (2004), The history of email.

[22] Elmasri & Navathe (2000), Section 24.1.2.

[23] Ghaemi, Reza; Milani Fard, Amin; Tabatabaee, Hamid; Sadeghizadeh, Mahdi (2008). "Evolutionary Query Optimization for Heterogeneous Distributed Database Systems" (PDF). *World Academy of Science, Engineering and Technology* (World Academy of Science, Engineering and Technology) (19): 43–49. Retrieved 2013-07-16.

[24] Andrews (2000), p. 10–11. Ghosh (2007), p. 4–6. Lynch (1996), p. xix, 1. Peleg (2000), p. xv. Elmasri & Navathe (2000), Section 24.

[25] Cormen, Leiserson & Rivest (1990), Section 30.

[26] Herlihy & Shavit (2008), Chapters 2-6.

[27] Lynch (1996)

[28] Cormen, Leiserson & Rivest (1990), Sections 28 and 29.

[29] Cole & Vishkin (1986). Cormen, Leiserson & Rivest (1990), Section 30.5.

[30] Andrews (2000), p. ix.

[31] Arora & Barak (2009), Section 6.7. Papadimitriou (1994), Section 15.3.

[32] Papadimitriou (1994), Section 15.2.

[33] Lynch (1996), p. 17–23.

[34] Peleg (2000), Sections 2.3 and 7. Linial (1992). Naor & Stockmeyer (1995).

[35] Lynch (1996), Sections 5–7. Ghosh (2007), Chapter 13.

[36] Lynch (1996), p. 99–102. Ghosh (2007), p. 192–193.

[37] Dolev (2000). Ghosh (2007), Chapter 17.

[38] Lynch (1996), Section 16. Peleg (2000), Section 6.

[39] Lynch (1996), Section 18. Ghosh (2007), Sections 6.2–6.3.

[40] Ghosh (2007), Section 6.4.

[41] Papadimitriou (1994), Section 19.3.

[42] R. G. Gallager, P. A. Humblet, and P. M. Spira (January 1983). "A Distributed Algorithm for Minimum-Weight Spanning Trees" (PDF). *ACM Transactions on Programming Languages and Systems* **5** (1): 66–77. doi:10.1145/357195.357200.

[43] Ephraim Korach, Shay Kutten, Shlomo Moran (1990). "A Modular Technique for the Design of Efficient Distributed Leader Finding Algorithms". *ACM Transactions on Programming Languages and Systems* **12** (1): 84–101. doi:10.1145/77606.77610.

[44] Hamilton, Howard. "Distributed Algorithms". Retrieved 2013-03-03.

[45] Lind P, Alm M (2006), "A database-centric virtual chemistry system", *J Chem Inf Model* **46** (3): 1034–9, doi:10.1021/ci050360b, PMID 16711722.

2.17.11 References

Books

- Andrews, Gregory R. (2000), *Foundations of Multithreaded, Parallel, and Distributed Programming*, Addison–Wesley, ISBN 0-201-35752-6.

- Arora, Sanjeev; Barak, Boaz (2009), *Computational Complexity – A Modern Approach*, Cambridge, ISBN 978-0-521-42426-4.

- Cormen, Thomas H.; Leiserson, Charles E.; Rivest, Ronald L. (1990), *Introduction to Algorithms* (1st ed.), MIT Press, ISBN 0-262-03141-8.

- Dolev, Shlomi (2000), *Self-Stabilization*, MIT Press, ISBN 0-262-04178-2.

- Elmasri, Ramez; Navathe, Shamkant B. (2000), *Fundamentals of Database Systems* (3rd ed.), Addison–Wesley, ISBN 0-201-54263-3.

- Ghosh, Sukumar (2007), *Distributed Systems – An Algorithmic Approach*, Chapman & Hall/CRC, ISBN 978-1-58488-564-1.

- Lynch, Nancy A. (1996), *Distributed Algorithms*, Morgan Kaufmann, ISBN 1-55860-348-4.

- Herlihy, Maurice P.; Shavit, Nir N. (2008), *The Art of Multiprocessor Programming*, Morgan Kaufmann, ISBN 0-12-370591-6.

- Papadimitriou, Christos H. (1994), *Computational Complexity*, Addison–Wesley, ISBN 0-201-53082-1.

- Peleg, David (2000), *Distributed Computing: A Locality-Sensitive Approach*, SIAM, ISBN 0-89871-464-8.

Articles

- Cole, Richard; Vishkin, Uzi (1986), "Deterministic coin tossing with applications to optimal parallel list ranking", *Information and Control* **70** (1): 32–53, doi:10.1016/S0019-9958(86)80023-7.

- Keidar, Idit (2008), "Distributed computing column 32 – The year in review", *ACM SIGACT News* **39** (4): 53–54, doi:10.1145/1466390.1466402.

- Linial, Nathan (1992), "Locality in distributed graph algorithms", *SIAM Journal on Computing* **21** (1): 193–201, doi:10.1137/0221015.

- Naor, Moni; Stockmeyer, Larry (1995), "What can be computed locally?", *SIAM Journal on Computing* **24** (6): 1259–1277, doi:10.1137/S0097539793254571.

Web sites

- Godfrey, Bill (2002). "A primer on distributed computing".

- Peter, Ian (2004). "Ian Peter's History of the Internet". Retrieved 2009-08-04.

2.17.12 Further reading

Books

- Coulouris, George et al. (2011), *Distributed Systems: Concepts and Design (5th Edition)*, Addison-Wesley ISBN 0-132-14301-1.

- Attiya, Hagit and Welch, Jennifer (2004), *Distributed Computing: Fundamentals, Simulations, and Advanced Topics*, Wiley-Interscience ISBN 0-471-45324-2.

- Faber, Jim (1998), *Java Distributed Computing*, O'Reilly: Java Distributed Computing by Jim Faber, 1998

- Garg, Vijay K. (2002), *Elements of Distributed Computing*, Wiley-IEEE Press ISBN 0-471-03600-5.

- Tel, Gerard (1994), *Introduction to Distributed Algorithms*, Cambridge University Press

- Chandy, Mani et al., *Parallel Program Design*

Articles

- Keidar, Idit; Rajsbaum, Sergio, eds. (2000–2009), "Distributed computing column", *ACM SIGACT News*.

- Birrell, A. D.; Levin, R.; Schroeder, M. D.; Needham, R. M. (April 1982). "Grapevine: An exercise in distributed computing" (PDF). *Communications of the ACM* **25** (4): 260–274. doi:10.1145/358468.358487.

Conference Papers

- C. Rodríguez, M. Villagra and B. Barán, Asynchronous team algorithms for Boolean Satisfiability, Bionetics2007, pp. 66–69, 2007.

2.17.13 External links

- Distributed computing at DMOZ

- Distributed computing journals at DMOZ

2.18 Database

A **database** is an organized collection of data.[1] It is the collection of schemes, tables, queries, reports, views and other objects. The data is typically organized to model aspects of reality in a way that supports processes requiring information, such as modelling the availability of rooms in hotels in a way that supports finding a hotel with vacancies.

A **database management system** (**DBMS**) is a computer software application that interacts with the user, other applications, and the database itself to capture and analyze data. A general-purpose DBMS is designed to allow the definition, creation, querying, update, and administration of databases. Well-known DBMSs include MySQL, PostgreSQL, Microsoft SQL Server, Oracle, Sybase and IBM DB2. A database is not generally portable across different DBMSs, but different DBMS can interoperate by using standards such as SQL and ODBC or JDBC to allow a single application to work with more than one DBMS. Database management systems are often classified according to the database model that they support; the most popular database systems since the 1980s have all supported the relational model as represented by the SQL language. Sometimes a DBMS is loosely referred to as a 'database'.

2.18.1 Terminology and overview

Formally, a "database" refers to a set of related data and the way it is organized. Access to this data is usually provided by a "database management system" (DBMS) consisting of an integrated set of computer software that allows users to interact with one or more databases and provides access to all of the data contained in the database (although restrictions may exist that limit access to particular data). The DBMS provides various functions that allow entry, storage and retrieval of large quantities of information as well as provides ways to manage how that information is organized.

Because of the close relationship between them, the term "database" is often used casually to refer to both a database and the DBMS used to manipulate it.

Outside the world of professional information technology, the term *database* is often used to refer to any collection of related data (such as a spreadsheet or a card index). This article is concerned only with databases where the size and usage requirements necessitate use of a database management system.[2]

Existing DBMSs provide various functions that allow management of a database and its data which can be classified into four main functional groups:

- **Data definition** – Creation, modification and removal of definitions that define the organization of the data.

- **Update** – Insertion, modification, and deletion of the actual data.[3]

- **Retrieval** – Providing information in a form directly usable or for further processing by other applications. The retrieved data may be made available in a form basically the same as it is stored in the database or in a new form obtained by altering or combining existing data from the database.[4]

- **Administration** – Registering and monitoring users, enforcing data security, monitoring performance, maintaining data integrity, dealing with concurrency control, and recovering information that has been corrupted by some event such as an unexpected system failure.[5]

Both a database and its DBMS conform to the principles of a particular database model.[6] "Database system" refers collectively to the database model, database management system, and database.[7]

Physically, database servers are dedicated computers that hold the actual databases and run only the DBMS and related software. Database servers are usually multiprocessor computers, with generous memory and RAID disk arrays used for stable storage. RAID is used for recovery of data if any of the disks fail. Hardware database accelerators, connected to one or more servers via a high-speed channel, are also used in large volume transaction processing environments. DBMSs are found at the heart of most database applications. DBMSs may be built around a custom multitasking kernel with built-in networking support, but modern DBMSs typically rely on a standard operating system to provide these functions. Since DBMSs comprise a significant economical market, computer and storage vendors often take into account DBMS requirements in their own development plans.

Databases and DBMSs can be categorized according to the database model(s) that they support (such as relational or XML), the type(s) of computer they run on (from a server cluster to a mobile phone), the query language(s) used to access the database (such as SQL or XQuery), and their internal engineering, which affects performance, scalability, resilience, and security

2.18.2 Applications

Databases are used to support internal operations of organizations and to underpin online interactions with customers and suppliers (see Enterprise software).

Databases are used to hold administrative information and more specialized data, such as engineering data or economic models. Examples of database applications include computerized library systems, flight reservation systems and computerized parts inventory systems.

Application areas of DBMS

1. Banking: For customer information, accounts, and loans, and banking transactions.

2. Airlines: For reservations and schedule information. Airlines were among the first to use databases in a geographically distributed manner - terminals situated around the world accessed the central database system through phone lines and other data networks.

3. Universities: For student information, course registrations, and grades.

4. Credit card transactions: For purchases on credit cards and generation of monthly statements.

5. Telecommunication: For keeping records of calls made, generating monthly bills, maintaining balances on prepaid calling cards, and storing information about the communication networks.

6. Finance: For storing information about holdings, sales, and purchases of financial instruments such as stocks and bonds.

7. Sales: For customer, product, and purchase information.

8. Manufacturing: For management of supply chain and for tracking production of items in factories, inventories of items in warehouses / stores, and orders for items.

9. Human resources: For information about employees, salaries, payroll taxes and benefits, and for generation of paychecks.[8]

2.18.3 General-purpose and special-purpose DBMSs

A DBMS has evolved into a complex software system and its development typically requires thousands of person-years of development effort.[9] Some general-purpose DBMSs such as Adabas, Oracle and DB2 have been undergoing upgrades since the 1970s. General-purpose DBMSs aim to meet the needs of as many applications as possible, which adds to the complexity. However, the fact that their development cost can be spread over a large number of users means that they are often the most cost-effective approach. However, a general-purpose DBMS is not always the optimal solution: in some cases a general-purpose DBMS may introduce unnecessary overhead. Therefore, there are many examples of systems that use special-purpose databases. A common example is an email system that performs many of the functions of a general-purpose DBMS such as the insertion and deletion of messages composed of various items of data or associating messages with a particular email address; but these functions are limited to what is required to handle email and don't provide the user with the all of the functionality that would be available using a general-purpose DBMS.

Many other databases have application software that accesses the database on behalf of end-users, without exposing the DBMS interface directly. Application programmers may use a wire protocol directly, or more likely through an application programming interface. Database designers and database administrators interact with the DBMS through dedicated interfaces to build and maintain the applications' databases, and thus need some more knowledge and understanding about how DBMSs operate and the DBMSs' external interfaces and tuning parameters.

2.18.4 History

Following the technology progress in the areas of processors, computer memory, computer storage and computer networks, the sizes, capabilities, and performance of databases and their respective DBMSs have grown in orders of magnitude. The development of database technology can be divided into three eras based on data model or structure: navigational,[10] SQL/relational, and post-relational.

The two main early navigational data models were the hierarchical model, epitomized by IBM's IMS system, and the CODASYL model (network model), implemented in a number of products such as IDMS.

The relational model, first proposed in 1970 by Edgar F. Codd, departed from this tradition by insisting that applications should search for data by content, rather than by following links. The relational model employs sets of ledger-style tables, each used for a different type of entity. Only in the mid-1980s did computing hardware become powerful enough to allow the wide deployment of relational systems (DBMSs plus applications). By the early 1990s, however, relational systems dominated in all large-scale data processing applications, and as of 2015 they remain dominant : IBM DB2, Oracle, mySQL and SQL server are the top DBMS.[11] The dominant database language, standardised SQL for the relational model, has influenced database languages for other data models.

Object databases were developed in the 1980s to overcome the inconvenience of object-relational impedance mismatch, which led to the coining of the term "post-relational" and also the development of hybrid object-relational databases.

The next generation of post-relational databases in the late 2000s became known as NoSQL databases, introducing fast key-value stores and document-oriented databases. A competing "next generation" known as NewSQL databases attempted new implementations that retained the relational/SQL model while aiming to match the high performance of NoSQL compared to commercially available relational DBMSs.

1960s, navigational DBMS

Further information: Navigational database
The introduction of the term *database* coincided with the

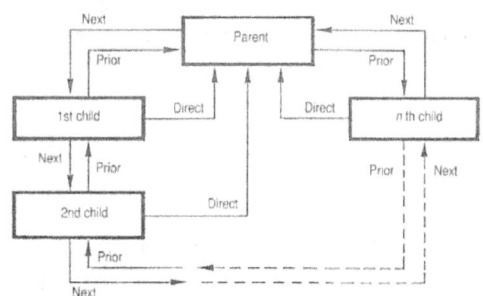

A closed chain of records in a navigational database model (e.g. CODASYL), with *next pointers*, *prior pointers* and *direct pointers* provided by keys in the various records.

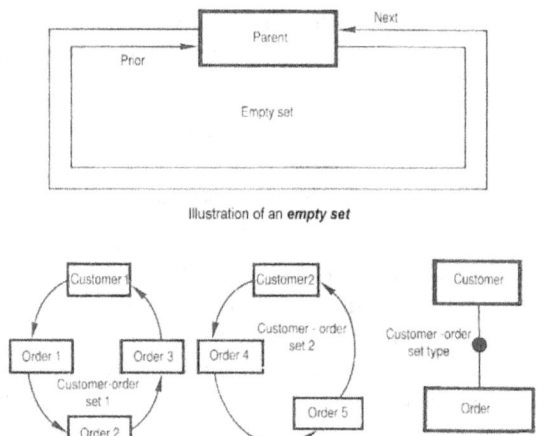

Illustration of an *empty set*

Illustration of a set type using a *Bachman diagram*

The record set, basic structure of navigational (e.g. CODASYL) databse model. A set consists of one parent record (also called "the owner"), and n child records (also called members records)

Basic structure of navigational CODASYL database model

availability of direct-access storage (disks and drums) from the mid-1960s onwards. The term represented a contrast with the tape-based systems of the past, allowing shared interactive use rather than daily batch processing. The Oxford English dictionary cites[12] a 1962 report by the System Development Corporation of California as the first to use the term "data-base" in a specific technical sense.

As computers grew in speed and capability, a number of general-purpose database systems emerged; by the mid-1960s a number of such systems had come into commercial use. Interest in a standard began to grow, and Charles Bachman, author of one such product, the Integrated Data Store (IDS), founded the "Database Task Group" within CODASYL, the group responsible for the creation and standardization of COBOL. In 1971 the Database Task Group delivered their standard, which generally became known as the "CODASYL approach", and soon a number of commercial products based on this approach entered the market.

The CODASYL approach relied on the "manual" navigation of a linked data set which was formed into a large network. Applications could find records by one of three methods:

1. Use of a primary key (known as a CALC key, typically implemented by hashing)

2. Navigating relationships (called sets) from one record to another

3. Scanning all the records in a sequential order

Later systems added B-Trees to provide alternate access paths. Many CODASYL databases also added a very straightforward query language. However, in the final tally, CODASYL was very complex and required significant training and effort to produce useful applications.

IBM also had their own DBMS in 1968, known as Information Management System (IMS). IMS was a development of software written for the Apollo program on the System/360. IMS was generally similar in concept to CODASYL, but used a strict hierarchy for its model of data navigation instead of CODASYL's network model. Both concepts later became known as navigational databases due to the way data was accessed, and Bachman's 1973 Turing Award presentation was *The Programmer as Navigator*. IMS is classified as a hierarchical database. IDMS and Cincom Systems' TOTAL database are classified as network databases. IMS remains in use as of 2014.[13]

1970s, relational DBMS

Edgar Codd worked at IBM in San Jose, California, in one of their offshoot offices that was primarily involved in the development of hard disk systems. He was unhappy with the navigational model of the CODASYL approach, notably the lack of a "search" facility. In 1970, he wrote a number of papers that outlined a new approach to database construction that eventually culminated in the groundbreaking *A Relational Model of Data for Large Shared Data Banks*.[14]

In this paper, he described a new system for storing and working with large databases. Instead of records being stored in some sort of linked list of free-form records as in CODASYL, Codd's idea was to use a "table" of fixed-length records, with each table used for a different type of

2.18. DATABASE

entity. A linked-list system would be very inefficient when storing "sparse" databases where some of the data for any one record could be left empty. The relational model solved this by splitting the data into a series of normalized tables (or *relations*), with optional elements being moved out of the main table to where they would take up room only if needed. Data may be freely inserted, deleted and edited in these tables, with the DBMS doing whatever maintenance needed to present a table view to the application/user.

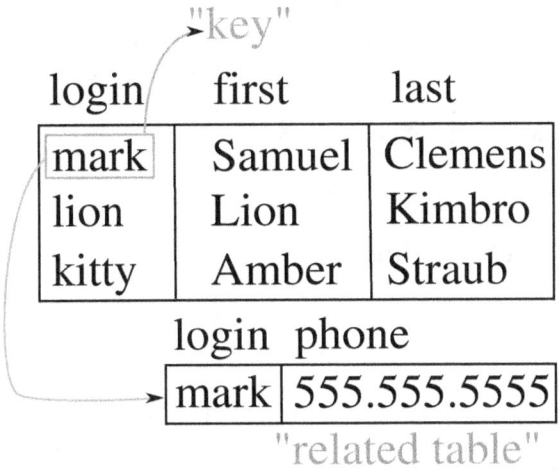

In the relational model, records are "linked" using virtual keys not stored in the database but defined as needed between the data contained in the records.

The relational model also allowed the content of the database to evolve without constant rewriting of links and pointers. The relational part comes from entities referencing other entities in what is known as one-to-many relationship, like a traditional hierarchical model, and many-to-many relationship, like a navigational (network) model. Thus, a relational model can express both hierarchical and navigational models, as well as its native tabular model, allowing for pure or combined modeling in terms of these three models, as the application requires.

For instance, a common use of a database system is to track information about users, their name, login information, various addresses and phone numbers. In the navigational approach all of these data would be placed in a single record, and unused items would simply not be placed in the database. In the relational approach, the data would be *normalized* into a user table, an address table and a phone number table (for instance). Records would be created in these optional tables only if the address or phone numbers were actually provided.

Linking the information back together is the key to this system. In the relational model, some bit of information was used as a "key", uniquely defining a particular record. When information was being collected about a user, information stored in the optional tables would be found by searching for this key. For instance, if the login name of a user is unique, addresses and phone numbers for that user would be recorded with the login name as its key. This simple "re-linking" of related data back into a single collection is something that traditional computer languages are not designed for.

Just as the navigational approach would require programs to loop in order to collect records, the relational approach would require loops to collect information about any *one* record. Codd's solution to the necessary looping was a set-oriented language, a suggestion that would later spawn the ubiquitous SQL. Using a branch of mathematics known as tuple calculus, he demonstrated that such a system could support all the operations of normal databases (inserting, updating etc.) as well as providing a simple system for finding and returning *sets* of data in a single operation.

Codd's paper was picked up by two people at Berkeley, Eugene Wong and Michael Stonebraker. They started a project known as INGRES using funding that had already been allocated for a geographical database project and student programmers to produce code. Beginning in 1973, INGRES delivered its first test products which were generally ready for widespread use in 1979. INGRES was similar to System R in a number of ways, including the use of a "language" for data access, known as QUEL. Over time, INGRES moved to the emerging SQL standard.

IBM itself did one test implementation of the relational model, PRTV, and a production one, Business System 12, both now discontinued. Honeywell wrote MRDS for Multics, and now there are two new implementations: Alphora Dataphor and Rel. Most other DBMS implementations usually called *relational* are actually SQL DBMSs.

In 1970, the University of Michigan began development of the MICRO Information Management System[15] based on D.L. Childs' Set-Theoretic Data model.[16][17][18] Micro was used to manage very large data sets by the US Department of Labor, the U.S. Environmental Protection Agency, and researchers from the University of Alberta, the University of Michigan, and Wayne State University. It ran on IBM mainframe computers using the Michigan Terminal System.[19] The system remained in production until 1998.

Integrated approach

Main article: Database machine

In the 1970s and 1980s attempts were made to build database systems with integrated hardware and software. The underlying philosophy was that such integration would provide higher performance at lower cost. Examples were IBM System/38, the early offering of Teradata, and the Britton Lee, Inc. database machine.

Another approach to hardware support for database management was ICL's CAFS accelerator, a hardware disk controller with programmable search capabilities. In the long term, these efforts were generally unsuccessful because specialized database machines could not keep pace with the rapid development and progress of general-purpose computers. Thus most database systems nowadays are software systems running on general-purpose hardware, using general-purpose computer data storage. However this idea is still pursued for certain applications by some companies like Netezza and Oracle (Exadata).

Late 1970s, SQL DBMS

IBM started working on a prototype system loosely based on Codd's concepts as *System R* in the early 1970s. The first version was ready in 1974/5, and work then started on multi-table systems in which the data could be split so that all of the data for a record (some of which is optional) did not have to be stored in a single large "chunk". Subsequent multi-user versions were tested by customers in 1978 and 1979, by which time a standardized query language – SQL – had been added. Codd's ideas were establishing themselves as both workable and superior to CODASYL, pushing IBM to develop a true production version of System R, known as *SQL/DS*, and, later, *Database 2* (DB2).

Larry Ellison's Oracle started from a different chain, based on IBM's papers on System R, and beat IBM to market when the first version was released in 1978.

Stonebraker went on to apply the lessons from INGRES to develop a new database, Postgres, which is now known as PostgreSQL. PostgreSQL is often used for global mission critical applications (the .org and .info domain name registries use it as their primary data store, as do many large companies and financial institutions).

In Sweden, Codd's paper was also read and Mimer SQL was developed from the mid-1970s at Uppsala University. In 1984, this project was consolidated into an independent enterprise. In the early 1980s, Mimer introduced transaction handling for high robustness in applications, an idea that was subsequently implemented on most other DBMSs.

Another data model, the entity–relationship model, emerged in 1976 and gained popularity for database design as it emphasized a more familiar description than the earlier relational model. Later on, entity–relationship constructs were retrofitted as a data modeling construct for the relational model, and the difference between the two have become irrelevant.

1980s, on the desktop

The 1980s ushered in the age of desktop computing. The new computers empowered their users with spreadsheets like Lotus 1-2-3 and database software like dBASE. The dBASE product was lightweight and easy for any computer user to understand out of the box. C. Wayne Ratliff the creator of dBASE stated: "dBASE was different from programs like BASIC, C, FORTRAN, and COBOL in that a lot of the dirty work had already been done. The data manipulation is done by dBASE instead of by the user, so the user can concentrate on what he is doing, rather than having to mess with the dirty details of opening, reading, and closing files, and managing space allocation."[20] dBASE was one of the top selling software titles in the 1980s and early 1990s.

1990s, object-oriented

The 1990s, along with a rise in object-oriented programming, saw a growth in how data in various databases were handled. Programmers and designers began to treat the data in their databases as objects. That is to say that if a person's data were in a database, that person's attributes, such as their address, phone number, and age, were now considered to belong to that person instead of being extraneous data. This allows for relations between data to be relations to objects and their attributes and not to individual fields.[21] The term "object-relational impedance mismatch" described the inconvenience of translating between programmed objects and database tables. Object databases and object-relational databases attempt to solve this problem by providing an object-oriented language (sometimes as extensions to SQL) that programmers can use as alternative to purely relational SQL. On the programming side, libraries known as object-relational mappings (ORMs) attempt to solve the same problem.

2000s, NoSQL and NewSQL

Main articles: NoSQL and NewSQL

The next generation of post-relational databases in the 2000s became known as NoSQL databases, including fast key-value stores and document-oriented databases.

XML databases are a type of structured document-oriented database that allows querying based on XML document attributes. XML databases are mostly used in enterprise database management, where XML is being used as the machine-to-machine data interoperability standard. XML database management systems include commercial software MarkLogic and Oracle Berkeley DB XML, and a

2.18. DATABASE

free use software Clusterpoint Distributed XML/JSON Database. All are enterprise software database platforms and support industry standard ACID-compliant transaction processing with strong database consistency characteristics and high level of database security.[22][23][24]

NoSQL databases are often very fast, do not require fixed table schemas, avoid join operations by storing denormalized data, and are designed to scale horizontally. The most popular NoSQL systems include MongoDB, Couchbase, Riak, Memcached, Redis, CouchDB, Hazelcast, Apache Cassandra and HBase,[25] which are all open-source software products.

In recent years there was a high demand for massively distributed databases with high partition tolerance but according to the CAP theorem it is impossible for a distributed system to simultaneously provide consistency, availability and partition tolerance guarantees. A distributed system can satisfy any two of these guarantees at the same time, but not all three. For that reason many NoSQL databases are using what is called eventual consistency to provide both availability and partition tolerance guarantees with a reduced level of data consistency.

NewSQL is a class of modern relational databases that aims to provide the same scalable performance of NoSQL systems for online transaction processing (read-write) workloads while still using SQL and maintaining the ACID guarantees of a traditional database system. Such databases include ScaleBase, Clustrix, EnterpriseDB, MemSQL, NuoDB[26] and VoltDB.

2.18.5 Research

Database technology has been an active research topic since the 1960s, both in academia and in the research and development groups of companies (for example IBM Research). Research activity includes theory and development of prototypes. Notable research topics have included models, the atomic transaction concept and related concurrency control techniques, query languages and query optimization methods, RAID, and more.

The database research area has several dedicated academic journals (for example, *ACM Transactions on Database Systems*-TODS, *Data and Knowledge Engineering*-DKE) and annual conferences (e.g., ACM SIGMOD, ACM PODS, VLDB, IEEE ICDE).

2.18.6 Examples

One way to classify databases involves the type of their contents, for example: bibliographic, document-text, statistical, or multimedia objects. Another way is by their application area, for example: accounting, music compositions, movies, banking, manufacturing, or insurance. A third way is by some technical aspect, such as the database structure or interface type. This section lists a few of the adjectives used to characterize different kinds of databases.

- An in-memory database is a database that primarily resides in main memory, but is typically backed-up by non-volatile computer data storage. Main memory databases are faster than disk databases, and so are often used where response time is critical, such as in telecommunications network equipment.[27] SAP HANA platform is a very hot topic for in-memory database. By May 2012, HANA was able to run on servers with 100TB main memory powered by IBM. The co founder of the company claimed that the system was big enough to run the 8 largest SAP customers.

- An active database includes an event-driven architecture which can respond to conditions both inside and outside the database. Possible uses include security monitoring, alerting, statistics gathering and authorization. Many databases provide active database features in the form of database triggers.

- A cloud database relies on cloud technology. Both the database and most of its DBMS reside remotely, "in the cloud", while its applications are both developed by programmers and later maintained and utilized by (application's) end-users through a web browser and Open APIs.

- Data warehouses archive data from operational databases and often from external sources such as market research firms. The warehouse becomes the central source of data for use by managers and other end-users who may not have access to operational data. For example, sales data might be aggregated to weekly totals and converted from internal product codes to use UPCs so that they can be compared with ACNielsen data. Some basic and essential components of data warehousing include extracting, analyzing, and mining data, transforming, loading and managing data so as to make them available for further use.

- A deductive database combines logic programming with a relational database, for example by using the Datalog language.

- A distributed database is one in which both the data and the DBMS span multiple computers.

- A document-oriented database is designed for storing, retrieving, and managing document-oriented, or semi structured data, information. Document-oriented databases are one of the main categories of NoSQL databases.

- An embedded database system is a DBMS which is tightly integrated with an application software that requires access to stored data in such a way that the DBMS is hidden from the application's end-users and requires little or no ongoing maintenance.[28]

- **End-user databases** consist of data developed by individual end-users. Examples of these are collections of documents, spreadsheets, presentations, multimedia, and other files. Several products exist to support such databases. Some of them are much simpler than full-fledged DBMSs, with more elementary DBMS functionality.

- A federated database system comprises several distinct databases, each with its own DBMS. It is handled as a single database by a federated database management system (FDBMS), which transparently integrates multiple autonomous DBMSs, possibly of different types (in which case it would also be a heterogeneous database system), and provides them with an integrated conceptual view.

- Sometimes the term *multi-database* is used as a synonym to federated database, though it may refer to a less integrated (e.g., without an FDBMS and a managed integrated schema) group of databases that cooperate in a single application. In this case typically middleware is used for distribution, which typically includes an atomic commit protocol (ACP), e.g., the two-phase commit protocol, to allow distributed (global) transactions across the participating databases.

- A graph database is a kind of NoSQL database that uses graph structures with nodes, edges, and properties to represent and store information. General graph databases that can store any graph are distinct from specialized graph databases such as triplestores and network databases.

- An array DBMS is a kind of NoSQL DBMS that allows to model, store, and retrieve (usually large) multidimensional arrays such as satellite images and climate simulation output.

- In a hypertext or hypermedia database, any word or a piece of text representing an object, e.g., another piece of text, an article, a picture, or a film, can be hyperlinked to that object. Hypertext databases are particularly useful for organizing large amounts of disparate information. For example, they are useful for organizing online encyclopedias, where users can conveniently jump around the text. The World Wide Web is thus a large distributed hypertext database.

- A knowledge base (abbreviated **KB**, **kb** or Δ[29][30]) is a special kind of database for knowledge management, providing the means for the computerized collection, organization, and retrieval of knowledge. Also a collection of data representing problems with their solutions and related experiences.

- A mobile database can be carried on or synchronized from a mobile computing device.

- Operational databases store detailed data about the operations of an organization. They typically process relatively high volumes of updates using transactions. Examples include customer databases that record contact, credit, and demographic information about a business' customers, personnel databases that hold information such as salary, benefits, skills data about employees, enterprise resource planning systems that record details about product components, parts inventory, and financial databases that keep track of the organization's money, accounting and financial dealings.

- A parallel database seeks to improve performance through parallelization for tasks such as loading data, building indexes and evaluating queries.

  > The major parallel DBMS architectures which are induced by the underlying hardware architecture are:
  > - **Shared memory architecture**, where multiple processors share the main memory space, as well as other data storage.
  > - **Shared disk architecture**, where each processing unit (typically consisting of multiple processors) has its own main memory, but all units share the other storage.
  > - **Shared nothing architecture**, where each processing unit has its own main memory and other storage.

- Probabilistic databases employ fuzzy logic to draw inferences from imprecise data.

- Real-time databases process transactions fast enough for the result to come back and be acted on right away.

- A spatial database can store the data with multidimensional features. The queries on such data include location based queries, like "Where is the closest hotel in my area?".

- A temporal database has built-in time aspects, for example a temporal data model and a temporal version of SQL. More specifically the temporal aspects usually include valid-time and transaction-time.

- A terminology-oriented database builds upon an object-oriented database, often customized for a specific field.

- An unstructured data database is intended to store in a manageable and protected way diverse objects that do not fit naturally and conveniently in common databases. It may include email messages, documents, journals, multimedia objects, etc. The name may be misleading since some objects can be highly structured. However, the entire possible object collection does not fit into a predefined structured framework. Most established DBMSs now support unstructured data in various ways, and new dedicated DBMSs are emerging.

2.18.7 Design and modeling

Main article: Database design

The first task of a database designer is to produce a conceptual data model that reflects the structure of the information to be held in the database. A common approach to this is to develop an entity-relationship model, often with the aid of drawing tools. Another popular approach is the Unified Modeling Language. A successful data model will accurately reflect the possible state of the external world being modeled: for example, if people can have more than one phone number, it will allow this information to be captured. Designing a good conceptual data model requires a good understanding of the application domain; it typically involves asking deep questions about the things of interest to an organisation, like "can a customer also be a supplier?", or "if a product is sold with two different forms of packaging, are those the same product or different products?", or "if a plane flies from New York to Dubai via Frankfurt, is that one flight or two (or maybe even three)?". The answers to these questions establish definitions of the terminology used for entities (customers, products, flights, flight segments) and their relationships and attributes.

Producing the conceptual data model sometimes involves input from business processes, or the analysis of workflow in the organization. This can help to establish what information is needed in the database, and what can be left out. For example, it can help when deciding whether the database needs to hold historic data as well as current data.

Having produced a conceptual data model that users are happy with, the next stage is to translate this into a schema that implements the relevant data structures within the database. This process is often called logical database design, and the output is a logical data model expressed in the form of a schema. Whereas the conceptual data model is (in theory at least) independent of the choice of database technology, the logical data model will be expressed in terms of a particular database model supported by the chosen DBMS. (The terms *data model* and *database model* are often used interchangeably, but in this article we use *data model* for the design of a specific database, and *database model* for the modelling notation used to express that design.)

The most popular database model for general-purpose databases is the relational model, or more precisely, the relational model as represented by the SQL language. The process of creating a logical database design using this model uses a methodical approach known as normalization. The goal of normalization is to ensure that each elementary "fact" is only recorded in one place, so that insertions, updates, and deletions automatically maintain consistency.

The final stage of database design is to make the decisions that affect performance, scalability, recovery, security, and the like. This is often called *physical database design*. A key goal during this stage is data independence, meaning that the decisions made for performance optimization purposes should be invisible to end-users and applications. Physical design is driven mainly by performance requirements, and requires a good knowledge of the expected workload and access patterns, and a deep understanding of the features offered by the chosen DBMS.

Another aspect of physical database design is security. It involves both defining access control to database objects as well as defining security levels and methods for the data itself.

Models

Main article: Database model
 A database model is a type of data model that determines the logical structure of a database and fundamentally determines in which manner data can be stored, organized, and manipulated. The most popular example of a database model is the relational model (or the SQL approximation of relational), which uses a table-based format.

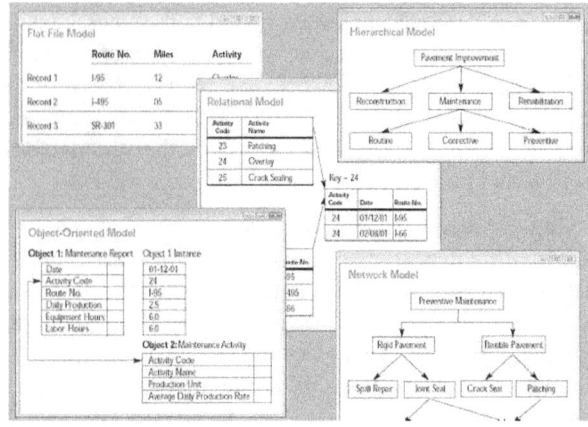

Collage of five types of database models

Common logical data models for databases include:

- Navigational databases
  - Hierarchical database model
  - Network model
  - Graph database
- Relational model
- Entity–relationship model
  - Enhanced entity–relationship model
- Object model
- Document model
- Entity–attribute–value model
- Star schema

An object-relational database combines the two related structures.

Physical data models include:

- Inverted index
- Flat file

Other models include:

- Associative model
- Multidimensional model
- Array model
- Multivalue model

Specialized models are optimized for particular types of data:

- XML database
- Semantic model
- Content store
- Event store
- Time series model

External, conceptual, and internal views

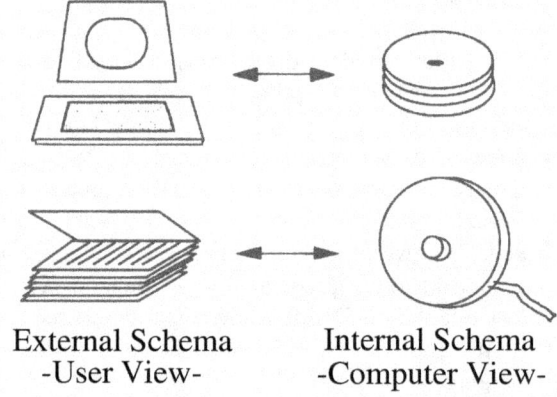

Traditional view of data[31]

A database management system provides three views of the database data:

- The **external level** defines how each group of end-users sees the organization of data in the database. A single database can have any number of views at the external level.

- The **conceptual level** unifies the various external views into a compatible global view.[32] It provides the synthesis of all the external views. It is out of the scope of the various database end-users, and is rather of interest to database application developers and database administrators.

- The **internal level** (or *physical level*) is the internal organization of data inside a DBMS (see Implementation section below). It is concerned with cost, performance, scalability and other operational matters. It deals with storage layout of the data, using storage structures such as indexes to enhance performance. Occasionally it stores data of individual views (materialized views), computed from generic data, if performance justification exists for such redundancy. It balances all the external views' performance requirements, possibly conflicting, in an attempt to optimize overall performance across all activities.

While there is typically only one conceptual (or logical) and physical (or internal) view of the data, there can be any number of different external views. This allows users to see database information in a more business-related way rather than from a technical, processing viewpoint. For example, a financial department of a company needs the payment details of all employees as part of the company's expenses, but does not need details about employees that are the interest of the human resources department. Thus different departments need different *views* of the company's database.

The three-level database architecture relates to the concept of *data independence* which was one of the major initial driving forces of the relational model. The idea is that changes made at a certain level do not affect the view at a higher level. For example, changes in the internal level do not affect application programs written using conceptual level interfaces, which reduces the impact of making physical changes to improve performance.

The conceptual view provides a level of indirection between internal and external. On one hand it provides a common view of the database, independent of different external view structures, and on the other hand it abstracts away details of how the data is stored or managed (internal level). In principle every level, and even every external view, can be presented by a different data model. In practice usually a given DBMS uses the same data model for both the external and the conceptual levels (e.g., relational model). The internal level, which is hidden inside the DBMS and depends on its implementation (see Implementation section below), requires a different level of detail and uses its own types of data structure types.

Separating the *external*, *conceptual* and *internal* levels was a major feature of the relational database model implementations that dominate 21st century databases.[32]

2.18.8 Languages

Database languages are special-purpose languages, which do one or more of the following:

- Data definition language – defines data types and the relationships among them
- Data manipulation language – performs tasks such as inserting, updating, or deleting data occurrences
- Query language – allows searching for information and computing derived information

Database languages are specific to a particular data model. Notable examples include:

- SQL combines the roles of data definition, data manipulation, and query in a single language. It was one of the first commercial languages for the relational model, although it departs in some respects from the relational model as described by Codd (for example, the rows and columns of a table can be ordered). SQL became a standard of the American National Standards Institute (ANSI) in 1986, and of the International Organization for Standardization (ISO) in 1987. The standards have been regularly enhanced since and is supported (with varying degrees of conformance) by all mainstream commercial relational DBMSs.[33][34]

- OQL is an object model language standard (from the Object Data Management Group). It has influenced the design of some of the newer query languages like JDOQL and EJB QL.

- XQuery is a standard XML query language implemented by XML database systems such as MarkLogic and eXist, by relational databases with XML capability such as Oracle and DB2, and also by in-memory XML processors such as Saxon.

- SQL/XML combines XQuery with SQL.[35]

A database language may also incorporate features like:

- DBMS-specific Configuration and storage engine management
- Computations to modify query results, like counting, summing, averaging, sorting, grouping, and cross-referencing
- Constraint enforcement (e.g. in an automotive database, only allowing one engine type per car)
- Application programming interface version of the query language, for programmer convenience

2.18.9 Performance, security, and availability

Because of the critical importance of database technology to the smooth running of an enterprise, database systems include complex mechanisms to deliver the required performance, security, and availability, and allow database administrators to control the use of these features.

Storage

Main articles: Computer data storage and Database engine

Database storage is the container of the physical materialization of a database. It comprises the *internal* (physical) *level* in the database architecture. It also contains all the information needed (e.g., metadata, "data about the data", and internal data structures) to reconstruct the *conceptual level* and *external level* from the internal level when needed. Putting data into permanent storage is generally the responsibility of the database engine a.k.a. "storage engine". Though typically accessed by a DBMS through the underlying operating system (and often utilizing the operating systems' file systems as intermediates for storage layout), storage properties and configuration setting are extremely important for the efficient operation of the DBMS, and thus are closely maintained by database administrators. A DBMS, while in operation, always has its database residing in several types of storage (e.g., memory and external storage). The database data and the additional needed information, possibly in very large amounts, are coded into bits. Data typically reside in the storage in structures that look completely different from the way the data look in the conceptual and external levels, but in ways that attempt to optimize (the best possible) these levels' reconstruction when needed by users and programs, as well as for computing additional types of needed information from the data (e.g., when querying the database).

Some DBMSs support specifying which character encoding was used to store data, so multiple encodings can be used in the same database.

Various low-level database storage structures are used by the storage engine to serialize the data model so it can be written to the medium of choice. Techniques such as indexing may be used to improve performance. Conventional storage is row-oriented, but there are also column-oriented and correlation databases.

Materialized views   Main article: Materialized view

Often storage redundancy is employed to increase performance. A common example is storing *materialized views*, which consist of frequently needed *external views* or query results. Storing such views saves the expensive computing of them each time they are needed. The downsides of materialized views are the overhead incurred when updating them to keep them synchronized with their original updated database data, and the cost of storage redundancy.

Replication   Main article: Database replication

Occasionally a database employs storage redundancy by database objects replication (with one or more copies) to increase data availability (both to improve performance of simultaneous multiple end-user accesses to a same database object, and to provide resiliency in a case of partial failure of a distributed database). Updates of a replicated object need to be synchronized across the object copies. In many cases the entire database is replicated.

Security

Main article: Database security

Database security deals with all various aspects of protecting the database content, its owners, and its users. It ranges from protection from intentional unauthorized database uses to unintentional database accesses by unauthorized entities (e.g., a person or a computer program).

Database access control deals with controlling who (a person or a certain computer program) is allowed to access what information in the database. The information may comprise specific database objects (e.g., record types, specific records, data structures), certain computations over certain objects (e.g., query types, or specific queries), or utilizing specific access paths to the former (e.g., using specific indexes or other data structures to access information). Database access controls are set by special authorized (by the database owner) personnel that uses dedicated protected security DBMS interfaces.

This may be managed directly on an individual basis, or by the assignment of individuals and privileges to groups, or (in the most elaborate models) through the assignment of individuals and groups to roles which are then granted entitlements. Data security prevents unauthorized users from viewing or updating the database. Using passwords, users are allowed access to the entire database or subsets of it called "subschemas". For example, an employee database can contain all the data about an individual employee, but one group of users may be authorized to view only payroll data, while others are allowed access to only work history and medical data. If the DBMS provides a way to interactively enter and update the database, as well as interrogate it, this capability allows for managing personal databases.

Data security in general deals with protecting specific chunks of data, both physically (i.e., from corruption, or destruction, or removal; e.g., see physical security), or the interpretation of them, or parts of them to meaningful information (e.g., by looking at the strings of bits that they comprise, concluding specific valid credit-card numbers; e.g., see data encryption).

Change and access logging records who accessed which attributes, what was changed, and when it was changed. Logging services allow for a forensic database audit later by keeping a record of access occurrences and changes. Sometimes application-level code is used to record changes rather than leaving this to the database. Monitoring can be set up to attempt to detect security breaches.

Transactions and concurrency

Further information: Concurrency control

Database transactions can be used to introduce some level of fault tolerance and data integrity after recovery from a crash. A database transaction is a unit of work, typically encapsulating a number of operations over a database (e.g., reading a database object, writing, acquiring lock, etc.), an abstraction supported in database and also other systems. Each transaction has well defined boundaries in terms of which program/code executions are included in that transaction (determined by the transaction's programmer via special transaction commands).

The acronym ACID describes some ideal properties of a database transaction: Atomicity, Consistency, Isolation, and Durability.

Migration

See also section Database migration in article Data migration

A database built with one DBMS is not portable to another DBMS (i.e., the other DBMS cannot run it). However, in some situations it is desirable to move, migrate a database from one DBMS to another. The reasons are primarily economical (different DBMSs may have different total costs of ownership or TCOs), functional, and operational (different DBMSs may have different capabilities). The migration involves the database's transformation from one DBMS type to another. The transformation should maintain (if possible) the database related application (i.e., all related application programs) intact. Thus, the database's conceptual and external architectural levels should be maintained in the transformation. It may be desired that also some aspects of the architecture internal level are maintained. A complex or large database migration may be a complicated and costly (one-time) project by itself, which should be factored into the decision to migrate. This in spite of the fact that tools may exist to help migration between specific DBMSs. Typically a DBMS vendor provides tools to help importing databases from other popular DBMSs.

Building, maintaining, and tuning

Main article: Database tuning

After designing a database for an application, the next stage is building the database. Typically an appropriate general-purpose DBMS can be selected to be utilized for this purpose. A DBMS provides the needed user interfaces to be utilized by database administrators to define the needed application's data structures within the DBMS's respective data model. Other user interfaces are used to select needed DBMS parameters (like security related, storage allocation parameters, etc.).

When the database is ready (all its data structures and other needed components are defined) it is typically populated with initial application's data (database initialization, which is typically a distinct project; in many cases using specialized DBMS interfaces that support bulk insertion) before making it operational. In some cases the database becomes operational while empty of application data, and data is accumulated during its operation.

After the database is created, initialised and populated it needs to be maintained. Various database parameters may need changing and the database may need to be tuned (tuning) for better performance; application's data structures may be changed or added, new related application programs may be written to add to the application's functionality, etc.

Backup and restore

Main article: Backup

Sometimes it is desired to bring a database back to a previous state (for many reasons, e.g., cases when the database is found corrupted due to a software error, or if it has been updated with erroneous data). To achieve this a **backup** operation is done occasionally or continuously, where each desired database state (i.e., the values of its data and their embedding in database's data structures) is kept within dedicated backup files (many techniques exist to do this effectively). When this state is needed, i.e., when it is decided by a database administrator to bring the database back to this state (e.g., by specifying this state by a desired point in time when the database was in this state), these files are utilized to **restore** that state.

Static Analysis

Static analysis techniques for software verification can be applied also in the scenario of query languages. In particular, the *Abstract interpretation framework has been extended to the field of query languages for relational databases as a way to support sound approximation techniques.[36] The semantics of query languages can be tuned according to suitable abstractions of the concrete domain of data. The abstraction of relational database system has many interesting applications, in particular, for security purposes, such as fine grained access control, watermarking, etc.

Other

Other DBMS features might include:

- Database logs

- Graphics component for producing graphs and charts, especially in a data warehouse system

- **Query optimizer** – Performs query optimization on every query to choose for it the most efficient *query plan* (a partial order (tree) of operations) to be executed to compute the query result. May be specific to a particular storage engine.

- Tools or hooks for database design, application programming, application program maintenance, database performance analysis and monitoring, database configuration monitoring, DBMS hardware configuration (a DBMS and related database may span computers, networks, and storage units) and related database mapping (especially for a distributed DBMS), storage allocation and database layout monitoring, storage migration, etc.

2.18.10 See also

Main article: Outline of databases

- Comparison of database tools

- Comparison of object database management systems

- Comparison of object-relational database management systems

- Comparison of relational database management systems

- Data hierarchy

- Data bank

- Data store

- Database theory

- Database testing

- Database-centric architecture

- Question-focused dataset

2.18.11 References

[1] "Database - Definition of database by Merriam-Webster". *merriam-webster.com*.

[2] Jeffrey Ullman 1997: *First course in database systems*, Prentice–Hall Inc., Simon & Schuster, Page 1, ISBN 0-13-861337-0.

[3] "Update - Definition of update by Merriam-Webster". *merriam-webster.com*.

[4] "Retrieval - Definition of retrieval by Merriam-Webster". *merriam-webster.com*.

[5] "Administration - Definition of administration by Merriam-Webster". *merriam-webster.com*.

[6] Tsitchizris, D. C. and F. H. Lochovsky (1982). *Data Models*. Englewood-Cliffs, Prentice–Hall.

[7] Beynon-Davies P. (2004). *Database Systems* 3rd Edition. Palgrave, Basingstoke, UK. ISBN 1-4039-1601-2

[8] Garcia-Molina, Hector; Ullman, Jeffrey D.; Widom, Jennifer (2009). "The Worlds of Database Systems" (PDF). *Database systems: the complete book* (2nd ed.). Upper Saddle River, N.J.: Pearson Prentice Hall. ISBN 978-0131873254.

[9] Raul F. Chong, Michael Dang, Dwaine R. Snow, Xiaomei Wang (3 July 2008). "Introduction to DB2". Retrieved 17 March 2013.. This article quotes a development time of 5 years involving 750 people for DB2 release 9 alone

[10] C. W. Bachmann (November 1973), "The Programmer as Navigator" (PDF), *CACM* (Turing Award Lecture 1973)

[11] "TOPDB Top Database index". *pypl.github.io*.

[12] "database, n". *OED Online*. Oxford University Press. June 2013. Retrieved July 12, 2013.

[13] IBM Corporation. "IBM Information Management System (IMS) 13 Transaction and Database Servers delivers high performance and low total cost of ownership". Retrieved Feb 20, 2014.

[14] Codd, E.F. (1970)."A Relational Model of Data for Large Shared Data Banks". In: *Communications of the ACM* 13 (6): 377–387.

[15] William Hershey and Carol Easthope, "A set theoretic data structure and retrieval language", Spring Joint Computer Conference, May 1972 in *ACM SIGIR Forum*, Volume 7, Issue 4 (December 1972), pp. 45–55, DOI=10.1145/1095495.1095500

[16] Ken North, "Sets, Data Models and Data Independence", *Dr. Dobb's*, 10 March 2010

[17] *Description of a set-theoretic data structure*, D. L. Childs, 1968, Technical Report 3 of the CONCOMP (Research in Conversational Use of Computers) Project, University of Michigan, Ann Arbor, Michigan, USA

[18] *Feasibility of a Set-Theoretic Data Structure : A General Structure Based on a Reconstituted Definition of Relation*, D. L. Childs, 1968, Technical Report 6 of the CONCOMP (Research in Conversational Use of Computers) Project, University of Michigan, Ann Arbor, Michigan, USA

[19] *MICRO Information Management System (Version 5.0) Reference Manual*, M.A. Kahn, D.L. Rumelhart, and B.L. Bronson, October 1977, Institute of Labor and Industrial Relations (ILIR), University of Michigan and Wayne State University

[20] Interview with Wayne Ratliff. The FoxPro History. Retrieved on 2013-07-12.

[21] Development of an object-oriented DBMS; Portland, Oregon, United States; Pages: 472 – 482; 1986; ISBN 0-89791-204-7

[22] "Oracle Berkeley DB XML" (PDF). Retrieved 10 March 2015.

[23] "ACID Transactions, MarkLogic". Retrieved 10 March 2015.

[24] "Clusterpoint Database at a Glance". Retrieved 10 March 2015.

[25] "DB-Engines Ranking". January 2013. Retrieved 22 January 2013.

[26] Proctor, Seth (2013). "Exploring the Architecture of the NuoDB Database, Part 1". Retrieved 2013-07-12.

[27] "TeleCommunication Systems Signs up as a Reseller of TimesTen; Mobile Operators and Carriers Gain Real-Time Platform for Location-Based Services". *Business Wire*. 2002-06-24.

[28] Graves, Steve. "COTS Databases For Embedded Systems", *Embedded Computing Design* magazine, January 2007. Retrieved on August 13, 2008.

[29] Argumentation in Artificial Intelligence by Iyad Rahwan, Guillermo R. Simari

[30] "OWL DL Semantics". Retrieved 10 December 2010.

[31] itl.nist.gov (1993) *Integration Definition for Information Modeling (IDEFIX)*. 21 December 1993.

[32] Date 1990, pp. 31–32

[33] Chapple, Mike. "SQL Fundamentals". *Databases*. About.com. Retrieved 2009-01-28.

[34] "Structured Query Language (SQL)". International Business Machines. October 27, 2006. Retrieved 2007-06-10.

[35] Wagner, Michael (2010), "1. Auflage", *SQL/XML:2006 – Evaluierung der Standardkonformität ausgewählter Datenbanksysteme*, Diplomica Verlag, ISBN 3-8366-9609-6

[36] R.Halder and A.Cortesi, Abstract Interpretation of Database Query Languages. COMPUTER LANGUAGES, SYSTEMS & STRUCTURES, vol. 38(2), pp. 123-–157, Elsevier Ed. (ISSN 1477-8424)

2.18.12 Further reading

- Ling Liu and Tamer M. Özsu (Eds.) (2009). "Encyclopedia of Database Systems, 4100 p. 60 illus. ISBN 978-0-387-49616-0.

- Beynon-Davies, P. (2004). Database Systems. 3rd Edition. Palgrave, Houndmills, Basingstoke.

- Connolly, Thomas and Carolyn Begg. *Database Systems*. New York: Harlow, 2002.

- Date, C. J. (2003). *An Introduction to Database Systems, Fifth Edition*. Addison Wesley. ISBN 0-201-51381-1.

- Gray, J. and Reuter, A. *Transaction Processing: Concepts and Techniques*, 1st edition, Morgan Kaufmann Publishers, 1992.

- Kroenke, David M. and David J. Auer. *Database Concepts*. 3rd ed. New York: Prentice, 2007.

- Raghu Ramakrishnan and Johannes Gehrke, *Database Management Systems*

- Abraham Silberschatz, Henry F. Korth, S. Sudarshan, *Database System Concepts*

- Discussion on database systems,

- Lightstone, S.; Teorey, T.; Nadeau, T. (2007). *Physical Database Design: the database professional's guide to exploiting indexes, views, storage, and more*. Morgan Kaufmann Press. ISBN 0-12-369389-6.

- Teorey, T.; Lightstone, S. and Nadeau, T. *Database Modeling & Design: Logical Design*, 4th edition, Morgan Kaufmann Press, 2005. ISBN 0-12-685352-5

2.18.13 External links

- Database at DMOZ
- DB File extension – informations about files with DB extension

2.19 Women in computing

Global concerns about current and future roles of **women in computing** occupations have gained more importance with the emerging information age. Historically, women played a crucial role in the evolution of computing, with many of the first programmers during the early 20th century being female.[1] These concerns motivated public policy debates addressing gender equality as computer applications exerted increasing influence in society. This dialogue helped to expand information technology innovations and to reduce the unintended consequences of perceived sexism.

2.19.1 Gender gap

A survey, conducted by SWIFT ("Supporting Women in Information Technology") based in Vancouver, Canada, asked 7,411 participants questions about their career choices. The survey found that females tend to believe that they lack the skill set needed to be successful in the field of computing. This provides a strong base for a positive correlation between perceived ability and career choice.[2] For more information about Canada in particular, see Women in computing in Canada.

A project based in Edinburgh, Scotland, "Strategies of Inclusion: Gender and the Information Society" (SIGIS) released its findings based on research conducted in 48 separate case studies all over Europe.[3] The findings focus on recruiting as well as retention techniques for women already studying in the field. These techniques range from the introduction of role models, advertisement campaigns, and the allocation of quotas, in order to make the computing field appear more gender neutral.[4] Educating reforms, which will increase the quality of the educating body and technological facilities, are also suggested.[4]

Research suggests that Malaysia has a much more equal split that varies around the half-way mark.[5] It is suggested that this may be due to the fact that Malaysian women view careers in information technology as a means of employment rather than a status symbol. A job in the computing industry also implies a safe work environment. Strong belief by the previous generation that IT would be a flourishing sector with many job opportunities caused parents to encourage their children to take a computing career, no matter the gender.[5]

In India, a growing number of women are studying and taking careers in technical fields. The percentage of women engineers graduating from IIT Bombay grew from 1.8% in 1972 to 8% in 2005.[6] Computer science is a popular subject among female students, as it utilizes mental rather than physical strength, and allows them to work indoors. Women with a good education and employment prospects are becoming more desirable as marriage partners. However, women remain underrepresented in information technology fields, possibly due to social constraints which allow women less freedom to study, and less access to resources and opportunities.[7]

Statistics in education

In the United States, the proportion of women represented in undergraduate computer science education and the white-collar information technology workforce peaked in the mid-1980s, and has declined ever since. In 1984, 37.1% of Computer Science degrees were awarded to women; the percentage dropped to 29.9% in 1989-1990, and 26.7% in 1997-1998.[8] Figures from the Computing Research Association Taulbee Survey indicate that fewer than 12% of Computer Science bachelor's degrees were awarded to women at U.S. PhD-granting institutions in 2010-11.[9]

Although teenage girls are now using computers and the Internet at rates similar to their male peers, they are five times less likely to consider a technology-related career or plan on taking post-secondary technology classes.[10] The National Center for Women & Information Technology (NCWIT) reports that of the SAT takers who intend to major in computer and information sciences, the proportion of girls has steadily decreased relative to the proportion of boys, from 20 percent in 2001 to 12 percent in 2006.[11] While this number has been decreasing, in 2001, the total number of these students (both boys and girls) reached its peak at 73,466.

According to a College Board report, in 2006 there were slightly more girls than boys amongst SAT takers that reported to having "course work or experience" in computer literacy, word processing, internet activity, and creating spreadsheets/databases.[12] It was also determined that more boys than girls (59% vs 41%) reported course work or experience with computer programming. Of the 146,437 students (13%) who reported having *no* course work or experience, 61% were girls and 39% were boys.

More boys than girls take Advanced Placement (AP) Computer Science exams. According to the College Board in 2006, 2,594 girls and 12,068 boys took the AP Computer Science A exam, while 517 girls and 4,422 boys took the more advanced AP Computer Science AB exam. From

1996 to 2004, girls made up 16–17% of those taking the AP Computer Science A exam and around 10% of those taking AP Computer Science AB exam.

Statistics in the workforce

Women's representation in the computing and information technology workforce has been falling from a peak of 38% in the mid-1980s. From 1993 through 1999, NSF's SESTAT reported that the percentage of women working as computer/information scientists (including those who hold a bachelor's degree or higher in an S&E field or have a bachelor's degree or higher and are working in an S&E field) declined slightly from 33.1% to 29.6% percent while the absolute numbers increased from 170,500 to 185,000.[13] Numbers from the Bureau of Labor Statistics and Catalyst in 2006 indicated that women comprise 27-29% of the computing workforce.[14][15] A National Public Radio report in 2013 stated that about 20% of all U.S. computer programmers are female.[16]

2.19.2 Benefits of gender diversity

A gender-diverse team is more likely to produce products that meet the needs of men and women. When women are underrepresented, many technical decisions are based on the experiences, opinions, and judgments of only men, which can result in products that meet the needs of only men.[17] In addition, a review of research on gender-diverse teams reveals that gender-diverse teams are more productive, more creative, and more able to stay on schedule and within budget, compared to homogenous teams.,[18] while other research review suggests that the results are mixed, with many studies showing no result, non-linear results or even negative results of gender diversity on team performances.[19] Research conducted by McKinsey & Company showed that companies with women in top management were more financially successful,[20] in contrast analysis of sample major US companies showed no effect of inclusion of women (or minority members) on financial performance.[21]

The book *Gender and Computers: Understanding the Digital Divide* states that the lack of participation of females in computing excludes them from the "new economy", which calls for sophisticated computer skills in exchange for high salary positions.[22]

2.19.3 Factors contributing to lack of female participation

Education

Diminished participation by women relative to men in computer science dates from about 1984[23] following mass marketing of personal computers to boys as toys to play games. Fiddling with computers by boys resulted in increased interest and readiness for computer science classes by young men.[24]

A study of over 7000 high school students in Vancouver, Canada showed that the degree of interest in the field of computer science for young women is comparably lower than that of young men.[25] The same effect is seen in higher education; for instance, only 4% of female college freshmen expressed intention to major in computer science in the US.[22] Research has shown that some aspects about computing may discourage women. One of the biggest turn-offs is the "geek factor". High school girls often envisage a career in computing as a lifetime in an isolated cubicle writing code. The "geek factor" affects both male and female high school students, but it seems to have more of a negative effect on the female students.[26] In addition, computer programmers depicted in popular media are overwhelmingly male, contributing to an absence of role models for would-be female computer programmers.

In part to qualify for federal education funding distributed through the states, most U.S. states and districts now focus on ensuring that all students are at least "proficient" in mathematics and reading, making it difficult for teachers to focus on teaching concepts beyond the test. According to a Rand Corporation study, such a concentration on testing can cause administrators to focus resources on tested subjects at the expense of other subjects (e.g., science) or distract their attention from other needs.[27] Thus, computational thinking is unlikely to be taught either standalone or as integrated into other areas of study (e.g., mathematics, biology) anytime in the near future. The National Center for Women & IT distributes free resources for increasing awareness of the need for teaching computer science in schools, including the "Talking Points" card, "Moving Beyond Computer Literacy: Why Schools Should Teach Computer Science".[28]

Female and male perspectives

According to a 1998–2000 ethnographic study by Jane Margolis and Allan Fisher at Carnegie Mellon University, men and women viewed computers very differently. Women interviewees were more likely to state that they saw the computer as a tool for use within a larger societal and/or interdisciplinary context than did the men interviewed. On the other hand, men were more likely to express an interest in the computer as a machine.[25][29] Moreover, women interviewed in this study perceived that many of their male peers were "geeks," with limited social skills. Females often disliked the idea that computers "become their life."[25] The students observed and interviewed in that study were probably not representative of students in general, since at that time, in order to be admitted to CMU Computer Science a student needed to have some programming experience. More research is needed to understand the ability to generalize Margolis' and Fisher's findings.

From a two-year research initiative published in 2000 by AAUW found that "Girls approach the computer as a "tool" useful primarily for what it can do; boys more often view the computer as a "toy" and/or an extension of the self. For boys, the computer is inherently interesting. Girls are interested in its instrumental possibilities, which may include its use as an artistic medium. They express scorn toward boys who confuse "real" power and power on a screen. "I see a computer as a tool," a high school girl declares. "You [might] go play Kung Fu Fighting, but in real life you are still a stupid little person living in a suburban way."[30] Still, the National Assessment of Educational Progress showed as far back as 2000 that boys and girls use computers at about the same rates, albeit for somewhat different purposes.

Nearly 1000 students in University of Akron were surveyed, and it was discovered that females hold a more negative attitude towards computers than males.[22] Another study assessed the computer-related attitude of over 300 students in University of Winnipeg and obtained similar results.[22]

This is thought to contribute to the gender disparity phenomenon in computing, in particular the females' early lack of interest in the field.[22]

Barriers to advancement

Research on the barriers that women face in undergraduate computing[31] has highlighted such factors as:

- Undergraduate classroom teaching in which the "weedout" practices and policies privileging competition over cooperation tend to advantage men.

- Laboratory climates in which women are seen as foreign and not belonging at best, and experience blatant hostility and sexism at worst.

- Well-meaning people who unwittingly create stereotype threat by reminding students that "women can do computing as well as men".

- Strong resistance to changing the system in which these and other subtle practices are continuously reproduced.

Just like in the pre-college situation, solutions are most often implemented outside of the mainstream (e.g., providing role models, mentoring, and women's groups), which can also create the perception among women, their male peers, and their professors that to be successful, women need "extra help" to graduate. Most people do not realize that the "extra help" is not academic, but instead access to the kind of peer networks more readily available to male students. Many women decline to participate in these extracurricular support groups because they do not want to appear deficient. In short, the conditions under which women (and underrepresented minority students) study computing are not the same as those experienced by men.

Lack of acknowledgment and promotion of skills

Women in technical roles often feel that the skills and feedback they bring to their jobs are not valued. According to a Catalyst report called "Women in Technology: Maximizing Talent, Minimizing Barriers", 65% of females in technical roles felt that those they reported to were receptive and responsive to their suggestions, as compared to 75% of women in non-technical roles.[15] This also speaks directly to the retention of females in the industry as females will commonly leave a company when they feel that what they are offering a company is not valued.[15] The report shows the concerns felt about this by sharing the following quote from an interviewee: "I would like to be involved with more projects than I am currently involved in; I feel that I am being underutilized. I would prefer my supervisor give me an opportunity to expand my skill sets and my responsibility at work".[15]

However, it is not enough to just acknowledge skills. Women also lack the support and advocacy needed to promote these skills.[32] Women feel alone and at a loss because they lack role models, networks, and mentors.[32] These support systems not only help women develop talent and opportunities for career advancement, but they are also needed to promote women to more senior roles.[32] It can be understood that advocacy is a major player in the advancement of females into senior tech roles.

Stereotyping computer scientists

Other research examines that undergraduates' stereotype of the people in computer science and how changing this stereotype through media can influence women's interest in computer science. Through this study they concluded that the image of computer science majors that is most prevalent in popular culture and in the minds of current undergraduates is someone who is highly intelligent, primarily obsessed with computers, and socially unskilled. This image can be considered to contrast with the more people-oriented, traditionally feminine image. According to this study, students continue to generate and propagate this stereotype when asked to describe people in computer science. Based on the results of their experiment based on this idea, they took a group of women and men undergraduates and had them read a stereotypical article and a non-stereotypical article. They found that women who read the non-stereotypical article were much more interested in computer science than those who read the article with the above-mentioned stereotypical computer science student. Overall, they concluded that the underrepresentation of women in computing not due to women's lack of interest. The study contests the perception that college major decisions are free choices, instead they discuss the implications that the major decisions are more constrained by the prevalent stereotypes. This has a negative consequence such that it prevents women from developing an interest in these technical fields. The finding suggests that the stereotypical image of the computer scientists is unattractive to women who would otherwise be interested if presented with a true representation or role model from the computer science field.[33]

2.19.4 Attracting women into computing

The majority of data collected about women in IT has been qualitative analysis such as interviews and case studies. This data has been used to create effective programs addressing the underrepresentation of women in IT.[34] Suggestions for incorporating more women in IT careers include formal mentoring, ongoing training opportunities, employee referral bonuses, multicultural training for all IT employees, as well as educational programs targeting women.[35]

The number of female college entrants expressing interest in majoring in computer science decreased in the 2000s to pre-1980's levels.[36] A research study was initialized by Allan Fisher, then Associate Dean for Undergraduate Computer Science Education at Carnegie Mellon University, and Jane Margolis, a social scientist and expert in gender equity in education, into the nature of this problem. The main issues discovered in interesting and retaining women in computer science were feelings of an experience gap, confidence doubts, interest in curriculum and pedagogy, and peer culture.[37] Universities across North America are changing their computer science programs to make them more appealing to women.[38] Proactive and positive exposures to early computer experiences, such as The Alice Project,[39] founded by the late Randy Pausch at Carnegie Mellon University, are thought to be effective in terms of retention and creation of enthusiasm for women who may later consider entering the field. Institutions of higher education are also beginning to make changes regarding the process and availability of mentoring to women that are undergraduates in technical fields.[40]

Another strategy for addressing this issue has been early outreach to elementary and high-school girls. Programs like all-girl computer camps, girls' after-school computer clubs, and support groups for girls have been instilled to create more interest at a younger age.[35] A specific example of this kind of program is the Canadian Information Processing Society outreach program, in which a representative is sent to schools in Canada, speaking specifically to grade nine girls about the benefits of Information Technology careers. The purpose is to inform girls about the benefits and opportunities within the field of information technology.[41] Companies like IBM also encourage young women to become interested in engineering, technology and science. IBM offers EX.I.T.E. (Exploring Interests in Technology and Engineering) camps for young women from the ages of 11 to 13.

Additionally, attempts are being made to make the efforts of female computer scientists more visible through events such as the Grace Hopper Celebration of Women conference series which allows women in the field to meet, collaborate and present their work. In the U.S., the Association for Women in Computing was founded in Washington, D.C. in 1978. Its purpose is to provide opportunities for the professional growth of women in computing through networking, and through programs on technical and career-oriented topics.[42] In the United Kingdom, the British Computer Society (BCS) and other organizations have groups which promote the cause of women in computing, such as BCSWomen, founded by Sue Black, and the BCS Women's Forum. In Ontario, Canada, the **Gr8 Designs for Gr8 Girls** program was founded to develop grade 8 girls' interest in computer science.

Recent efforts

The National Center for Women & IT (NCWIT) is currently one of the lead supporters of women's entry and retention in computing. Their goal is to help to create academic and work environments that are welcoming and fair for women. Their research shows that encouragement is one of the key elements to help women enter a primarily male-dominated field. They found women report more often than their male-counterpart that they entered computer science due to the influence of a teacher, family member, or friend's encouragement. Their findings conclude that support can make the difference in a woman's belief that she is competent enough to compete in computing. Thus, the NCWIT developed a program called Aspirations in Computing in order to provide girls with the necessary encouragement, a network of support, and female role models. In a survey done, nearly half of the girls polled said they would feel uncomfortable being the only girl in a group or class, one of the Aspirations main goals is to enable girls to feel less isolated in these predicaments. They have found that creating a sense of belonging or "fitting in" is fundamental for interest and current retention. The NCWIT Aspirations Award was created in order to involve women in a national competition, awardees are selected for their computing and IT aptitude, leadership skills, academics, and plans for graduate schooling. Due to their reach and awareness of the program, they saw a 54% increase in the girls applying in the 2013 season compared to the previous year.[43]

In September 2013, Ada Developers Academy, a tuition-free 1 year intensive school in software development for women was launched by Technology Alliance in Seattle, and students could even apply to receive a $1000-per-month-stipend. The first half of the course focuses on HTML/CSS, JavaScript, Ruby on Rails and computer science fundamentals.

Having started in the US, Girl Develop It is a network of city chapters that teach women from all parts of the country learn to develop software with HTML and CSS, Javascript, Ruby on Rails, Python, and Android. The organization was co-founded by Sara Chipps and Vanessa Hurst in 2010. As of 2013, it has 17 city chapters running regular courses and events.[44] The programs offered by Girl Develop It are all taught by volunteers that are employed in the technology field. Structural and content resources used to teach the programs have been developed and are offered for free both on their website and on GitHub.com.

Hackbright Academy is an intensive, women-only 10-week programming course in San Francisco.[45] A *Moms in Tech* sponsorship for Hackbright Academy is also available for mothers who are former IT professionals and wish to retrain and return to work as a technically hands-on lead or manager, sponsored by Facebook.

Geek Girl is an organization that was started in March 2006 by Leslie Fishlock. It is an organization that acts as a technology resource for women. The organization strives to empower women of all ages through making technology easy to understand and use. These services are provided entirely by women. Though the target audience tends to be female and the organization was founded on the goal to empower women, men are also encouraged to participate in any of the events or services the organization offers. Geek Girl hosts localized events, meetups, and conferences. The organization also supports a video channel titled GeekGirl TV that provides workshops about technological tools as well as provides coverage for their events for those who are unable to attend. Additionally, Geek Girl's website hosts a blog that provides technology-related news and information that is accessible to a reader with minimal technology experience.[46]

CodeEd is a non-profit organization that focuses on teaching computer science to young girls in underserved communities. The organization partners with schools and programs to help provide volunteer teachers, computer science course offerings, and computers. The organization was co-founded by Angie Sciavoni and Sep Kamvar in 2010. CodeEd provides courses in HTML and CSS, and provides the curriculum and course material for free under a Creative Commons Attribution license. The organization offers classes that are taught by a team of two volunteer teachers, provide lessons in one hour blocks that may be dispensed in a way that works for the receiving school, and teachers through fun and experimental projects. Code Ed currently offers services in New York City, Boston, and San Francisco.[47]

she++ is an organization that facilitates a community driven to inspire women to take on a role in the computer sciences. The organization was founded at Stanford University by now-alumnae Ellora Israni and Ayna Agarwal, who spearheaded the organization's inaugural conference in April 2012. The conference featured female speakers who held tech positions in companies like Google, Pinterest, and Facebook and was well attended. The conference inspired its organizers to continue with and expand upon she++ and now facilitates participation initiatives through hosting additional events such as a 2013 conference, curating a video library that features inspirational stories from technology professionals, and by offering a mentorship program. The organization is run by a collection of female students and Stanford University.[48]

Nerd Girls was launched in 2000 by Dr. Karen Panetta, a Professor of Electrical and Computer Engineering at Tufts University. It is an organization that is represented by a group of female engineering students each year and encourages women to take on roles in the engineering and technology profession. The organization celebrates the coincidence of science knowledge and femininity. Participating members solve real-world problems as a group by addressing and fixing technology related issues in the community.[49] Nerd Girls has gained national attention since its launch and has been approached by media producers to create a reality show based off the organization's problem-solving activities.[50][51] Nerd Girls is sponsored by the Institute of Electrical and Electronics Engineers (IEEE).

Femgineer was started in 2007 by Poornima Vijayashanker. It was originally developed as a blog that focused on engineers, which evolved into an organization that supports women in technology careers. Femgineers is now an education-focused organization that offers workshops, free teaching resources on the topic of technology, supports forums and Meetups, an a team has been developed to continue to expand on the original blog.[52] Poornima Vijayashanker is an avid public speaker and regularly speaks at technology-related conferences and events about the technology industry and about Femgineer itself. In addition to founding Femgineer, she also founded a startup called BizeeBee in 2010 that supports growing fitness businesses, teaches technology workshops for tech-driven organizations around the country,[53] and was named one of the ten women to watch in tech in 2013 by Inc Magazine.[54]

Numerous higher education institutions have seen development of student-run organizations that focus on the advancement of women in computer science. In addition to she++ based out of Stanford University, Rochester Institute of Technology (RIT) supports a chapter of the organization called Women In Computing. The campus's chapter of the organization is composed of students, faculty and staff at RIT and they strive to support and further develop the culture of computing to women. This effort is not only focused on their campus, but in the larger community. They host events both on their campus located in Henrietta, New York, and within surrounding Rochester schools.[55] RIT is among a national list of schools that host a chapter of Women in Computing, which is founded in the organization Association of Computing Machinery's committee for women in computing (ACM-W).[56] Harvard University hosts the organization titled Harvard Undergraduate Women in Computer Science (WiSC). The organization aims to promote women in computing across a variety of schools and industries, educate women on the profession of computer science, and provide opportunities for women in technical fields. WiCS supports the annual conference named WECode, a conference that aims to promote women's involvement in computer science.[57][58]

In an effort to improve the gender composition in computing, the Women & Information Technology (NCWIT) created a nationwide U.S. program called "Pacesetters." Through this program, twenty-four academic and corporate organizations added close to 1,000 "Net New Women" to the field of computer science by 2012. These Net New Women are women in the sciences that had not originally intended on pursuing a computer science degree. The Pacesetters is the first program of its kind where different organizations come together to identify effective ways to broaden the participation of women in computer science. There are currently more than 300 corporations, academic institutions, government agencies and non-profit organizations devoted to this cause. Together they build internal teams in order to develop and fund the needed programs and share their overall results. Pacesetters organizations include some very prestigious companies such as AT&T, Intel, Microsoft, Google, Georgia Tech, Pfizer, and IBM IBM to name a few. These are a few examples of their results due to the work with Pacesetters: • Google: built a new programs for undergraduate women and held a career development panel of engineers which gave women the chance to participate in mock interviews. Due to these efforts, the number of women applicants grew and Google doubled the number of women in their software engineering summer internship program in 2011 compared to 2010. • Intel: piloted a program called Command Presence Workshop in which senior technical women participated in specialized training, • Virginia Tech: created a team of CS faculty, advisors, and student mentors to interact with potential female undergraduates and high school students. They say a 56% increase in the number of female students who showed interest in their science programs. [59]

2.19.5 Relation to gender theory

There are a number of thinkers who engage with gender theories and issues related to women and technology. Such thinkers include, for example, Donna Haraway, Sadie Plant, Julie Wosk, Sally L. Hacker, Evelyn Fox Keller, Janet Abbate, Thelma Estrin, and Thomas J. Misa, among others.[60] A 2008 book titled *Gender and Information Technology: Moving Beyond Access to Co-Create Global Partnership* uses Riane Eisler's cultural transformation theory to offer an interdisciplinary, social systems perspective on issues of access to technology.[61] The book explores how shifting from dominator towards partnership systems — as reflected in four primary social institutions (communication, media, education, and business) - might help society move beyond the simplistic notion of access to co-create a real digital revolution worldwide.[61]

A 2000 book titled *Athena Unbound*[62] provides a life-course analysis (based on interviews and surveys) of women in the sciences from an early childhood interest, through university, to graduate school and finally into the academic workplace. The thesis of this book is that "women face a special series of gender related barriers to entry and success in scientific careers that persist, despite recent advances".[62]

Computer scientist Karen Petrie, from University of Dundee, has developed an argument to illustrate why an attack on sexism in computing is not an attack on men.[63] Ian Gent, University of St Andrews, has described this idea which is key to the argument as the "Petrie Multiplier".[64]

According to J. McGrath Cohoon, senior research scientist for the National Center for Women & Information Technology, there are a few possible hypotheses for why women are underrepresented in computer sciences attributed to already established theories about the influence of gender and technology stereotypes. One gender related hypothesis is that women find it more difficult than men to contribute to the intellectual life of the field in the sense that reviewers of their work are unconsciously downgraded due to their status as women or those women have lower confidence in this field that inhibits women's willingness to publicly present their technical findings. Due to this barrier of women as second-class citizens in the computing world, it creates an environment that is not accessible to women.[65] A study by the Psychology of Women Quarterly backs this hypothesis up by concluding that even the enduring effect of single brief exposures to stereotypical role models leaves a strong mark. Their findings reported that the most important factor in recruiting women to the computer science field is that women meet with a potential role model, regardless of gender of that role model, that conveys to the woman a sense of belonging in the field. This finding suggests that support and encouragement are the two most important aspects that can influence women participation in computing. In order for women to be more receptive to the field is if the environment became a more welcoming place by their male counterparts.[66]

Another argument for why women are less prevalent in computer science is the ill-defined nature of computing according to Paul De Palma. In his article Why Women Avoid Computer Science, he postulates that women find careers in computing unattractive. He finds that among the many reasons offered, he believes the nature of computing is what drives them away. He claims that young men who are drawn to computer science and engineering are those that like to tinker, those who like to use tools to create and dismantle objects. He further claims that computing is not a true profession, that traditional career paths such as law, business, and medicine are more certain and profitable on average than computing. He compares it to using a computer, computers nowadays do not come with lengthy manuals on the inner workings of the modern day computer, in fact our tools are always more complicated than their what they are used for, thus the tinkering nature of men, the drive born from gender stereotyping from birth, has made men successful in this field for they are more inclined to spend endless hours of tinkering with software and hardware. His claim revolves around the focus that boys and girls fall into gender stereotypes, girls who usually are given dolls and boys who are given trucks and toy tool boxes. He claims that these gender roles placed on children is one of the primary causes for the gender gap seen in computer science. He postulates that if we were to see more girls playing with trucks and other "boy-related" toys that perhaps we would see an increase in this tinkering nature and therefore more participation of women in the computer science field.[67]

2.19.6 Worldwide timeline

- 1842: Ada Lovelace (1815–1852) was an analyst of Charles Babbage's analytical engine and considered the "first computer programmer."[68]

- 1893: Henrietta Swan Leavitt joined the Harvard

A poster encouraging women to pursue technology studies at University of Valle, Cali, Colombia. It reads: "If it's not appropriate for women, it's not appropriate. Women and technology." c. 2000.

"computers", a group of women engaged in the production of astronomical data at Harvard. She was instrumental in discovery of the cepheid variable stars, which are evidence for the expansion of the universe.

- 1926: Grete Hermann published the foundational paper for computerized algebra. It was her doctoral thesis, titled "The Question of Finitely Many Steps in Polynomial Ideal Theory", and published in Mathematische Annalen.[69]

- 1940s: American women were recruited to do ballistics calculations and program computers during WWII. Around 1943-1945, these women "computers" used a Differential Analyzer in the basement of the Moore School of Electrical Engineering to speed up their calculations, though the machine required a mechanic to be totally accurate and the women often rechecked the calculations by hand.[70]

- 1942: Hedy Lamarr (1913–2000), was an actress and the co-inventor of an early form of spread-spectrum broadcasting.

- 1943: Women worked as WREN Colossus operators

Ada Lovelace, considered to be the first computer programmer.

during WW2 at Bletchley Park.[71]

- 1943: The wives of scientists at Los Alamos were first organized as "computers" on the Manhattan Project.

- 1943: Gertrude Blanch led the Mathematical Tables Project group from 1938 to 1948. During World War II, the project operated as a major computing office for the U.S. government and did calculations for the Office of Scientific Research and Development, the Army, the Navy, the Manhattan Project and other institutions.[72]

- 1946: Betty Jennings, Betty Snyder, Frances Spence, Kay McNulty, Marlyn Wescoff, and Ruth Lichterman were the original programmers of the ENIAC. Adele Goldstine, also involved in the programming, wrote the program manual for the ENIAC.[73]

- 1948: Kathleen Booth writes the assembly language for the ARC2 computer.

- 1949: Grace Hopper (1906–1992), was a United States Navy officer and the first programmer of the Harvard Mark I, known as the "Mother of COBOL". She developed the first-ever compiler for an electronic computer, known as A-0. She also popularized the term "debugging" – a reference to a moth extracted from a relay in the Harvard Mark II computer.[74]

- 1949: Evelyn Boyd Granville was the second African-American woman in the U.S. to receive a PhD in mathematics. From 1956 to 1960, she worked for IBM on the Project Vanguard and Project Mercury space programs, analyzing orbits and developing computer procedures.

- 1950: Ida Rhodes was a pioneer in the analysis of systems of programming. She designed the C-10 language in the early 1950s for the UNIVAC I – a computer system that was used to calculate the census. She also designed the original computer used for the Social Security Administration.

- 1958: Orbital calculations for the United States' Explorer 1 satellite were solved by the NASA Jet Propulsion Laboratory's all-female "computers", many of whom were recruited out of high school. Mechanical calculators were supplemented with logarithmic calculations performed by hand.[75][76]

- 1961: Dana Ulery (1938–), was the first female engineer at Jet Propulsion Laboratory, developing realtime tracking systems using a North American Aviation Recomp II, a 40-bit word size computer.

- 1962: Jean E. Sammet (1928–), developed the FORMAC programming language. She was also the first to write extensively about the history and categorization of programming languages in 1969, and became the first female president of the Association for Computing Machinery in 1974.

- 1962: Dame Stephanie "Steve" Shirley (1933–), founded the UK software company F.I. She was concerned with creating work opportunities for women with dependents, and predominantly employed women, only 3 out of 300-odd programmers were male, until that became illegal. She adopted the name "Steve" to help her in the male-dominated business world. From 1989 to 1990, she was President of the British Computer Society. In 1985, she was awarded a Recognition of Information Technology Award.

- 1965: Mary Allen Wilkes was the first person to use a computer in a private home (in 1965) and the first developer of an operating system (LAP) for the first minicomputer (LINC).

- 1965: Sister Mary Kenneth Keller (1914?–1985) became the first American woman to earn a PhD in Computer Science in 1965.[77] Her thesis was titled "Inductive Inference on Computer Generated Patterns."[78]

- 1966: Margaret R. Fox was appointed Chief of the Office of Computer Information in 1966, part of the Institute for Computer Science and Technology of NBS. She held the post until 1975. She was also actively involved in the Association for Computing Machinery (ACM) and served as the first Secretary for the American Federation of Information Processing Societies (AFIPS).

- 1969: Margaret Hamilton developed on-board flight software for the Apollo space program. Her work prevented an abort of the Apollo 11 moon landing by using robust architecture. Later, she was awarded the NASA Exceptional Space Act Award for her scientific and technical contributions. The award included a check for $37,200, the largest amount awarded to any individual in NASA's history.[79][80][81]

- 1971: Erna Schneider Hoover is an American mathematician notable for inventing a computerized telephone switching method which "revolutionized modern communication" according to several reports. At Bell Laboratories, where she worked for over 32 years, Hoover was described as an important pioneer for women in the field of computer technology. She was awarded one of the first patents for computer software.

- 1972: Mary Shaw became the first woman to get a Ph.D. in Computer Science from Carnegie Mellon University.

- 1972: Adele Goldberg (1945–), was one of the designers and developers of the Smalltalk language.[82]

- 1972: Karen Spärck Jones (1935–2007), was a pioneer of information retrieval and natural language processing.

- 1972: Sandra Kurtzig founded ASK Computer Systems, an early Silicon Valley startup.

- 1973: Susan Nycum co-authored *Computer Abuse*, a minor classic that was one of the first studies to define and document computer-related crime.[83][84]

- 1973: Lynn Conway (1938–), led the "LSI Systems" group, and co-authored *Introduction to VLSI Systems*.

- 1974: Elizabeth Feinler and her team defined a simple text file format for Internet host names.[85] The list evolved into the Domain Name System and her group became the naming authority for the top-level domains of .mil, .gov, .edu, .org, and .com.

- 1975?: Phyllis Fox worked on the PORT portable mathematical/numerical library.

- 1975: Irene Greif became the first woman to get a Ph.D. in computer science from the Massachusetts Institute of Technology.[86]

- 1978: Sophie Wilson (1957–), is a British computer scientist. She is known for designing the Acorn Micro-Computer, as well as the instruction set of the ARM processor.

- 1979: Carol Shaw (?), was a game designer and programmer for Atari Corp. and Activision.

- 1980: Carla Meninsky (?), was the game designer and programmer for Atari 2600 games *Dodge 'Em* and *Warlords*.

- 1982?: Lorinda Cherry worked on the Writer's Workbench (wwb) for Bell Labs.

- 1983: Janese Swanson (with others) developed the first of the Carmen Sandiego games. She went on to found Girl Tech. Girl Tech develops products and services that encourage girls to use new technologies, such as the Internet and video games.[87]

- 1984: Roberta Williams (1953–), did pioneering work in graphical adventure games for personal computers, particularly the King's Quest series.

- 1984: Susan Kare (1954–), created the icons and many of the interface elements for the original Apple Macintosh in the 1980s, and was an original employee of NeXT, working as the Creative Director.

- 1985: Radia Perlman (1951–), invented the Spanning Tree Protocol. She has done extensive and innovative research, particularly on encryption and networking. She received the USENIX Lifetime Achievement Award in 2007, among numerous others.

- 1985: Irma Wyman (~1927–), was the first Honeywell CIO.

- 1987: Monica S. Lam receives a Ph.D. for her work on optimising compilers. She has since then performed influential research in many areas of computer science as well as co-authored a famous textbook on compilers.

- 1988: Éva Tardos (1957–), was the recipient of the Fulkerson Prize for her research on design and analysis of algorithms.

- 1989: Frances E. Allen (1932–), became the first female IBM Fellow in 1989. In 2006, she became the first female recipient of the ACM's Turing Award.

- 1989: Frances Brazier, professor of Computer Science at the Vrije Universiteit in Amsterdam, is one of the founder of NLnet, the first Internet service provider in the Netherlands.

- 1992: Donna Dubinsky (1955–), CEO and co-founder of Palm, Inc., co-founder of Handspring, co-founder of Numenta, Harvard Business School's Alumni Achievement Award winner for "introducing the first successful personal digital assistant (PDA) and who is now developing a computer memory system modeled after the human brain".

- 1993: Shafi Goldwasser (1958–), a theoretical computer scientist, is a two-time recipient of the Gödel Prize for research on complexity theory, cryptography and computational number theory, and the invention of zero-knowledge proofs.

- 1993: Barbara Liskov, together with Jeannette Wing, developed the Liskov substitution principle. Liskov was also the winner of the Turing Prize in 2008.[88]

- 1994: Sally Floyd (~1953–), is known for her work on Transmission Control Protocol.

- 1996: Xiaoyuan Tu (1967–), was the first female recipient of ACM's Doctoral Dissertation Award.[89]

- 1997: Anita Borg (1949–2003), was the founding director of the Institute for Women and Technology (IWT).

- 1998: LinuxChix an international organization for women who use Linux and women and men who want to support women in computing was founded by Deb Richardson.

- 1999: Marissa Mayer (1975–), was the first female engineer hired at Google, and was later named Vice President of Search Product and User Experience. She is currently the CEO of Yahoo!.

- 2003: Ellen Spertus earned a PhD in Electrical Engineering and Computer Science from MIT in 1998 with the notable thesis "ParaSite: Mining the structural information on the World-Wide Web".

- 2004: Jeri Ellsworth (1974–), is a self-taught computer chip designer and creator of the C64 Direct-to-TV.

- 2005: Audrey Tang (1981–), was the initiator and leader of the Pugs project.

- 2005: Mary Lou Jepsen (1965–), was the founder and chief technology officer of One Laptop Per Child (OLPC), and the founder of Pixel Qi.

- 2005: Ruchi Sanghvi became the first female engineer at Facebook.[90]

- 2006: Maria Klawe (1951–), was the first woman to become President of the Harvey Mudd College since its founding in 1955 and was ACM president from 2002 until 2004.

- 2006: Melanie Rieback's research concerns the security and privacy of Radio Frequency Identification (RFID) technology, she is known to have program the first virus to infect RFID devices.[91]

- 2006: Joanna Rutkowska presented Blue Pill, a rootkit based on x86 virtualization, at the Black Hat Briefings computer security conference.

- 2014: Kimberley Bolton became the first woman to win a Microsoft Apprentice of the Year award, winning in the "Medium Business Category".[92]

2.19.7 Notable organizations

- Ada Initiative

- Anita Borg Institute for Women and Technology, group for support of women, runs the Grace Hopper Celebration of Women in Computing yearly conference.

- Association for Computing Machinery (ACM) Committee on Women

- Association for Women in Computing: one of the first professional organizations for women in computing. AWC is dedicated to promoting the advancement of women in the computing professions.[93]

- BCSWomen, a women-only Specialist Group of the British Computer Society

- Black Girls Code, non-profit focused on providing technology education to young African-American women.

- Center for Women in Technology, university center focused on increasing the representation of women in the creation of technology.

- Computing Research Association's Committee on the Status of Women in Computing Research (CRA-W), group focused on increasing the number of women participating in Computer Science and Engineering (CSE) research and education at all levels.

- Girl Geek Dinners, an International group for women of all ages.

- LinuxChix, a women-oriented community in the open source movement.

- Systers, a moderated listserv dedicated to mentoring women in the Systers community.

- Women in Technology International, global organization dedicated to the advancement of women in business and technology.

- Women's Technology Empowerment Centre (W.TEC), non-profit organisation focused on providing technology education and mentoring to Nigerian women and girls.[94]

2.19.8 See also

- Discrimination
- List of female mathematicians
- List of female scientists
- List of organizations for women in science
- List of prizes, medals, and awards for women in science
- Women in engineering
- Women in science
- Women in the workforce
- Women in venture capital
- Women and video games

2.19.9 References

[1] Grurer, Denis (1995) "Pioneering Women in Computer Science" ACM.

[2] Chan, Vania; Stafford, Katie; Klawe, Maria; Chen, Grace (2000). "Gender Differences in Vancouver Secondary Students' Interests Related to Information Technology Careers". Department of Computer Science, University of British Columbia.

[3] Faulkner, Wendy (2004). "Strategies of Inclusion: Gender and the Information Society - Final Report", SIGIS, University of Edinburgh.

[4] Prof Robin Williams. "Getting More Women in Computer Science and Engineering" (PDF). University of Edinburgh.

[5] Prof. Vivian Anette Lagesen. "A Cyberfeminist Utopia?: Perceptions of Gender and Computer Science among Malaysian Women Computer Science Students and Faculty". Sage Publications.

[6] Simard, Caroline. "The state of women and technology fields around the world" (PDF). Anita Borg Institute.

[7] Varma, Roli (2010). "Computing self-efficiency among women in India" (PDF). *Journal of Women and Minorities in Science and Engineering* **16**: 257–274. doi:10.1615/jwomenminorscieneng.v16.i3.40.

[8] Camp, Tracy (2001). "Women in Computer Science: Reversing the Trend". Colorado School of Mines.

[9] "Computing Degree and Enrollment Trends", 2010-2011 CRA Taulbee Survey. The Computing Research Association.

[10] Melkymuka, Kathleen (8 January 2001). "If Girls Don't Get IT, IT Won't Get Girls", Computer World.

[11] Stross, Randall (15 November 2008). "What Has Driven Women Out of Computer Science?", The New York Times.

[12] 2006 College-Bound Seniors - Total Group Profile Report, CollegeBoard SAT.

[13] "Characteristics of Scientists and Engineers in the US", National Science Foundation.

[14] Thomas J. Misa, ed. (2010). *Gender Codes: Why Women Are Leaving Computing*. Wiley/IEEE Computer Society Press. pp. 32-34.

[15] Foust-Cummings, Heather; Sabattini, Laura; Carter, Nancy (2008). "Women in Technology: Maximizing Talent, Minimizing Barriers". Catalyst.

[16] Laura Sydell (Director) (2013-04-29). "Blazing The Trail For Female Programmers". *All Tech Considered*. National Public Radio. Retrieved 2013-06-07.

[17] "Solving the Equation: The Variables for Women's Success in Engineering and Computing". Retrieved 10 August 2015.

[18] "What Is the Impact of Gender Diversity on Technology Business Performance?: Research Summary" (PDF). Retrieved 10 August 2015.

[19] "RECEIVED WISDOM AND THE RELATIONSHIP BETWEEN DIVERSITY AND ORGANIZATIONAL PERFORMANCE". Retrieved 25 August 2015.

[20] "Is there a payoff from top-team diversity?". Retrieved 10 August 2015.

[21] "The Gender and Ethnic Diversity of US Boards and Board Committees and Firm Financial Performance". Retrieved 25 August 2015.

[22] Cooper, J.; Weaver, K. (2003). *Gender and Computers: Understanding the Digital Divide*. Lawrence Erlbaum Associates. ISBN 0-8058-4427-9

[23] "TABLE 33. Computer sciences degrees awarded, by degree level and sex of recipient: 1966–2010" (PDF). *http://www.nsf.gov/statistics". NSF. Retrieved December 26, 2014.*

[24] Steve Henn (October 21, 2014). "When Women Stopped Coding". *Morning Edition* (NPR). Retrieved December 26, 2014. The share of women in computer science started falling at roughly the same moment when personal computers started showing up in U.S. homes in significant numbers.

[25] Handcock, Mark S. et al. (2004). "Focus on Women in Computer Science", University of British Columbia. Archived from the original on 10 May 2012.

[26] Dean, Cornelia (17 April 2007). "Computer Science Takes Steps to Bring Women to the Fold". *New York Times*.

[27] Stecher, B. M. (2002). "Consequences of large-scale, high-stakes testing on school and classroom practice". In: Hamilton, L. S., B. M. Stecher, and S. P. Klein (Eds.). *Making sense of test-based accountability in education*. Santa Monica, CA: Rand Corporation.

[28] Moving Beyond Computer Literacy: Why Schools Should Teach Computer Science, National Center for Women & Information Technology.

[29] Margolis, J. et al. (1999). *Unlocking the Clubhouse*. The MIT Press. p.4.

[30] AAUW Educational Foundation Commission on Technology, Gender, and Teacher Education (2000). "Tech Savvy: Educating Girls in the New Computer Age", p.8.

[31] Cohoon, J. McGrath; Aspray, William (2006). *Women and Information Technology: Research on Underrepresentation*, Chapter 5. The MIT Press.

[32] (2003). "Bit by Bit: Catalyst's Guide to Advancing Women in High Tech Companies". Catalyst.

[33] Cheryan, Sapna, et al. "The Stereotypical Computer Scientist: Gendered Media Representations As A Barrier To Inclusion For Women." Sex Roles 69.1/2 (2013): 58. Publisher Provided Full Text Searching. Web. 16 Jan. 2015.

[34] Moody, J W; Beise, C M; Woszczynski, A B; Myers, M E. (2003). "Diversity and the information technology workforce: Barriers and opportunities", p.3. *The Journal of Computer Information Systems*.

[35] Ramsey, N.; McCorduck, P. (2005). "Where are the women in Information Technology?". Anita Borg Institute.

[36] Eggers, Andy (17 November 2008). "Interest in computer science is volatile". The Institute of Quantitative Social Science. Archived from the original on 10 May 2012.

[37] Blum, Lenore (2001). "Women in Computer Science: The Carnegie Mellon Experience", Carnegie Mellon School of Computer Science.

[38] http://www.npr.org/2014/10/23/358238982/to-get-women-to-work-in-computer-science-schools-get-them-to-class

[39] The Alice Project, Carnegie Mellon University.

[40] Sullivan, Patricia; Kristen Moore (2013). "Time Talk: On Small Changes that Enact Infrastructural Mentoring for Undergraduate Women in Technical Fields". *Journal of Technical Writing & Communication* 43 (3): 333–354. doi:10.2190/TW.43.3.f. Retrieved 30 September 2013.

[41] "Women in IT", Canada's Association of IT Professionals.

[42] "Association for Women in Computing". Awc-hq.org. Retrieved 2013-10-02.

[43] DuBow, Wendy M., et al. "Bringing Young Women Into Computing Through The NCWIT Aspiratiogns In Computing Program." Communications of the ACM 56.12 (2013): 34-37. Business Source Premier. Web. 16 Jan 2015.

[44] Girl Develop It site.

[45] "Hackbright Academy". *Hackbright Academy*. Retrieved 26 October 2014.

[46] Made with love the Geek Girls. "Geek Girl Tech Conferences Education Training for Women". *Geek Girl*. Retrieved 26 October 2014.

[47] "CodeEd". Retrieved 26 October 2014.

[48] "she++". Retrieved 26 October 2014.

[49] "About -". Retrieved 26 October 2014.

[50] "Karen Panetta: Bringing Geek Chic Into Style". Retrieved 26 October 2014.

[51] http://www.todaysengineer.org/2010/Jul/Nerd-Girls.asp

[52] "Femgineer". Retrieved 26 October 2014.

[53] "Poornima Vijayashanker: Femgineer & Top Ten Woman to Watch in Tech". Retrieved 26 October 2014.

[54] "10 Women to Watch in Tech in 2013". Retrieved 26 October 2014.

[55] "Women in Computing". Retrieved 26 October 2014.

[56] "Home". Retrieved 26 October 2014.

[57] "Harvard's WECode conference welcomes more women into tech". *Boston.com*. Retrieved 26 October 2014.

[58] "Closing the gender gap in computer science". *Harvard Gazette*. Retrieved 26 October 2014.

[59] "Improving Gender Composition in Computing." Communications Of The ACM 55.4 (2012): 29-31.Business Source Premier. Web. 15 Jan. 2015

[60] Smith, Erika E (2013). "Recognizing a Collective Inheritance through the History of Women in Computing". *CLCWeb: Comparative Literature and Culture* 15 (1). doi:10.7771/1481-4374.1972.

[61] Kirk, Mary (2008). *Gender and Information Technology: Moving Beyond Access to Co-Create Global Partnership*. Hershey, PA: IGI Global. ISBN 978-1-59904-786-7

[62] Etzkowitz, Henry; Kemelgor, Carol; Uzzi, Brian (2000). *Athena Unbound - The advancement of women in science and technology*, Cambridge University Press. ISBN 0-511-03833-X

[63] Petrie, Karen (2013). *Attack on sexism not an attack on men*, The Scotsman, 27 November 2013, http://www.scotsman.com/news/attack-on-sexism-not-an-attack-on-men-1-3209552

[64] Gent, Ian (2013) *The Petrie Multiplier: Why an Attack on Sexism in Tech is NOT an Attack on Men*, Posted on Ian Gent's Blog, 13 October 2013, http://iangent.blogspot.co.uk/2013/10/the-petrie-multiplier-why-attack-on.html

[65] "Gender And Computing Conference Papers." Communications of the ACM 54.8 (2011): 72-80. Business Source Premier. Web. 15 Jan. 2015

[66] Cheryan, Sapna, Benjamin J. Drury, and Marissa Vichayapai. "Enduring Influence Of Stereotypical Computer Science Role Models on Women's Academic Aspirations." Psychology Of Women Quarterly 37.1 (2013): 72-79. ERIC. Web. 16 Jan. 2015.

[67] De Palma, Paul. "Why Women Avoid Computer Science." Communications Of the ACM 44.6 (2001): 27-29. Business Source Premier. Web. 16 Jan. 2015

[68] Fuegi, J.; Francis, J. (asd). *Lovelace & Babbage and the creation of the 1843 'notes'*. Annals of the History of Computing **25** (4). pp. 18–26. doi:10.1109/MAHC.2003.1253887. Check date values in: |date= (help)

[69] Grete Hermann (1926). "Die Frage der endlich vielen Schritte in der Theorie der Polynomideale". *Mathematische Annalen* **95**: 736–788. doi:10.1007/bf01206635.

[70] Gumbrecht, Jamie (8 February 2011). "Rediscovering WWII's female 'computers'". CNN. Archived from the original on 10 May 2012.

[71] Copeland, Jack B. (2010). *Colossus: The Secrets of Bletchley Park's Code Breaking Computers*. Oxford University Press.

[72] Grier, David Alan (1998). "The Math Tables Project of the Work Projects Administration: The Reluctant Start of the Computing Era". *IEEE Ann. Hist. Comput.* **20** (3): 33–50. doi:10.1109/85.707573. ISSN 1058-6180.

[73] Light, Jennifer S. (1999). "When Computers Were Women". *Technology and Culture* **40** (3): 469 Extra |pages= or |at= (help).

[74] "bug". Catb.org. 1947-09-09. Retrieved 2013-10-02.

[75] "JPL Computers". NASA JPL.

[76] Conway, Erik (27 March 2007). "Women Made Early Inroads at JPL". NASA/JPL. Archived from the original on 10 May 2012.

[77] Steel, Martha Vickers (2001). "Women in Computing: Experiences and Contributions Within the Emerging Computing Industry" (PDF). Computing History Museum.

[78] "UW-Madison Computer Science Ph.D.s Awarded, May 1965 - August 1970". UW-Madison Computer Sciences Department. Retrieved 2010-11-08.

[79] NASA Administrator Sean O'Keefe has commented saying "The concepts she and her team created became the building blocks for modern software engineering. It's an honor to recognize Ms. Hamilton for her extraordinary contributions to NASA.".

[80] NASA Press Release "NASA Honors Apollo Engineer" (September 03, 2003)

[81] *Michael Braukus* NASA News "NASA Honors Apollo Engineer" (Sept. 3, 2003)

[82] Oakes, Elizabeth H. (2002). *International encyclopedia of women scientists*. New York, NY: Facts on File. pp. 136–137. ISBN 0816043817.

[83] Parker, Donn B.; Nycum, Susan (1973). *Computer Abuse*. Stanford Research Institute.

[84] Cortada, James W. (2007). *The Digital Hand, Vol 3 : How Computers Changed the Work of American Public Sector Industries*. Oxford University Press. pp. 133–134, 390. ISBN 978-0-19-803709-5.

[85] "DoD INTERNET HOST TABLE SPECIFICATION". Retrieved 10 August 2015.

[86] Rosen, Rebecca J.. (2014-03-05) The First Woman to Get a Ph.D. in Computer Science From MIT - Rebecca J. Rosen. The Atlantic. Retrieved on 2014-03-25.

[87] "Lemelson-MIT Program". Retrieved 26 October 2014.

[88] "Official ACM Turing award website". *http://amturing.acm.org"*. ACM. Retrieved 14 February 2015.

[89] ACM Awards 1996, ACM.

[90] Kottoor, Naveena (2012-05-18). "BBC News - Ruchi Sanghvi: Facebook's pioneer woman". Bbc.co.uk. Retrieved 2013-10-02.

[91] Rieback, M., Crispo, B., Tanenbaum, A., (2006), " Is Your Cat Infected with a Computer Virus?", Vrije Universiteit Amsterdam

[92] "First Female to Win a Microsoft Apprentice of the Year Award". *MarketWatch*. Retrieved 26 October 2014.

[93] "Association for Women in Computing". Retrieved 10 August 2015.

[94] "The Women's Technology Empowerment Centre – W.TEC". Retrieved 26 October 2014.

2.19.10 Further reading

- Cooper, Joel; Weaver, Kimberlee D. (2003). *Gender and Computers: Understanding the Digital Divide*. Philadelphia: Lawrence Erlbaum Associates. ISBN 0-8058-4427-9.

- Galpin, Vashti (2002). "Women in computing around the world". *ACM SIGCSE Bulletin* **34** (2): 94–100. doi:10.1145/543812.543839.

- Light, Jennifer S. (1999). "When Computers Were Women". *Technology and Culture* **40** (3): 455–483.

- Margolis, Jane; Fisher, Allan (2002). *Unlocking the Clubhouse: Women in Computing*. Cambridge, MA: MIT Press. ISBN 978-0262632690.

- Misa, Thomas J., ed. (2010). *Gender Codes: Why Women Are Leaving Computing*. Wiley/IEEE Computer Society Press. ISBN 978-0-470-59719-4.

- Moses, L. E. (1993). "Our computer science class rooms: Are they friendly to female students?". *SIGCSE Bulletin* **25** (3). pp. 3–12.

- Newitz, Annalee (ed.); Anders, Charlie (ed.) (2006). *She's Such a Geek: Women Write About Science, Technology, and Other Nerdy Stuff*. Seal Press. ISBN 978-1580051903.

- Varma, Roli; Galindo-Sanchez, Vanessa (2006). "Native American Women in Computing" (PDF). University of New Mexico.

2.19.11 External links

- Carnegie Mellon Project on Gender and Computer Science
- National Center for Women & Information Technology US
- Equate Scotland
- Institute for Women in Trades, Technology and Science
- MNT - Mulheres na Tecnologia Brazil
- Resources related to Women in Computing US
- Society for Canadian Women in Science and Technology
- Women in Science, Engineering, and Technology UK
- Women's Engineering Society UK
- When Woman Stopped Coding

Chapter 3

Text and image sources, contributors, and licenses

3.1 Text

- **Computer science** *Source:* https://en.wikipedia.org/wiki/Computer_science?oldid=680630199 *Contributors:* AxelBoldt, Derek Ross, LC~enwiki, Lee Daniel Crocker, Tuxisuau, Brion VIBBER, Mav, Robert Merkel, Espen, The Anome, Tarquin, Taw, Jzcool, DanKeshet, Andre Engels, Khendon, LA2, Jkominek, Aldie, Fubar Obfusco, SolKarma, SimonP, Peterlin~enwiki, Hannes Hirzel, Ole Aamot, Camembert, B4hand, Hephaestos, Olivier, Stevertigo, Ghyll~enwiki, DrewT2, JohnOwens, Ted~enwiki, Michael Hardy, Erik Zachte, Gretyl, Kwertii, JakeVortex, Dante Alighieri, Fuzzie, Rp, Bensmith, Mic, Ixfd64, Phoe6, Sannse, TakuyaMurata, Delirium, Loisel, 7265, Minesweeper, Pcb21, Kvikeg, MartinSpamer, Ahoerstemeier, Haakon, Stan Shebs, Docu, J-Wiki, Kazuo Moriwaka, Angela, Jdforrester, Salsa Shark, Glenn, Cyan, LouI, Poor Yorick, Nikai, Azazello, Kwekubo, Jiang, Cryoboy, Rob Hooft, Jonik, Mxn, BRG, Denny, Dgreen34, Schneelocke, Nikola Smolenski, Revolver, Popsracer, Charles Matthews, Guaka, Timwi, Dcoetzee, Sbwoodside, Dysprosia, Jitse Niesen, Jay, Daniel Quinlan, Michaeln, Greenrd, Quux, HappyDog, Tpbradbury, Maximus Rex, Cleduc, Morwen, Buridan, Ed g2s, Persoid, Mikez80, Wakka, Wernher, Bevo, Spikey, Traroth, Shizhao, Farmerchris, Dbabbitt, Raul654, Jim Mahoney, Marc Girod~enwiki, Guppy, Carbuncle, ThereIsNoSteve, RadicalBender, Robbot, Sdedeo, Fredrik, Hobbes~enwiki, Soilguy2, R3m0t, RedWolf, Troworld, Altenmann, Naddy, Lowellian, Chris Roy, Mirv, MathMartin, Merovingian, Hellotoast, Rfc1394, Academic Challenger, Texture, Bethenco, Diderot, Hadal, Nerval, Borislav, MOiRe, Pps, Bshankaran, Anthony, Lupo, HaeB, TexasDex, Guy Peters, Xanzzibar, Iain.mcclatchie, Pengo, Tobias Bergemann, Applegoddess, Ancheta Wis, Decumanus, Honta, Gbali, Giftlite, Thv, Fennec, Kenny sh, Netoholic, Abigail-II, Levin, Lupin, Zigger, Everyking, Henry Flower, Guanaco, Eequor, Matt Crypto, Just Another Dan, Arvind Singh, Wmahan, Neilc, Quackor, Andycjp, Dullhunk, Bact, Kjetil r, Mineminemine, Antandrus, BozMo, Thray, Billposer, APH, Josephgrossberg, Kntg, Bumm13, Sovereigna, Eiserlohpp, Leire Sánchez, Robin klein, Fvilim~enwiki, Andreas Kaufmann, Zondor, Grunt, EagleOne, Bluemask, Corti, Perl guy, Mike Rosoft, Jwdietrich2, MichaelMcGuffin, Smimram, Erc, Discospinster, Leibniz, Notinasnaid, SocratesJedi, Michael Zimmermann, Mani1, BBB~enwiki, Bender235, ESkog, Android79, Kbh3rd, S.K., Mattingly23, Project2501a, Relix~enwiki, Barfooz, Linn~enwiki, Barcelova, Briséis~enwiki, RoyBoy, Bookofjude, Matteh, Aaronbrick, Coolcaesar, Bobo192, Smalljim, Shenme, Matt Britt, Maureen, NattyBumppo, Sam Korn, Haham hanuka, Pearle, Mpeisenbr, Nsaa, Mdd, Passw0rd, Poweroid, Alansohn, Liao, Pinar, Samuel.Jones, Tek022, Jason Davies, Hellhound, TheVenerableBede, Walkerma, InShaneee, Hu, Katefan0, DoesPHalt, Caesura, Polyphilo, Shinjiman, Wtmitchell, Velella, Shepshep, Cburnett, CloudNine, Mikeo, Versageek, MIT Trekkie, HenryLi, Bookandcoffee, Oleg Alexandrov, SimonW, Ott, Alex.g, Novacatz, Soultaco, Marasmusine, Woohookitty, Debuggar, Uncle G, Robert K S, Ruud Koot, JeremyA, Orz, MONGO, Nakos2208~enwiki, Shmitra, Al E., TreveX, Ralfipedia, Sega381, Z80x86, Graham87, Qwertyus, Chun-hian, SixWingedSeraph, OMouse, Reisio, Rjwilmsi, Mayumashu, MarSch, Materdaddy, Nneonneo, Ddawson, Jhballard, Bubba73, Brighterorange, The wub, Mkehrt, Kwharris, Sango123, Oo64eva, Leithp, Sheldrake, FayssalF, Johnnyw, Old Moonraker, Mathbot, Crazycomputers, Vsion, Makkuro, TheDJ, Intgr, SpectrumDT, BMF81, Jersey Devil, Bgwhite, Gwernol, Flcelloguy, Jayme, Eray~enwiki, The Rambling Man, Wavelength, Spacepotato, Angus Lepper, Phantomsteve, RussBot, Jeffhoy, Hyad, Piet Delport, Epolk, SpuriousQ, Thoreaulylazy, Stephenb, Gaius Cornelius, Bovineone, Wimt, Anomalocaris, CarlHewitt, Vanished user kjdioejh329io3rksdkj, Mipadi, Grafen, Jaxl, Ino5hiro, Bobbo, Hakkinen, Anetode, Yym, Jstrater, Jpbowen, JulesH, E rulez, Petr.adamek, Mgnbar, Tigersshrike, Light current, MCB, Sterling, Shimei, The Fish, Claygate, GraemeL, Joshua bigamo, Bachmann1234, Donhalcon, Katieh5584, Kungfuadam, Junglecat, Zvika, DVD R W, Finell, Hide&Reason, Thijswijs, SmackBot, Wilycoder, Sparkz08, Rtc, Slashme, Zanter, Olorin28, K-UNIT, McGeddon, Brick Thrower, Mmeri, CapitalSasha, Jpvinall, Powo, Gilliam, Ohnoitsjamie, Skizzik, RickiRich, Tv316, Somewherepurple, Bluebot, Nympheta, Crashuniverse, Jprg1966, Technotaoist, Miquonranger03, Fluri, LaggedOnUser, Nbarth, Spellchecker, Dzonatas, Krallja, A. B., Dfletter, Rrelf, Fireduck, Can't sleep, clown will eat me, Readams, Andri12, Vanished User 0001, Edivorce, Allan McInnes, Wen D House, Cybercobra, Jonovision, "alyosha", MisterCharlie, Dreadstar, Richard001, Tompsci, Iridescence, Brycedrm, JohnC1987, Ultraexactzz, Sigma 7, Zito ta xania, Fyver528, Nazgul533, Lambiam, ArglebargleIV, SilverStar, Harryboyles, Kuru, Treyt021, IAENG, AlphaTwo, Msc44, Evanx, IronGargoyle, Edenphd, Physis, Ekrub-ntyh, Ckatz, 16@r, JHunterJ, Slakr, Emerybob, Avs5221, Dicklyon, Tee Owe, Allamericanbear, Eridani, Dhp1080, RichardF, Xionbox, Beefyt, Hu12, Lucid, Levineps, DouglasCalvert, Siebrand, OnBeyondZebrax, Iridescent, Onestone, Markan~enwiki, Xsmith, Joseph Solis in Australia, Pegasus1138, Aeternus, Igoldste, Crippled Sloth, Courcelles, FairuseBot, Tawkerbot2, Jwalls, CRGreathouse, Ahy1, CBM, Banedon, NaBUru38, NickW557, Requestion, Leujohn, Myasuda, Simeon, Gregbard, Mac010382, Bobthesmiley, Porco-esphino, Gogo Dodo, Blaisorblade, Christian75, Chrislk02, Garik, Kozuch, Daven200520, Omicronpersei8, EnglishEfternamn, Epbr123, ClosedEyesSeeing, Hunan131,

3.1. TEXT

Headbomb, Newton2, Louis Waweru, Ideogram, Thiaguwin, Mikeeg555, Druiloor, Klausness, Dawnseeker2000, Escarbot, AntiVandalBot, BokicaK, Luna Santin, Seaphoto, Olexandr Kravchuk, Poshzombie, Superzohar, Mihas, Kdano, Carewolf, Hermel, JAnDbot, Niaz, Husond, Jimothytrotter, Nthep, Mark Shaw, Rstevens27, Aviroop Ghosh, Fourchannel, Dream Focus, Bookinvestor, Raanoo, 4jobs, Bongwarrior, VoABot II, Nyq, Necklace, JamesBWatson, Appraiser, Jlenthe, Cadsuane Melaidhrin, Rivertorch, Nikevich, Indon, Nucleophilic, ArchStanton69, Allstarecho, Bmeguru, JaGa, Kgfleischmann, Esanchez7587, D.h, Calltech, Pavel Jelínek, Gwern, Hdt83, MartinBot, Mouhanad alramli, Anaxial, CommonsDelinker, Pacdude9, Erkan Yilmaz, J.delanoy, Pedrito, Trusilver, Metamusing, Sandeepgupta, Ps ttf, Maurice Carbonaro, Rodhilton, Mike.lifeguard, Christian Storm, Tparameter, The Transhumanist (AWB), NewEnglandYankee, Hennessey, Patrick, Brian Pearson, Sanscrit1234, Jevansen, Bonadea, Dzenanz, User77764, Regenspaziergang, Neil Dodgson, Cromoser, Idioma-bot, Sheliak, Wikieditor06, Vranak, 28bytes, Hersfold, Fossum~enwiki, Balaji7, MagicBanana, Barneca, Philip Trueman, TXiKiBoT, Coder Dan, Austin Henderson, The Original Wildbear, Technopat, Sparkzy, Tomsega, Tms9980, Ocolon, T-Solo202, Ferengi, Metalmaniac69, Jackfork, Psyche825, Noformation, Everything counts, The Divine Fluffalizer, ARUNKUMAR P.R, Hankhuck, Andy Dingley, Julcia, Yk Yk Yk, Wolfrock, Piecemealcranky, Careercornerstone, Lake Greifen, Oldwes, Nighthawk19, Insanity Incarnate, Sebastjanmm, Pjoef, Palaeovia, E. H.-A. Gerbracht, Demize, NHRHS2010, Matthe20, D. Recorder, S.Örvarr.S, SieBot, EllenPetersen, Dawn Bard, Poisoncarter, Bruchowski, Ham Pastrami, Jerryobject, Happysailor, Flyer22, Radon210, JCLately, JetLover, JSpung, Aruton, Oxymoron83, Anjin-san, Vpovilaitis, Lightmouse, Poindexter Propellerhead, Ceas webmaster, StaticGull, Mori Riyo~enwiki, Maxime.Debosschere, Denisarona, Savie Kumara, Kayvan45622, Martarius, Sfan00 IMG, ClueBot, MBD123, Bwfrank, Foxj, The Thing That Should Not Be, Chocoforfriends, Keeper76, HairyFotr, Diana cionoiu, Meisterkoch, Ndenison, Keraunoscopia, R000t, WDavis1911, Der Golem, Uncle Milty, Agogino, SuperHamster, Niceguyedc, Zow, Amomam, Darkstar56, Jmcangas, Masterpiece2000, Excirial, Pumpmeup, Bedwanimas214, Diderot's dreams, Jusdafax, Waiwai933, Farisori, John Nevard, Jakraay, Hezarfenn, Muhandes, Buscalade, Alejandrocaro35, Sun Creator, Turnipface, Brianbjparker, Hans Adler, Morel, H.Marxen, ChrisHamburg, Thehelpfulone, GlasGhost, La Pianista, Thingg, Hunhot, PCHS-NJROTC, Apparition11, DumZiBoT, AzraelUK, XLinkBot, Spitfire, Pichpich, Mohammadshamma, Rror, Pasha11, Pimpedshortie99, Dhall1245, Little Mountain 5, Srikant.sharma, Dimoes, MCR789, Skarebo, WikHead, Galzigler, Airplaneman, Branrile09, Ackmenm, Max the tenken, Maimai009, Addbot, Some jerk on the Internet, DOI bot, Farzan mc, Betterusername, Elsendero, CanadianLinuxUser, MrOllie, Download, LaaknorBot, Favonian, West.andrew.g, 5 albert square, Unknown483, Gusisgay, Cupat07, Systemetsys, Tide rolls, Bfigura's puppy, Verbal, Teles, Jarble, Luckas-bot, Yobot, OrgasGirl, Fraggle81, MarioS, Cyanoa Crylate, SergeyJ, Jnivekk, KamikazeBot, Khalfani khaldun, Sajibcse, Backslash Forwardslash, AnomieBOT, DemocraticLuntz, Jim1138, IRP, Galoubet, Royote, JackieBot, 9258fahsflkh917fas, Piano non troppo, Danielt998, Law, Flewis, Lilgip01, Giants27, Materialscientist, Rtyq2, Salem F, Danno uk, Citation bot, Neurolysis, Roxxyroxursox, Quebec99, Xqbot, WikiNSK, Hubbard rox 2008, DSisyphBot, Grim23, Raj Wijesinghe, Blix1ms0ns, Tyrol5, Miym, Deadbeatatdawn, Лев Дубовой, Shirik, Mathonius, Erstats, Amaury, Doulos Christos, Dontknoa, Shadowjams, Methcub, CSgroup7, Luminique, Remshad, Velblod, CES1596, ESpublic013, FrescoBot, Skylark2008, Vitomontreal, Tobby72, Mark Renier, ToxicOranges, Recognizance, Vacuunaut, MTizz1, Machine Elf 1735, Louperibot, OgreBot, Citation bot 1, Dilaksan, MacMed, Pinethicket, Kiefer.Wolfowitz, BRUTE, Achraf52, Ezrdr, Serols, SpaceFlight89, Talbg, Meaghan, RandomStringOfCharacters, Jauhienij, Weylinp, Keri, Trappist the monk, SchreyP, Si23mk4n32i, Alexmilt, Lotje, Keith Cascio, Thefakeeditor, Ladies gifts, Weedwhacker128, Mttcmbs, Lysander89, Yondonjamts, DARTH SIDIOUS 2, Rednas1234, Saywhatman, Иъ Лю Ха, Sarang, John.legal, Star-Syrup, Gnabi82, EmausBot, John of Reading, Acather96, WikitanvirBot, Pfuchs722, Surlyduff50, Ibbn, Tinytn, Xiaogaozi, Pratapy, Solarra, Tommy2010, Lightdarkend, Wikipelli, K6ka, Djembayz, Lucas Thoms, Sciprecision, AaronLLF, Namastheg, BigMattyO, Cogiati, Spykeretro, Fæ, Josve05a, Bijuro, Steave77, H3llBot, Dennis714, Bveedu, Prashant Dey, Jay-Sebastos, Vanished user fijtji34toksdcknqrjn54yoimascj, Donner60, Junip~enwiki, Orange Suede Sofa, Rangoon11, Tijfo098, Danushka99999, Srshetty94, TYelliot, 28bot, BigMatty93, Scotty16-2007, GreenEdu, Petrb, Hughleat, Signalizing, ClueBot NG, Gareth Griffith-Jones, LogX, This lousy T-shirt, Satellizer, Sdht, Jcrwaford5, Fauzan, Hon-3s-T, Astew10, Dfarrell07, Bergbra, Rinaku, Cntras, Cnkids, O.Koslowski, Mcasswidmeyer, Widr, Tonywchen, Ashish Gaikwad, Ajjuddn, Lawsonstu, Saketmitra, Jk2q3jrklse, Helpful Pixie Bot, HMSSolent, Jkimdgu, Wald, Wbm1058, Jiule0, Trunks ishida, Lowercase sigmabot, BG19bot, Furkhaocean, ISTB351, MusikAnimal, J991, Neutral current, FutureTrillionaire, Sickdartzepic, Cadiomals, Mayuri.sandhanshiv, CalaD33, Kairi p, Mihai.stefanache, Salesvery1, Bryson1410, Zhenyanwang1, Sreedharram, Carso empires, Isacdaavid, Abilngeorge, Klilidiplomus, Pavankbk1113, Anbu121, XIN3N, LloydOlivier, BattyBot, Computer tower, Mburkhol, Alkafrifiras, ComputerScienceForum, Valueindian, Fagitcasey, E prosser, Varagrawal, Cyberbot II, The Illusive Man, GoShow, Chitraproject, JYBot, Tow, Dexbot, Mogism, Mani306, BlackHawkToughbook, Lugia2453, אלקים, Jamesx12345, Elcashini, Zziccardi, Itoula, Snehlata1102, Phamnhatkhanh, Ekips39, Faizan, Epicgenius, Babara150504, Crap12321, Littlejimmylel, Maggots187, Perfecshun, Netiru, Agenbola1, Red-eyed demon, RG3Redskins, Eyesnore, PhantomTech, Tiberius6996, Satassi, Tentinator, Dad29, JpurvisUM, Nbak, Kanoog, NJIT HUM dad29, Backendgaming, DavidLeighEllis, Diptytiw, Hollylilholly, Sibekoe, Spyglasses, ㄏㄏㄏ, Ginsuloft, Quenhitran, MrLinkinPark333, Dannyruthe, Manul, TCMemoire, Rons corner, Jaaron95, Ritik2345678, Philroc, Sbrankov05, Magicalbeakz1, JaconaFrere, Indiasian mbe mafia, 7Sidz, Eaglepuffs, Kgeza71, CompSci, Bobobobobobobdup, Monkbot, Wigid, Vieque, Ahsannaweed101, James.hochadel, 1908rs, BobVermont, Swet.anzel mee, NishantRM, Stuartbrade, Chacha2001, Typherix, Crfranklin, Susith Chandira Gts, Antithesisx, Offy284, Robie024, Nigerhoe, Psychedgrad, ChamithN, Crystallizedcarbon, Prachi2812, Rider ranger47, Yilinglou, Iman.haghdost, Hansguyholt, Yaourrrt, Pishcal, ErickaAgent, Rimavich, Astrachano, Yuil.Tr, K scheik, Swagkid1010, ABWarrick, Niceguy69, KasparBot, Jamieddd, PACIFICASIAWiki, Brahma Pacey, Zakzak1112, Vinodcd1, Lr0^^k, Gtouchan94, Arun po, GalacticGamer774 and Anonymous: 1400

- **History of computer science** *Source:* https://en.wikipedia.org/wiki/History_of_computer_science?oldid=680041806 *Contributors:* Edward, Sbwoodside, David costanzo, Greenrd, E23~enwiki, Topbanana, Dina, Giftlite, Jorend, Hugh Mason, Discospinster, Rich Farmbrough, Martpol, Bobo192, Guy Harris, Andrewpmk, Wtmitchell, DanShearer, Bsadowski1, Quirkie, Hq3473, Davidkazuhiro, Ruud Koot, WadeSimMiser, KymFarnik, Rjwilmsi, Koavf, Elsan, Johnnyw, Viznut, Wavelength, RadioFan, Stephenb, Gaius Cornelius, Rsrikanth05, Dialectric, Trovatore, RazorICE, Ragesoss, Daniel Mietchen, Jpbowen, Aldux, Raven4x4x, Mhkay, Rwwww, SmackBot, Emeraldemon, Jagged 85, Delldot, Commander Keane bot, Rdj999, Hmains, JMiall, Somewherepurple, Miquonranger03, Dzonatas, Rrelf, Allan McInnes, Jonovision, Astroview120mm, Ckatz, JHunterJ, R~enwiki, Benplowman, CapitalR, Eastlaw, CmdrObot, CBM, Jaxad0127, Gregbard, Yaris678, Epbr123, Ishdarian, AntiVandalBot, Pmt6sbc, Politicaljunkie23, JAnDbot, Kaobear, ThomasO1989, The Transhumanist, Bongwarrior, VoABot II, Schwarzbichler, KConWiki, 28421u2232nfenfcenc, EstebanF, Fluxguy2005, J.delanoy, Pharaoh of the Wizards, Ginsengbomb, Rushforth1967, Dogsgomoo, Tricky Victoria, MusicScience, Anna Lincoln, !dea4u, Dj711, Logarkh, Happysailor, Flyer22, Oxymoron83, CharlesGillingham, Cyfal, Maxime.Debosschere, Athenean, Stuartjnoall, ClueBot, Shatree, Fyyer, Quinxorin, CristianCantoro, Niceguyedc, Excirial, Universityuser, KyuubiSeal, Wazupman, XLinkBot, NellieBly, Addbot, Cst17, Torla42, Netzwerkerin, Luckas-bot, Yobot, Fraggle81, Iroony, AnomieBOT, Jim1138, IRP, Kingpin13, Materialscientist, ImperatorExercitus, Xqbot, Poetaris, Miym, Omnipaedista, Endothermic, CES1596, Prari, FrescoBot, Thiagupillai, Kwiki, HamburgerRadio, Citation bot 1, Pinethicket, I dream of horses, RedBot, Full-date unlinking bot, Abc518, Dalakov,

Krassotkin, Vrenator, RichNick, Jeffrd10, RjwilmsiBot, EmausBot, NotAnonymous0, Joshfinnie, A930913, L Kensington, Donner60, Floydvirginia, Petrb, ClueBot NG, Smtchahal, Wcherowi, Satellizer, VanishedUser sdu8asdasd, Kevin Gorman, ScottSteiner, Helpful Pixie Bot, DBigXray, BG19bot, Mark Arsten, Chip123456, BattyBot, StarryGrandma, ChrisGualtieri, Khazar2, Thom2729, Dexbot, Frosty, Yosoyyosbel, Vanamonde93, Zalunardo8, Ironeyes16, B14709, AmySmiles, AddWittyNameHere, JaconaFrere, Monkbot, Yu,Kevin, Kansiime, Ammara shahid, KH-1, Sayamsethi, Spumuq, Seanpatrickgray, Yellowjacket2323, Geeks On Hugs and Anonymous: 240

- **Philosophy of computer science** *Source:* https://en.wikipedia.org/wiki/Philosophy_of_computer_science?oldid=664373591 *Contributors:* Gandalf61, Ruud Koot, Thane, PaulJones, SmackBot, JzG, OlegSmirnov, Aeternus, Gregbard, Steel1943, Logan, Niceguyedc, Addbot, Ptbotgourou, Amirobot, AnomieBOT, WikiNSK, Crzer07, Omnipaedista, Sophus Bie, FrescoBot, Zero Thrust, WikitanvirBot, Cat4567nip, Serketan, Cogiati, Petra oftenlungs, Ladyhilbert, Helpful Pixie Bot, Jochen Burghardt, SucreRouge, Liz, Allevirgi, Aliensyntax and Anonymous: 11

- **Outline of computer science** *Source:* https://en.wikipedia.org/wiki/Outline_of_computer_science?oldid=679687401 *Contributors:* Andre Engels, Khendon, Hfastedge, DrewT2, Lexor, Vera Cruz, Alfio, TraxPlayer, Cadr, Timwi, Topbanana, Robbot, Murray Langton, Telemakh0s, Elf, Ssd, Andycjp, Andreas Kaufmann, EagleOne, D6, Ronaldo~enwiki, Discospinster, ZeroOne, CanisRufus, Storm Rider, Liao, Diego Moya, Mnemo, Deathphoenix, Mahanga, Woohookitty, Ruud Koot, Quiddity, Bubba73, Mkehrt, Wavelength, Hyad, Welsh, AlMac, Moe Epsilon, Pegship, Searchme, Fmccown, Zzuuzz, Donhalcon, Rwwww, David Kernow, Rmosler2100, Fplay, JonHarder, Allan McInnes, Cybercobra, Nexus Seven, Fagstein, A Clown in the Dark, JeffW, Dp462090, CRGreathouse, CBM, Cydebot, Porco-esphino, Ideogram, The Transhumanist, True Genius, Ceros, Sman789, The Transhumanist (AWB), Merzul, Sintaku, Sychen, Palaeovia, Jimmi Hugh, Drothlis, Taemyr, Anchor Link Bot, DeXXus, Robert Skyhawk, Brianbjparker, Ivanpranav, Legobot, DemocraticLuntz, OllieFury, Raven1977, J04n, Lwoodyiii, Thehelpfulbot, John of Reading, RockMagnetist, Petrb, IjonTichyIjonTichy, Amrit Ghimire Ranjit, Josiahsprague, PhoenixFF and Anonymous: 50

- **Theoretical computer science** *Source:* https://en.wikipedia.org/wiki/Theoretical_computer_science?oldid=677598917 *Contributors:* Stan Shebs, David.Monniaux, Tobias Bergemann, Giftlite, Mahanga, Ruud Koot, Arbor, Protez, SLi, Intgr, Lmatt, RussBot, Dv82matt, SamuelRiv, Haon, JLaTondre, Bsod2, SmackBot, Impaciente, Renku, Powo, OrangeDog, Arindamp, Salt Yeung, SpyMagician, RekishiEJ, Zhoadon~enwiki, Irwangatot, BeenAroundAWhile, Gregbard, GPhilip, Pascal.Tesson, Christian75, Kilva, Ideogram, Ben1220, Hermel, JAnDbot, Cic, David Eppstein, Maurice Carbonaro, Mrseacow, Merzul, Squids and Chips, Jimmaths, Jaime v torres heredia~enwiki, Robertekraut, Palaeovia, Ivan Štambuk, Arapajoe, Maxime.Debosschere, Sbshah25, ClueBot, EoGuy, Niceguyedc, Brianbjparker, Addbot, Yobot, Legobot II, Pcap, AnomieBOT, DemocraticLuntz, HRV, Papppfaffe, Miym, Thore Husfeldt, Лев Дубовой, Prari, FrescoBot, Kiefer.Wolfowitz, Zedoul, RobinK, SchreyP, EmausBot, Surlyduff50, Chricho, Cogiati, Ian Rastall, Sarimurat, Fortnow, Helpful Pixie Bot, Neutral current, Mejoribus, Rodrigo Folha, Jeff Erickson, Computhematics, Brirush, Balamurugan Kanakaraj, Andywear1, KasparBot, Klairh.fr, Udubey and Anonymous: 63

- **Theory of computation** *Source:* https://en.wikipedia.org/wiki/Theory_of_computation?oldid=678081872 *Contributors:* Michael Hardy, Tobias Bergemann, Zondor, Discospinster, DcoetzeeBot~enwiki, Rajah, Jonsafari, Helix84, Diego Moya, Sligocki, Cromwellt, Oleg Alexandrov, Ron Ritzman, Ruud Koot, Graham87, Rjwilmsi, Protez, SLi, Chobot, DaGizza, 4C~enwiki, Yahya Abdal-Aziz, Mikeblas, Arthur Rubin, That Guy, From That Show!, Sardanaphalus, SmackBot, Hydrogen Iodide, DCDuring, Readams, SingCal, Physis, EricR, Britannica~enwiki, WikiKatateochi, SkyWalker, CRGreathouse, CBM, Gregbard, Julian Mendez, Mattisse, Kilva, Urdutext, Pmt6sbc, Harborsparrow, JAnDbot, Kirrages, Cic, David Eppstein, Abatasigh, Ntalamai, SparsityProblem, Gombang, Rwessel, Cometman, VasilievVV, Dindon~enwiki, Jmath666, Dmcq, SieBot, Ivan Štambuk, Oxymoron83, Anchor Link Bot, XDanielx, XLinkBot, Jlazerus, Thebestofall007, Multipundit, Addbot, MrVanBot, Jamiltonio, Luckas-bot, Yobot, Fraggle81, The Grumpy Hacker, Pcap, AnomieBOT, HRV, Materialscientist, Citation bot, Taeshadow, ArthurBot, Janet Davis, Miym, Ute in DC, Thomas.ohland, HamburgerRadio, Eser.aygun, LcawteHuggle, EmausBot, Udqbpn, ClueBot NG, Helpful Pixie Bot, CitationCleanerBot, Brirush, Telfordbuck, Phamnhatkhanh, Csreseracher, Cubism44, MasaComp, Velvel2, Broswald, Nbro and Anonymous: 85

- **Information theory** *Source:* https://en.wikipedia.org/wiki/Information_theory?oldid=678086001 *Contributors:* AxelBoldt, Brion VIBBER, Timo Honkasalo, Ap, Graham Chapman, XJaM, Toby Bartels, Hannes Hirzel, Edward, D, PhilipMW, Michael Hardy, Isomorphic, Kku, Bobby D. Bryant, Varunrebel, Vinodmp, AlexanderMalmberg, Karada, (, Iluvcapra, Minesweeper, StephanWehner, Ahoerstemeier, Angela, LittleDan, Kevin Baas, Poor Yorick, Andres, Novum, Charles Matthews, Guaka, Bemoeial, Ww, Dysprosia, The Anomebot, Munford, Hyacinth, Ann O'nyme, Shizhao, AnonMoos, MH~enwiki, Robbot, Fredrik, Rvollmert, Seglea, Chancemill, Securiger, SC, Lupo, Wile E. Heresiarch, ManuelGR, Ancheta Wis, Giftlite, Lee J Haywood, COMPATT, KuniShiro~enwiki, SoWhy, Andycjp, Ynh~enwiki, Pcarbonn, OverlordQ, L353a1, Rdsmith4, APH, Cihan, Elektron, Creidieki, Neuromancien, Rakesh kumar, Picapica, D6, Jwdietrich2, Imroy, CALR, Noisy, Rich Farmbrough, Guanabot, NeuronExMachina, Ericamick, Xezbeth, MisterSheik, Crunchy Frog, El C, Spoon!, Simon South, Bobo192, Smalljim, Rbj, Maureen, Nothingmuch, Photonique, Andrewbadr, Haham hanuka, Pearle, Mpeisenbr, Mdd, Msh210, Uncle Bill, Pouya, BryanD, PAR, Cburnett, Jheald, Geraldshields11, Kusma, DV8 2XL, Oleg Alexandrov, FrancisTyers, Velho, Woohookitty, Linas, Mindmatrix, Ruud Koot, Eatsaq, Eyreland, SeventyThree, Kanenas, Graham87, Josh Parris, Mayumashu, SudoMonas, Arunkumar, HappyCamper, Bubba73, Alejo2083, Chris Pressey, Mathbot, Annacoder, Nabarry, Srleffler, Chobot, Commander Nemet, FrankTobia, Siddhant, YurikBot, Wavelength, RobotE, RussBot, Michael Slone, Loom91, Grubber, ML, Yahya Abdal-Aziz, Raven4x4x, Moe Epsilon, DanBri, Allchopin, Light current, Mceliece, Arthur Rubin, Lyrl, GrinBot~enwiki, Sardanaphalus, Lordspaz, SmackBot, Imz, Henri de Solages, Incnis Mrsi, Reedy, InverseHypercube, Cazort, Gilliam, Metacomet, Octahedron80, Spellchecker, Colonies Chris, Jahiegel, Unnikrishnan.am, LouScheffer, Calbaer, EPM, Djcmackay, Michael Ross, Tyrson, Jon Awbrey, Het, Bidabadi~enwiki, Chungc, SashatoBot, Nick Green, Harryboyles, Sina2, Lachico, Almkglor, Bushsf, Sir Nicholas de Mimsy-Porpington, FreezBee, Dicklyon, E-Kartoffel, Wizard191, Matthew Verey, Isvish, ScottHolden, CapitalR, Gnome (Bot), Tawkerbot2, Marty39, Daggerstab, CRGreathouse, Thermochap, Ale jrb, Thomas Keyes, Mct mht, Pulkitgrover, Grgarza, Maria Vargas, Roman Cheplyaka, Hpalaiya, Vanished User jdksfajlasd, Nearfar, Heidijane, Thijs!bot, N5iln, WikiIT, James086, PoulyM, Edchi, D.H, Jvstone, HSRT, JAnDbot, BenjaminGittins, RainbowCrane, Jthomp4338, Buettcher, MetsBot, David Eppstein, Pax:Vobiscum, MartinBot, Tamer ih~enwiki, Sigmundg, Jargon777, Policron, Useight, VolkovBot, Joeoettinger, JohnBlackburne, Jimmaths, Constant314, Starrymessenger, Kjells, Magmi, AllGloryToTheHypnotoad, Bemba, Lamro, Radagast3, Newbyguesses, SieBot, Ivan Štambuk, Robert Loring, Masgatotkaca, Pcontrop, Algorithms, Anchor Link Bot, Melcombe, ClueBot, Fleem, Ammarsakaji, Estirabot, 7&6=thirteen, Oldrubbie, Vegetator, Singularity42, Dziewa, Lambtron, Johnuniq, SoxBot III, HumphreyW, Vanished user uih38riiw4hjlsd, Mitch Ames, Addbot, Deepmath, Peerc, Eweinber, Sun Ladder, C9900, L.exsteens, Xlasne, Egoistorms, Luckas-bot, Quadrescence, Yobot, TaBOT-zerem, Taxisfolder, Carleas, Twohoos, Cassandra Cathcart, Dbln, Materialscientist, Informationtricks, Jingluolaodao, Expooz, Raysonik, Xqbot, Isheden, Informationtricks, Dani.gomezdp, PHansen, Masrudin, FrescoBot, Nageh, Tiramisoo, Sanpitch, Gnomehacker, Pinethicket, Momergil, SkyMachine, SchreyP, Lotje, Miracle Pen, Vanadiumho, Kastchei, Djjr, EmausBot, WikitanvirBot, Jmencisom, Bethnim, Quondum, Henriqueroscoe, Terra Novus, ClueBot NG, MelbourneStar,

3.1. TEXT

BarrelProof, TimeOfDei, Frietjes, Thepigdog, Pzrq, MrJosiahT, Lawsonstu, Helpful Pixie Bot, Leopd, BG19bot, Wiki13, Trevayne08, CitationCleanerBot, Brad7777, Schafer510, BattyBot, Bankmichael1, SFK2, Jochen Burghardt, Limit-theorem, Phamnhatkhanh, Szzoli, 314Username, Roastliras, Eigentensor, Comp.arch, SakeUPenn, Logan.dunbar, Prof. Michael Bank, DanBalance, JellydPuppy, KasparBot, Lr0^^k and Anonymous: 263

- **Coding theory** *Source:* https://en.wikipedia.org/wiki/Coding_theory?oldid=680179935 *Contributors:* Andre Engels, Drahflow, Michael Hardy, Raven in Orbit, Charles Matthews, Xiaodai~enwiki, Phil Boswell, Kaol, Altenmann, Giftlite, DavidCary, Sam Hocevar, D6, Rich Farmbrough, LindsayH, Bender235, CanisRufus, Bobo192, Photonique, Pouya, Cburnett, Jheald, Xiaoyanggu, Oleg Alexandrov, GregorB, BD2412, Salix alba, Mathbot, Jpkotta, YurikBot, Gene.arboit, Gaius Cornelius, Aaron Brenneman, Kevmo, Einsteinsatheesh, Ott2, SmackBot, Incnis Mrsi, InverseHypercube, Relaxing, RDBrown, SEIBasaurus, Jlpayton, Drewnoakes, Leiting, Dicklyon, CRGreathouse, CBM, Jesse Viviano, Phatom87, Icazzi, Nearfar, Thijs!bot, Epbr123, Andyjsmith, Bobblehead, Gdickeson, Careless hx, Applrpn, STBot, Chiswick Chap, NewEnglandYankee, DavidCBryant, Selinger, Magmi, Picojeff, Spur, Jamessungjin.kim, JackSchmidt, OKBot, Alexkrules1234, Martarius, Justin W Smith, SteveJothen, Addbot, RPHv, Vavlap, Uncia, Ramses68, Teles, Zorrobot, Yobot, AnomieBOT, Keithbob, Merisiscute, Isheden, SchnitzelMannGreek, Solarium2, FrescoBot, Mmillier, Nageh, Sławomir Biały, Zero Thrust, RedBot, Lotje, Yatescr, Zink Dawg, John of Reading, GoingBatty, Bethnim, ZéroBot, Ahughes6, Devanshuhpandey, L Kensington, Bomazi, ChuispastonBot, Rezabot, Helpful Pixie Bot, Neutral current, Drift chambers, CitationCleanerBot, BattyBot, ChrisGualtieri, Madhurasuresh, Harikine, Brirush, Trapmoth, Joeinwiki, Phamnhatkhanh, 314Username, Ahasn, Mark-W-T, Gmk7, Anurag Bishnoi, Monkbot, BlueFenixReborn, KasparBot and Anonymous: 65

- **Programming language theory** *Source:* https://en.wikipedia.org/wiki/Programming_language_theory?oldid=679449336 *Contributors:* K.lee, Fredrik, Quackor, Spayrard, AshtonBenson, Gary, Diego Moya, Ruud Koot, SDC, Dysepsion, Seidenstud, Jrtayloriv, EngineerScotty, Tom Duff, Edgar181, JonHarder, Allan McInnes, Zophar1, Cybercobra, Antonielly, DagErlingSmørgrav, CmdrObot, Pgr94, Thijs!bot, Bot-maru, Headbomb, Gwern, R'n'B, Warlordwolf, Bonadea, Steven shaw, Andy Dingley, ClueBot, Prof Wrong, Galzigler, Addbot, Lightbot, Luckas-bot, Yobot, Denispir, Pcap, PMLawrence, AnomieBOT, Eumolpo, Miym, Schmonyon, Thehelpfulbot, LittleWink, VanishedUser sdu9aya9fs787232, ZéroBot, Cogiati, ChuispastonBot, Hossein bardareh, Akmalzhon, Helpful Pixie Bot, MilerWhite, Vagobot, Alan Moraes, ⁇, Offy284, H662 and Anonymous: 36

- **Formal methods** *Source:* https://en.wikipedia.org/wiki/Formal_methods?oldid=680085322 *Contributors:* Torfason, Vkuncak, Michael Hardy, TakuyaMurata, Minesweeper, Topbanana, Ashley Y, Michael Snow, Bogdanb, Khalid hassani, Kelson, Leibniz, Project2501a, Mdd, Qwertyus, Jim Huggins, GeorgeBills, Vonkje, YurikBot, Wavelength, Robert Will, Stephenb, SteveLoughran, CarlHewitt, Jpbowen, Robertbyrne, Nikkimaria, SmackBot, Bluebot, DHN-bot~enwiki, Allan McInnes, Sspecter, FlyHigh, Derek farn, Antonielly, Huperniketes, RichardDenney, Amakuru, AGK, Pce3@ij.net, Gioto, Dylan Lake, VictorAnyakin, Jcarnelian, Damyot, MartinBot, ARC Gritt, J.delanoy, Adavidb, Daniel5Ko, Mufka, Erhasalz, Jimmaths, SieBot, NuclearWarfare, Carriearchdale, Bdongol, XLinkBot, Dekart, Addbot, MrOllie, FSVZ, Yobot, Pcap, Pablomics~enwiki, Ayda D, Xqbot, Zouxiaohui, Mark Renier, Annaamalia, ComputScientist, Vasywriter, MastiBot, Danielbruns, TjBot, Airsplit, T.krilavicius, Waeswaes, EmausBot, ZéroBot, JohnGDrever, Helpful Pixie Bot, Wbm1058, Brad7777, Mburkhol, Phamnhatkhanh, Fgegypt, Ragerdl, Andyed 2003, MadScientistX11, David.r.cok, Sofia Koutsouveli and Anonymous: 77

- **Artificial intelligence** *Source:* https://en.wikipedia.org/wiki/Artificial_intelligence?oldid=680716800 *Contributors:* AxelBoldt, TwoOneTwo, The Cunctator, Derek Ross, WojPob, Sodium, Lee Daniel Crocker, Brion VIBBER, Mav, Bryan Derksen, Robert Merkel, Zundark, The Anome, Koyaanis Qatsi, Taw, RK, Andre Engels, Poiman, Arvindn, Toby Bartels, Dlloader~enwiki, MadSurgeon, M~enwiki, Little guru, ChangChienFu, Axon, Ellmist, Imran, Heron, Ryguasu, Mintguy, Netesq, KF, Tzartzam, Olivier, Chuq, Stevertigo, Hfastedge, Frecklefoot, Edward, AdSR, D, JohnOwens, Michael Hardy, EvanProdromou, Oliver Pereira, Lexor, David Martland, Nixdorf, Liftarn, Gabbe, Bobby D. Bryant, Ixfd64, Evanherk, Karada, Paul A, Minesweeper, Looxix~enwiki, Ellywa, Mdebets, Ahoerstemeier, Mac, Ronz, Nanshu, Docu, Snoyes, Jebba, Ugen64, ZENDELBACH, Jagdeepyadav, Poor Yorick, Tkinias, Evercat, [212], BAxelrod, EdH, ArtificioSapiens, Hike395, Emperorbma, Rene halle, Novum, Martha2000, Timwi, Dcoetzee, Dmsar, Jm34harvey, Dysprosia, Fuzheado, Hgamboa, Selket, Tkorrovi, Tpbradbury, Maximus Rex, Furrykef, Populus, Melody, Horris, Fvw, Stormie, Dpbsmith, Olathe, Marc Girod~enwiki, David.Monniaux, MD87, Francs2000, Lumos3, Shantavira, Phil Boswell, Unknown, Nufy8, Robbot, MrJones, Sander123, Pigsonthewing, R3m0t, RedWolf, Chocolateboy, Psychonaut, Dessimoz, Chris Roy, Chopchopwhitey, Academic Challenger, Kneiphof, Nach0king, Rholton, KellyCoinGuy, Aniu~enwiki, DHN, Rasmus Faber, Hadal, Wikibot, Borislav, Witbrock, Bjklein, Insomniak, Wile E. Heresiarch, MikeCapone, Tobias Bergemann, Javidjamae, Marc Venot, Psb777, Matthew Stannard, Centrx, Giftlite, Muness, DavidCary, Qartis, 0x0077BE, Orangemike, Herbee, Risk one, Everyking, Anville, Emuzesto~enwiki, Maver1ck, Rick Block, Vidstige~enwiki, Wikiwikifast, Eoghan, Guanaco, Bovlb, Remy B, Finn-Zoltan, AlistairMcMillan, Jackol, SWAdair, Bobblewik, JRR Trollkien, MichalJurosz, Gyrofrog, Wmahan, Lenehey, Neilc, Gadfium, Utcursch, Alexf, Bact, Mendel, Gdm, Vanished user svinet8j3ogifm98wjfgoi3tjosfg, Nx7000~enwiki, Yardcock, Indyfitz, Antandrus, Beland, Joeblakesley, ThG, Loremaster, Piotrus, Ihavenolife, Karol Langner, YoungFreud, IYY, APH, EisenKnoechel, Khaydarian, Anythingyouwant, Gene s, Bornslippy, DanielDemaret, Simoneau, Kevin143, Sam Hocevar, Asbestos, Leire Sánchez, Herschelkrustofsky, Robin klein, McCart42, Kevyn, MakeRocketGoNow, Ratiocinate, GreenReaper, Jake11, Barnaby dawson, Trevor MacInnis, Grunt, ELApro, AAAAA, Jayjg, Poccil, Eyrian, Neckelmann, Erc, Discospinster, Rich Farmbrough, Rhobite, Guanabot, Michal Jurosz, Vsmith, Pluke, Loki en, Nondescript, SocratesJedi, Mani1, Harriv, Bender235, ESkog, Khalid, ZeroOne, FrankCostanza, JoeSmack, Gridlinked, Neko-chan, Ylee, Rgarvage, Livajo, El C, Shanes, Susvolans, RoyBoy, Nickj, Matteh, Bootedcat, Jpgordon, Semper discens, Sole Soul, Bobo192, Stephane.magnenat, Jordan123~enwiki, Mike Schwartz, Smalljim, Bustter, John Vandenberg, BrokenSegue, Shenme, R. S. Shaw, Polocrunch, Maurreen, Dejitarob, Pokrajac, Jojit fb, Rajah, WikiLeon, Sam Korn, JesseHogan, Mdd, Klafubra, Jumbuck, Markus.Waibel, Vesal, Alansohn, Gary, Anthony Appleyard, Thüringer, Jamyskis, Arthena, AzaToth, Lectonar, Axl, Shpiget, Curious1i, B3virq3b, Wdfarmer, Hu, Bootstoots, Schaefer, Judson, Wtmitchell, Monkee13, Yuckfoo, Sciurinæ, LFaraone, Liger~enwiki, BDD, Leondz, SteinbDJ, MIT Trekkie, Redvers, Ceyockey, Oleg Alexandrov, Ott, Loxley~enwiki, Daranz, Zntrip, MilesMi, NorrYtt, Gmaxwell, Conskeptical, Angr, Velho, CygnusPius, OwenX, Mindmatrix, Jason Palpatine, Olethros, ApLundell, Kzollman, Benbest, Ruud Koot, Urod, WadeSimMiser, Brentdax, Acerperi, Gengiskanhg, Wikiklrsc, Emir Arven, SDC, CharlesC, Tokek, Stefanomione, Eluchil, Reidgsmith, Rlw, Rafael.perez.rosario, Marudubshinki, MassGalactusUniversum, Stoni, Graham87, Cuchullain, Bforte, Qwertyus, Chun-hian, CoderGnome, Kane5187, Drbogdan, Rjwilmsi, Nightscream, Koavf, Robotwisdom, Phileas, Hulagutten, Eyu100, Healeyb, Stardust8212, Sdornan, Bruce1ee, DonSiano, Benpryde, DouglasGreen~enwiki, SeanMack, Madd4Max, Bensin, The wub, Dar-Ape, Sango123, Mrvasin, Dionyseus, FlaBot, Jsun027, Harmil, Dpupek, SouthernNights, Nivix, SportsMaster, RexNL, Gurch, Qswitch426, Jrtayloriv, Jagginess, Preslethe, Nabarry, Diza, GreyCat, Kri, Gareth E Kegg, King of Hearts, Chobot, Theo Pardilla, Garas, Gwernol, Tone, Interested~enwiki, YurikBot, Wavelength, Pspoulin, Sceptre, Cabiria, Jimp, Charles Gaudette, RussBot, Arado, Sillybilly, TheDoober, Piet Delport, SnoopY~enwiki, DanMS, Tsch81, Hydrargyrum, Bill52270, Gaius Cornelius, CambridgeBayWeather, Pseudomonas, Thane, CarlHewitt, LauriO~enwiki, ENeville, Wiki alf, Boneheadmx, Grafen, Tailpig, ImGz, Introgressive, Srinivasasha, Darker Dreams, John Newbury, RabidDeity, Thiseye, Robert McClenon, Nick, Banes, Daniel Mietchen, Jpbowen, Larry laptop, Aldux, Iyerakshay, MarkAb, Tony1, Supten, Syrthiss, Linweizhen, Gadget850, DeadEyeArrow, Gzabers, Dv82matt, Searchme, Richardcavell, Zaklog, Pawyilee, Jvoegele, K.Nevelsteen, Zzuuzz, Nikkimaria, Arthur Rubin, ColinMcMillen, Xaxafrad, Jogers, Saizai, GraemeL, CWenger, HereToHelp, ArielGold, Dublinclontarf, Hamster Sandwich., Allens, Banus, Ásgeir IV.~enwiki, Anniepoo, NeilN, Kingboyk, GrinBot~enwiki, Jonathan Métillon, Bo Jacoby, D Monack, DVD R W, Teo64x, Oldhamlet, SmackBot, Mmernex, Shannonbonannon, Haymaker, Moxon, Mneser, 1dragon, InverseHypercube, Inego~enwiki, Hydrogen Iodide, McGeddon, Martinp, Jared555, Bbewsdirector, Davewild, Pkirlin, CommodiCast, Cacuija, Vilerage, Took, Edgar181, Alsandro, Moralis, W3bj3d1, Gilliam, Betacommand, Rpmorrow, ERcheck, Grokmoo, Mirokado, Chris the speller, Shaggorama, NCurse, Thumperward, Stevage, J. Spencer, DHN-bot~enwiki, Darth Panda, Zsinj, Pegua, Can't sleep, clown will eat me, Erayman64, Onorem, MJBurrage, JonHarder, EvelinaB, Nunocordeiro, RedHillian, Edivorce, Normxxx, Memming, COMPFUNK2, Freek Verkerk, PrometheusX303, Jaibe, Shadow1, Richard001, Taggart Transcontinental, NapoleonB, Freemarket, Lacatosias, StephenReed, Jon Awbrey, Metamagician3000, Salamurai, LeoNomis, Curly Turkey, Ck lostsword, Pilotguy, Kukini, Ohconfucius, Dankonikolic, William conway bcc, Nishkid64, Baby16, Harryboyles, Titus III, John, Jonrgrover, AmiDaniel, Geoinline, Yan Kuligin, Madhukaleeckal, Tazmaniacs, Gobonobo, Disavian, NewTestLeper79, ChaoticLogic, Chessmaniac, Goodnightmush, Ripe, Mr. Vernon, Newkidd11, Special-T, WMod-NS, Owlbuster, Mr Stephen, Dicklyon, Emurph, Daphne A, Dee Jay Randall, AdultSwim, Condem, Glen Pepicelli, Zapvet, Digsdirt, Nabeth, Peyre, Caiaffa, Andreworkney, Hu12, Burto88, Levineps, Vespine, Mjgilson, Clarityfiend, Sierkejd, Joseph Solis in Australia, Ralf Klinkenberg, Snoutholder, Igoldste, Rnb, Wfructose, Marysunshine, Dream land2080, Tawkerbot2, Dlohcierekim, GerryWolff, Eastlaw, Myncknm, 8754865, Rahuldharmani, CRGreathouse, CmdrObot, Eggman64, Wafulz, Makeemlighter, Discordant~enwiki, Mudd1, Ruslik0, El aprendelenguas, ShelfSkewed, Pgr94, MeekMark, Casper2k3, Fordmadoxfraud, Myasuda, Livingston7, Abdullahazzam, Gregbard, Shanoman, Cydebot, AndyPardoe, Peripitus, Abeg92, Besieged, Beta Trom, Peterdjones, Kaldosh, Gogo Dodo, Corpx, Ivant, Rzwitserloot, JamesLucas, Julian Mendez, Josephorourke, LaserBeams, WikiNing, Robertinventor, Bubba2323, Bryan Seecrets, Bitsmart, Gimmetrow, PamD, Michael Fourman, Thijs!bot, Epbr123, Mercury~enwiki, ConceptExp, Daniel, Hervegirod, Sagaciousuk, N5iln, Mojo Hand, Atamyrat~enwiki, Marek69, Zzthex, GTof~enwiki, Mailseth, I already forgot, David D., Mschures, Mac-steele, AntiVandalBot, Tabortiger, Luna Santin, Seaphoto, Opelio, Prolog, 17Drew, Nosirrom, Jj137, Ykalyan, TurntableX, Science History, Theropod-X, Spinningobo, Myanw, Steelpillow, MikeLynch, JAnDbot, Jimothytrotter, MattBan, MTuffield, Barek, Sarnholm, MER-C, CosineKitty, Mrsolutions, Schlegel, The Transhumanist, Davespice, 100110100, Greensburger, TAnthony, .anacondabot, Acroterion, Wasell, Coffee2theorems, Magioladitis, Bongwarrior, VoABot II, Cobratom, Farquaadhnchmn, Gamkiller, Redaktor, Tedickey, Johannes Simon, Tremilux, Rootxploit, Cic, Crunchy Numbers, Nposs, BatteryIncluded, Robotman1974, ArthurWeasley, Johnkoza1992, Jroudh, Allstarecho, Adamreiswig, Wookiee cheese, Joydurgin, Siddharthsk2000, Talon Artaine, DerHexer, Tommy Herbert, TheRanger, Francob, MartinBot, IanElmore, Bradgib, ARC Gritt, Naohiro19, Rettetast, Bissinger, Mschel, Kostisl, CommonsDelinker, Amareshjoshi, KTo288, Lilac Soul, LegendGamer, Mausy5043, Pacas, J.delanoy, JuniorMonkey, Trusilver, Anandcv, Gustavo1255, Richiekim, Jiuguang Wang, Uncle Dick, Public Menace, Yonidebot, Laurusnobilis, Jkaplan, Dispenser, Eric Mathews Technology, DarkGhost08, Ignatzmice, Touisiau, Tdewey, Pogowitwiz, Mikael Häggström, Ypetrachenko, Tarotcards, Topazxx, ColinClark, AntiSpamBot, Zubenelgenubi, Tobias Kuhn, Lewblack, The Transhumanist (AWB), Hthth, Bobianite, Jorfer, Sbennett4, Sunderland06, Chuckino, Wesleymurphy, Burzmali, Remember the dot, Walter Fritz, Riccardopoli, Andy Marchbanks, Inwind, Useight, Leontolstoy2, Halmstad, RJASE1, Funandtrvl, Idarin, VolkovBot, Paranoid600, Stephen G Graham, Jeff G., Maghnus, Gogarburn, Philip Trueman, Kramlovesmovies, Sweetness46, TXiKiBoT, Coder Dan, Vrossi1, Master Jaken, Java7837, Alan Rockefeller, Technopat, Olinga, Lordvolton, BarryList, Una Smith, Sirkad, DonutGuy, Eroark, Seb az86556, Cremepuff222, TheSix, Jeeny, The Divine Fluffalizer, Bugone, CO, Eubulides, Kurowoofwoof111, Andy Dingley, Dirkbb, Haseo9999, Graymornings, Falcon8765, MCTales, Cvdwalt, Harderm, Dmcq, LittleBenW, Pjoef, AlleborgoBot, Symane, Szeldich, Darthali, Iceworks, SieBot, RHodnett, Frans Fowler, JamesA, Tiddly Tom, WereSpielChequers, Paradoctor, Blackshadow153, Viskonsas, WBTheFROG, Yintan, Soler97, Grundle2600, Purbo T, DavidBourguignon, Yungjibbz, Mr.Z-bot, Wadeduck, Flyer22, Darth Chyrsaor, Jojalozzo, Taemyr, Arthur Smart, Oxymoron83, Ioverka, Scorpion451, Ddxc, Harry~enwiki, MiNombreDeGuerra, Steven Crossin, Lightmouse, Yankee-Bravo, Xobritbabeox10, RyanParis, Svick, Smallclone2, CharlesGillingham, Macduffman, Wyckster, Voices cray, Searchmaven, Cheesefondue, Neo., Denisarona, Finetooth, Emptymountains, ImageRemovalBot, Hpdl, Elassint, ClueBot, Fribbler, Rumping, Prohlep, Avenged Eightfold, The Thing That Should Not Be, Logperson, Ezavarei, Ndenison, Unbuttered Parsnip, Willingandable, Grantbow, Drmies, VQuakr, Mild Bill Hiccup, Malignedtruth, Boing! said Zebedee, Mayfly may fly, Nappy1020, Arne Heise, Neverquick, Thomas Kist, Yakota21, Pooya.babahajyani, Time for action, Jdzarlino, Excirial, Gnome de plume, Hezarfenn, Vivio Testarossa, Thunderhippo, Nayanraut, Xklsv, NuclearWarfare, Jotterbot, Iohannes Animosus, Sebaldusadam, Renamed user 3, Mr.Sisgay, Mullhawk, Chaosdruid, Aitias, EPIC MASTER, Ranjithsutari, Scalhotrod, Johnuniq, HumphreyW, Apparition11, Sparkygravity, MasterOfHisOwnDomain, Escientist, XLinkBot, AgnosticPreachersKid, Basploeger, Sgunteratparamus.k12.nj.us, Spitfire, Pichpich, Alex naish, Rror, Ost316, Libcub, Dheer7c, Noctibus, Thede, Truthnlove, D.M. from Ukraine, Addbot, Barsoomian, DOI bot, Guoguo12, Kimveale, Betterusername, Ashish krazzy, Coolcatfish, AndrewHZ, DougsTech, Elsendero, TutterMouse, CanadianLinuxUser, Leszek Jańczuk, Fluffernutter, Damiens.rf, Me pras, Sebastian scha., MrOllie, Aykantspel, LaaknorBot, Nuclear Treason, The world deserves the truth, Glane23, AndersBot, Favonian, Kyle1278, LinkFA-Bot, Rbalcke, AgadaUrbanit, Tassedethe, Brianjfox, Jan eissfeldt, Ricvelozo, Jarble, KarenEdda, Ben Ben, Luckas-bot, PetroKonashevich, Yobot, Worldbruce, Themfromspace, Ptbotgourou, Fraggle81, Twexcom, Obscuranym, Leoneris, Rinea, Mmxx, Taxisfolder, THEN WHO WAS PHONE?, Vini 17bot5, MHLU, PluniAlmoni, Pravdaverita, AnomieBOT, Macilnar, Floquenbeam, 1exec1, Ai24081983, Frans-w1, Jim1138, IRP, Galoubet, Fraziergeorge122, Palace of the Purple Emperor, AdjustShift, ChristopheS, Glenfarclas, Flewis, Materialscientist, Citation bot, Kjellmikal, Devantheryv, Vivohobson, Eumolpo, Ankank, ArthurBot, Xqbot, Tinucherian-Bot II, AVBAI, Roesslerj, Capricorn42, TracyMcClark, Staberind, Renaissancee, Taylormas229, Oxwil, Wyklety, The Evil IP address, Turk oğlan, Isheden, S0aasdf2sf, Crzer07, A157247, Hi878, IntellectToday, J04n, GrouchoBot, Armbrust, Wizardist, Diogeneselcinico42, Omnipaedista, Shirik, RibotBOT, Chris.urs-o, Mathonius, Shadowjams, Chicarelli, WhatisFeelings?, AlGreen00, Dougofborg, Fillepa, FrescoBot, FalconL, Hobsonlane, Recognizance, Nojan, Ilcmuchas, Zero Thrust, HJ Mitchell, Steve Quinn, Yoyoscool, Lightbound, Juno, Spectatorbot13, Intrealm, Cannolis, Philapathy, HamburgerRadio, Citation bot 1, DeStilaDo, RCPayne, Lylodo, MacMed, Pinethicket, WaveRunner85, Jonesey95, Rameshngbot, Skyerise, Staflorin, Serols, Agemoi, Farmer21, Bubwater, Fartherred, Reconsider the static, IJBall, Cnwilliams, Bqdemon, JCAILLAT, TobeBot, Puzl bustr, SchreyP, Compvis, LogAntiLog, ItsZippy, Lotje, Javierito92, Emarus, Fox Wilson, Vrenator, Lynn Wilbur, Robot8888, Gregman2, Fricanod, Stroppolo, Wikireviewer99, BrightBlackHeaven, DARTH SIDIOUS 2, Chucks91, Mean as custard, RjwilmsiBot, Humanrobo, Иъ Лю Ха, Theyer, BertSeghers, Rollins83, Nistra, DASHBot, EmausBot, John of Reading, Orphan Wiki, WikitanvirBot, Syncategoremata, GoingBatty, Implements, Wikicolleen, Olof nord, Gimmetoo, Tommy2010, K6ka, Azlan Iqbal, Thecheesykid, Werieth, Evanh2008, AvicBot, Vfrias, AVGavrilov, Josve05a, Shuipzv3, Lateg, Annonnimus, Habstinat, Unreal7, Foryourinfo, Tolly4bolly, Thine Antique Pen, Staszek Lem, Δ, Coasterlover1994, Westwood25, L Kensington, Donner60, Casia wyq, Rangoon11, Keidax, Lilinjing cas, Terraflorin,

3.1. TEXT

JonRichfield, ClueBot NG, Xzbobzx, Tillander, ClaretAsh, Astrobase36, MelbourneStar, Satellizer, Mostlymark, James childs, Robiminer, Tideflat, Aloisdimpflmoser, Prakashavinash, Delusion23, Widr, Danim, Heldrain, Helpful Pixie Bot, Adam Roush, SecretStory, Whitehead3, IrishStephen, Calabe1992, Jeraphine Gryphon, Technical 13, BG19bot, Virtualerian, Jwchong, Starship.paint, Juro2351, Mr.TAMER.Shlash, MangoWong, ElphiBot, MusikAnimal, Josvebot, Piguy101, Treva26, Reckiz, Cadiomals, Drift chambers, Altaïr, Cassianp, Wiki-uoft, Snow Blizzard, TheProfessor, NotWith, Mschuldt, Glacialfox, Peter Baum, Devonmann101, Avery.mabojie, Wannabemodel, Maarten Rail, Batty-Bot, StarryGrandma, Simbara, E prosser, Varagrawal, Cyberbot II, Ideafarmcity, Brookeweiner, Fireboy3015, Psych2012Joordens, Marktindal, IjonTichyIjonTichy, RichardKPSun, Dexbot, Oritnk, Acrognale, Lugia2453, Sly1993, Mark Bao, Iskand26, SFK2, Dineshhi, Yassu66, Henrifrischborno, Clin18, Reatlas, Samee, Joeinwiki, Faizan, ChassonR, Epicgenius, Newtesteditor, Allaroundtheworld123, Amandapan1, Snatoon, Son$\hat{\text{g}}$anto, Melonkelon, Kingfaj, Silas Ropac, Weightlessjapan1337, Satassi, Jiayuliu, Tentinator, Rosenblumb1, Kogmaw, Syntaxerrorz, Msundqvist, Shrikarsan, Dustin V. S., Mamadoutadioukone, Laper1900, Gaurang2904, Riddhi-gupta, Babitaarora, Megerler, IWishIHadALife, Orion dude, Mrm7171, MarinMersenne, ????, Aniruddhmanishpatel, Mandruss, Ginsuloft, Mintiematt, Aubreybardo, Francois-Pier, Healybd, Cows12345, Zourcilleux, Fixuture, Mellon2030, Lakun.patra, Balaji4894, FelixRosch, Wyn.junior, JacwanaKL, ????, 22merlin, MadScientistX11, Hnchinmaya, Monkbot, Lucyloo10, SantiLak, Jfishel, TheQ Editor, YdJ, T lanuza, BioMeow, Madan Pokharel, Pbravo2, Dodynamic, Evolutionvisions, Wstevens2090, Zeus000000, Charmingpianist, ChamithN, Feynman1918, Shrestha sumit, Yoon Aris, Dorianluparu, Junbibi, Pythagoros, SpRu01, Comp-heur-intel, Praneshyadav1, Kmp302, Devwebtel, KayleighwilliamsLS, Easeit7, Zortwort, Illiteration, Spectrum629, CV9933, Miguelsnchz723, Newwikieditor678, KenTancwell, Demdim0, Eobasanya, KasparBot, Pianophage, Csisawesome, Pmaiden, Συντάκτης Βικιλεξικό, Ray engh 302, Vahagn125, Skyshines, Andyjin2002, Aviartm, Chhana Tlau and Anonymous: 1618

- **Computer architecture** *Source:* https://en.wikipedia.org/wiki/Computer_architecture?oldid=680714371 *Contributors:* Robert Merkel, Rjstott, Youssefsan, Toby Bartels, William Avery, Mudlock, Ray Van De Walker, SimonP, Hannes Hirzel, Stevertigo, Edward, RTC, Michael Hardy, Mahjongg, Ixfd64, Dori, CesarB, Mdebets, Ahoerstemeier, Ideyal, Cameronc, Raul654, Robbot, Murray Langton, Jmabel, JesseW, Iain.mcclatchie, Fabiform, Giftlite, Brouhaha, DavidCary, Harp, Lee J Haywood, VampWillow, Neilc, ConradPino, Togo~enwiki, Rich Farmbrough, Guanabot, Pj.de.bruin, Dyl, ESkog, ZeroOne, Neko-chan, LeonardoGregianin, MPerel, Quaternion, Mdd, Honeycake, Alansohn, Liao, Atlant, Pion, Hu, Bart133, Andrewmu, Velella, Brock, Cburnett, Bsadowski1, Oleg Alexandrov, Justinlebar, Uncle G, Ruud Koot, JeremyA, Wikiklrsc, Dionyziz, Eyreland, Graham87, Kbdank71, Reisio, Quiddity, ABot, The wub, FlaBot, Gnikhil, Margosbot~enwiki, BMF81, Yurik-Bot, Salsia, Gaius Cornelius, Stassats, Danny31415, Nick, Matthiku, Aaron Schulz, DeadEyeArrow, Tetracube, Neomagus00, LeonardoRob0t, Whaa?, GrinBot~enwiki, Dkasak, SpLoT, SmackBot, Kellen, Incnis Mrsi, Prodego, Gilliam, Hmains, Jcarroll, Kurykh, TimBentley, Thumperward, EncMstr, Newbyman, Nbarth, DHN-bot~enwiki, Dfletter, Can't sleep, clown will eat me, RyanEberhart, David Morón, Frap, Q uant, AcidPenguin9873, JonHarder, Zvar, Edivorce, Allan McInnes, SundarBot, Zachbenman, Krashlandon, Feradz, NongBot~enwiki, Robert Bond, Shoeofdeath, Igoldste, Tawkerbot2, SkyWalker, CRGreathouse, Ahy1, Unixguy, Tuvas, Rdv, HenkeB, Michael B. Trausch, Xaariz, Tawkerbot4, Akhilesh043658647, Thijs!bot, Kubanczyk, Renaissongsman, Ideogram, Liquid-aim-bot, Prolog, Dylan Lake, Skarkkai, Res2216firestar, JAnDbot, Gopal1035, The Transhumanist, Cmgomes, Bongwarrior, VoABot II, Nickmalik, CommonsDelinker, J.delanoy, Trusilver, Daufman, McSly, Plasticup, L.W.C. Nirosh, Su-steveri, VolkovBot, Su-steve, Jigabooda, MagicBanana, TedColes, Miko3k, AlleborgoBot, Biasoli, Jimmi Hugh, Logan, Hazel77, TheStarman, ThorstenStaerk~enwiki, Fanatix, Chickendude1313, Meldor, Gerakibot, Mark w69, Jerryobject, Masgatotkaca, Allmightyduck, Vanished user kijsdion3i4jf, Kumioko, Svick, Denisarona, TheWILSE, Conniejlewis, ClueBot, Rilak, Czarkoff, Excirial, Ykhwong, NuclearWarfare, Dmyersturnbull, Razorflame, Rrccflores, Gereon K., Xxray03, Dsimic, Addbot, Melab-1, AkhtaBot, Leszek Jańczuk, Fluffernutter, Glane23, AnnaFrance, Favonian, Upulcranga, Tide rolls, Lightbot, Luckas-bot, Yobot, OrgasGirl, Fraggle81, Nanju123, Amirobot, Pcap, Mmxx, AnomieBOT, Li1939108, Fahadsadah, Materialscientist, Citation bot, Tharindunisal, Groovenstein, Joehms22, Shadowjams, TheAmplidude, Erik9bot, FrescoBot, Aubencheulobois, Alxeedo, HJ Mitchell, DrilBot, Pinethicket, Rameshngbot, Strenshon, Qazwsxedcrfv1, Merlion444, FoxBot, GlikD, SchreyP, ??, Vrenator, Quafios, DARTH SIDIOUS 2, Anurag golipkar, Rjwilmsibot, EmausBot, Nuujinn, Racerx11, Sohaib.mohd, Slawekb, Cogiati, Fæ, Alpha Quadrant, Elektrik Shoos, A930913, Microprocessor Man, L Kensington, Donner60, Tot12, ClamDip, 28bot, ClueBot NG, CocuBot, Phonedigs, Nickspoon0, Vacation9, Delusion23, Zynwyx, Robin400, Widr, Jgowdy, Helpful Pixie Bot, HMSSolent, Aalomaim, Wbm1058, AvocatoBot, Neutral current, Benzband, Dentalplanlisa, XIN3N, Orderkim, BattyBot, L8starter, Pratyya Ghosh, ChrisGualtieri, Codename Lisa, ZaferXYZ, Phamnhatkhanh, Mahbubur-r-aaman, Faizan, Forgot to put name, Greengreengreenred, Wenzchen, Pokechu22, VirtualAssist, ScotXW, G S Palmer, Olenyash, Abc 123 def 456, Trax support, Lich counter, Haosjaboeces, Esicam, Kylemanel, Bobby1234abcd, KasparBot, Boehm, Jpskycak, Srinivas blaze and Anonymous: 323

- **Computer engineering** *Source:* https://en.wikipedia.org/wiki/Computer_engineering?oldid=680601722 *Contributors:* Jlinton, DavidLevinson, Camembert, Hephaestos, Edward, Michael Hardy, Seav, Ahoerstemeier, DavidWBrooks, Darkwind, Andres, Grin, Andrewman327, Wernher, Bevo, Joy, Stephane Simard, Fredrik, Aaron Pannell, Hadal, Filemon, Giftlite, DocWatson42, Niteowlneils, Brockert, Jackol, Scurra, Utcursch, Bact, CryptoDerk, Jfliu, Yayay, Klox, Robin klein, McCart42, Trevor MacInnis, Corti, Mike Rosoft, Discospinster, Rich Farmbrough, Sgauria, El C, GTubio, A-Day, Slipperyweasel, Sam Korn, Haham hanuka, Pearle, Mdd, Pion, Bart133, Snowolf, Velella, Cburnett, Versageek, Redvers, TheCoffee, Kenyon, Oleg Alexandrov, Commander Keane, Ruud Koot, Scm83x, Prashanthns, Graham87, Rsg, Sjö, Astronaut, KamasamaK, XP1, Bruce1ee, Bubba73, Yamamoto Ichiro, FayssalF, Titoxd, RexNL, Czar, Malhonen, Wrightbus, Hall Monitor, Dúnadan, ATH500, YurikBot, Wavelength, Tamzid, MMuzammils, Crazytales, Skyhoper, Arado, NawlinWiki, InformationalAnarchist, Jpbowen, Voidxor, Tony1, JHCaufield, Dbfirs, Samir, ICberg7, Marcelo-Silva, Typer 525, Bakkster Man, Light current, Demus Wiesbaden, Willtron, Katieh5584, ScottWinder~enwiki, Palapa, Veinor, SmackBot, Prodego, Prestinian, KnowledgeOfSelf, Hydrogen Iodide, Blue520, Oceanm, Jhwilliams, Vilerage, Timotheus Canens, Powo, Gilliam, Skizzik, Rmosler2100, Keegan, MK8, JDCMAN, Jprg1966, Rhoeg, Xbxg32000, Shion Uzuki, Rrelf, Can't sleep, clown will eat me, Bsodmike, Sephiroth BCR, JonHarder, Rrburke, Rsm99833, Allan McInnes, Easwarno1, Weregerbil, DMacks, Imecs, Supaplex~enwiki, Molerat, Kuru, Euchiasmus, Disavian, RCX, Melody Concerto, Callred, Csyberblue, Meco, Tmcw, Dcflyer, Drdestiny77, Zorxd, Squirepants101, Informationplusgood, KJS77, BranStark, Iridescent, Mintaddict, Aaronsells, Tawkerbot2, Pi, Mkuusela, Ashok2006, Vanamyn, TysK, Tuvas, TheJMan, Cydebot, MC10, Travelbird, Skittleys, Tawkerbot4, Shirulashem, Christian75, Garik, Septagram, Omicronpersei8, Epbr123, Andyjsmith, Mojo Hand, Marek69, John254, Nick Number, J Clear, AntiVandalBot, Davidoff, Widefox, Seaphoto, NightwolfAA2k5, Maksud, Res2216firestar, CombatWombat42, Dreadengineer, MER-C, Fadikaouk, Hut 8.5, Bookinvestor, Geniac, Magioladitis, Bongwarrior, Blaserules, Loonymonkey, User A1, Hi mostafa, Ahmad87, Talon Artaine, DerHexer, Patstuart, IKBixo, TheBot, Iboixo, ShaunL, Anaxial, R'n'B, ZThomas1234987, Mausy5043, Erkan Yilmaz, J.delanoy, Pharaoh of the Wizards, Trusilver, Juangaman, Storm9, Newsmen~enwiki, Slithymatt, Shay Guy, Mimigu, Chriswiki, Tonyshan, Aervanath, Johonn, Potatoswatter, KylieTastic, Remember the dot, Vanished user 39948282, Funandtrvl, Burlywood, Philip Trueman, Technopat, Neo63, L46kok, Figureskatingfan, Mwilso24, Suriel1981, Andy Dingley, @pple, IndulgentReader, Tiddly Tom, Smudd, Luker3, Triwbe, Yintan, Vanished User 8a9b4725f8376,

Calabraxthis, Keilana, Bentogoa, Cocomaxwater, Flyer22, Radon210, Arbor to SJ, Momo san, Oxymoron83, Pac72, Techman224, Alex.muller, Vanished user kijsdion3i4jf, Svick, TrevorPace, Superbeecat, Pinkadelica, Denisarona, Atif.t2, Martarius, Tanvir Ahmmed, Elassint, Clue-Bot, Vorik111, Mfaridh, The Thing That Should Not Be, R000t, Boing! said Zebedee, Ottawahitech, N najjar85, Excirial, Eeekster, Hanifbbz, Robertdodson, Winston365, Gtstricky, JK-RULZ, Ykhwong, GeneralMacAwesome, Arjayay, Kryptonian250, Aitias, Andrew Jameson, Scalhotrod, Versus22, SoxBot III, Nafsadh, XLinkBot, Fastily, Rror, Baudday, Karaku, Mitch Ames, Mifter, Dekart, JinJian, Dwilso, Adam-Cox9, Addbot, Some jerk on the Internet, Thomas888b, Hda3ku, Silikonvadisi~enwiki, Jonathanasdf, Ronhjones, Moosehadley, EconoPhysicist, UserDœ, Blakecyrus, Tide rolls, Lightbot, Luckas Blade, Vanuan, Jarble, Yobot, 2D, Fraggle81, Aa223, Noah03, AnomieBOT, Floquenbeam, Jim1138, Piano non troppo, AdjustShift, Kingpin13, Law, Materialscientist, Matt365, Danno uk, Aff123a, Citation bot, Qproq, Capnleonardo, Bagumba, Zad68, Cureden, JimVC3, Capricorn42, Gilo1969, Coretheapple, GCompsupport, Omnipaedista, Mferyo, بپووی, Doulos Christos, Shadowjams, 55h1lkasf97a1lhflas7fal2ha, FrescoBot, Mark Renier, HJ Mitchell, Cannolis, HamburgerRadio, Laciportbus, EagleEye96, Joaopelicano, Pinethicket, I dream of horses, Edderso, Serols, Colin.holzman, Rick1653, IJBall, Bucko94, SchreyP, Thái Nhi, Dark Lord of the Sith, Sumone10154, Vrenator, Jd0gg9, Quafios, DARTH SIDIOUS 2, AXRL, Onel5969, Jtsandlund, Mazgard, Lbrown123, Autumnalmonk, AndyHe829, John of Reading, Immunize, Philowiki, Super48paul, Racerx11, ΓιάννηςΚαραμήτρος, RenamedUser01302013, Illogicalpie, Tommy2010, Wikipelli, Anirudh Emani, John Cline, Daonguyen95, Wumbotom, MIT-Alumini, Kiwi128, Njit352, FILTHY JACK SPARROW, Dr.Franklin R. Thomason ll, Wayne Slam, Frigotoni, Tolly4bolly, Isarra, Butterflylunch, Computer Engineering, MaGa, Donner60, Jack sparrow mit, Puffin, Carmichael, Peter Karlsen, TYelliot, DASHBotAV, Freemankevin15, Davey2010, ClueBot NG, Vacation9, Repseki, Talvinder.grewaal, Duecre, Widr, Reify-tech, Ashish Gaikwad, MerlIwBot, Oddbodz, HMSSolent, Calabe1992, Devojam, BZTMPS, BG19bot, Krenair, Sasan Geranmehr, JohnChrysostom, Ajith P V, Red Rover112, Mark Arsten, OneThousandTwentyFour, Kidloco3214, Cynthia627, Eduardofeld, Cyberbot II, ChrisGualtieri, Mediran, Cossr, Fabianhjr, Hksuj91, Take of pants manager, Bobaseth, Uzidon92, User051828339, Lugia2453, The Triple M, Wywin, Siggy13, Samee, Phamnhatkhanh, Faizan, Quantum Fox, Waqasbeyg, Salience129, Jordyced, Ruby Murray, Infamous Castle, Kritimailbox, Babitaarora, Baconfry, My name is not dave, YiFeiBot, AliH121, JaconaFrere, Skr15081997, Hpham122, Monkbot, NATHANWASHERE2014, BethNaught, Shivaaa1123, Joven parazo, Ajosh02, Crystallizedcarbon, StewdioMACK, Gurnoor kaur, TDRinfinity, Wiki1tikitaka, KasparBot, Ryytdnbd fsb, Brecapla000, JeremiahY and Anonymous: 895

- **Computer performance** *Source:* https://en.wikipedia.org/wiki/Computer_performance?oldid=675400304 *Contributors:* Edward, Kku, Raul654, Jeffq, Phil Boswell, Robbot, DavidCary, Woohookitty, Mindmatrix, Mandarax, Intgr, BMF81, Chobot, RussBot, Rsrikanth05, Arichnad, Voidxor, Derek1G, SmackBot, KD5TVI, EncMstr, A5b, Derek farn, 16@r, Kozuch, Thijs!bot, Kdakin, CosineKitty, The Transhumanist, ChrisLoosley, RockMFR, Hoopygreen, UnitedStatesian, Skgbafa, Martin J Roth, Sanya3, Luis v silva, PipepBot, The Thing That Should Not Be, Drmies, Mild Bill Hiccup, Boing! said Zebedee, Niceguyedc, PatMurphy, Meaganmurphy, Ykhwong, Avoided, Zodon, Addbot, Fgnievinski, MrOllie, Zorrobot, Luckas-bot, Yobot, Cflm001, Deicool, S0aasdf2sf, Kyng, FrescoBot, Fortdj33, Jonkerz, EmausBot, WikitanvirBot, John Cline, Anir1uph, Makecat, OnePt618, ClueBot NG, Wbm1058, BG19bot, Justincheng12345-bot, Codename Lisa, Telfordbuck, BobVermont, ComsciStudent and Anonymous: 23

- **Computer graphics (computer science)** *Source:* https://en.wikipedia.org/wiki/Computer_graphics_(computer_science)?oldid=674606906 *Contributors:* Eloquence, Zundark, The Anome, Drj, Karl E. V. Palmen, Enchanter, Maury Markowitz, B4hand, Youandme, ChrispyH, Edward, Patrick, Michael Hardy, Blueshade, Mahjongg, Nixdorf, Ixfd64, Graue, Karada, Arpingstone, Alfio, Egil, Ellywa, Ronz, Nanshu, Theresa knott, Александър, Poor Yorick, Rossami, [212], Rl, Charles Matthews, Dcoetzee, Tedius Zanarukando, Clivehayward, DJ Clayworth, Grendelkhan, SEWilco, Bevo, Optim, Robbot, Mazin07, Astronautics~enwiki, RedWolf, ZimZalaBim, Altenmann, Sverdrup, Rholton, AndreasB, SoLando, Connelly, Giftlite, Levork, Mark Richards, Marcika, No Guru, Endlessnameless, FrYGuY, Jorge Stolfi, AlistairMcMillan, Uranographer, MrMambo, Quadell, Collino, Sonett72, Chmod007, Eep², Rindis, Slady, Discospinster, Rich Farmbrough, Kurainosaru, Mike Capp, Mani1, Pavel Vozenilek, JoeSmack, BACbKA, STHayden, PhilHibbs, RoyBoy, Bobo192, Cmdrjameson, .:Ajvol:., Phlake, Brlcad, Minghong, BlueNovember, Stephen Bain, Mdd, Espoo, Jumbuck, JYolkowski, Kanie, Darco, Clubmarx, Yuckfoo, Woodstone, MIT Trekkie, Stemonitis, Marasmusine, Nuno Tavares, Pinball22, Aaronh, Phillipsacp, Ruud Koot, Jeff3000, Graham87, BD2412, Yurik, Reisio, Sadangel, Graibeard, The wub, Wheger, GeorgeBills, Yamamoto Ichiro, Reedbeta, Strangnet, Vfxblog, Gurch, Fosnez, Intgr, Viznut, Alvin-cs, JackyJ, Gwernol, Wavelength, RobotE, Jeffthejiff, Manop, Wimt, ALoopingIcon, Janke, Megapixie, Irishguy, Nick, Bert Macklin, Davechatting, Daniel Mietchen, Felsir, MaxVeers, Cheeser1, MaxDZ8, Googl, Yonidebest, Zzuuzz, Closedmouth, JLaTondre, ArielGold, Profero, Chris Chittleborough, Veinor, SmackBot, Classicfilms, Mihai cartoaje, Nomad421, Jhhays, Dagnode, Chris the speller, Bluebot, NCurse, Octahedron80, Robth, Royboycrashfan, HeavyD14, Nixeagle, Mallicos, Design tutor, MichaelBillington, Mikebrands, RandomP, Tompsci, Bidabadi~enwiki, Acidburn24m, Wibbble, Queens finest, Psashikumar, Melody Concerto, Ckatz, Gilles Tran, 16@r, Rainwarrior, Saxbryn, MrDolomite, Cglinux, IvanLanin, Tawkerbot2, Ahy1, Zarex, Van helsing, Keithh, Gogo Dodo, Alanbly, PKT, AntiVandalBot, Luna Santin, Jayron32, Farosdaughter, Alphachimpbot, Gregorof, HanzoHattori, JAnDbot, Cvanegas, Mfabbri77, Rpgsimmaster, Nismo~enwiki, Meredyth, JNW, Atifiqbal, Oicumayberight, Jdigital, Valarauka, EyeSerene, TheEgyptian, R'n'B, Mange01, WarthogDemon, Prince wiki thai, Laurusnobilis, Good-afternun!, Boldupdater, C quest000, Bhteam, Artsgrie, DadaNeem, Cometstyles, Wiki187, Diego, Visedit, Mas Ahmad, Sheliak, Remi0o, Trevorgoodchild, TheMindsEye, TXiKiBoT, Mmfidler, Rebornsoldier, Willoughbyorama, HHH-DX, SockManForLife, Trendspotter, SieBot, ToePeu.bot, Masgatotkaca, Dhatfield, D3av, Lightmouse, Comtemporaryaxa, EmanWilm, Martarius, ClueBot, Wwclrulescaw, Temp432, Terrencewiki, ZillurRehman, Skymartin, BOTarate, DumZiBoT, AgnosticPreachersKid, BodhisattvaBot, Danbob00, Addbot, Dhanake, NjardarBot, AndersBot, SirGudi, Godfather21~enwiki, Tassedethe, Yorche 1999, Luckas-bot, Yobot, AnomieBOT, Instantaneous, FrescoBot, HRoestBot, SchreyP, Lotje, Porusjpatell, EmausBot, WikitanvirBot, Moswento, ClueBot NG, Snotbot, Juan56, EricEnfermero, Dexbot, Brianlevis, KasparBot, Agencjareklamowa, Gguayaqu and Anonymous: 250

- **Computer security** *Source:* https://en.wikipedia.org/wiki/Computer_security?oldid=679996281 *Contributors:* Tobias Hoevekamp, Derek Ross, Tuxisuau, Brion VIBBER, Eloquence, Zardoz, Mav, Robert Merkel, The Anome, Stephen Gilbert, Taw, Arcade~enwiki, Graham Chapman, Dachshund, Arvindn, PierreAbbat, Fubar Obfusco, SimonP, Ben-Zin~enwiki, Ant, Ark~enwiki, Heron, Dwheeler, Chuq, Iorek~enwiki, Frecklefoot, Edward, Michael Hardy, Pnm, Kku, Ixfd64, Dcljr, Dori, Arpingstone, CesarB, Haakon, Ronz, Snoyes, Yaronf, Nikai, Smaffy, Qwert, Mydogategodshat, Jengod, JidGom, Aarontay, Gingekerr, Taxman, Joy, Vaceituno, Khym Chanur, Pakaran, Robbot, Yas~enwiki, Fredrik, ZimZalaBim, Rursus, Texture, KellyCoinGuy, 2501~enwiki, Hadal, Tobias Bergemann, David Gerard, Honta, Wolf530, Tom harrison, Dratman, Mike40033, Siroxo, C17GMaster, Matt Crypto, SWAdair, Bobblewik, Wmahan, Mu, Geni, Antandrus, Beland, Mako098765, CSTAR, GeoGreg, Marc Mongenet, Gscshoyru, Joyous!, Bluefoxicy, Squash, Strbenjr, Mike Rosoft, Kmccoy, Monkeyman, Pyrop, Rich Farmbrough, Rhobite, Leibniz, FT2, Jesper Laisen, ArnoldReinhold, YUL89YYZ, Jwalden, Zarutian, MeltBanana, Sperling, Bender235, ZeroOne, Moa3333, JoeSmack, Danakil, Omnifarious, Jensbn, El C, Joanjoc~enwiki, Marcok, Perspective, Spearhead, EurekaLott, Nigelj, Stesmo, Smalljim,

Rvera~enwiki, Myria, Adrian~enwiki, Boredzo, ClementSeveillac, JohnyDog, Poweroid, Alansohn, Quiggles, Arthena, Lightdarkness, Cdc, Mrholybrain, Caesura, Gbeeker, Raraoul, Filx, Proton, M3tainfo, Suruena, HenkvD, 2mcm, Wikicaz, H2g2bob, Condor33~enwiki, Bsdlogical, Johntex, Dan100, Woohookitty, Daira Hopwood, Al E., Prashanthns, Zhen-Xjell, Palica, Kesla, Vininim, Graham87, Clapaucius, BD2412, Icey, Sjakkalle, Rjwilmsi, Seidenstud, Koavf, Guyd, DeadlyAssassin, Dookie~enwiki, Edggar, Oblivious, QuickFox, Kazrak, Ddawson, Ligulem, Smtully, Aapo Laitinen, Ground Zero, RexNL, Alvin-cs, BMF81, JonathanFreed, Jmorgan, J.Ammon, Hall Monitor, Digitalme, Gwernol, FrankTobia, Elfguy, Wavelength, NTBot~enwiki, Alan216, StuffOfInterest, Foxxygirltamara, Stephenb, Gaius Cornelius, Ptomes, Morphh, Salsb, Wimt, Bachrach44, AlMac, Irishguy, Albedo, Rmky87, Amcfreely, Romal, Peter Schmiedeskamp, Zzuuzz, Gorgonzilla, Papergrl, Arthur Rubin, Ka-Ping Yee, Juliano, GraemeL, Rlove, JoanneB, Whouk, NeilN, SkerHawx, SmackBot, Mmernex, Tripletmot, Reedy, KnowledgeOfSelf, TestPilot, Kosik, McGeddon, Stretch 135, Ccalvin, Manjunathbhatt, Gilliam, Ohnoitsjamie, Skizzik, Lakshmin, Kurykh, Autarch, Snori, Miquonranger03, Deli nk, Jenny MacKinnon, Kungming2, Jonasyorg, Timothy Clemans, Frap, Ponnampalam, Nixeagle, KevM, JonHarder, Wine Guy, Cpt~enwiki, Krich, Bslede, Richard001, Stor stark7, Newtonlee, Doug Bell, Harryboyles, Kuru, Geoinline, Disavian, Robofish, Joffeloff, Kwestin, Mr. Lefty, Beetstra, Jadams76, Ehheh, Boxflux, Kvng, Chadnibal, Wfgiuliano, Dthvt, IvanLanin, DavidHOzAu, Lcamtuf, CmdrObot, Tional, ShelfSkewed, Michael B. Trausch, Phatom87, Cydebot, Mblumber, Future Perfect at Sunrise, Blackjackmagic, UncleBubba, Gogo Dodo, Anonymi, Anthonyhcole, GRevolution824, Clovis Sangrail, SpK, Njan, Ebyabe, Thijs!bot, Epbr123, The Punk, Kpavery, Wistless, Oarchimondeo, RichardVeryard, EdJohnston, Druiloor, SusanLesch, I already forgot, Sheridbm, AntiVandalBot, Obiwankenobi, Shirt58, Marokwitz, Khhodges, Ellenaz, Manionc, Chill doubt, Dmerrill, SecurityGuy, JAnDbot, Jimothytrotter, Barek, MER-C, The Transhumanist, Technologyvoices, Tqbf, Dave Nelson, Acroterion, Raanoo, VoABot II, Ukuser, JNW, Michi.bo, Szh~enwiki, Hubbardaie, Arctific, Froid, JXS, AlephGamma, Rohasnagpal, Catgut, WhatamIdoing, Marzooq, Gerrardperrett, Thireus, Devmem, Dharmadhyaksha, DerHexer, JaGa, Rcseacord, XandroZ, Gwern, SolitaryWolf, CliffC, =JeffH, Sjjupadhyay~enwiki, Bertix, Booker.ercu, J.delanoy, Gam2121, Maurice Carbonaro, Public Menace, Jesant13, Jreferee, JA.Davidson, Katalaveno, Touisiau, Ansh1979, Toon05, Mufka, Largoplazo, Dubhe.sk, YoavD, Bonadea, Red Thrush, RJASE1, Cralar, Javeed Safai, ABF, Wiki-ay, Davidwr, Zifert, Crazypete101, Dictouray, Shanata, Haseo9999, Falcon8765, Pctechbytes, Sapphic, Donnymo, FutureDomain, Smith bruce, Kbrose, JonnyJD, Lxicm, Whitehatnetizen, Jargonexpert, SecurInfos~enwiki, Ml-crest, Immzw4, Sephiroth storm, Graceup, Yuxin19, Agilmore, JohnManuel, Flyer22, Jojalozzo, Riya.agarwal, Corp Vision, Lightmouse, KathrynLybarger, Mscwriter, Soloxide, StaticGull, Capitalismojo, PabloStraub, Rinconsoleao, Denisarona, White Stealth, Ishisaka, WikipedianMarlith, Sfan00 IMG, Elassint, ClueBot, Shonharris, PipepBot, TransporterMan, Supertouch, Add32, Emantras, Tanglewood4, Mild Bill Hiccup, Niceguyedc, Dkontyko, Trivialist, Gordon Ecker, DragonBot, Dwcmsc, Excirial, Socrates2008, Dcampbell30, Moomoo987, Dr-Mx, Rbilesky, DanielPharos, Versus22, HarrivBOT, Fathisules, Raysecurity, XLinkBot, BodhisattvaBot, Solinym, Skarebo, Wingfamily, WikiDao, MystBot, Dsimic, JimWalker67, Addbot, Cst17, MrOllie, Passport90, Favonian, Torla42, AgadaUrbanit, Tassedethe, Jarble, Ben Ben, Tartarus, Luckas-bot, Yobot, OrgasGirl, The Grumpy Hacker, Librsh, Cyanoa Crylate, Grammaton, THEN WHO WAS PHONE?, Dr Roots, Sweerek, AnomieBOT, JDavis680, Jim1138, Galoubet, Dwayne, Piano non troppo, AdjustShift, Rwhalb, Quantumseven, HRV, Vijay Varadharajan, Materialscientist, Aneah, Stationcall, ArthurBot, Cameron Scott, Intelati, Securitywiki, Hi878, Coolkidmoa, Zarcillo, Mark Schierbecker, Pradameinhoff, Amaury, George1997, Architectchamp, =Josh.Harris, Shadowjams, President of hittin' that ass, FrescoBot, Bingo-101a, Nageh, Ionutzmovie, Cudwin, Expertour, Intelligentsium, Pinethicket, I dream of horses, Edderso, Access-bb, Yahia.barie, RedBot, MastiBot, Wlalng123, Mentmic, Dac04, Banej, Codemaster32, Tjmannos, Nitesh13579, Lotje, Sumone10154, Arkelweis, Ntlhui, Aoidh, Endpointsecurity, Tbhotch, Jesse V., DARTH SIDIOUS 2, Ripchip Bot, Panda Madrid, DASHBot, Julie188, EmausBot, Timtempleton, Dewritech, Active Banana, P@ddington, Susfele, Dolovis, Cosmoskramer, Alxndrpaz, AvicAWB, Bar-abban, Ocaasi, Solipsys, Tolly4bolly, Sharpie66, DennisIsMe, Veryfoolish, Geohac, ChuispastonBot, Pastore Italy, Tentontunic, Sepersann, Gadgad1973, Rocketrod1960, Jramio, ClueBot NG, AAriel42, Name Omitted, Enfcer, Iliketurtlesmeow, Widr, Helpful Pixie Bot, TechGeek70, Curb Chain, Calabe1992, BG19bot, Mollsiebee, M0rphzone, Rubmum, Mohilekedar, Karlomagnus, IraChesterfield, Sburkeel, Zune0112, Venera Seyranyan, Wondervoll, Mihai.scridonesi, Jtlopez, Nfirdosian, Alessandra Napolitano, Wannabemodel, Keeper03, BattyBot, Popescucalin, Arr4, Mrt3366, Cyberbot II, Khazar2, Peter A. Wolff, Soulparadox, Ilker Savas, BIG ISSUE LADY, Saturdayswiki, Dexbot, Jmitola, Mogism, Pete Mahen, Lugia2453, Doopbridge, Sbhalotra, SFK2, Arjungiri, Jamesx12345, ElinaSy, Patna01, Dr Dinosaur IV, Pdecalculus, Mbmexpress, Idavies007, RaheemaHussain, Cyberlawjustin, Rkocher, MoHafesji, ResearcherQ, Westonbowden, Peter303x, Karinera, OccultZone, LukeJeremy, Robevans123, Chima4mani, ClyderRakker46, Jonathan lampe, Jppcap, Leejjung86, Azulfiqar, IrvingCarR, Nyashinski, Monkbot, Nitzy99, Carpalclip3, RicardoBanchez, Owais Khursheed, Oushee, 405Duke, BrettofMoore, Gr3yHatf00l, Thetechgirl, Fimatic, Hchaudh3, AndrewKin, JRPolicy, Pacguy, HVanIderstine, Leeemily, FormerPatchEditor, Pixelized frog, ABCDEFAD, Johngot, Bmore84, Informationsystemgeeks, PardonTheComma, Nemoanon, JohnEvans79, Hatebott, Ajay Yankee, Nbyrd2000, Soderbounce, Tejalpatel and Anonymous: 694

- **Cryptography** *Source:* https://en.wikipedia.org/wiki/Cryptography?oldid=680522233 *Contributors:* AxelBoldt, WojPob, LC~enwiki, Brion VIBBER, Mav, Uriyan, Zundark, The Anome, Taw, Ap, Tao~enwiki, Ted Longstaffe, Dachshund, Arvindn, Gianfranco, PierreAbbat, Ortolan88, Roadrunner, Boleslav Bobcik, Maury Markowitz, Imran, Graft, Heron, Sfdan, Stevertigo, Nevilley, Patrick, Chas zzz brown, Michael Hardy, GABaker, Dante Alighieri, Liftarn, Ixfd64, Cyde, TakuyaMurata, Karada, Dori, (, Goatasaur, Card~enwiki, Ahoerstemeier, DavidWBrooks, ZoeB, Theresa knott, Cferrero, Jdforrester, Julesd, Glenn, Kylet, Nikai, Andres, Cimon Avaro, Evercat, Delifisek, Dgreen34, Schneelocke, Norwikian, Revolver, Novum, Htaccess, Timwi, Wikiborg, Dmsar, Ww, Dysprosia, Jitse Niesen, Phr, The Anomebot, Greenrd, Dtgm, Tpbradbury, GimmeFuel, K1Bond007, Tempshill, Ed g2s, Raul654, Rbellin, Pakaran, Jeffq, Ckape, Robbot, Fredrik, Chris 73, RedWolf, Donreed, Altenmann, Kuszi, Securiger, Georg Muntingh, MathMartin, Jsdeancoearthlink.net, Academic Challenger, Meelar, Timrollpickering, Rasmus Faber, Cyrius, Mattflaschen, Ludraman, Tobias Bergemann, Dave6, Snobot, Giftlite, Dbenbenn, Jacoplane, HippoMan, Wolfkeeper, Netoholic, Farnik, Peruvianllama, Michael Devore, Yekrats, Per Honor et Gloria, Sietse, Mboverload, Ferdinand Pienaar, Matt Crypto, Mobius, Neilc, Gubbubu, Geni, CryptoDerk, Antandrus, Beland, Vanished user 1234567890, Pale blue dot, Rdsmith4, APH, Mzajac, Euphoria, SimonLyall, Oiarbovnb, TiMike, Ta bu shi da yu, Freakofnurture, Monkeyman, Blokhead, Heryu~enwiki, Mark Zinthefer, Moverton, Discospinster, Rich Farmbrough, Guanabot, MaxMad, ArnoldReinhold, YUL89YYZ, Ivan Bajlo, Paul August, DcoetzeeBot~enwiki, Bender235, TerraFrost, Surachit, JRM, Prsephone1674, Bobo192, Stesmo, Harley peters, AnyFile, John Vandenberg, Myria, Jericho4.0, Davidgothberg, Slipperyweasel, Wrs1864, ClementSeveillac, M5, Stephen G. Brown, LoganK, Msh210, Wereldburger758, Alansohn, JYolkowski, Dhar, Mo0, Fg, Seamusandrosy, Complex01, ABCD, Logologist, InShaneee, Avenue, Snowolf, Super-Magician, Saga City, Zyarb, Daedelus, Egg, H2g2bob, Vadim Makarov, Richwales, Oleg Alexandrov, Zntrip, Woohookitty, Mindmatrix, Justinlebar, Deeahbz, Jacobolus, Madchester, E=MC^2, Brentdax, Duncan.france, Nfearnley, Shmitra, Jok2000, Wikiklrsc, Mangojuice, SDC, Plrk, DarkBard, Cedrus-Libani, Stefanomione, Turnstep, Jimgawn, Tslocum, Graham87, Abach, FreplySpang, Vyse, JIP, Sinar~enwiki, Jorunn, Sjakkalle, Ner102, Rjwilmsi, Demian12358, Adjusting, MarSch, Mike Segal, Edggar, Miserlou, HappyCamper, Brighterorange, The wub, DoubleBlue, Volfy, CBR1kboy, Vuong Ngan Ha, RobertG, Mathbot, Gouldja, PleaseSendMoneyToWikipedia, Crazycomputers, Jameshfisher, RobyWayne, KFP, King of Hearts, Chobot, Manscher, Roboto de Ajvol, Siddhant, Wavelength, Laurentius, Auyongcheemeng, Mukkakukaku, RussBot, Lpmusix, Pigman, Manop, The1physicist, Gaius Cornelius, Chaos, Zeno of Elea, NawlinWiki, Welsh, Joel7687, Exir Kamalabadi, Proidiot, ONEder Boy, Schlafly, DavidJablon, Thiseye, Dhollm, Peter Delmonte, Misza13, Grafikm fr, Xompanthy, Deckiller, BOT-Superzerocool, Jeremy Visser, FF2010, 21655, Papergrl, Closedmouth, Nemu, CharlesHBennett, Aeon1006, Peyna, Bernd Paysan, Echartre, Anclation~enwiki, Wbrameld, Who-is-me, MagneticFlux, Crazyquesadilla, Endymi0n, Dr1819, DVD R W, ChemGardener, Yakudza, A bit iffy, SmackBot, Sean.nobles, Mmernex, Nihonjoe, 1dragon, Impaciente, Uncle Lemon, Jacek Kendysz, Jagged 85, Jrockley, David G Brault, BiT, JohnMac777, Mauls, Peter Isotalo, Gilliam, Ohnoitsjamie, Hmains, Skizzik, Chaojoker, Lakshmin, Chris the speller, Ciacchi, Agateller, Hibbleton, Thumperward, Delfeye, Snori, Alan smithee, PrimeHunter, Iago4096, NYKevin, DevSolar, Vkareh, ZachPruckowski, DrDnar, Wes!, Rashad9607, Alieseraj, Kazov, Wonderstruck, Maxt, DRLB, OutRIAAge, Sovietmah, Bidabadi~enwiki, Chungc, Andrewrabbott, Harryboyles, Dr. Sunglasses, Molerat, Fatespeaks, Ksn, Sidmow, JoshuaZ, Minna Sora no Shita, ManiF, Michael miceli, Jacopo, Ryanwammons, Slayemin, Chrisd87, Eltzermay, Meco, TastyPoutine, Dhp1080, Serlin, DeathLoofah, Drink666, Hectorian, DouglasCalvert, RudyB, Judgesurreal777, Pegasus1138, Detach, Shenron, Nightswatch, Gilabrand, Tawkerbot2, Chetvorno, Jafet, Powerslide, Sansbras, CRGreathouse, Hermitage17, Crownjewel82, BeenAroundAWhile, Thehockeydude44, CWY2190, Saoirse11, Raghunath88, Blackvault, Grandexandi, Cydebot, Ntsimp, Mblumber, John Yesberg, Gogo Dodo, Corpx, Tawkerbot4, XP105, Kozuch, Brad101, Omicronpersei8, Robertsteadman, Antura, Pallas44, Saber Cherry, Oerjan, Mojo Hand, Lotte Monz, Dgies, DPdH, Scircle, AntiVandalBot, Luna Santin, Jj137, Dylan Lake, Oddity-, G Rose, JAnDbot, Monkeymonkey11, Komponisto, WPIsFlawed, Hut 8.5, GurchBot, SCCC, Jahoe, Richard Burr, Acroterion, KooIkirby, Calcton, Hong ton po, MoleRat, CrazyComputers, Heinze~enwiki, MooCowz69, Connormah, Bongwarrior, VoABot II, Nyq, Michi.bo, Doug Coldwell, Nyttend, Homunq, KConWiki, David Eppstein, NoychoH, Havanafreestone, JaGa, Mmustafa~enwiki, BetBot~enwiki, Rettetast, Speck-Made, David Nicoson, Glrx, CommonsDelinker, Artaxiad, J.delanoy, Hans Dunkelberg, Maurice Carbonaro, Syphertext, Cadence-, Darth Mike, Salih, MezzoMezzo, Touisiau, AntiSpamBot, SJP, Wilson.canadian, Chandu iiet, R Math, Treisijs, Ross Fraser, Adam7117, Remi0o, Reddy212, Cralar, Tw mama, Mrstoltz, VolkovBot, Thomas.W, Macedonian, DSRH, JohnBlackburne, Jimmaths, Greatdebtor, Mercurish, TXiKiBoT, Oshwah, GimmeBot, MPA Neto, Xnquist, Qxz, DavidSaff, Ocolon, TedColes, Praveen pillay, Abdullais4u, Msanford, LeaveSleaves, Geometry guy, Bkassay, Rich5411, Symane, Legoktm, NHRHS2010, Radagast3, Botev, SieBot, TJRC, Nihil novi, Moonriddengirl, James Banogon, Caltas, Yintan, Browner87, Mayevski, Yob kejor, Branger~enwiki, Enti342, WannabeAmatureHistorian, Lightmouse, Skippydo, StaticGull, Hamiltondaniel, Secrefy, PerryTachett, Tom Reedy, Joel Rennie, Dlrohrer2003, Leranedo, WikipedianMarlith, ClueBot, Binksternet, The Thing That Should Not Be, JuPitEer, Niceguyedc, Mspraveen, Sv1xv, Excirial, Infomade, Ziko, Lunchscale, Jpmelos, Kakofonous, Unmerklich, Aitias, Johnuniq, MasterOfHisOwnDomain, Skunkboy74, Bletchley, XLinkBot, Hotcrocodile, IAMTrust, Bill431412, Kbdankbot, IsmaelLuceno, B Fizz, Addbot, Ghettoblaster, Some jerk on the Internet, DOI bot, Mabdul, CL, Madmax8712, Blethering Scot, TutterMouse, Gus Buonafalce, Fieldday-sunday, D0762, Bte99, Leszek Jańczuk, Harrymph, MrOllie, Protonk, AndersBot, Porkolt60, Maslen, 5 albert square, Hollerme, Tide rolls, Artusstormwind, Luckas-bot, Yobot, 2D, MarioS, Amirobot, Anypodetos, Maxí, AnomieBOT, BeEs1, Rubinbot, Jim1138, Galoubet, AdjustShift, Gowr, Wiki5d, Materialscientist, Rohitnwg, Citation bot, Clickey, Xtremejames183, Xqbot, Tomasz Dolinowski, Cluckkid, Capricorn42, Permethius, Jessicag12, ProtectionTaggingBot, Omnipaedista, Shirik, Brandon5485, Kernel.package, Smallman12q, Aaron Kauppi, WhatisFeelings?, StevieNic, 00mitpat, FrescoBot, Dogposter, Tobby72, Nageh, Krj373, Mark Renier, D'ohBot, Mohdavary, LaukkuTheGreit, DivineAlpha, HamburgerRadio, Citation bot 1, Geoffreybernardo, Quartekoen, Pinethicket, Jonesey95, Hoo man, Rochdalehornet, Pbsouthwood, Strigoides, Pezanos, Lightlowemon, FoxBot, Wsu-dm-a, كاشف عقیل, Lotje, PPerviz, Vrenator, Aoidh, Diannaa, Socialworkerking, Sonam.r.88, Dienlei, Episcopus~enwiki, RjwilmsiBot, VernoWhitney, Church074, Skamecrazy123, EmausBot, John of Reading, Immunize, Udopr, Japs 88, GoingBatty, Slightsmile, Beleary, MithrandirAgain, Akerans, DanDao, OnePt618, Msaied75, FrankFlanagan, Donner60, Dev-NJITWILL, Herk1955, Jramio, Rememberway, ClueBot NG, Wcherowi, Frapter, Nikola1891, Lord Roem, Ap375-NJITWILL, Braincricket, Widr, Mvoorzanger, Kapanidze, Dzu33, Strike Eagle, Sprishi, BG19bot, 2pem, Hdrugge, Chrisbx1, Wiki13, Anubhab91, Mm32pc, ZipoBibrok5x10^8, Drift chambers, Difbobatl, Brad7777, Sciguystfm, Giacomo.vacca, Winston Chuen-Shih Yang, Melenc, Sam Edward c, OldishTim, Dexbot, Kushalbiswas777, Denis Fadeev, Numbermaniac, Bobanobahoba, Frosty, Hamerbro, WiHkibew, JustAMuggle, Fshtea, Phamnhatkhanh, Faizan, Sachin Hariharan1992, Ac130195, Tentinator, Hendrick 99, JohnMarkOckerbloom, SelfishSeahorse, Raseman~enwiki, R00stare, Abdalla Dabdoub, Alidad1261, NorthBySouthBaranof, Orhanozkilic, Bryanrutherford0, Jianhui67, Whizz40, محمد علي العراقي, ⌽, GrantWishes, Joineir, Ninja1123, JohnDoe4000, Buddy mohit, Claw of Slime, Monkbot, Cayelr, Jordanbailey123456789, BrayLockBoy, Shammie23, Ephemeratta, Hannasnow, Garfield Garfield, Phayzfaustyn, Je.est.un.autre, Redkilla007, Whikie, Suspender guy, Crystallizedcarbon, TD-Linux, Bagulbol, Crypto Funcault, Sizzy1337, TheCoffeeAddict, Opalraava, JellyPatotie, SoSivr, Gauntman1, Zabineph, Sweepy, Cryptic Scripture and Anonymous: 699

- **Distributed computing** *Source:* https://en.wikipedia.org/wiki/Distributed_computing?oldid=678289726 *Contributors:* Damian Yerrick, TwoOneTwo, Szopen, Koyaanis Qatsi, Snorre, Greg Lindahl, SimonP, Kurt Jansson, Heron, Formulax~enwiki, Metz2000, Bernfarr, DennisDaniels, Edward, Derek~enwiki, Marvinfreeman, Lexor, Nixdorf, Kku, Wapcaplet, Ixfd64, Dori, Anonymous56789, SebastianHelm, Alfio, Nanshu, CatherineMunro, Darkwind, Glenn, Whkoh, Rotem Dan, EdH, Rob Hooft, Ghewgill, Adam Conover, Timwi, Reddi, Ww, Greenrd, Hao2lian, David Shay, Dbabbitt, Optim, Raul654, Frazzydee, Jni, Donarreiskoffer, Robbot, MrJones, Brent Gulanowski, Fredrik, Kizor, R3m0t, Kristof vt, Vespristiano, Nurg, Kuszi, Hadal, Wikibot, Dbroadwell, Michael2, Giftlite, Dbenbenn, Thv, Herbee, Curps, Waxmop, Dawidl, Mboverload, Khalid hassani, Matt Crypto, Edcolins, Lupine1647, Barneyboo, Beland, Jacob grace, APH, Maximaximax, Nickptar, M1ss1ontomars2k4, Eggstasy, D6, AlexChurchill, Freakofnurture, Spiffy sperry, Mark Zinthefer, Vague Rant, Chrischan~enwiki, YUL89YYZ, Bender235, S.K., Darkness Productions, Evice, Bobdoe, El C, Walden, Drektor2oo3, Gyll, Stesmo, BrokenSegue, Viriditas, Cmdrjameson, Mrdude, Haham hanuka, Paullaw, Mdd, Wayfarer, Autopilots, Ellisonch, Redxiv, Guy Harris, Atlant, Andrewpmk, DLJessup, Flata, InShaneee, Irdepesca572, Stephan Leeds, Suruena, Evil Monkey, 4c27f8e656bb34703d936fc59ede9a, SimonHova, Nigini, Nuno Tavares, Daira Hopwood, Decrease789, JonH, Ruud Koot, Jeff3000, AlbertCahalan~enwiki, Qwertyus, Kbdank71, Iflipti, Rjwilmsi, Indiedan, Karmachrome, Vary, John Nixon, Pascal76, Brighterorange, AlisonW, Fred Bradstadt, FayssalF, FlaBot, JFromm, Ewlyahoocom, Bihzad, Glenn L, Chobot, DVdm, Garas, Bgwhite, YurikBot, Wavelength, Mdsmedia, Spl, Bhny, Gaius Cornelius, Bovineone, CarlHewitt, SEWilcoBot, Mkbnett, Ichatz, Neum, Voidxor, Amwebb, Nethgirb, Jeh, Tim Watson, Georgewilliamherbert, Cdiggins, Ninly, Juliano, Wsiegmund, Wikiant, Joysofpi, JoanneB, Rwwww, SmackBot, Ariedartin, David Woolley, Powo, CrypticBacon, Gilliam, RDBrown, PrimeHunter, EncMstr, LaggedOnUser, Scwlong, Allan McInnes, Cybercobra, Rajrajmarley, Kasperd, Dreadstar, Bejnar, Howdoesthiswo, Kuru, Sosodank, Iosef aetos, Statsone, Codepro, Bjankuloski06en~enwiki, Hazzeryoda, MikeHearn, Beetstra, Trey56, Skabraham, Lee Carre, Quaeler, Buyya, Tawkerbot2, Flubeca, Gangesmaster, Page Up, Only2sea, Pmerson, WeggeBot, Ezrakilty, SuperMidget, Gortsack, CaptainMooseInc, Markov12, Stevag, Vanished User jdksfajlasd, D104, Thijs!bot, Hervegirod, Andyjsmith, Ideogram, Hala54, Papipaul, Alphachimpbot, Sorry Go Fish, JAnDbot, CosineKitty, Magioladitis, Greg Ward, Nyq, SirDuncan, Geozapf, Tedickey, Cic, David Eppstein, Jacobko, Unfactual POV, Sahkuhnder, Chocmah, Chtfn, Softguyus, LedgendGamer, Cadence-, Cpiral, McSly, Akiezun, Aervanath, Shamjithkv, DorganBot, LightningDragon, VolkovBot, Lee.Sailer, AlnoktaBOT,

3.1. TEXT

Philip Trueman, DragonLord, ChuckPheatt, VanishedUserABC, Spinningspark, Palaeovia, Kbrose, YonaBot, EwokiWiki, Ajtouchstone, Monkeypooisgood, Flyer22, JCLately, Hello71, Xe7al, Dust Filter, WikiLaurent, Vladrassvet~enwiki, Tanvir Ahmmed, The Thing That Should Not Be, TallMagic, Nonlinear149, Worldwidegrid, Dominikiii, Alexbot, Ahmed abbas helmy, WalterGR, Warrior4321, Aitias, SoxBot III, DumZiBoT, Darkicebot, XLinkBot, Wonderfulsnow, WikHead, Slashem, RealityDysfunction, NonNobisSolum, Addbot, Proofreader77, Ramu50, Some jerk on the Internet, DOI bot, Maria C Mosak, EjsBot, AkhtaBot, MrOllie, Kisbesbot, Jarble, Frehley, Legobot, PlankBot, Luckas-bot, Yobot, AnomieBOT, Nit634, Materialscientist, CoMePrAdZ, Citation bot, ArthurBot, Hahutch298, Xqbot, Capricorn42, Julianhyde, Mika au, Gilo1969, GrabBrain, Miguel in Portugal, Miym, Wizardist, AreThree, Felix.rivas, Toonsuperlove, Doulos Christos, D'ohBot, Sae1962, Wifione, Jomifica, Neilksomething, Citation bot 1, Guarani.py, I dream of horses, Jonesey95, Sohil it, RedBot, Île flottante, Jandalhandler, Trappist the monk, Yunshui, Diannaa, Tbhotch, Jesse V., Shafigoldwasser, TjBot, Eng azza, EmausBot, Kinshuk jpr19, Janakan86, Goudron, JordiGH, Cincybluffa, Wakebrdkid, Unobjectionable, ClueBot NG, Matthiaspaul, MelbourneStar, Gilderien, Advuser14, Widr, ساجد امجد ساجد, Helpful Pixie Bot, Mellorf, BG19bot, Cognitivecarbon, PlasmaTime, Kitisco, Riley Huntley, Khiladi 2010, Boufal, ChrisGualtieri, Mtriana, Dexbot, Catclock, Frosty, Malhelo, Maxcommejesus, Phamnhatkhanh, Mario.virtu, Dudewhereismybike, Narendra22, Dtngo, Ma2369, Spmeu, Crystallizedcarbon, Meyerjo, Lr0^^k, Unsaved.work and Anonymous: 373

- **Database** *Source:* https://en.wikipedia.org/wiki/Database?oldid=680049216 *Contributors:* Paul Drye, NathanBeach, Dreamyshade, LC~enwiki, Robert Merkel, Zundark, The Anome, Stephen Gilbert, Sjc, Andre Engels, Chuckhoffmann, Fubar Obfusco, Ben-Zin~enwiki, Maury Markowitz, Waveguy, Imran, Leandrod, Stevertigo, Edward, Ubiquity, Michael Hardy, JeffreyYasskin, Fuzzie, Pnm, Ixfd64, TakuyaMurata, SebastianHelm, Pcb21, CesarB, MartinSpamer, ArnoLagrange, Ahoerstemeier, Haakon, Nanshu, Angela, Bogdangiusca, Cyan, Poor Yorick, Mxn, Mulad, Feedmecereal, Jay, Greenrd, Wik, DJ Clayworth, Tpbradbury, E23~enwiki, Furrykef, Morwen, Sandman~enwiki, Finlay McWalter, Jni, Chuunen Baka, Robbot, Noldoaran, Sander123, Craig Stuntz, Chrism, Chris 73, Vespristiano, Chocolateboy, Netizen, Nurg, Romanm, Lowellian, Pingveno, Tualha, Rursus, Rothwellisretarded, Jondel, TittoAssini, Hadal, Vikreykja, Mushroom, HaeB, Pengo, SpellBott, Tobias Bergemann, Stirling Newberry, Psb777, Giftlite, Graeme Bartlett, SamB, Sarchand~enwiki, Arved, Inter, Kenny sh, Levin, Peruvianllama, Everyking, Ciciban, Ssd, Niteowlneils, Namlemez, Mboverload, SWAdair, Bobblewik, Wmahan, Gadfium, SarekOfVulcan, Quadell, Kevins, Antandrus, Beland, OverlordQ, Rdsmith4, APH, Troels Arvin, Gscshoyru, Ohka-, Sonett72, Trevor MacInnis, Canterbury Tail, Bluemask, Zro, Grstain, Mike Rosoft, DanielCD, Shipmaster, EugeneZelenko, AnjaliSinha, KeyStroke, Discospinster, Rich Farmbrough, Rhobite, Lovelac7, Pak21, C12H22O11, Andrewferrier, Mumonkan, Kzzl, Paul August, Edgarde, Djordjes, S.K., Elwikipedista~enwiki, CanisRufus, *drew, MBisanz, Karmafist, Kiand, Cpereyra, Tom, Causa sui, Chrax, PatrikR, Hurricane111, Mike Schwartz, Smalljim, Wipe, John Vandenberg, Polluks, Ejrrjs, JeffTan, Nk, Franl, Alphax, Railgun, Sleske, Sam Korn, Nsaa, Mdd, HasharBot~enwiki, Jumbuck, Storm Rider, Alansohn, Tablizer, Etxrge, Guy Harris, Arthena, Keenan Pepper, Ricky81682, Riana, AzaToth, Zippanova, Kocio, PaePae, Velella, Skybrian, Helixblue, Filx, Frankman, Danhash, Max Naylor, Harej, Mathewforyou, W mccall, Ringbang, Chirpy, Djsasso, Dan100, Brookie, Isfisk, Marasmusine, Simetrical, Reinoutr, Woohookitty, Mindmatrix, Camw, Arcann, 25or6to4, Decrease789, Mazca, Pol098, Commander Keane, Windsok, Ruud Koot, Tabletop, Bbatsell, KingsleyIdehen, DeirdreGerhardt, GregorB, AnmaFinotera, Plrk, Crucis, Prashanthns, TrentonLipscomb, Turnstep, PeregrineAY, Dysepsion, Mandarax, Wulfila, MassGalactusUniversum, Graham87, Qwertyus, DePiep, Jclemens, Sjakkalle, Rjwilmsi, Koavf, DeadlyAssassin, Vary, Carbonite, GlenPeterson, Feydey, Eric Burnett, Jb-adder, ElKevbo, The wub, Sango123, FlaBot, Doc glasgow, Latka, GnuDoyng, Jstaniek, RexNL, AndriuZ, Intgr, Antrax, Ahunt, Imnotminkus, JonathanFreed, King of Hearts, Chobot, Visor, Phearlez, DVdm, Bkhouser, NSR, Cornellrockey, Rimonu, YurikBot, Wavelength, Sceptre, JarrahTree, Phantomsteve, Michael Slone, Woseph, Fabartus, Toquinha, GLaDOS, SpuriousQ, RadioFan2 (usurped), Akamad, Stephenb, Rsrikanth05, Cryptic, Cpuwhiz11, BobStepno, Wimt, SamJohnston, RadioKirk, NawlinWiki, Wiki alf, Jonathan Webley, Jaxl, Milo99, Welsh, Joel7687, SAE1962, Journalist, Nick, Aaron Brenneman, RayMetz100, Matticus78, Larsinio, Mikeblas, Ezeu, Zwobot, Supten, Dbfirs, JMRyan, Bluerocket, LindaEllen, Samir, DeadEyeArrow, Werdna, User27091, Mugunth Kumar, SimonMorgan, Lod, Twelvethirteen, Deville, Theodolite, Zzuuzz, Mike Dillon, Closedmouth, Arthur Rubin, Fang Aili, Th1rt3en, GraemeL, JoanneB, Alasdair, Echartre, JLaTondre, ArielGold, Stuhacking, Kungfuadam, Mhkay, Bernd in Japan, GrinBot~enwiki, DVD R W, Jonearles, CIreland, Victor falk, Pillefj, SmackBot, Hydrogen Iodide, McGeddon, WikiuserNI, Unyoyega, Pgk, AnonUser, Davewild, AutumnSnow, Brick Thrower, Stifle, Jab843, PJM, Kslays, Edgar181, Lexo, David Fuchs, Siebren, Yamaguchi??, Gilliam, Donama, Ohnoitsjamie, Chaojoker, Chris the speller, TimBentley, MikeSy, Thumperward, Nafclark, Oli Filth, MalafayaBot, Silly rabbit, Robocoder, Xx236, Deli nk, Jerome Charles Potts, Baa, Robth, DHN-bot~enwiki, Methnor, Colonies Chris, Darth Panda, Can't sleep, clown will eat me, Chlewbot, Paul E Ester, Edivorce, Allan McInnes, Pax85, Mugaliens, Khoikhoi, COMPFUNK2, Soosed, Cybercobra, Jwy, Jdlambert, Dreadstar, Insineratehymn, Hgilbert, BryanG, Ultraexactzz, RayGates, Daniel.Cardenas, Kukini, Kkailas, SashatoBot, Krashlandon, Jasimab, Srikeit, Kuru, Jonwynne, Microchip08, Tazmaniacs, Gobonobo, PeeAeMKay, Sir Nicholas de Mimsy-Porpington, Lguzenda, Tim Q. Wells, Minna Sora no Shita, Joffeloff, HeliXx, IronGargoyle, 16@r, MarkSutton, Slakr, Tasc, Beetstra, Noah Salzman, Wikidrone, Babbling.Brook, Childzy, Optakeover, Waggers, Ryulong, ThumbFinger, DougBarry, Asyndeton, Dead3y3, Iridescent, Mrozlog, TwistOfCain, Paul Foxworthy, Igoldste, Benni39, Dwolt, DEddy, Courcelles, Linkspamremover, Navabromberger, Dkastner, Tawkerbot2, Flubeca, LessHeard vanU, Megatronium, FatalError, JForget, Comps, VoxLuna, Spdegabrielle, Thatperson, Ahy1, CmdrObot, Ale jrb, Ericlaw02, Iced Kola, KyraVixen, Kushal one, GHe, Constructive, Dgw, Argon233, FlyingToaster, Moreschi, Sewebster, Simeon, Joshnpowell, Ubiq, Cantras, Mato, Gogo Dodo, Parzi, Chasingsol, Pascal.Tesson, Dancter, SymlynX, Tawkerbot4, Shirulashem, DumbBOT, Chrislk02, Alaibot, IComputerSaysNo, SpK, Omicronpersei8, UberScienceNerd, Cavanagh, Click23, Mattisse, Thijs!bot, Epbr123, Qwyrxian, HappyInGeneral, Andyjsmith, CynicalMe, Mojo Hand, Philippe, Eric3K, Peashy, Maxferrario, Mentifisto, AntiVandalBot, Majorly, Luna Santin, Widefox, Seaphoto, Turlo Lomon, MrNoblet, EarthPerson, Kbthompson, Credema, Spartaz, Lfstevens, Deadbeef, JAnDbot, Eric Bekins, MER-C, BlindEagle, The Transhumanist, Blood Red Sandman, RIH-V, Andonic, PhilKnight, Saiken79, LittleOldMe, Jdrumgoole, Magioladitis, Karlhahn, Bongwarrior, VoABot II, Hasek is the best, JamesBWatson, Think outside the box, Lucyin, Twsx, WODUP, Cic, Jvhertum, Bubba hotep, Culverin, Danieljamesscott, Adrian J. Hunter, 28421u2232nfenfcenc, Stdazi, Wwmbes, Cpl Syx, Kunaldeo, Kozmando, Chris G, DerHexer, JaGa, Ahodgkinson, Oroso, Leaderofearth, MartinBot, Ironman5247, Arjun01, NAHID, Poeloq, CableCat, Rettetast, R'n'B, NetManage, Tgeairn, J.delanoy, Pharaoh of the Wizards, Trusilver, Rohitj.iitk, Bogey97, Ayecee, Uncle Dick, Maurice Carbonaro, Jesant13, Ginsengbomb, Darth Mike, Gzkn, Bcartolo, BrokenSphere, Kataleveno, Afluegel, Chriswiki, DamnRandall, Girl2k, NewEnglandYankee, SJP, Gregfitzy, Kraftlos, Madth3, Madhava 1947, Jackacon, Juliancolton, Cometstyles, Ryager, Raspalchima, Seanust 1, Lamp90, Bonadea, Aditya gopal3, Pdcook, Ja 62, TheNewPhobia, DigitalEnthusiast, Squids and Chips, CardinalDan, Ryanslater, Ryanslater2, Siteobserver, Lights, VolkovBot, Amaraiel, Thedjatclubrock, Alain Amiouni, Indubitably, JustinHagstrom, WOSlinker, Barneca, N25696, Erikrj, Philip Trueman, Lingwitt, TXiKiBoT, Wiki tiki tr, Moogwrench, Vipinhari, Technopat, Caster23, GDonato, ScMeGr, Olinga, Ann Stouter, Anonymous Dissident, Cyberjoac, Qxz, Gozzy345, Lradrama, Sintaku, Clarince63, Twebby, DragonLord, Jackfork, LeaveSleaves, Wya 7890, Mannafredo, Amd628, Zhenqinli, Hankhuck, Gwizard, Synthebot, Kingius, Bblank, Why Not A Duck, Atkinsdc, Pjoef, Aepanico, Logan, HybridBoy, Thehulkmonster, D. Recorder, Calutuigor, SieBot, Fooker69, Calliopejen1, Praba tuty, Kimera

Kat, Jauerback, LeeHam2007, Caltas, Eagleal, Triwbe, Yintan, TalkyLemon, Keilana, Bentogoa, Flyer22, Radon210, Oda Mari, JCLately, Jojalozzo, Hxhbot, Le Pied-bot~enwiki, Sucker666, Theory of deadman, KoshVorlon, 10285658sdsaa, Mkeranat, Fratrep, Macy, Chorizo-Lasagna, Autumn Wind, Maxime.Debosschere, Spazure, Paulinho28, Vanished User 8902317830, G12kid, Pinkadelica, Treekids, Denisarona, Escape Orbit, Levin Carsten, Kanonkas, VanishedUser sdu9aya9fs787sads, Explicit, Beeblebrox, CluBot, Frsparrow, Phoenix-wiki, Hugsandy, Strongsauce, Avenged Eightfold, The Thing That Should Not Be, Buzzimu, Jan1nad, Poterxu, Supertouch, Unbuttered Parsnip, Garyzx, Zipircik, SuperHamster, Boing! said Zebedee, Doddsy1993, Niceguyedc, Sam Barsoom, Blanchardb, Dylan620, Mikey180791, Puchiko, Mspraveen, Vivacewwxu~enwiki, Veryprettyfish, Robert Skyhawk, Drumroll99, Excirial, Pumpmeup, M4gnum0n, Dbates1999, LaosLos, Northernhenge, Eeekster, Tyler, Odavy, Cenarium, Lunchscale, Peter.C, Jotterbot, MECiAf., Huntthetroll, Tictacsir, Thehelpfulone, Inspector 34, Thingg, Aitias, DerBorg, Subash.chandran007, Versus22, Burner0718, Johnuniq, SoxBot III, Apparition11, DumZiBoT, Jmanigold, XLinkBot, EastTN, Gsallis, PrePress, Avoided, Pee Tern, Galzigler, Noctibus, Qwertykris, Dsimic, Osarius, HexaChord, Rakeki, Addbot, Proofreader77, Pyfan, Willking1979, Some jerk on the Internet, Betterusername, Captain-tucker, Ngpd, Fgnievinski, Fieldday-sunday, JephapE, Xhelllox, Vishnava, CanadianLinuxUser, Fluffernutter, Cevalsi, Cambalachero, CarsracBot, DFS454, Glane23, FiriBot, SDSWIKI, Roux, Favonian, Doniago, Exor674, AtheWeatherman, Jasper Deng, Hotstaff, Evildeathmath, Tide rolls, Nicoosuna, Kivar2, Matěj Grabovský, Dart88, Gail, David0811, Duyanfang, Jarble, Arbitrarily0, LuK3, Informatwr, Ben Ben, Luckas-bot, Yobot, Sudarevic, 2D, OrgasGirl, Bunnyhop11, Fraggle81, Gishac, MarcoAurelio, Pvjohnson, Nallimbot, SwisterTwister, Srdju001, Peter Flass, Bbb23, N1RK4UDSK714, AnomieBOT, AmritasyaPutra, Rubinbot, Sonia, Jim1138, JackieBot, Piano non troppo, Kingpin13, Ulric1313, Imfargo, Flewis, Bluerasberry, Materialscientist, Kimsey0, Citation bot, OllieFury, BlurTento, Clark89, Darthvader023, Xqbot, Anders Torlind, Kimberly ayoma, Sythy2, Llyntegid, Addihockey10, Capricorn42, Bcontins, 4twenty42o, Craftyminion, Grim23, Yossman007, Preet91119, Tonydent, GrouchoBot, Call me Bubba, Kekekecakes, Bjcubsfan, Earlypsychosis, Prunesqualer, Crashdoom, Amaury, Doulos Christos, Sophus Bie, The Wiki Octopus, IElonex!, Shadowjams, М И Ф, Oho1, Dougofborg, Al Wiseman, Chtuw, Captain-n00dle, Gonfus, Prari, FrescoBot, Sock, Riverraisin, Fortdj33, Blackguard SF, Dogposter, Mark Renier, StaticVision, HJ Mitchell, Sae1962, Wifione, Weetoddid, ZenerV, Kwiki, Javert, ZooPro, Winterst, Shadowseas, Pinethicket, I dream of horses, HRoestBot, Grsmca, LittleWink, 10metreh, Supreme Deliciousness, Hamtechperson, Sissi's bd, 28nebraska, Jschnur, Xfact, RedBot, Btilm, MastiBot, Rotanagol, Bharath357, Σ, 05winsjp, Psaajid, Meaghan, Abhikumar1995, Jandalhandler, Refactored, FoxBot, TobeBot, Mercy11, كاشف عقيل, KotetsuKat, ItsZippy, Lotje, Callanecc, Writeread82, Vrenator, Reidh21234, Reaper Eternal, Luizfsc, TheGrimReaper NS, Xin0427, Suffusion of Yellow, SnoFox, BluCreator, Colindolly, TheMesquito, Minimac, Thinktdub, Heysim0n, RazorXX8, DARTH SIDIOUS 2, Lingliu07, KILLERKEA23, Onel5969, Leonnicholls07, Mean as custard, Helloher, ArwinJ, Kvasilev, Regancy42, FetchcommsAWB, Timbits82, Aj.robin, Salvio giuliano, Skamecrazy123, Rollins83, EmausBot, John of Reading, FFGeyer, Armen1304, Heymid, ScottyBerg, Lflores92201, Beta M, Dewritech, GoingBatty, RA0808, RenamedUser01302013, Itafran2010, Knbanker, Winner 42, Carbo1200, Wikipelli, K6ka, Sheeana, Ceyjan, Serketan, AsceticRose, Anirudh Emani, Tudorol, Komal.Ar, Pete1248, Savh, Ravinjit, Joshwa1234567890, Fæ, NicatronTg, M.badnjki, Alpha Quadrant (alt), Tuhl, Makecat, Ocaasi, OnePt618, Tolly4bolly, W163, TyA, L Kensington, Mayur, Donner60, Mentibot, MainFrame, Nz101, Matthewrbowker, Peter Karlsen, GregWPhoto, GrayFullbuster, Rishu arora11, DASHBotAV, Kellyk99, 28bot, Rocketrod1960, Diamondland, ClueBot NG, SpikeTorontoRCP, Mechanical digger, Jack Greenmaven, MelbourneStar, Satellizer, Dancayta, Chester Markel, Name Omitted, Bwhynot14, Millermk, Theimmaculatechemist, Lsschwar, Bowlderizer, Zhoravdb, Widr, Danim, Ugebgroup8, CasualVisitor, Vibhijain, Franky21, Jk2q3jrklse, Cammo33, Oddbodz, Lbausalop, Cambapp, Strike Eagle, Calabe1992, Doorknob747, Lowercase sigmabot, BG19bot, Freebiekr, MilerWhite, Machdohvah, Tomatronster, Northamerica1000, Wiki13, MusikAnimal, Frze, Dan653, AwamerT, Allecher, Mark Arsten, Somchai1029, Vincent Liu, Compfreak7, 110808028 amol, Altaïr, Foxfax555, Rj Haseeb, Alzpp, Bfugett, Jbrune, Thomasryno, Afree10, Glacialfox, Admfirepanther, Era7bd, Soumark, Maxmarengo, Manikandan 2030, Branzman, Melucky2getu, Fylbecatulous, Plavozont, Carliitaeliza, IkamusumeFan, Several Pending, Pratyya Ghosh, Zhaofeng Li, Mrt3366, VNeumann, ChrisGualtieri, Christophe.billiottet, Lovefamosos, Maty18, Mediran, Khazar2, Deathlasersonline, Saturdayswiki, ???, Mukherjeeassociates, Cerabot~enwiki, Malvikiran, Cheolsoo, R3miixasim, Pebau.grandauer, TwoTwoHello, Lugia2453, Frosty, SFK2, Graphium, Rafaelschp, 069952497a, Reatlas, Phamnhatkhanh, Epicgenius, P2Peter, Acetotyce, Rockonomics, Eyesnore, Moazzam chand, JamesMoose, Jabby11, EvergreenFir, Menublogger, Backendgaming, PappaAvMin, Mike99999, Gburd, Babitaarora, MJunkCat, Boli1107, JJdaboss, Ray Lightyear, BentlijDB, Hshoemark, Melody Lavender, Ginsuloft, D Eaketts, Eddiecarter1, Eddiejcarter, Mwaci11, Gajurahman, Manul, IrfanSha, AddWittyNameHere, Dkwebsub, JunWan, WPGA2345, Verajohne, Phinicle, Title302, JaconaFrere, ElijahLloyd97, Suelru, 7Sidz, Monkbot, JewishMonster69, Rajat Kant Singh, Davidcopperfield123, Sunrocket89, Nomonomnom, Samster0708, Krushna124, Cabral88, MisteArndon, KizzyCode, Uoy ylgu dratsab, Hillysilly, FSahar, Thedinesh4u, Boybudz321, Jesseminisis, ChamithN, Crystallizedcarbon, Eurodyne, JensLechtenboerger, Papapasan, Is8ac, Torvolt, Rgeurts, MaurolepisDreki, Top The Ball, Godfarther48, Jack0898, Rob12467, Gfsfg, Uthinkurspecial, Asdafsd, KasparBot, SaltySloth, Jrgreene2, Timoutiwin, Smedley Rhyse-Frockmorton, Communal t, BadSprad, AldrinRemoto, Vinurarulz, Yeshii 909, Cani talk and Anonymous: 2063

- **Women in computing** *Source:* https://en.wikipedia.org/wiki/Women_in_computing?oldid=680201496 *Contributors:* Ed Poor, Frecklefoot, Edward, Fred Bauder, Lquilter, ZoeB, Kingturtle, Greenrd, Espertus, Jake Nelson, Fredrik, Geeklizzard, Ancheta Wis, Giftlite, Quasarstrider, Sj, WiseWoman, Tapo, Beland, Kaldari, Icairns, Mcannella, Grm wnr, D6, 4pq1injbok, MeltBanana, Bender235, Irrbloss, Cje~enwiki, John Vandenberg, Viriditas, Giraffedata, Sam Korn, Pearle, Pouya, Hu, Idont Havaname, Vedant, Nkour, TSP, Robert K S, Ruud Koot, Mangojuice, GregorB, Graham87, BD2412, Rjwilmsi, MarSch, Funge, Marlow4, Bgwhite, Wavelength, RussBot, RadioFan, Elcaset~enwiki, Jpbowen, MaxVeers, Lockesdonkey, BABair, Ott2, Genjix, ArielGold, Mardus, SmackBot, Eperotao, Classicfilms, Eug, Chris the speller, Smallbones, OrphanBot, JonHarder, Gobonobo, Aeternus, Pudeo, Pmerson, Myasuda, Matrix61312, Teratornis, Kirk Hilliard, Kubanczyk, Opabinia regalis, Missvain, Michael A. White, Ablonus, Onasraou, Alphachimpbot, ElComandanteChe, Magioladitis, Nikevich, David Eppstein, Thibbs, CCS81, Icorey, RJBurkhart3, Junkstar, Jbowski18, Random user123, Nieske, Bonadea, Angorian, Steel1943, 28bytes, Drzzy, Fences and windows, T-bonham, TedColes, Girona7, Garish, Lightbreather, Flyer22, Faradayplank, Cyfal, Nn123645, ClueBot, Drmies, Ottawahitech, Spock of Vulcan, Shawis, Duncan, Dthomsen8, Sonjabern, G7huiben, Alvinlin123, Addbot, Hannah dee, DOI bot, Policy111116, Angelia2041, LaaknorBot, Torla42, Calculuslover, Spideralex, Lightbot, Ben Ben, Yobot, WikiDan61, AnomieBOT, MyComputerGirl, Prokurator11, Citation bot, Martychamberlain, Fstonedahl, Kirkma55, SisqoDd, FrescoBot, Fortdj33, Medanat, Liiiii, Rcmulcrone, LizzieBabes419, Kurtbeyer, Tinton5, Skyerise, Smithe2 98, GWW57, SchreyP, Laofmoonster, Lotje, Akim Demaille, Wikeithpedia, EmausBot, John of Reading, Dewritech, GoingBatty, Selena Deckelmann, Djembayz, Rmercuri, Dante8, RockMagnetist, Dlu776, ClueBot NG, ClaretAsh, Catlemur, Escapepea, Widr, Torontostudent24, WestLakeGirl, Megalibrarygirl, BG19bot, Rdachere, Nylrc, Gabriel Yuji, Compfreak7, OttawaAC, Quest Atkinson, Morengab, Cth027, BattyBot, Ema--or, Sawol, Msoreoluwa, ChrisGualtieri, DoctorKubla, Padenton, Dominiktesla, Mogism, DiggingUpAStar, Jochen Burghardt, DamascusGirlGeek, Zziccardi, Tiatastic, Sharimo1, Ruby Murray, Pattylopez, Jodosma, Srbraker, Djoverton, Matty.007, Comp.arch, Vaasu123, Melody Lavender, Lolz690, Someone not using his real name, Lcp30582, BrickiLee, Go0dwin6504, Thenamesdanie, Adoverm, Pfletch 43,

Superdinomomma, Johnb1122, Krsharp66, CorneliaBoldyreff, Kimmoir, JaconaFrere, Monkbot, Demoniccathandler, Abickel, Meglerner2, Corky001, OlyBin, Amybelotti, Vanisheduser00348374562342, Kaçkar, Thetechgirl, Teresan, Godsy, Michaelacaulfield, Nicolas Hrechko, Charlie Kellner, Poppenhe and Anonymous: 154

3.2 Images

- **File:16th_century_French_cypher_machine_in_the_shape_of_a_book_with_arms_of_Henri_II.jpg** *Source:* https://upload.wikimedia.org/wikipedia/commons/a/a2/16th_century_French_cypher_machine_in_the_shape_of_a_book_with_arms_of_Henri_II.jpg *License:* CC BY-SA 3.0 *Contributors:* Own work, photographed at Musee d'Ecouen *Original artist:* Uploadalt

- **File:1u04-argonaute.png** *Source:* https://upload.wikimedia.org/wikipedia/commons/0/02/1u04-argonaute.png *License:* CC-BY-SA-3.0 *Contributors:* Self created from PDB entry 1U04 using the freely available visualization and analysis package VMD raytraced with POV-Ray 3.6 *Original artist:* Opabinia regalis

- **File:2008-09_Kaiserschloss_Kryptologen.JPG** *Source:* https://upload.wikimedia.org/wikipedia/commons/a/ad/2008-09_Kaiserschloss_Kryptologen.JPG *License:* CC BY-SA 3.0 *Contributors:* Own work *Original artist:* Ziko

- **File:3-Tastenmaus_Microsoft.jpg** *Source:* https://upload.wikimedia.org/wikipedia/commons/a/aa/3-Tastenmaus_Microsoft.jpg *License:* CC BY-SA 2.5 *Contributors:* Own work *Original artist:* Darkone

- **File:6n-graf.svg** *Source:* https://upload.wikimedia.org/wikipedia/commons/5/5b/6n-graf.svg *License:* Public domain *Contributors:* Image:6n-graf.png simlar input data *Original artist:* User:AzaToth

- **File:Ada_lovelace.jpg** *Source:* https://upload.wikimedia.org/wikipedia/commons/0/0f/Ada_lovelace.jpg *License:* Public domain *Contributors:* www.fathom.com *Original artist:* Alfred Edward Chalon

- **File:Al-kindi_cryptographic.png** *Source:* https://upload.wikimedia.org/wikipedia/commons/7/76/Al-kindi_cryptographic.png *License:* Public domain *Contributors:* en:Image:Al-kindi_cryptographic.gif *Original artist:* Al-Kindi

- **File:Ambox_current_red.svg** *Source:* https://upload.wikimedia.org/wikipedia/commons/9/98/Ambox_current_red.svg *License:* CC0 *Contributors:* self-made, inspired by Gnome globe current event.svg, using Information icon3.svg and Earth clip art.svg *Original artist:* Vipersnake151, penubag, Tkgd2007 (clock)

- **File:Ambox_important.svg** *Source:* https://upload.wikimedia.org/wikipedia/commons/b/b4/Ambox_important.svg *License:* Public domain *Contributors:* Own work, based off of Image:Ambox scales.svg *Original artist:* Dsmurat (talk · contribs)

- **File:Animation2.gif** *Source:* https://upload.wikimedia.org/wikipedia/commons/c/c0/Animation2.gif *License:* CC-BY-SA-3.0 *Contributors:* Own work *Original artist:* MG (talk · contribs)

- **File:ArtificialFictionBrain.png** *Source:* https://upload.wikimedia.org/wikipedia/commons/1/17/ArtificialFictionBrain.png *License:* CC-BY-SA-3.0 *Contributors:* No machine readable source provided. Own work assumed (based on copyright claims). *Original artist:* No machine readable author provided. Gengiskanhg assumed (based on copyright claims).

- **File:Artificial_neural_network.svg** *Source:* https://upload.wikimedia.org/wikipedia/commons/e/e4/Artificial_neural_network.svg *License:* CC-BY-SA-3.0 *Contributors:* This vector image was created with Inkscape. *Original artist:* en:User:Cburnett

- **File:Automated_online_assistant.png** *Source:* https://upload.wikimedia.org/wikipedia/commons/8/8b/Automated_online_assistant.png *License:* Attribution *Contributors:*

    The text is adapted from the Wikipedia merchandise page (this automated customer service itself, however, is fictional), and pasted into a page in Wikipedia:

    Original artist: Mikael Häggström

- **File:Babbage40.png** *Source:* https://upload.wikimedia.org/wikipedia/commons/6/67/Babbage40.png *License:* Public domain *Contributors:* The Mechanic's Magazine, Museum, Register, Journal and Gazette, October 6, 1832-March 31, 1833. Vol. XVIII. *Original artist:* AGoon, derivative work, original was 'Engraved by Roffe, by permifsion from an original Family Painting' 1833

- **File:Binary_entropy_plot.svg** *Source:* https://upload.wikimedia.org/wikipedia/commons/2/22/Binary_entropy_plot.svg *License:* CC-BY-SA-3.0 *Contributors:* original work by Brona, published on Commons at Image:Binary entropy plot.png. Converted to SVG by Alessio Damato *Original artist:* Brona and Alessio Damato

- **File:Binary_erasure_channel.svg** *Source:* https://upload.wikimedia.org/wikipedia/commons/b/b6/Binary_erasure_channel.svg *License:* Public domain *Contributors:* Own work *Original artist:* David Eppstein

- **File:Binary_symmetric_channel.svg** *Source:* https://upload.wikimedia.org/wikipedia/commons/b/b5/Binary_symmetric_channel.svg *License:* Public domain *Contributors:* Own work *Original artist:* David Eppstein

- **File:Blochsphere.svg** *Source:* https://upload.wikimedia.org/wikipedia/commons/f/f3/Blochsphere.svg *License:* CC-BY-SA-3.0 *Contributors:* Transferred from en.wikipedia to Commons. *Original artist:* MuncherOfSpleens at English Wikipedia

- **File:Braille_closeup.jpg** *Source:* https://upload.wikimedia.org/wikipedia/commons/4/4c/Braille_closeup.jpg *License:* CC BY-SA 3.0 *Contributors:* Own work *Original artist:* Lrcg2012

- **File:CDSCRATCHES.jpg** *Source:* https://upload.wikimedia.org/wikipedia/commons/5/5a/CDSCRATCHES.jpg *License:* Public domain *Contributors:* English Wikipedia <a href='//en.wikipedia.org/wiki/en:Image:CDSCRATCHES.JPG' class='extiw' title='w:en:Image:CDSCRATCHES.JPG'>here</a> *Original artist:* en:user:Jam01

- **File:Chess.svg** *Source:* https://upload.wikimedia.org/wikipedia/commons/0/05/Chess.svg *License:* LGPL *Contributors:* http://ftp.gnome.org/pub/GNOME/sources/gnome-themes-extras/0.9/gnome-themes-extras-0.9.0.tar.gz *Original artist:* David Vignoni
- **File:Chomsky-hierarchy.svg** *Source:* https://upload.wikimedia.org/wikipedia/commons/9/9a/Chomsky-hierarchy.svg *License:* CC BY-SA 3.0 *Contributors:* Own work *Original artist:* J. Finkelstein
- **File:CodasylB.png** *Source:* https://upload.wikimedia.org/wikipedia/commons/d/d6/CodasylB.png *License:* CC-BY-SA-3.0 *Contributors:* "CIM: Principles of Computer Integrated Manufacturing", Jean-Baptiste Waldner, John Wiley & Sons, 1992 *Original artist:* Jean-Baptiste Waldner
- **File:Comm_Channel.svg** *Source:* https://upload.wikimedia.org/wikipedia/commons/4/48/Comm_Channel.svg *License:* Public domain *Contributors:* en wikipedia *Original artist:* en:Dicklyon
- **File:Commons-logo.svg** *Source:* https://upload.wikimedia.org/wikipedia/en/4/4a/Commons-logo.svg *License:* ? *Contributors:* ? *Original artist:* ?
- **File:Commutative_diagram_for_morphism.svg** *Source:* https://upload.wikimedia.org/wikipedia/commons/e/ef/Commutative_diagram_for_morphism.svg *License:* Public domain *Contributors:* Own work, based on en:Image:MorphismComposition-01.png *Original artist:* User:Cepheus
- **File:Compiler.svg** *Source:* https://upload.wikimedia.org/wikipedia/commons/6/6b/Compiler.svg *License:* CC-BY-SA-3.0 *Contributors:* self-made SVG version of Image:Ideal compiler.png by User:Raul654. Incorporates Image:Computer n screen.svg and Image:Nuvola mimetypes source.png. *Original artist:* Surachit
- **File:Complexity_subsets_pspace.svg** *Source:* https://upload.wikimedia.org/wikipedia/commons/6/6e/Complexity_subsets_pspace.svg *License:* Public domain *Contributors:* Own work by uploader, intended to replace bitmap image illustrating same thing *Original artist:* Hand drawn in Inkscape Qef
- **File:Computer-aj_aj_ashton_01.svg** *Source:* https://upload.wikimedia.org/wikipedia/commons/c/c1/Computer-aj_aj_ashton_01.svg *License:* CC0 *Contributors:* ? *Original artist:* ?
- **File:Cornellbox_pathtracing_irradiancecaching.png** *Source:* https://upload.wikimedia.org/wikipedia/en/e/e3/Cornellbox_pathtracing_irradiancecaching.png *License:* PD *Contributors:*
I created this work entirely by myself. I created this work entirely by myself!
Original artist:
Trevorgoodchild (talk)
- **File:Corner.png** *Source:* https://upload.wikimedia.org/wikipedia/commons/5/5f/Corner.png *License:* Public domain *Contributors:* http://en.wikipedia.org/wiki/File:Corner.png *Original artist:* Retardo
- **File:Crypto_key.svg** *Source:* https://upload.wikimedia.org/wikipedia/commons/6/65/Crypto_key.svg *License:* CC-BY-SA-3.0 *Contributors:* Own work based on image:Key-crypto-sideways.png by MisterMatt originally from English Wikipedia *Original artist:* MesserWoland
- **File:DFAexample.svg** *Source:* https://upload.wikimedia.org/wikipedia/commons/9/9d/DFAexample.svg *License:* Public domain *Contributors:* Own work *Original artist:* Cepheus
- **File:Database_models.jpg** *Source:* https://upload.wikimedia.org/wikipedia/commons/3/3b/Database_models.jpg *License:* CC BY-SA 3.0 *Contributors:* Own work *Original artist:* Marcel Douwe Dekker
- **File:Diffie_and_Hellman.jpg** *Source:* https://upload.wikimedia.org/wikipedia/commons/8/88/Diffie_and_Hellman.jpg *License:* CC-BY-SA-3.0 *Contributors:* ? *Original artist:* ?
- **File:Distributed-parallel.svg** *Source:* https://upload.wikimedia.org/wikipedia/commons/c/c6/Distributed-parallel.svg *License:* CC BY-SA 3.0 *Contributors:* Own work *Original artist:* Miym
- **File:Edit-clear.svg** *Source:* https://upload.wikimedia.org/wikipedia/en/f/f2/Edit-clear.svg *License:* Public domain *Contributors:* The *Tango!* Desktop Project. *Original artist:*
The people from the Tango! project. And according to the meta-data in the file, specifically: "Andreas Nilsson, and Jakub Steiner (although minimally)."
- **File:Elliptic_curve_simple.png** *Source:* https://upload.wikimedia.org/wikipedia/commons/7/76/Elliptic_curve_simple.png *License:* CC-BY-SA-3.0 *Contributors:* Upload from English Wikipedia. The original description is/was here. *Original artist:* Created by Sean κ. + 23:33, 27 May 2005 (UTC)
- **File:Encoded_letter_of_Gabriel_Luetz_d_Aramon_after_1546_with_partial_deciphering.jpg** *Source:* https://upload.wikimedia.org/wikipedia/commons/b/b8/Encoded_letter_of_Gabriel_Luetz_d_Aramon_after_1546_with_partial_deciphering.jpg *License:* CC BY-SA 3.0 *Contributors:* Own work, photographed at Ecouen Museum *Original artist:* Uploadalt
- **File:Encryption_-_decryption.svg** *Source:* https://upload.wikimedia.org/wikipedia/commons/b/bf/Encryption_-_decryption.svg *License:* CC-BY-SA-3.0 *Contributors:* based on png version originally uploaded to the English-language Wikipedia by mike40033, and moved to the Commons by MichaelDiederich. *Original artist:* odder
- **File:English.png** *Source:* https://upload.wikimedia.org/wikipedia/commons/0/0a/English.png *License:* Public domain *Contributors:* ? *Original artist:* ?
- **File:Enigma.jpg** *Source:* https://upload.wikimedia.org/wikipedia/commons/a/ae/Enigma.jpg *License:* Public domain *Contributors:* User:Jszigetvari *Original artist:* ?
- **File:Fivestagespipeline.png** *Source:* https://upload.wikimedia.org/wikipedia/commons/2/21/Fivestagespipeline.png *License:* CC-BY-SA-3.0 *Contributors:* ? *Original artist:* ?

3.2. IMAGES

- **File:Flowchart.png** *Source:* https://upload.wikimedia.org/wikipedia/commons/9/9d/Flowchart.png *License:* CC SA 1.0 *Contributors:* ? *Original artist:* ?
- **File:Folder_Hexagonal_Icon.svg** *Source:* https://upload.wikimedia.org/wikipedia/en/4/48/Folder_Hexagonal_Icon.svg *License:* Cc-by-sa-3.0 *Contributors:* ? *Original artist:* ?
- **File:GFO_taxonomy_tree.png** *Source:* https://upload.wikimedia.org/wikipedia/commons/9/9e/GFO_taxonomy_tree.png *License:* CC BY-SA 3.0 *Contributors:* Transferred from en.wikipedia; transferred to Commons by User:Shizhao using CommonsHelper. *Original artist:* Original uploader was Leechuck at en.wikipedia
- **File:HONDA_ASIMO.jpg** *Source:* https://upload.wikimedia.org/wikipedia/commons/0/05/HONDA_ASIMO.jpg *License:* CC-BY-SA-3.0 *Contributors:* ? *Original artist:* ?
- **File:Hamming.jpg** *Source:* https://upload.wikimedia.org/wikipedia/commons/3/39/Hamming.jpg *License:* Public domain *Contributors:* Own work *Original artist:* Josiedraus
- **File:Hierarchical-control-system.svg** *Source:* https://upload.wikimedia.org/wikipedia/en/7/76/Hierarchical-control-system.svg *License:* CC-BY-3.0 *Contributors:*
Image:Hierarchical-control-system.jpg *Original artist:*
user:Pbroks13
- **File:Human_eye,_rendered_from_Eye.png** *Source:* https://upload.wikimedia.org/wikipedia/commons/5/51/Human_eye%2C_rendered_from_Eye.png *License:* CC-BY-SA-3.0 *Contributors:* Eye.svg
Original artist: Kenny sh at English Wikipedia
- **File:International_Data_Encryption_Algorithm_InfoBox_Diagram.svg** *Source:* https://upload.wikimedia.org/wikipedia/commons/a/af/International_Data_Encryption_Algorithm_InfoBox_Diagram.svg *License:* Public domain *Contributors:* Transfered from en.wikipedia *Original artist:* Original uploader was Surachit at en.wikipedia
- **File:Internet_map_1024.jpg** *Source:* https://upload.wikimedia.org/wikipedia/commons/d/d2/Internet_map_1024.jpg *License:* CC BY 2.5 *Contributors:* Originally from the English Wikipedia; description page is/was here. *Original artist:* The Opte Project
- **File:Julia_iteration_data.png** *Source:* https://upload.wikimedia.org/wikipedia/commons/4/47/Julia_iteration_data.png *License:* GFDL *Contributors:* Own work *Original artist:* Adam majewski
- **File:Kismet_robot_at_MIT_Museum.jpg** *Source:* https://upload.wikimedia.org/wikipedia/commons/b/b8/Kismet_robot_at_MIT_Museum.jpg *License:* CC-BY-SA-3.0 *Contributors:* ? *Original artist:* ?
- **File:KnnClassification.svg** *Source:* https://upload.wikimedia.org/wikipedia/commons/e/e7/KnnClassification.svg *License:* CC-BY-SA-3.0 *Contributors:* Own work *Original artist:* Antti Ajanki AnAj
- **File:Lambda_lc.svg** *Source:* https://upload.wikimedia.org/wikipedia/commons/3/39/Lambda_lc.svg *License:* Public domain *Contributors:* The Greek alphabet *Original artist:* User:Luks
- **File:LampFlowchart.svg** *Source:* https://upload.wikimedia.org/wikipedia/commons/9/91/LampFlowchart.svg *License:* CC-BY-SA-3.0 *Contributors:* vector version of Image:LampFlowchart.png *Original artist:* svg by Booyabazooka
- **File:Lorenz-SZ42-2.jpg** *Source:* https://upload.wikimedia.org/wikipedia/commons/4/4d/Lorenz-SZ42-2.jpg *License:* Public domain *Contributors:* ? *Original artist:* ?
- **File:Lorenz_attractor_yb.svg** *Source:* https://upload.wikimedia.org/wikipedia/commons/5/5b/Lorenz_attractor_yb.svg *License:* CC-BY-SA-3.0 *Contributors:* ? *Original artist:* ?
- **File:MIPS_Architecture_(Pipelined).svg** *Source:* https://upload.wikimedia.org/wikipedia/commons/e/ea/MIPS_Architecture_%28Pipelined%29.svg *License:* Public domain *Contributors:* Own work *Original artist:* Inductiveload
- **File:Maquina.png** *Source:* https://upload.wikimedia.org/wikipedia/commons/3/3d/Maquina.png *License:* Public domain *Contributors:* en.wikipedia *Original artist:* Schadel (http://turing.izt.uam.mx)
- **File:Monitor_padlock.svg** *Source:* https://upload.wikimedia.org/wikipedia/commons/7/73/Monitor_padlock.svg *License:* CC BY-SA 3.0 *Contributors:* Transferred from en.wikipedia; transferred to Commons by User:Logan using CommonsHelper.
Original artist: Lunarbunny (talk). Original uploader was Lunarbunny at en.wikipedia
- **File:Motherboard.jpg** *Source:* https://upload.wikimedia.org/wikipedia/commons/3/32/Motherboard.jpg *License:* Public domain *Contributors:* Own work (Original text: *I created this work entirely by myself.*) *Original artist:* Simpsons contributor (talk)
- **File:NOR_ANSI.svg** *Source:* https://upload.wikimedia.org/wikipedia/commons/6/6c/NOR_ANSI.svg *License:* Public domain *Contributors:* Own Drawing, made in Inkscape 0.43 *Original artist:* jjbeard
- **File:Naphthalene-3D-balls.png** *Source:* https://upload.wikimedia.org/wikipedia/commons/3/3e/Naphthalene-3D-balls.png *License:* Public domain *Contributors:* ? *Original artist:* ?
- **File:Neuron.svg** *Source:* https://upload.wikimedia.org/wikipedia/commons/b/b5/Neuron.svg *License:* CC-BY-SA-3.0 *Contributors:* ? *Original artist:* ?
- **File:Nicolas_P._Rougier'{}s_rendering_of_the_human_brain.png** *Source:* https://upload.wikimedia.org/wikipedia/commons/7/73/Nicolas_P._Rougier%27s_rendering_of_the_human_brain.png *License:* GPL *Contributors:* http://www.loria.fr/~{}rougier *Original artist:* Nicolas Rougier
- **File:Nuvola_apps_edu_mathematics_blue-p.svg** *Source:* https://upload.wikimedia.org/wikipedia/commons/3/3e/Nuvola_apps_edu_mathematics_blue-p.svg *License:* GPL *Contributors:* Derivative work from Image:Nuvola apps edu mathematics.png and Image:Nuvola apps edu mathematics-p.svg *Original artist:* David Vignoni (original icon); Flamurai (SVG convertion); bayo (color)

- **File:Nuvola_apps_kcmsystem.svg** *Source:* https://upload.wikimedia.org/wikipedia/commons/7/7a/Nuvola_apps_kcmsystem.svg *License:* LGPL *Contributors:* Own work based on Image:Nuvola apps kcmsystem.png by Alphax originally from [1] *Original artist:* MesserWoland
- **File:Nuvola_apps_ksim.png** *Source:* https://upload.wikimedia.org/wikipedia/commons/8/8d/Nuvola_apps_ksim.png *License:* LGPL *Contributors:* http://icon-king.com *Original artist:* David Vignoni / ICON KING
- **File:Nuvola_apps_package_games_strategy.png** *Source:* https://upload.wikimedia.org/wikipedia/commons/5/5e/Nuvola_apps_package_games_strategy.png *License:* LGPL *Contributors:* http://icon-king.com *Original artist:* David Vignoni / ICON KING
- **File:Office-book.svg** *Source:* https://upload.wikimedia.org/wikipedia/commons/a/a8/Office-book.svg *License:* Public domain *Contributors:* This and myself. *Original artist:* Chris Down/Tango project
- **File:Open_book_nae_02.svg** *Source:* https://upload.wikimedia.org/wikipedia/commons/9/92/Open_book_nae_02.svg *License:* CC0 *Contributors:* OpenClipart *Original artist:* nae
- **File:Operating_system_placement.svg** *Source:* https://upload.wikimedia.org/wikipedia/commons/e/e1/Operating_system_placement.svg *License:* CC BY-SA 3.0 *Contributors:* Own work *Original artist:* Golftheman
- **File:Oxygen_devices.svg** *Source:* https://upload.wikimedia.org/wikipedia/commons/4/4c/Oxygen_devices.svg *License:* LGPL *Contributors:* KDE oxygen icons *Original artist:* Nuno Pinheiro <nuno@oxygen-icons.org>, David Vignoni <david@icon-king.com>, David Miller <miller@oxygen-icons.org>, Johann Ollivier Lapeyre <johann@oxygen-icons.org>, Kenneth Wimer <kwwii@bootsplash.org>, Riccardo Iaconelli <riccardo@oxygen-icons.org>
- **File:ParseTree.svg** *Source:* https://upload.wikimedia.org/wikipedia/commons/6/6e/ParseTree.svg *License:* Public domain *Contributors:* en: Image:ParseTree.jpg *Original artist:* Traced by User:Stannered
- **File:People_icon.svg** *Source:* https://upload.wikimedia.org/wikipedia/commons/3/37/People_icon.svg *License:* CC0 *Contributors:* OpenClipart *Original artist:* OpenClipart
- **File:PersonalStorageDevices.agr.jpg** *Source:* https://upload.wikimedia.org/wikipedia/commons/8/87/PersonalStorageDevices.agr.jpg *License:* CC-BY-SA-3.0 *Contributors:* I took this photograph of artifacts in my possession *Original artist:* --agr 15:53, 1 Apr 2005 (UTC)
- **File:Phrenology1.jpg** *Source:* https://upload.wikimedia.org/wikipedia/commons/f/fa/Phrenology1.jpg *License:* Public domain *Contributors:* Friedrich Eduard Bilz (1842–1922): Das neue Naturheilverfahren (75. Jubiläumsausgabe) *Original artist:* scanned by de:Benutzer:Summi
- **File:Portal-puzzle.svg** *Source:* https://upload.wikimedia.org/wikipedia/en/f/fd/Portal-puzzle.svg *License:* Public domain *Contributors:* ? *Original artist:* ?
- **File:Public_key_encryption.svg** *Source:* https://upload.wikimedia.org/wikipedia/commons/f/f9/Public_key_encryption.svg *License:* Public domain *Contributors:* ? *Original artist:* ?
- **File:Python_add5_syntax.svg** *Source:* https://upload.wikimedia.org/wikipedia/commons/e/e1/Python_add5_syntax.svg *License:* Copyrighted free use *Contributors:* http://en.wikipedia.org/wiki/Image:Python_add5_syntax.png *Original artist:* Xander89
- **File:Quark_wiki.jpg** *Source:* https://upload.wikimedia.org/wikipedia/commons/c/cb/Quark_wiki.jpg *License:* CC BY-SA 3.0 *Contributors:* Own work *Original artist:* Brianzero
- **File:Question_book-new.svg** *Source:* https://upload.wikimedia.org/wikipedia/en/9/99/Question_book-new.svg *License:* Cc-by-sa-3.0 *Contributors:*

  Created from scratch in Adobe Illustrator. Based on Image:Question book.png created by User:Equazcion *Original artist:*
  Tkgd2007
- **File:Relational_key_SVG.svg** *Source:* https://upload.wikimedia.org/wikipedia/commons/4/4c/Relational_key_SVG.svg *License:* CC BY-SA 3.0 *Contributors:* Own work *Original artist:* IkamusumeFan
- **File:Roomba_original.jpg** *Source:* https://upload.wikimedia.org/wikipedia/commons/f/f5/Roomba_original.jpg *License:* CC BY-SA 3.0 *Contributors:* © 2006 Larry D. Moore *Original artist:* Larry D. Moore
- **File:SIMD.svg** *Source:* https://upload.wikimedia.org/wikipedia/commons/2/21/SIMD.svg *License:* CC-BY-SA-3.0 *Contributors:* Own work in Inkscape *Original artist:* en:User:Cburnett
- **File:Shadow_Hand_Bulb_large.jpg** *Source:* https://upload.wikimedia.org/wikipedia/commons/c/c5/Shadow_Hand_Bulb_large.jpg *License:* CC-BY-SA-3.0 *Contributors:* http://www.shadowrobot.com/media/pictures.shtml *Original artist:* Richard Greenhill and Hugo Elias (myself) of the Shadow Robot Company
- **File:SimplexRangeSearching.png** *Source:* https://upload.wikimedia.org/wikipedia/commons/4/48/SimplexRangeSearching.png *License:* Public domain *Contributors:* Transferred from en.wikipedia to Commons. *Original artist:* Gfonsecabr at English Wikipedia
- **File:Singly_linked_list.png** *Source:* https://upload.wikimedia.org/wikipedia/commons/3/37/Singly_linked_list.png *License:* Public domain *Contributors:* Copied from en. Originally uploaded by Dcoetzee. *Original artist:* Derrick Coetzee (User:Dcoetzee)
- **File:Sky.png** *Source:* https://upload.wikimedia.org/wikipedia/commons/0/08/Sky.png *License:* CC BY-SA 2.5 *Contributors:* selbst gemacht. own work. *Original artist:* Manuel Strehl
- **File:Skytala&EmptyStrip-Shaded.png** *Source:* https://upload.wikimedia.org/wikipedia/commons/b/b2/Skytala%26EmptyStrip-Shaded.png *License:* CC-BY-SA-3.0 *Contributors:* ? *Original artist:* ?
- **File:Sorting_quicksort_anim.gif** *Source:* https://upload.wikimedia.org/wikipedia/commons/6/6a/Sorting_quicksort_anim.gif *License:* CC-BY-SA-3.0 *Contributors:* originally upload on the English Wikipedia *Original artist:* Wikipedia:en:User:RolandH
- **File:Sorting_quicksort_anim_frame.png** *Source:* https://upload.wikimedia.org/wikipedia/commons/1/1e/Sorting_quicksort_anim_frame.png *License:* CC-BY-SA-3.0 *Contributors:* Image:Sorting quicksort anim.gif *Original artist:* en:User:RolandH

3.2. IMAGES

- **File:Stanford_bunny_qem.png** *Source:* https://upload.wikimedia.org/wikipedia/commons/1/1b/Stanford_bunny_qem.png *License:* Public domain *Contributors:* Own work (Original text: *I created this work entirely by myself.*) *Original artist:* Trevorgoodchild (talk)
- **File:Symbol_book_class2.svg** *Source:* https://upload.wikimedia.org/wikipedia/commons/8/89/Symbol_book_class2.svg *License:* CC BY-SA 2.5 *Contributors:* Mad by Lokal_Profil by combining: *Original artist:* Lokal_Profil
- **File:Symbol_list_class.svg** *Source:* https://upload.wikimedia.org/wikipedia/en/d/db/Symbol_list_class.svg *License:* Public domain *Contributors:* ? *Original artist:* ?
- **File:Symbol_template_class.svg** *Source:* https://upload.wikimedia.org/wikipedia/en/5/5c/Symbol_template_class.svg *License:* Public domain *Contributors:* ? *Original artist:* ?
- **File:Symbol_venus.svg** *Source:* https://upload.wikimedia.org/wikipedia/commons/7/74/Symbol_venus.svg *License:* CC-BY-SA-3.0 *Contributors:* Own work *Original artist:* By Rei-artur (talk · contribs).
- **File:Symmetric_key_encryption.svg** *Source:* https://upload.wikimedia.org/wikipedia/commons/2/27/Symmetric_key_encryption.svg *License:* CC0 *Contributors:* Own work *Original artist:* Phayzfaustyn
- **File:TLS_indicator_in_Firefox_34.png** *Source:* https://upload.wikimedia.org/wikipedia/commons/6/66/TLS_indicator_in_Firefox_34.png *License:* MPL 1.1 *Contributors:* Mozilla Firefox *Original artist:* Mozilla
- **File:TSP_Deutschland_3.png** *Source:* https://upload.wikimedia.org/wikipedia/commons/c/c4/TSP_Deutschland_3.png *License:* Public domain *Contributors:* https://www.cia.gov/cia/publications/factbook/maps/gm-map.gif *Original artist:* The original uploader was Kapitän Nemo at German Wikipedia
- **File:Telecom-icon.svg** *Source:* https://upload.wikimedia.org/wikipedia/commons/4/4e/Telecom-icon.svg *License:* Public domain *Contributors:* ? *Original artist:* ?
- **File:Text_document_with_red_question_mark.svg** *Source:* https://upload.wikimedia.org/wikipedia/commons/a/a4/Text_document_with_red_question_mark.svg *License:* Public domain *Contributors:* Created by bdesham with Inkscape; based upon Text-x-generic.svg from the Tango project. *Original artist:* Benjamin D. Esham (bdesham)
- **File:Traditional_View_of_Data_SVG.svg** *Source:* https://upload.wikimedia.org/wikipedia/commons/4/4d/Traditional_View_of_Data_SVG.svg *License:* CC BY-SA 3.0 *Contributors:* Own work *Original artist:* IkamusumeFan
- **File:Utah_teapot_simple_2.png** *Source:* https://upload.wikimedia.org/wikipedia/commons/5/5f/Utah_teapot_simple_2.png *License:* CC BY-SA 3.0 *Contributors:* Own work *Original artist:* Dhatfield
- **File:Wang_tiles.png** *Source:* https://upload.wikimedia.org/wikipedia/commons/0/06/Wang_tiles.png *License:* Public domain *Contributors:* ? *Original artist:* ?
- **File:Wiki_letter_w_cropped.svg** *Source:* https://upload.wikimedia.org/wikipedia/commons/1/1c/Wiki_letter_w_cropped.svg *License:* CC-BY-SA-3.0 *Contributors:*
- Wiki_letter_w.svg *Original artist:* Wiki_letter_w.svg: Jarkko Piiroinen
- **File:Wikibooks-logo-en-noslogan.svg** *Source:* https://upload.wikimedia.org/wikipedia/commons/d/df/Wikibooks-logo-en-noslogan.svg *License:* CC BY-SA 3.0 *Contributors:* Own work *Original artist:* User:Bastique, User:Ramac et al.
- **File:Wikibooks-logo.svg** *Source:* https://upload.wikimedia.org/wikipedia/commons/f/fa/Wikibooks-logo.svg *License:* CC BY-SA 3.0 *Contributors:* Own work *Original artist:* User:Bastique, User:Ramac et al.
- **File:Wikinews-logo.svg** *Source:* https://upload.wikimedia.org/wikipedia/commons/2/24/Wikinews-logo.svg *License:* CC BY-SA 3.0 *Contributors:* This is a cropped version of Image:Wikinews-logo-en.png. *Original artist:* Vectorized by Simon 01:05, 2 August 2006 (UTC) Updated by Time3000 17 April 2007 to use official Wikinews colours and appear correctly on dark backgrounds. Originally uploaded by Simon.
- **File:Wikiquote-logo.svg** *Source:* https://upload.wikimedia.org/wikipedia/commons/f/fa/Wikiquote-logo.svg *License:* Public domain *Contributors:* ? *Original artist:* ?
- **File:Wikisource-logo.svg** *Source:* https://upload.wikimedia.org/wikipedia/commons/4/4c/Wikisource-logo.svg *License:* CC BY-SA 3.0 *Contributors:* Rei-artur *Original artist:* Nicholas Moreau
- **File:Wikiversity-logo-Snorky.svg** *Source:* https://upload.wikimedia.org/wikipedia/commons/1/1b/Wikiversity-logo-en.svg *License:* CC BY-SA 3.0 *Contributors:* Own work *Original artist:* Snorky
- **File:Wikiversity-logo.svg** *Source:* https://upload.wikimedia.org/wikipedia/commons/9/91/Wikiversity-logo.svg *License:* CC BY-SA 3.0 *Contributors:* Snorky (optimized and cleaned up by verdy_p) *Original artist:* Snorky (optimized and cleaned up by verdy_p)
- **File:Wiktionary-logo-en.svg** *Source:* https://upload.wikimedia.org/wikipedia/commons/f/f8/Wiktionary-logo-en.svg *License:* Public domain *Contributors:* Vector version of Image:Wiktionary-logo-en.png. *Original artist:* Vectorized by Fvasconcellos (talk · contribs), based on original logo tossed together by Brion Vibber
- **File:Woman-power_emblem.svg** *Source:* https://upload.wikimedia.org/wikipedia/commons/4/41/Woman-power_emblem.svg *License:* Public domain *Contributors:* Made by myself, based on a character outline in the (PostScript Type 1) "Fnord Hodge-Podge Discordian fonts version 2" by **toa267** (declared by them to be Public Domain). I chose the color to be kind of equally intermediate between red, pink, and lavender (without being any one of the three...). *Original artist:* AnonMoos, toa267
- **File:Women_and_technology_poster_colombia.jpg** *Source:* https://upload.wikimedia.org/wikipedia/commons/6/63/Women_and_technology_poster_colombia.jpg *License:* CC BY 2.0 *Contributors:* http://www.flickr.com/photos/nachoeuropa/5815949513/sizes/z/ *Original artist:*

    De todos los Colores ::

3.3 Content license

- Creative Commons Attribution-Share Alike 3.0

www.ingramcontent.com/pod-product-compliance
Lightning Source LLC
Chambersburg PA
CBHW080911170526
45158CB00008B/2071